Boy of the Year
Competing for a Dream

By

Willie Chavez
(aka Guillermo Daniel Chavez and Bill Chavez)

Copyright © 2019 All rights reserved.

Houston, Texas

For Alex, Chris, Dash and Vince

Acknowledgements

For most of my life, I have felt a compelling need to write *Boy of the Year; Competing for a Dream*. I could never have finished it without the help of many of the friends who are featured in the book. I want here to acknowledge their assistance and to express my profound gratitude for what they did to help me complete the book and thus my life-long passion.

First, my thanks go to the Boy of the Year contestants who inspired me to no end during our Boys' Club days and who graciously allowed me to interview them: Richard Lopez, Ignacio Chavez, Joe Renteria, Sergio Reza, Juan Uranga, Dionicio Manuel Alvarez, Salvador E. Garcia, Mario M. Lewis, Xavier Bañales, Manuel Ontiveros, Homer Reza, Antonio Stephens and Raymundo Velarde.

My thanks also go to the other Boys' Club friends who shared those memorable days with me and who also permitted me to interview them: Hector Armijo, Fernando A. Casas, Eloiso De Avila, Bernie Del Hierro, Luis Cesar Labrado, Gilbert Montes, Lionel Nava, Jesus M. Reza and El Muchacho.

I am equally appreciative for the help I received from the two Boys' Club staff members from the 1960's who I managed to find and who also allowed me to interview them: Lane W. Smith and Dan Hightower.

I thank also all who looked at preliminary versions of the book and who gave me their valuable input: Fernando A. Casas, Hilda Luz Chavez, Ignacio Chavez, Richard Lopez, Elizabeth Jennings Reina, Joe Renteria, Sergio Reza, Dennis Ruhl and Maria Luisa Yanar.

Table of Contents

Introduction — page 5

Chapter 1-The Willie Chavez View of the World in the late 1950's — page 8

Chapter 2-Our Move to the West Side-1957 — page 34

Chapter 3-The Paisano Projects — page 46

Chapter 4-Time to Move Again — page 76

Chapter 5-Jobs I got as a Kid — page 82

Chapter 6-The El Paso Boys' Club — page 104

Chapter 7-Unit 2 Takes Off — page 121

Chapter 8-My Years as a Club Member — page 159

Chapter 9-The Jr. Toastmasters Club — page 209

Chapter 10-Crossroads of the Americas — page 238

Chapter 11-The Jefferson High School Band — page 255

Chapter 12-Other Enriching Experiences and People — page 260

Chapter 13-The National Boy of the Year Contest — page 308

Chapter 14-Why This Surge of Juvenile Decency? — page 345

Epilogue: Where the Boys Are Today — page 349

Introduction

My name is Willie Chavez. The following is a narrative about me when I was a kid. First and foremost, it's a memoir in which I indulge freely and intimately in recalling some of the best days of my life. Since I decided to entitle my story *Boy of the Year* and since it's a memoir, the reader might anticipate that I or one of my childhood friends will somehow assert a claim to that title, whatever it happens to mean. While some of the kids mentioned in my story really did earn an award from the *Boys' Clubs of America* that carried that particular title, most did not. The reader will eventually learn that the reference to *"Boy of the Year"* in the title of this book really refers to the *life experience* that my friends and I went through when we were boys. I believe that the notion that each of us could be a *"Boy of the Year"* was compelling and almost all-consuming for many of us and that it drove us to strive to be so much better than the kids we otherwise might have become. I was nothing more than one set of eyes and ears that captured the events and the personalities of the people involved in that experience. I now merely offer the reader my version of what occurred. But my narrative is also somewhat of an old and timeless story. It's old because the events covered in the story occurred more than a half-century ago. And it is timeless because it's about the American dream--that same aspiration that has been around as long as America has existed and which most of us have pursued to one degree or another.

But my story is also the story of a bunch of other kids. We all happened to find ourselves growing up during the same period of time—late fifties and early sixties—and in the same neighborhood—the south side of El Paso, Texas. We had lots in common: The vast majority of us were Mexican-Americans. That is, we were of Mexican ancestry but were also extremely proud Americans living in the US and intending to remain in the US forever. Our parents were mostly recent immigrants who spoke little or no English, had very limited educations, had difficulty finding good jobs, could afford only the cheapest (and therefore generally substandard) housing but who invariably believed that America was the place where they wanted to be and stay in and where they wanted to raise their kids.

Although this bunch of kids--like most kids—believed that the bounty of America was limitless, the prevailing outlook among most of us at that time-- and to most outsiders as well--was that little would change as we grew up and tried to find our places in society. Historically, as each generation of Mexican-Americans attempted to assimilate, they struggled mightily. If anyone had studied our history, they would almost certainly have learned that it was extremely unlikely that the succeeding generations would break the well-established pattern of not being able to graduate from high school and, therefore, not being able to ascend to a significantly higher socio-economic status. It was enormously difficult for the American dream to become a reality for us. I can still recall how happy, optimistic and carefree kids in elementary school became timid, reticent and even cynical as they went into high school and realized that assimilation, higher education, socio-economic escalation and full participation in the fabled "pursuit of happiness," were not going to happen easily. Indeed, there was a common belief among the barrio youth that regardless of how hard one worked, there was a very high probability that a Mexican-American kid would forever remain in the barrio.

Yet, for many, many reasons—some of which I can and will intimately expound upon—this bunch of kids did indeed break that historic pattern. The same factors that had hobbled previous generations of Mexican-American kids growing up in South El Paso seemed to let up dramatically during those years.

There were many factors that affected this group as they grew up in that neighborhood but I believe that the most prominent common denominator was the *El Paso Boys' Club*. We were all members between 1959 and roughly 1967, and all of us were profoundly impacted by the people that we encountered there as well as the activities and events we experienced within the Club. Perhaps the most significant experience revolved around the annual "Boy of the Year" competition. This contest sought to identify the most outstanding Boys' Club member in the entire country from candidates submitted from local Boys' Clubs throughout the US. The winner would be given the title of *National Boy of the Year*, would be awarded a huge college scholarship from the *Reader's Digest Foundation* and would receive national recognition including a meeting with the President of the United States.

In essence, it is my view that the Boy of the Year *contest* prompted an intense desire on the part of most of us to be the best. I know that during those years, I certainly felt an unusually strong desire to do well, to try harder and to aim more intently to please anyone and everyone who came in contact with me. The competition gave me a clear objective with a huge potential for meaningful rewards. It had great legitimacy and support from seemingly everyone everywhere. And the prospects for success seemed extremely attractive.

In my mind, the Boy of the Year contest also sparked a fierce yet friendly competition among us to be better than our peers. Whether we, the boys, found ourselves in the school environment, the Boys' Club or elsewhere in the El Paso community, competing in academics, sports or extra-curricular activities, we seemed to be unusually focused on outdoing each other while pursuing a very wholesome set of values. The end result was an exceptional crop of young men whose accomplishments generally exceeded the traditional objectives of the Boys' Club and the barrio and who went on to become real contributors in the fabric of American society. Most of us in this bunch of kids from El Paso eventually did indeed manage to firmly wrap our arms around the American dream.

I am very proud of my story and of the story about these kids. But I am also keenly aware of and extremely grateful for the efforts expended by certain very special men and women and some very generous institutions which unquestionably enabled me and the other kids to ignore and sometimes even to defy those forces which easily could have caused the story you are about to read to end differently.

Chapter 1- The Willie Chavez View of the World in the late 1950's

I was eleven years old in 1958 when mi Papá (my Dad) delivered to me the most wonderful news of my life. He had gathered the family and, with some dejection, told us that by the end of the summer, we would be living in the *project*s. The *"projects?"* As in "housing for the underprivileged or the economically disadvantaged?" The *"projects?"* As in "some of the most dangerous neighborhoods in El Paso?" The *"projects*?" As in "that place where people usually are trying very hard to move away from?" Yes indeed! We were heading for the *projects* and despite the somber attitude of mi Papá, I could not possibly have been happier.

Mi Papá, on the other hand, probably could not have felt worst when he told my family and me about the impending move. He had always somehow managed to avoid having to rely on public assistance in order to provide for his family. At this point, however, he really had no other way to give his family a decent place to live other than moving us to the projects. By doing this, he was being forced to admit that he was a failure as a provider and I know that he was not at all happy about that. But there was another reason why mi Papá must have felt badly. Mi Mamá (my Mom) was also completely distressed about the impoverished way we were living. Many years later I found out from older friends and relatives that she had told mi Papá that if we did not find another place in which to live by the end of that summer, she would leave him and return to her family home in Mexico and take the three kids with her. All these circumstances forced mi Papá to swallow his pride and to move us into the projects.

By summer's end, we would be living in a 2-bedroom apartment at the Paisano Housing Project right where Paisano Drive and Hammett Boulevard used to intersect. In those days, the *Housing Authority of the City of El Paso* operated a number of subsidized housing projects. The Paisano Project was one of them. It was common then to refer to each housing project as the "projects" or in Spanish "los proyectos." I was truly thrilled to no end at the prospect of moving there. Why? Because I felt that finally we were going to live in a "real" home. I genuinely believed then that the brick construction of the relatively new apartment buildings that comprised the projects were what real homes were supposed to be made from. I also firmly believed that a real home was not supposed to have a grocery store attached to the front as our home had had for as long as I could remember. But that was only part of my reasoning. Even at the ripe age of 11, I sensed that the projects were a ready-made community of families that seemed even to me to be culturally and economically as homogeneous as possible. Moreover, I believed that in such an environment, where everyone's home was so superficially similar, it would be easier to hide or disguise the very advanced age and the handicap of mi Papá as well as the frail health and the inability of mi Mamá to speak English. At that time, all of these factors weighed heavily in my eleven-year-old mind. In order to appreciate why I felt as I did, it is necessary to consider what the rest of my world was like at that time.

Mi Papá

A year earlier, in 1957, when I was 10 years old, Mi Papá was a huge disappointment to me and he had been that for as long as I could remember. He wasn't a mean father and he really never neglected his family. His problem was that he was blind and old. And, I resented that he had not provided us with a nice home at least during my lifetime up to that point. Like most adolescents, I wanted much more than what I had and I placed upon mi Papá the blame for our impecunious economic state.

Ygnacio Desiderio Chavez, born in 1899, was mi Papá. He was born in Asención, Chihuahua, Mexico, a small town just south of the Mexico-New Mexico border. He came to the US in 1908 when his father (my grandfather) brought his wife and their four children in a covered wagon to Silver City in the New Mexico territory. The family had left Mexico because of the political instability that existed there at the time. There were at least three powerful Mexican politicians who claimed the national presidency and they each had armies that constantly sought to expand their constituencies. My grandfather lived in constant fear that any of those armies would storm into his home and demand that they declare who they supported. He was afraid that the wrong answer would result in immediate death for him and possibly his family and so he fled north across the border.

Mi Papá never got beyond the 8th grade in school. Between 1908 and 1944, he lived in New Mexico or California earning a living in a variety of jobs although he did best and earned the most money as a meat cutter. For some reason unknown to me, everyone who did business with him called him "Charlie." Mi Mamá and close friends and relatives, however, called him "Nacho." He married mi Mamá in February, 1944, in Los Mochis, Sinaloa, Mexico. They spent their honeymoon in Culiacán, Sinaloa, where mi Mamá had to go to get the permit to travel to the US. As soon as her papers were in order, they headed for California, but not before picking up mi Mamá's 8-year-old niece, Alma Lorena Kelly, in Los Mochis and taking her with them. Alma was the daughter of mi Mamá's older sister, Catalina, and her husband Juan Kelly. Alma ended up staying with my parents until she graduated from high school in El Paso in 1957.

Once settled in Los Angeles, my parents gave birth to Ignacio ("Nachito") in 1945. In 1946, mi Papá took his family and fled to El Paso in order to avoid having to pay alimony under a California judgment brought by a woman who claimed that mi Papá was her common law husband. Once in El Paso, my parents produced two more children, Guillermo ("Willie") (me) born in 1947 and Hilda Luz born in 1954.

In his 30's mi Papá had become afflicted with Retinitis Pigmentosa and his vision, therefore, had been steadily deteriorating. By 1958, at age 59, he was legally blind and he could only get around with his red and white cane or with someone to guide him. So, in that year, at about the time I wanted and needed a strong father figure the most, all I had was what I thought was nothing more than an old, partially blind man.

Then, to top it all off, mi Papá seemed to me to have great difficulty earning a decent living for his family. In a period of 6 or 7 years beginning in 1951, he had made two attempts at operating a small grocery store and both had failed badly. The first of these was *Albro's Grocery* on Alameda Avenue in El Paso, Texas. It was a typical Mom & Pop store of the 50's which included a 2-bedroom house with a bathroom immediately to the rear of the store. We shared that bathroom with another family who lived in an apartment behind our house. That was our home for 5 or 6 years until 1957 when, after losing most of his steady customers to new supermarkets like the *Food Mart* at the *Del Camino* shopping center a few blocks east on Alameda Ave., mi Papá decided that we could not afford the rent and had to find a cheaper store elsewhere. At about that time, we moved to the west side of town near *Texas Western College* where he opened *Tex-Western Gro.* on West Main Street. After one year, that venture also ended in failure which led him to give up on the grocery store business forever in 1958.

Operating a grocery store apparently did not completely consume all of the waking hours of mi Papá. He also happened to love to make music. I seem to remember that every day he would pull out the ebony flute that he owned and play it for at least an hour. I also remember vividly that he did not play it very well. Our house was small and so when he practiced, there really was no way to get away so as not to listen. He would play the same song over and over desperately attempting to master it. He did not read music. Instead, he relied strictly on his hearing and on his memory to reproduce any song. I remember listening to his attempts as he continued for hours at a time, and because he relied on his memory, he repeated his errors more often than not. Never do I recall hearing a song coming out of his flute that I would say sounded pretty. On the contrary; I remember repeatedly hearing him as he vainly attempted to reach some unreachable note. He would try over and over and over and he would miss the note over and over and over. My tender eardrums surely were damaged as a result of his dedication to that flute.

I really was sick and tired of listening to that flute during that part of my life. Yet, as I think about it now, I have nothing but respect and admiration for mi Papá who, even though he had no genuine musical talent, persisted in trying to create music. He even tried to play his flute whenever he got together with his musician buddies. Most of these musician buddies were also blind and even though they considered themselves to be musicians, most listeners probably did not. In a later chapter, I will provide more details about this musical group.

Today, I wish that even if I did not have the talent to play it, I could have mi Papá's enthusiasm for the flute. I can only imagine the amount of pleasure that he got from that flute. As he grew older, his passion for the flute only seemed to intensify. When we lived in the projects, I remember that he had not one but two ebony flutes. So, during that period, should either flute suffer a misfortune and be rendered unplayable, there was always a backup. I listened to him play the flute regularly until the day I went off to college. I think he attempted to continue playing long after that, but it became more difficult since he moved frequently. I have no idea what ever happened to those flutes. What I do know is that the last few times I saw mi Papá he was in his mid-eighties and he did not have a flute, although I don't think that he could've played one even if he did.

During the 1950s and 1960s, mi Papá was quite the entertainer. In addition to playing the ebony flute, he loved to sing, was the leader of the band of blind musicians and, he loved to recite poetry.

I remember clearly how my parents (and we, the kids) would go to parties at friends' homes, or friends would come to parties at our home and mi Papá always seemed to be smack in the middle of any entertainment activities. He would either be singing or telling jokes or helping make music. But the most entertaining thing that he did was to recite poetry in Spanish. There were at least three poems that he had memorized and that he loved to deliver at such gatherings. One of those poems was a comedy about a feud between a mother and her son-in-law entitled *La Suegra Y el Yerno*. In the late 1950s, when my sister, Hilda Luz, was 6 or 7 years old, he taught her to recite the part of the mother, while he played the son-in-law. The performance was always very well received. The second poem was one entitled *El Brindis del Bohemio* by Guillermo Aguirre y Fierro. The third one was *Porqúe Me Alejé Del Vicio*.

As the aforementioned parties progressed, I remember people becoming more relaxed, happier and more intimate with each other, thanks to the presence of alcohol, an abundance of food and the passage of time. Toward the end of the parties, when everyone was feeling totally relaxed and when most people had forgotten about the everyday problems that they were inevitably having, someone would suggest that it was time for mi Papá to recite a poem. It seems that even though many of these people had heard these recitations many times before, when someone announced that it was time for mi Papá to recite, everyone--including the young kids--would gather quickly into the main room where mi Papá was preparing to do his thing.

Mi Papá was actually quite an accomplished orator and actor. And, since he had delivered these recitations perhaps hundreds of times in his life, by the time that I got to hear them, he had become quite good at doing it.

His favorite poem, *El Brindis del Bohemio,* is a remarkable story about a gathering of six bohemians who, while drinking and having a good time at a new year's celebration, decided to individually offer a toast to whatever each of them considered important in their respective lives. I will not go into great detail about the poem and I certainly won't attempt now to translate it, but the poem is really a wonderfully dramatic and tear-jerking tribute to mothers.

Whenever mi Papá delivered his recitation of this poem, he would act out the parts of the six bohemians and he would also act as the narrator. The poem starts with a very happy and animated tempo. His audience would always be completely in tune with the story he was telling. As the story progressed, the drama intensified. Toward the end of the poem, the bohemian who is then reciting a toast to his mother, becomes extremely emotional. As he remembers his mother and as he tells stories about her, he actually begins to cry and since he is remembering his mother who has passed away, the burden that he is carrying as the recitation progresses actually brings the actor down to one knee. When mi Papá would reach this part of the recitation, I believed in the bottom of my heart that he was really crying. And the entire audience, whether they were men or women, seemed to weep along with him.

As the play reaches the climax, the toasting, disconsolate bohemian now down on one knee is converted into the narrator. As mi Papá would transition from one role to the other, it always amazed me how interesting it was for him to be totally overwhelmed with emotion and crying at one point in time and on the next second be on his feet as the narrator, calmly concluding the recitation. Immediately after he would recite the last word, there would be a moment of total silence followed by an outburst of cheers and applause.

Being the child that I was, I never appreciated what mi Papá was doing. In fact, I always thought that all of his recitations were silly, corny, and the cause of great embarrassment to me. Today, my appreciation for what he did then is huge. Not only do I feel amazement at the fact that he had an artistic interest and that he could act and recite quite well, but I feel that it is even more remarkable that he was able to do all this even though he was blind. I believe that he memorized all of these poems many years earlier when he was still able to see, which means that he did that even before I was born. But somehow, he retained these poems in his mind well into his seventies. When one considers the length of this particular poem, one cannot help but be impressed with the ability that he must have had in order to retain it in his mind.

Apparently, during the first half of the twentieth century, particularly in Mexico, the recitation of dramatic poetry was a very common form of entertainment. I suspect that in some parts of Latin-America or Spain, this may still be true. However, in the United States today—even in the Mexican-American communities--I can't imagine anyone reciting poetry at a party.

Mi Papá was simply quite an entertainer. He passionately loved to do all sorts of things in order to make people laugh or cry. He also liked to do things simply to impress an audience. In his repertoire was another of his favorite acts: to entertain guests by demonstrating how smart his children were.

Although mi Papá did not have an extensive formal education, he was a strong believer in the power of knowledge. At some point in my life--a point too early for me to recall precisely--mi Papá started to drill my brother and me with historical facts and information. We apparently spent lots of time interacting with him and so the opportunity for discourse was ample. He would tell us a few historical facts over and over and then he would query us about them. It was a simple exercise that proved effective because of simple--and seemingly interminable--repetition. At every opportunity, he would tell us a fact. Later he would ask us about it. I guess that if that's done often enough, a child will retain a whole lot of that stuff. Once he felt satisfied that we had memorized a sufficient amount of historical data, the fun would begin.

I assume that he would teach us these things for the right reason: to educate us. We went along with him for a completely different reason: to make a little money. The way this would work was as follows. He would invite my brother and/or me to stand in front of an audience. The audience could be a single person such as a walk-in stranger or potential customer at our grocery store or it could be a houseful of guests at a party. Then, he would ask us those historical questions that we had been drilling earlier. To the amazement of all, we would produce the right answer even though we were probably still too young to know how to wipe our little bottoms. It was customary to reward young entertainers not only by smiling approvingly and by applauding, but also by giving the child a few pennies as a reward. And so, during these entertaining sessions, mi Papá would be gratified by demonstrating how smart his children were, and his children were gratified by receiving some pocket change for very little effort.

In those days, I suppose I felt inconvenienced and annoyed whenever mi Papá would interrupt me in whatever I was doing in order to ask me these historical questions. However, I was a disciplined boy and I always minded mi Papá. And so, I always played along with him. After all, it took very little time or work for me to respond to the questions he would throw at me and there was always that chance that I might even make a little money. But I never really understood and I never appreciated what he was actually doing. I was learning history and didn't even know it.

Today, I recall those times very fondly. I can even recall the specific questions and answers that we recited. Unfortunately, I only can remember a few of the questions and answers although I know that there were many more that I had memorized back then.

So here are a few that I do recall.

Question: Who discovered America? Answer: Christopher Columbus. (That was a no-brainer and no one was ever particularly impressed by that exchange.)

Question: On what year was America discovered? Answer: 1492. (Again, mostly mundane data; not impressive.)

Question: Who was the last King of Spain? Answer: Alfonso XIII. (That particular dialog would invariably raise eyebrows and impress the audience.)

Question: Who was the conqueror of Mexico? Answer: Hernán Cortez. (In the Mexican-American community where we lived, this was common knowledge and therefore not impressive.)

Question: What were the names of the three wise men (Los trés Reyes magos)? Answer: Melchior, Balthazar and Gaspar. (Somewhat impressive)

Question: Who is a Prime Minister of Russia? Answer: Joseph Stalin (at that time). (Once again, somewhat impressive for a preschooler.)

Question: Who was the first president of the United States? Answer: George Washington. (Not impressive, every kid knew that.)

Question: Who said "Respect for the rights of others is peace"? Answer: Don Benito Juárez. (Once again, not bad, particularly since the answer included the title "Don" which in those days was the title of respect associated with males who somehow found themselves in an elevated social position.)

Question: Who liberated the Negroes? Answer: Abraham Lincoln. (Not bad again for a snotty preschooler.)

Question: Who is the President of the Republic of Mexico? Answer: Adolfo Ruiz Cortines (He was President from 1952-1958 which is when all this was happening. This question demonstrated the continuing interest mi Papá had in Mexican matters.)

Question: What's the ancient capital of Turkey? Answer: Constantinople. (That always impressed the audience.)

Question: How do you spell Constantinople? Answer: I would invariably spell it correctly *and* do it in a musical sing-song. (The audience would usually start applauding.)

Question: What river separates Mexico from the United States? Answer: The Rio Grande as it is known in the United States; the Rio Bravo as it is known in Mexico. (Once again, somewhat impressive in its completeness.)

Question: What's the biggest river in the United States? Answer: The Mississippi. This would be immediately followed with: How do you spell it? And I would invariably spell it correctly and again in a musical sing-song.

To conclude the session with a bang, mi Papá would ask the following: Who said, "La cuesta mía patria está perduta per la mala gobernata"? Answer: Benito Mussolini. (Wow! The kid even speaks Italian! I am certain that it is not proper Italian and I am almost certain that Mussolini never said that.)

With that, everyone was happy. Mi Papá was pleased to show off his obviously gifted progeny; the audience had to have been impressed and entertained; and I and/or my brother could now go back to playing games with perhaps a shiny nickel or more to show for our effort.

Questions and answers would usually total fifteen or twenty before the session was over and I suppose the audience would invariably be impressed. Unfortunately, my memory has failed to retain any of the other questions and answers that he taught us. Of course, when one really looks into the matter, there was nothing very impressive about it all. Even in those days, kids our age were like sponges as far as knowledge was concerned, and when further motivated by a little bit of approval, recognition and reward, any child probably would have done the same.

One variation that mi Papá used to like to do was to ask the questions in Spanish and in English to coincidentally show our bilingual capabilities. The fact is that not only did we learn historical data, but we also sharpened infinitely our ability to speak comfortably in both languages in front of people.

It is customary in countries where Spanish is the first language for individuals to have a first name, followed by a middle name, followed by the father's first surname and followed finally by the mother's first surname. Mi Papá and mi Mamá did not follow that tradition. They instead adopted the American tradition of giving their children a first name followed by a middle name followed by mi Papá s first surname. However, they—like most other parents in the Mexican-American community--apparently made no attempt to give their children English names. I wondered all my life whether they gave us decidedly Spanish or bilingual names because they were confident that the Spanish culture would eventually obliterate the Anglo culture or whether they viewed the family's sojourn in the US as strictly temporary. In any event, my brother's birth certificate says: Ignacio Enrique Chavez; mine says: Guillermo Daniel (fortunately Daniel is spelled the same in Spanish as well as in English) Chavez; and my sister's: Hilda (another bilingual name) Luz Chavez. Our surname, Chavez, technically should have an accent mark over the "a" (i.e. "Chávez") but I suppose that such things became less important as we became assimilated. And so, in today's world I hardly ever use or require the accent mark when my surname is written.

But in naming his children, mi Papá also saw another opportunity to have fun. It all started even before my brother and I were old enough to pronounce our names or to understand what he was doing. What he did was this: After I was born, he created a preposterously long name: *Daniel Luís Guillermo*

Elias Romero Alcalde Chavez de la Garza Cárdenas García. The name has some connection to reality since my complete name is indeed embedded in it as is mi Mamá's maiden name (Romero Alcalde). But the composite is otherwise totally fabricated. Then he got my brother and me to memorize that long name while we were so young that we could barely pronounce it. Once we had committed the name to memory, he would grab every opportunity to introduce us to others. Even though my brother normally went by the name "Nachito" and I had become known as "Willie," whenever mi Papá introduced us to another adult, we would jump into the routine that he had taught us, inhale deeply and then let out that torrent of names. The response was almost always the same: amazement on the part of the stranger followed by raucous laughter. I know this routine endeared us as well as mi Papá to those strangers and maybe even created another customer relationship for mi Papá's grocery store.

Today, I feel deeply impressed and appreciative of what mi Papá did to my brother, my sister and me along these lines way back when. I don't know of any other Dad who would do anything like this. Mi Papá was far from being a perfect man; however, he did do many things that today I find amazing. That history lesson that he afforded us when we were young as well as that crazy, long name that he taught us were just some of those amazing things.

And so, on those pivotal years 1957 and 1958, despite mi Papá's best efforts, the business at *Tex-Western Gro.* simply did not work out. There were very few customers and yet we always had the unavoidable operating costs. And so, at the end of the one-year lease, for business reasons and probably because of an ultimatum given to him by mi Mamá, mi Papá ended up doing what he had avoided for so long but what seemed to me to be one of the best things that ever happened to me: we moved into federally subsidized housing at the Paisano Projects.

Mi Mamá

So, if mi Papá was having great difficulty earning an income, what about mi Mamá? Why could she not get a job and help out? Well, Mi Mamá had more than her fair share of problems.

Mi Mamá's name was Julia Daria Romero Alcalde Chavez. As far as I know, everyone called her "Dari" (pronounced "Dottie"). She was born in 1916. Her birthplace was the little town in Sinaloa known as Sinaloa de Leyva in her father's ranch called "Las Playitas." She had two brothers Victor and Genaro and one sister Catalina. Her education was modest and rural and she never got beyond the 8th grade.

My parents arrived in El Paso in late 1946 or early 1947. They lived on Frutas Street across from *Guardian Angel School* until the early 1950's. From then until 1958, they tried to make a living by operating the grocery stores mentioned earlier. Mi Mamá—who spoke no English--was the home maker, while mi Papá—who spoke English well--tried to run the grocery stores. If he was ever absent, she would be in charge and the three children would help as necessary, particularly when it came to translating for her. In addition, mi Mamá became a skilled seamstress who catered to the dress needs of neighbors and friends and thereby managed to supplement the family income modestly. While living at our store on Alameda, her best client was Lena Gray.

Lena and her husband Herman were very close friends of mi Mamá and mi Papá. They were an African-American couple—actually the only black folks we knew--and they were probably the wealthiest family in our entire neighborhood. They certainly had the nicest home in the neighborhood. It was a three-story structure made of gray granite on a huge lot right next to the Franklin canal on Tobin Street. The house of the Grays had really fancy wooden floors and beautiful wooden staircases and banisters. It was probably 50 years old then. Why the Grays chose to live in our neighborhood was a mystery to me although now I can guess that it was because they were not welcome in the nice Anglo neighborhoods of El Paso. They were the only black family in our neighborhood which was mostly Mexican-American. They never had children.

Herman and Lena were both extremely large people. When we knew them on Alameda Avenue, Herman was probably in his late forties or early fifties. He was well over 6ft. tall and weighed more than 350lb. He was an employee of the *Southern Pacific Railroad*, a company well known for its generous wages and benefits. Herman had a reputation for being--and in fact, was--an excellent cook. His specialty was barbecued beef and pork. Frequently, when he prepared it, he would bring huge portions of it to our home.

Lena was a few years younger than Herman, of normal stature (around 5'6"), but she tipped the scales at well over 500lb. I was always amused when Lena came to our home because she could only sit on our chrome and vinyl dinette chairs. Any wooden chair was likely to collapse under her.

It was Lena's extreme obesity that brought her to mi Mamá. Lena could not buy off-the-rack clothing and had to have everything made to order. Mi Mamá became her seamstress. The relationship was wonderful for both.

Lena was very pleased that mi Mamá could make anything for her to wear. And mi Mamá was delighted to take Lena's money for her work.

Mi Mamá and Lena would have long chats sipping coffee and discussing the dresses Lena needed. Since mi Mamá could not speak English and Lena could not speak Spanish, they always needed an interpreter. Mi Papá was the usual person to handle that task but when he wasn't available, they would let me or Nachito to do it. Despite this language difference, Lena and mi Mamá would exchange jokes, sad stories and the news of the day. After a long conversation that required translation by Nachito or me, Lena would always give us a tip (a quarter, maybe) for our effort. In addition, Lena would always compliment us generously for being bilingual. She thought it was so cool.

As Nachito and I became bigger boys, Herman and Lena would hire us to do odd jobs in their huge home. We would clean up the backyard or mow the lawn or rake the leaves or wash their cars, etc. But they were generous to us and they always gave us a fantastic lunch. Herman and Lena always followed the activities of the neighborhood schools and when we were in High School, they were really proud of Nachito and me for our accomplishments since they had no children of their own.

Herman and Lena each drove their own Buicks. Hers was the large four-door model; his was a slightly smaller two-door model. Both cars had the driver seat positioned all the way back so that it almost touched the rear seat bench. I always found it somewhat entertaining--given my age--to watch them get out of their respective cars. They never came to see us in one car. They would always drive over in two separate cars. We always assumed that they did that because both of them could not fit in one car.

They were probably among the sweetest and happiest people I have ever met. They laughed constantly and vigorously and made everyone around them laugh with them. Herman, however, probably had a drinking problem. He seemed to be drunk most of the time. And he would drive drunk frequently. Mi Mamá always cautioned us not to get into his car with him. He would offer to pick us up and take us to his home to do the odd jobs and we always told him that we would instead ride our bikes. I know mi Mamá was extremely fond of Lena and I remember well how mi Papá and Herman would sit and drink beer and laugh boisterously for hours in the living room while mi Mamá was doing sewing work and visiting with Lena in the kitchen.

I remember mi Mamá as a perfectly normal, although perhaps slightly overweight mother who loved her family dearly but who missed her home in Mexico very much also. In fact, mi Mamá, my sister and I made a number of trips to Mexico during the summers of those years so she could stay connected to her family.

She was an extremely sweet person that everyone seemed to like. She was loving and kind to us, her children, although I remember a few occasions when she felt the need to discipline us and occasionally to spank us with a belt. I don't necessarily recall those spankings with bitterness. While we never enjoyed them, they never were really that devastating so as to permanently scar any of us either physically, mentally or emotionally. What I do remember, is that she was very affectionate with all of us all the time.

She was a very traditional Mexican mother. She would prepare three meals a day every day. She would cook beans at every meal. For the evening meal every day she would make flour tortillas that would last until the next evening meal. When we became adolescents, she would not actually sit down to eat a meal with us but instead would stand by the stove ready to refill our dishes or give us more tortillas. After the meal, she would sit at the table alone or with Hilda Luz and eat after mi Papá, my brother and I had run off to do stuff. One of her favorite dishes consisted of a corn tortilla that she would heat over a gas flame on the stove top until it was charred. Then she would butter it. She would eat this with a cup of coffee and would give the impression that she was in heaven. Until I went to college, I remember helping with the dishes unless some school activity called me away.

Mi Mamá never learned to speak English. It was probably for that reason that her children all learned Spanish. All of us could not only speak Spanish but we could also read and write Spanish, which was somewhat unusual even in our old Mexican neighborhood. The first Spanish lessons she ever gave me were when I was learning to read English and in conjunction with correspondence she maintained for the longest time with her older sister, Catalina, who lived in Los Mochis, Sinaloa, Mexico. Mi Mamá would receive a letter from her every few months and frequently she would read it to the children. I liked very much to hold those letters and to have mi Mamá read specific lines to me. Eventually, I started to actually read the lines by myself despite my aunt's awful penmanship. Later, mi Mamá would help me write a line or two in the letters she would write to Catalina. By the time I started taking Spanish classes in high school, I felt a great advantage from what mi Mamá had taught me.

She loved to watch television even though she didn't understand very much of it. I think her favorite program was *I Love Lucy*. After all, you didn't have to understand Lucy in order to laugh at her and did mi Mamá ever laugh at her. She would laugh so hard that she rocked from side to side as she sat on the sofa watching those programs. And, very frequently she laughed until she cried. I remember being very happy when she was that happy.

Until I was 12, mi Mamá would actually sew all the shirts that I would wear. Since these shirts were homemade, they did not look exactly like store-bought shirts. I found the difference to be somewhat humiliating. I did not want to wear them since they looked so different from the shirts that other kids wore. I was ashamed that we could not buy what other kids' parents were able to buy. My teachers and other parents, on the other hand, thought my shirts were beautiful. I was so wrong at those times for not appreciating what mi Mamá was doing. Only now do I fully appreciate the love and the effort that mi Mamá put into making those shirts. I am really glad that I was able to tell her how much I appreciated what she did many years later before she passed away.

Mi Mamá, like so many other Mexican mothers, was deeply religious. She prayed a rosary every day and went to Mass on Sundays until she was too sick to go. But then she insisted that her children go to Mass on Sunday by themselves. She was convinced that the good fortunes that fell on her children were nothing more than answers to her prayers. In 1967, when I was a first-year cadet at West Point, she disclosed to me that she believed I was alive because of a promise she had made to the Virgin of Guadalupe when I was an infant. She told me that I had been suffering from severe bronchitis and that she truly feared that I would not make it through the night. So, she prayed passionately to the Virgin of Guadalupe and promised that if I survived the night, she would one day make a pilgrimage to Mexico City to visit her shrine. Mi Mamá never forgot her promise. In the summer between my first and second years at West Point, mi Mamá, my little sister and I went to Mexico City where mi Mamá discharged her obligation to the Virgin of Guadalupe.

Although both she and mi Papá had very little formal education, they seemed to be of one mind when it came to the early education of my siblings and me. They preferred that we attend a Catholic school (Guardian Angel) rather than the public schools and, for as long as they could afford it, we did. That cousin of mine, Alma, who came with my parents from Mexico when they got married, actually graduated from a prestigious catholic girls' school in El Paso. When mi Papá started to struggle with his grocery store business, my older brother and I were pulled from Guardian Angel and we started going to a public school, Burleson Elementary. We did well at Burleson and economic reality dictated that we would never return to the parochial schools even though my parents would have preferred that we did. Since my brother and I seemed to be self-motivated, I don't remember ever having a conversation with either of my parents regarding the importance of an education or of completing high school.

Like so many other members of the Mexican-American community, mi Mamá became a great fan of John F. Kennedy. Again, even though she could not understand what Kennedy was saying, she loved to watch him on television and to listen to his speeches. His characteristic voice was something that everyone came to love and enjoy. She felt particularly blessed when my brother, Nachito, actually met Kennedy in 1963. The details of that meeting are set forth in a later part of this book.

I also recall that mi Mamá had quite a sense of humor. She laughed frequently and vigorously. One time, mi Papá played a prank on one of his buddies named Elias Garrido. We apparently threw a party at our home on Alameda and invited a bunch of people including Elias and his family. Elias had a reputation for being extremely fearful of rats. Before the party started mi Papá had placed a rubber rat behind the stove in our kitchen but left it so that it was barely visible. The party progressed through the evening and Elias, as usual, had a few too many beers. Late in the evening, somehow, the rat caught the eye of Elias and Elias, upon seeing it, sprung from his seat on the sofa, let out a loud scream and in terror flung his can of beer at the rat. The can was open and as it flew toward its target, it spewed a spiral of foaming brew in all directions. The can landed with a clang close to the rat but obviously caused no reaction from the toy. Mi Mamá witnessed all this, and instead of being upset at a guest spraying beer all over her kitchen, she laughed uproariously along with all others who saw the spectacle. I witnessed all this and was frightened at the beginning but ended up laughing hysterically along with all the others when it was all over.

Beginning around 1955, mi Mamá started having seizures. They were unpredictable and mostly uncontrollable despite the fact that she took medication for them. For all of us, the seizures were terrifying. They would begin with a blood-curdling scream that she would let out as the seizure started. She would then shake violently and fall unconscious to the floor where the convulsions would continue for a few seconds. She would roll her eyes and foam at the mouth and bite her tongue. Even if we were near her, there was nothing we could do until the seizure passed. Afterward, we would have to tend to the injuries that she sustained from the fall and from biting her tongue. Once in a while, the seizure would be so severe that we had to call an ambulance to take her to the hospital. Fortunately, the seizures only occurred once or twice a year. Since we could not afford anything better, the medical care that she required was covered by El Paso County. That was good in some respects, but one has to wonder whether she was receiving the best care available. After all, her doctors were never able to determine what was causing her seizures. It was only after she died in 1968 that they discovered a tumor in her brain.

The seizures and living in fear of them were a huge burden on mi Mamá but they also created a profound strain in the rest of us. Mi Papá probably felt the pressure most because of his blindness. One time, while my parents were in our living room and I was sitting by the kitchen table, mi Mamá had a seizure. As I heard her scream, I dashed into the living room. She had already fallen to the floor in convulsions. Then I saw Mi Papá on his knees frantically searching for her with outstretched arms. But he was nowhere near her. He was simply searching in a place other than where she lay. Afterward, when things had quieted down again and mi Mamá was resting comfortably, mi Papá tearfully lamented how he may have been able to catch her as she fell if only he could have been able to see.

My brother, sister and I also felt an enormous encumbrance as we tried to cope with the seizures. I remember on many occasions waking in the middle of the night because mi Mamá was snoring too loudly. I would go and awaken her to ensure that she had not suffered a seizure. My poor little sister, who was barely a child and who naturally was extremely close to mi Mamá probably suffered the greatest stress. The 3 kids and mi Papá constantly re-arranged our schedules to make sure that one of us was always at the side of mi Mamá in case she suffered a seizure. We were always immensely grateful that she never had a seizure away from home.

All through my high school years, mi Mamá struggled with her illness. 1963 was particularly a tough year for her. In early November, she suffered a seizure while she slept. Her convulsions caused her to fall from the bed and she landed face down on the hard wood floor of the bedroom. I remember that the thud of her fall awakened me. We knew she was having a seizure. When I arrived from my bedroom and turned on the light, I found mi Papá still groping in the dark trying to find mi Mamá on the floor. She was wedged between the queen bed where she and mi Papá slept and the twin bed where Hilda Luz slept. We all tried to help her but she was still convulsing. After the spasms passed, we turned her over on the floor and saw that she had fallen from the bed on her face and that she was bleeding badly. Eventually, an ambulance arrived and took her to Thomason General Hospital where she spent a few days before coming back home.

When she returned home, she stayed in bed most of the time recovering from her injuries. After a few days, she was able to come downstairs and lie on the sofa where she could watch TV. Then the worst event of my youth took place. On November 22, 1963, President John F. Kennedy was assassinated. The whole country went into a state of shock and depression and so did mi Mamá. For reasons that no one will ever know for certain, she suffered another seizure in the days following the assassination. While this time she did not fall, she did somehow injure her arm and shoulder as a result of the seizure. Those injuries stayed with her until she died in 1968.

As difficult as 1963 was for her in terms of her illness, that year was also most likely the best and most memorable for other reasons. 1963 was the year when my brother Nachito was named national Boy of the Year by the *Boys' Clubs of America*. Her son, despite having been brought up in humble circumstances, became the object of national recognition and fame. She witnessed with great pride how Nachito met and was praised by huge public figures such as *The Tonight Show* host Johnny Carson, Vice President Lyndon B. Johnson, FBI Director J. Edgar Hoover and most significant of all, President John F. Kennedy.

She also must have felt wonderful in 1963 when she learned that Nachito had received a scholarship from the *Boys' Clubs of America*. A complete education for her children had always been a priority in her life even though I truly do not believe that she fully understood what college entailed nor how much it cost or how she and mi Papá would ever be able to afford it. Perhaps to her, a college education for her kids was simply a part of that bigger abstract ambition we called the "American dream." We all wanted to realize it even if we did not know precisely what it was or how to do it.

During the last five years of her life, she experienced a mixture of events that are, even in these days, common to loving mothers. Her two sons, Nachito and I, graduated from high school and probably did so with lots more distinction than most of our peers. As Nachito and I continued our development in college, we both chose paths that were heavily laced with military content. Nachito spent a year at *New Mexico Military Institute* before getting an appointment and reporting to the *United States Naval Academy* at Annapolis, Maryland. I spent a year in the Corps of Cadets at *Texas A&M University* before reporting to the *United States Military Academy* at West Point, New York. That series of academic achievements must have made her feel good. But there was a war evolving in Vietnam and she knew that her sons would most likely end up there sooner or later. That possibility must have been a massive emotional weight for her. She also must have worried a lot about her mysterious seizures and the pressure that they brought to mi Papá and my sister Hilda Luz, who would now have to cope with all that without the benefit of Nachito or me to help.

Ironically, she did not have to worry about finances. Even though Nachito and I were no longer able to supplement the family income, mi Mamá was able to make ends meet. The family was so impoverished that we were receiving financial assistance from the county and subsidized housing from the *El Paso Housing Authority*. That, coupled with mi Papá's Social Security pension and his sales activities with the *Lighthouse for the Blind* enabled my parents and Hilda Luz to do OK.

Mi Mamá died on March 29th, 1968. I was in my second year at West Point. I saw her for the last time around Christmas time 1967 when I spent a few weeks at home while on Christmas leave from the Academy. I have innumerable memories of her but the one that stands out the most is how she frequently reassured me that there was no kid smarter or better looking than me and how there was nothing in this world that I could not do.

My Cousin Alma

Alma was that 8-year-old niece that mi Mamá brought with her from Mexico in 1944 when she married mi Papá. I guess Alma was brought along to ensure that mi Papá did not pull off any stunts like deserting his new wife once they arrived in America. So, in the late 1950's, Alma must have been a very big part of our family. Even though Alma lived with us for the first 10 years of my life, I do not remember very much about her or the role she played within our household. She was seven years older than me and therefore, from my perspective, she was just another adult. I have to believe that she pulled her weight around the house and grocery store whenever she was needed and, at the same time, was privileged enough to attend a private catholic girls' school. Since the income that mi Papá was able to generate from the store had to be modest at best, Alma's parents back in Los Mochis, Sinaloa, Mexico, probably sent money to mi Mamá regularly to cover Alma's expenses, particularly her school tuition. However, I do not recall that she ever did any income-producing work outside of our home and store. I am certain that she frequently worked as a store clerk at mi Papá's store and as a babysitter for the three children in our home especially for the youngest, Hilda Luz.

While Alma was in high school, she met a guy named Serafín Avitia III. Serafín at the time was a student at *El Paso High School*. I don't know how they met but I do recall that he was one cool dude. First of all, he was an all-around nice guy that always seemed to be smiling and saying nice things to everyone. Everyone seemed to like him. Also, he was a handsome young man from what I can remember although I don't think he was any kind of athlete. One thing that he was recognized for in El Paso was that he was a lap-top puppeteer/ventriloquist who performed in small venues around town. Finally--and most important--he had one of the coolest cars that could be seen anywhere in El Paso at the time. It was a 1946 Chevy two-door coupe that he had painted red with a grey top. The color of the car made it stand out and clearly identified the owner as a really swell and nifty guy. I admired Serafín a whole lot.

Alma and Serafín started to date and, as far as I know, they did so in the most traditional sense. I remember that he would come to our house at appropriate times, park his Chevy on Alameda Avenue directly in front of our store and come inside the house to visit with Alma in the presence of my parents. He would always leave at an appropriate time too. Occasionally, they would go out on dates accompanied by Nachito or me as chaperones. In 1955, soon after Alma graduated from high school and Serafin returned from a military stint in Japan with the US Army, they got married. They lived in El Paso for a couple of years where Serafin was employed by the *Orkin* pest exterminator company doing residential treatments. Then Serafin applied for and got a job with the US Government in Washington, DC, applying technical skills that he acquired while he was in the Army. They moved to Maryland where they lived the rest of their lives.

Big Brother

Because in those days in the late 1950's I perceived so many deficiencies in mi Papá's ability to head our household, and because mi Mamá's health was so unsteady, I often felt that our home was like a boat adrift at sea without a helmsman. But more and more that void began to get filled by my big brother, Nachito.

Nachito, only a year and a half older than me, was extremely mature even then. I suppose that due to simple necessity, Nachito was frequently required to participate in many of the decisions that had to be made in order for our family to function. He regularly was the eyes for mi Papá and went with him as a guide whenever mi Papá had to go anywhere. He was called upon constantly to read any correspondence that the family received and to not only read and interpret the contents for mi Papá, but also to translate it for mi Mamá. As the oldest child, he was responsible often for taking care of my little sister and me.

And, even then, Nachito had put together a pretty impressive history of earning a little money that was used by our parents to help with the financial household needs. *Albro's Grocery* and our house were located at the 4500 block of Alameda Avenue about 2-3 miles east of downtown El Paso. There was a city bus that passed by right in front of *Albro's* every 15-20 minutes. Nachito, beginning when he was around 9 years of age and equipped with his home-made shoe shine box, was dispatched on that bus into town on Saturdays and Sundays by mi Papá to earn whatever he could by shining shoes at the downtown parks, bars and restaurants. As I grew older, my parents would also send me along as Nachito's sidekick. I suppose they believed that two boys were stronger than one if the need ever arose to defend ourselves or maybe they just figured that one of us could always be counted upon to report on the activities of the other. In any event, at 5 cents a shine, the proceeds of these business ventures were indeed helpful to the family.

When my family lived on Alameda Avenue, we used to regularly engage in small carpentry projects either as a necessity (in order to keep my father's store operating) or as a means of having fun. I was very young and I really liked to play with hammers and nails and small pieces of wood to create little wooden objects that I could then play with.

I shall never forget how much fun I had when I built my first shoe-shine box. I was probably under five years old and I know I got lots of help from mi Papá and from Nachito. The most memorable part of the building process has to do with where my building materials came from. In those days, we received vegetables such as tomatoes or squash to sell in the store. They usually came packed in small wooden crates that were approximately 24 inches long by 18 inches wide by 5 inches high. The two end-pieces of each crate were 1"x5"x18" pieces of reasonably good wood and they actually held the entire crate together. Thinner and cheaper slabs of wood were then nailed to those end-pieces to form the crates. All of these pieces of wood were held together by 1-inch black nails. So, when a crate was taken apart carefully, you got a good amount of wood and some nails to fool-around with.

Mi Papá's store would probably go through three or four of these crates per week and therefore, they provided a fairly large amount of small, useful pieces of wood. Mi Papá would remove the nails, separate the cheap wood from the better wood and then allow us to play with any of those materials to make the stuff that we wanted.

Here's how I built my first shoe-shine box. I started with the two end-pieces of a vegetable crate. They comprised the front and the back of the shoe-shine box. I then sawed each of those two pieces so that they looked like a little house, that is, the sides were parallel up to the midpoint of the plank and then they were pitched toward the middle but with a 2-inch wide top. I would then take three other end-pieces and they would comprise the bottom and the two sides of the box. A small 2-inch strip that I would cut from yet another end-piece would then constitute the top of the shoe-shine box.

With that, the main structure of the shoe-shine box was done and special features could then be added to it. For example, I could close up the sides of the box (the sides which corresponded to the roof of the house) by nailing down one of them on one side and attaching the other as a hinged door on the opposite side to permit access to the interior of the shoe-shine box. The hinges were made of small squares of leather from a belt that mi Papá had discarded. Also, I could fashion a piece of wood shaped like the sole of the shoe and affix it to the top of the shoe-shine box at a slight angle. That's where the customer could place his foot and I could shine his shoes, one at a time. Finally, a really essential feature was to take the rest of that leather belt and attach it to the front and back of the shoe-shine box so as to form a sling that I could place over my shoulder to facilitate carrying the shoe-shine box around. To properly promote the service that I offered, I would take the black liquid shoe polish container and with the applicator that came with it, write the following on the two top panels of the shoe-shine box: **SHOE SHINE 5¢**.

Nachito and I each had our own shoe-shine boxes. The two of us would lug our shoe-shine boxes and board the city bus and head for the parks, bars and restaurants in the downtown area of El Paso. There we would wait near the park benches or outside the front entrances of the bars and restaurants and, as patrons left or entered, we would accost them to see if they required a shoe-shine. Invariably, there would be some number of customers who, even if they didn't get the best shoe-shine of their lives, they probably found it somewhat amusing to see a pair of brothers just past the toddler age hawking their services. I remember doing this only a few times but, on each occasion, bringing home a little bit of loose change that would help supplement the family income. I suppose those shoe-shining excursions also provided us with invaluable growing-up experience although we were probably much too young to be doing these things around local bars.

It may sound strange but shoe-shining really did play a somewhat pivotal role in my life. My shoe-shining life is divided into two phases. The first phase--which took up my early years up until the time I became a freshman in high school—was basically the phase that I call the "Conventional Era." In this Conventional Era, shoe-shining was accomplished very simply by first brushing (with a cleaning brush) the dust and dirt off of the surface of the leather, then applying with an applicator brush a sudsy soapy solution to the surface of the shoe to loosen any dirt or grease. Before permitting that solution to penetrate the leather, I would dry it in preparation for the next step.

The next step was to apply the liquid shoe polish that came in small bottles with applicators affixed to the screw-on tops. Then, the shoe would be brushed to a reasonable gloss with a different buffing brush. Next, a paste wax from a little flat *Shinola* tin can in the appropriate color would be applied using the index and middle fingertips of the right hand. That shoe, now waxed, would be permitted to dry for a few minutes while the above-described process was undertaken for the other shoe. When that same process was done for the other shoe, attention would be directed back to the first shoe which was now dry and ready for buffing.

The final buff would start with the buffing brush again and then be followed with a buffing using a strip of soft cloth about 3 inches wide and 12 inches long. I would hold the two ends of that cloth with each of my hands and move the cloth back and forth over the toe of the shoe in a repetitive left and right motion until the shoe gleamed like glass. When the shoe was finished, I would give a gentle tap on the front of the sole of the shoe indicating to the customer that the job was finished. The whole process rarely took more than ten minutes and always resulted in much better-looking shoes.

The most significant potential problem arose when a customer wore white or light-colored socks. The shiner had to be careful not to get shoe polish on the socks. Some kids would insert a small piece of cardboard to protect the socks. "Real men/boys" never did that. They just managed the shoe-shine materials and tools in such a way so as to ensure that only leather got shined. I recall that on various occasions the customer showed me where I had stained his socks. But I suppose I was so young and cute that they paid–and tipped—me anyway.

The second phase of my shoe-shining life came as I entered high school. That phase is what I call the "Spit-Shine Era." I describe it in great detail in a later chapter where I cover my high school days. It was during that period that spit-shining skill really paid me big dividends.

Notwithstanding the riches to be made, providing shoe-shining services to others did not gratify me anywhere near as much as shining my own shoes. All that started when I was very young. I somehow became a bit obsessed with wanting to always keep my shoes shined brilliantly. Perhaps mi Papá instilled that idea in me. Regardless, I believed strongly that shiny shoes were an essential part of any gentleman's proper bearing. Nevertheless, I fondly remember shining shoes when I was young and to this day, consider myself a world-class shoe-shiner.

It was also during those days when Nachito was no more than 5 or 6 that mi Papá started placing other pretty significant responsibilities on his tiny shoulders. *Albro's Grocery* was a small operation by any standard but it was open daily from 8AM until 10PM. Mi Papá was the principal operator but he relied heavily on mi Mamá and on my cousin, Alma, to also be there when customers appeared. Nachito and I were also always there because we lived there. However, as soon as we were old enough to attend to customers and to make change, we too became part of the retail staff. Mi Papá kiddingly named Nachito as the assistant manager of the store at about the same time that Nachito started the first grade. His first set of chores included mostly sweeping, mopping and cleaning and stocking of shelves but he was nevertheless interfacing with customers extensively. By the time he was in the third grade Nachito was able to service any customer regardless of what the customer needed. This included cutting, weighing and selling meat and cheese from the huge meat refrigerator. I followed in Nachito's footsteps a few years later and leaned heavily on Nachito as I learned the ropes, but Nachito had to learn all that on his own and this undoubtedly enabled him to mature more quickly and with a keen eye for making money.

Nachito was also an altar boy at Guardian Angel Catholic Church and on weekends would bring home additional small change from having assisted in the celebration of baptisms. He simply was a fine all-around boy and I was fortunate to have him near to keep me safe and generally on a healthy and constructive growth path.

Little Sister

On that day in 1958 when mi Papá announced the plan to move to the projects, I also had a little sister, Hilda Luz, who was around 3 ½ years old. She certainly was a cute and joyous part of our family. At that point, Hilda Luz was too young to be a factor in anything that was happening. Mi Papá was still living his dream having brought a daughter, finally, into his life. And, I am sure that mi Mamá and my brother were thrilled greatly with the presence of this little girl. But I honestly do not remember being either especially close or distant to her. Hilda Luz was too young to be a playmate for me, but more significantly she was, after all, a girl and a baby girl at that. She was just a cute little kid who was blessed with a mother who made the most amazing and beautiful dresses for her as frequently as she could.

If there is any person in my life that I have completely taken for granted it would have to be my sister Hilda Luz. It certainly was not done deliberately. However, from the earliest of times that I can remember her, I have always felt that she did not need my attention since mi Papá, mi Mamá, and my older brother, Nacho, always seemed to be spoiling her. And so, I essentially ignored her.

I do not know this for a fact and I actually do not believe this to be the case, but her birth may have been unplanned by my parents. Of course, that type of planning in those days was unheard of. But the fact is that mi Papá was struggling in his business and for some reason they waited seven years to conceive Hilda Luz so, I always have believed that she came as a surprise.

As I look back on the days when she arrived in our household, I remember feeling robbed. I felt robbed of the attention that I had previously been getting from everyone whether family or friends. She was a curiosity when she came into our lives and I didn't hate her nor did any nasty things to her but I know I was not terribly excited about her being around.

Coincidentally, it was shortly after Hilda Luz's birth that mi Mamá started to suffer those epileptic-like seizures. I certainly do not blame Hilda Luz for having any connection with those seizures. It was not until much later in life that I considered the possibility that my Mom's illness had been caused by childbirth since mi Mamá was 39 years old when Hilda Luz was born. Yet, there is no proof that Hilda Luz's birth and mi Mamá's illness were related. I believe mi Mamá just became ill as many people normally do late in middle age.

Mi Mamá was naturally thrilled to the max when finally, after bringing two boys into the world, she had a little girl. I distinctly remember that Hilda Luz had the nicest dresses of all of the girls in the neighborhood and in her school. Mi Mamá sewed the prettiest things for her. In a way, Hilda Luz was her "doll" and she dressed her up to perfection. I don't think this created any resentment on my part since I really did not like to wear the clothes mi Mamá would make for me.

Mi Papá, who was 55 years old when Hilda Luz was born, was also completely beside himself with excitement. He actually wrote a song entitled *Oh, Linda Hilda Luz*, to commemorate her birth. I can hum it even as I write this and I recall a few of the lyrics. At that time, I was actually pretty impressed by the fact that she had had a song written for her. In fact, I remember on many occasions joining the rest of the family as we sang Hilda

Luz's song whenever we had company. Interestingly, the song also actually makes note of her two brothers. Maybe mi Papá was trying to make sure we did not get jealous of the new infant.

As I stated earlier, I took Hilda Luz's happiness and well-being completely for granted, unwittingly as it may have been, because she had always been under the very close care of our Mother. Even when mi Mamá was ill, Hilda Luz was always her first concern. During those days when I was in elementary school, I suppose I became almost completely self-absorbed as I contemplated my current predicament as well as my future.

Years later, when I left home to attend college, things were relatively calm at home even though mi Mamá was not well. Hilda Luz was ten years old by then and I do not even remember what school she was attending. But my future was bright and so I just took off without giving one second thought to Hilda Luz's well-being. Fortunately, things remained calm for the next few years and Hilda Luz grew up in a relatively normal environment.

However, in March, 1968, all hell broke loose for all of us. Mi Mamá suddenly died. I was away at West Point when it happened. It was a horrible shock and loss to me but I completely failed to appreciate how devastating mi Mamá's death must have been to Hilda Luz. Hilda Luz was thirteen years old. She was at exactly the age when a young girl probably needs her Mother the most. Even if I had been sensitive, there probably wasn't much that I could have done to help. Fortunately, my brother, who three weeks before had been commissioned a second lieutenant in the US Army, was able to get a compassionate re-assignment and get stationed at Fort Bliss in El Paso to care for my little sister and our disabled father. Hilda Luz's life during the next 17 months was relatively normal, living with Nachito, and some time also with our Papá.

In August of 1969, Nachito decided to extend his military obligation in order to volunteer to do a service tour in Vietnam, primarily in order to assist himself to overcome some financial difficulties that he had assumed since Mamá's death. This, however, required that arrangements be made to care for Hilda Luz. So, he contacted our cousin, Alma, who lived in Maryland with her family and arranged for Hilda Luz to live with them until he returned from Vietnam. Unfortunately, that arrangement did not work very well for anyone.

My family was very fortunate in that we had a younger brother of mi Papá who also lived in El Paso. Clemente Salvador Chavez, or Uncle Sal, as we used to call him, was in many respects exactly what mi Papá was not. Uncle

Sal served in World War II, had a steady job as an optometrist/technician, provided well for his family and whenever mi Papá needed help he was always around. Hilda Luz came back from Maryland and lived with our Uncle Sal and his family for a while. Unfortunately, Hilda Luz's year or two there were also pretty miserable for many reasons.

As I think back today on what Hilda Luz must have been going through in those years, I shudder. Eventually, however, Hilda Luz earned the degree of Doctor of Naturopathy and has had a successful practice in the El Paso area for 38 years.

Anyway, back in mid-1957, as my family contemplated the move to West Main Street where mi Papá was going to try to open and operate yet another grocery store, I felt cheated. Somehow, I was living in a world that had no promise. What friends I had then were about to be taken away from me, Mi Mamá was sick with a mysterious ailment, Mi Papá was an old blind man that would probably never earn a decent living and we were moving into a hovel. I also was very disappointed that we were not moving to the projects. I must have known for a while that we had no money and that the government offers apartments in the projects for families like mine. While that normally would not be a nice place to move, I had many friends and classmates who lived in the projects and I could think of many worse places in which to live.

As my family prepared to leave *Albro's Grocery* and move to *Tex-Western Gro.* on West Main Street, I wrote a letter to my 4th grade classmates. The 1956-1957 school term at Burleson Elementary School had just ended and I knew that the letter would not be delivered or read to my former classmates until September. Still, I wrote it in late May because I felt very sad and hurt that I was being moved away from the only home and friends that I had ever known. I wanted to make sure that they knew that they were my friends forever and that I would never replace them with other friends. That letter was a clear expression of my dissatisfaction with what was happening in my life. Yet, I never sent that letter because I could not figure out how to mail it to the Burleson Elementary fifth grade homeroom that would not come to existence until three months later.

So, that's the way my world seemed to be around 1957 when I was 10 years old. I was not terribly excited with the way things were at home because I could see and feel that my family was having a tough time. Yet, I remember feeling very excited about the future. My family and I were about to undertake a momentous change and I suppose I was old enough to realize that any change carried with it a high probability that things would get better.

Chapter 2- Our Move to the West Side-1957

So, as I mentioned earlier, mi Papá opened his second grocery store, *Tex-Western Grocery,* in June, 1957. This grocery store was a veritable dive on West Main Street just south of the *Texas Western College* (now the *University of Texas at El Paso or UTEP*) campus. Not only was the store old and dilapidated, but it also was situated where few potential customers could be found. Just in front of the store, West Main Street went from a paved 2-lane street to a dirt road. Yet, mi Papá somehow believed that he could make a go of it and signed a one-year lease.

In many respects, this new venture represented a considerable setback from his previous business effort. This store was in need of lots of repairs and basic updating (it had no heating system) and was situated on a dirt road with very few neighbors close by. However, I have to give mi Papá credit for envisioning a business opportunity. The married-student housing section of the college was located in that neighborhood and there were no stores anywhere near to keep them supplied with groceries. He had the right idea. However, nothing profitable ever materialized.

Opening the store provided me with my first opportunity to practice my sign-making skills. Stashed in the shed right next to the store, we found a huge tin panel nailed to a wooden frame that measured approximately 1 ft. by 10 ft. It was painted white. I asked mi Papá to allow me to make the marquee sign to place in front of the store to tell the world that we were now open for business. He put the task in my young and inexperienced hands. I proceeded to use my best skills to paint the name of the store on this panel. My intention was to paint "Tex-Western Grocery Store". My failure to properly plan the project left me short of space. The sign therefore only read "Tex-Western Gro." Nevertheless, we erected it above the entrance to the store and hoped for the best.

Our nearest neighbor was next door on the north side of the store. Mr. and Mrs. Hilario Pozo and their rather large Mexican-American family lived there. Mr. and Mrs. Pozo were somewhat elderly. They had children that were fully grown (in their 20s-30s) but they also had one son who was only 9 years old at the time. His name was Carlos Pozo but everyone called him "Bucky." I was just a year or two older than Bucky and so he and I became good friends and playmates. This was the only family in the neighborhood that owned a TV. My brother, Nachito, and I on many occasions would stand outside their living room screen door leaning our faces into the screen to watch the afternoon cartoon programs on that TV. After causing two ugly head-sized indentations on the screen door, Mrs. Pozo eventually routinely would let us come in and sit on the floor with Bucky to watch TV.

One day, Bucky's parents came to Nachito and offered to hire him to chaperone Bucky to the movies in downtown El Paso on Sunday afternoons. They made this offer to Nachito right in front of me. Nachito agreed. The deal was that Bucky's parents would pay for bus fare, movies and popcorn for Nachito and Bucky. They very conspicuously failed to mention me. I remember I was heartbroken because I knew that my parents did not have the money to pay for the costs of including me. But the Pozos must have been impressed by my sad eyes because they said it was OK for Nachito to also take me along. And so, we went to the movies every Sunday for many months thereafter at the expense of the Pozo family.

Another thing that I remember about the Pozo family was that Bucky had two sisters who had graduated from high school but still lived at home. I can't remember their names but I remember their faces and their extremely attractive bodies quite well. I remember that they would always flirt with me and drive me crazy.

Tex Western Gro. was located so far out in the boonies that a trading-stamp company used to burn redeemed trading-stamp books in a vacant lot very close to our backyard. Every so often, a truck would dump thousands of books filled with trading-stamps into the lot and the driver would then set the books on fire. Back then, trading-stamps were offered by most grocery stores with any purchases made. For every 10¢ spent, a purchaser would get one trading-stamp. The purchaser would then lick and stick the stamps into a book and, when the book was filled, would trade in the book for a huge assortment of different gifts. It was such a common practice, that even mi Papá offered these stamps at his humble stores. The two most popular stamps were *Green Stamps* and *Frontier Stamps*. I remember that whenever the trading-stamps were discarded in that lot near our back yard and set on fire, there would invariably be a lot of books that would not be ruined. After the ashes cooled, I would collect these and give them to mi Mamá so she could re-redeem them. Those books never lost their smoky smell even as mi Mamá was re-redeeming them.

A few feet away from the vacant lot where these trading-stamps were burned was a railroad right-of-way. The train would pass through two or three times a day. What kid in his right mind would not love to have a train in his backyard? We used to put all sorts of things on the railroad tracks to watch them get squashed by the train. Fortunately, we were not crazy. The biggest thing that we ever put on the track was a steering wheel of a car. The train neatly sliced the wheel in two. I also remember placing lots of pennies on the tracks and then recovering them in a totally-squashed form.

Immediately on the other side of the tracks was a large ice-making facility that produced huge blocks of ice measuring 2 feet high, 1 foot wide and 3 feet long. Big conveyor belt systems would bring these blocks of ice to an outside platform where workers with pincher tools would pull and push them into railroad freight cars getting them ready to take on perishable loads of food and other stuff to be transported all over the country. On many occasions, Nachito and I gathered large pieces of ice that had broken off and fallen to the ground and brought them to the store to use in the ice boxes where mi Papá stored soft drinks.

A little farther west beyond the ice factory was *Globe Mills*, a 4-story flour mill that was erected in 1910. By the 1950's—and during the time we lived nearby--it had become a cottonseed processing facility. Apparently, after cotton is picked and the cotton fibers are removed, a whole bunch of seeds are left over. The seeds can be processed to extract cottonseed oil from them. This factory--not more than a hundred yards from our house--was constantly processing these seeds. I remember very fondly the smell of that cottonseed oil being processed. It was actually a very pleasant smell that eventually I came to associate with home. I haven't smelled cottonseed oil in 40 years but I will never forget how much I enjoyed it. The *Globe Mills* building remained intact for many decades thereafter and was easily spotted as one drove on Interstate 10 just north of downtown El Paso. It was finally razed in 2016.

By late May, 1958, we had been trying without success to operate *Tex-Western Gro.* for almost a year. Mi Mamá had given mi Papá that ultimatum during the winter of 1957-1958: "We either move out of this house or I go back to Mexico." I am not surprised that mi Mamá might have felt so extremely desperate. I distinctly remember that winter. Our living quarters--located directly behind and attached to the grocery store--were so poorly constructed that freezing drafts constantly raced through it taking with them whatever small amount of heat the kitchen stove could produce. We had no furnace and relied entirely on the kitchen oven to keep us warm. The winters in El Paso are generally mild but we had an extraordinarily nasty one that year. We wore jackets indoors all the time and the stove oven was always on with the oven door open so it could also heat parts of the house. I recall that at any given time during that winter, at least one member of the family was sick with some malady related to the cold.

No doubt, mi Mamá's ultimatum was also tied to the harsh economic reality that we faced that year. The many prospective customers that lived in the nearby "married-student housing area," never materialized. Even the neighbors did not seem interested in buying groceries from our store. To this day, it is inexplicable to me how mi Papá made enough money each month to pay the rent. After all, the store was the only source of income for us. he was only 58 years old and, therefore, was not yet qualified for *Social Security* benefits.

The year that my family spent trying to make a living at *Tex-Western Gro.* was for me a rich mix of experiences that I treasure deeply. During that year, I attended an elementary school called *Vilas*. I was in the fifth grade. It was a generally uneventful year spent doing what fifth-graders might do. For example, there was a kid at school that everybody picked on. I remember feeling then that he deserved every bit of abuse that he got since he was a real loser. One day, I decided that I wanted to fight with him to establish my own reputation as a cool winner. So, he and I scheduled a fight a few days later after school. I then went to my brother Nachito, who was in the 7th grade at *Morehead Intermediate School*, and asked him to train me for the fight. Every afternoon thereafter until the day of the fight, in the large patch of dirt directly in front of the store, Nachito trained me by essentially punching me with no mercy. But on the day of the fight I was ready. The usual after-school fight crowd gathered at a nearby alley and the sides formed and the other kid and I confronted each other. I was ready to fight and I could feel my adrenaline surging. But much to my surprise, my opponent conceded without me having to deliver a single punch. I was smart enough to accept victory under those terms although it would have been much better for my reputation if I had kicked his butt all over the playground. But even at that tender age, I realized that sometimes the best of plans go awry. And so, rather than risk finding out that my brother's training might not have prepared me adequately, I shook his hand and was declared the victor. As I look back to that sequence of events, it is clear that this kid was getting bullied and that I had been one of the bullies. This is a dark chapter in my life and I am deeply ashamed of it.

Mi Papá Teaches Me a Lesson

In those days, a huge residential area had mushroomed just west of downtown and it was called *Sunset Heights*. The residential area contained some really old but nice homes occupied mostly by solid members of the middle class. By that I mean that *Sunset Heights* was an almost exclusively Anglo-American community. Over the years, *Sunset Heights* had grown physically up to the point where canyons and deep ravines of the foothills prevented any further growth. And so, *Sunset Heights* remained that way for many years.

Texas Western College was situated a little bit farther north and west from *Sunset Heights*. The campus was relatively nice although still somewhat on the small side. Access to the college for many years was limited to Mesa Street which went directly from downtown to the heart of the college.

Sometime shortly before we moved there, a road was built to access the college directly from *Sunset Heights*. That was West Main Street. It approached the college from the southwest edge of the campus. What separated the campus from *Sunset Heights* was a deep ravine that dropped probably 150ft. from the *Sunset Heights* level and then rose that same distance back up to the campus. West Main Street was the only artery that traversed this ravine. It consisted of a two-lane blacktop road that started at *Sunset Heights*, plunged north to the bottom of the ravine, then rose once again to the southwestern edge of the campus. The top of the ravine right at the southwestern edge of the campus was where mi Papá's new grocery store was actually located. The boundary line with Mexico was less than ½ mile directly west from our store.

There was no city bus service to our home. That was probably due to the newness of the area and the steepness of the ravine section of West Main Street. Access was limited even more because some of the roads near our neighborhood were still dirt and gravel. Whenever any of us in our neighborhood needed to go into town, we either drove our private vehicles (if we had one) or we walked the length of West Main Street that was in the ravine all the way to *Sunset Heights* from where we could catch the *Sunset Heights* bus to downtown. In our neighborhood, our family was the only family that did not have a car.

The distance from the bus stop on *Sunset Heights* to the front of our house was approximately one mile. I used to walk that distance every day when I attended *Vilas Elementary School*. Whenever anybody else in my family-- including mi Mamá and four-year-old sister--needed to shop downtown, they also had to endure that miserable walk down the ravine and up to *Sunset Heights* to catch the bus. Over time, we accepted that ritual as part of our normal routine.

Now, I can get to the heart of my story. Because mi Papá was nearly totally blind, my brother, Nachito, or I always had to accompany him whenever he left the store. There were many reasons why he would leave the store on any given day. For example, he often needed to go to *Sunset Heights* to shop for more stock for the store or to obtain loans or to visit friends.

I was eleven years old. I was cocky and felt absolutely invincible. Mi Papá knew that and like any father, he respected and encouraged me for being that way. But he also must have known that at that age, my limitations far exceeded my capabilities.

It was a relatively nice day, probably on a weekend afternoon, when mi Papá and I had just gotten off the bus at *Sunset Heights* and had started the long walk home. I was chomping at the bit to get home. I remember feeling that I had wasted my entire day being the seeing-eye boy for mi Papá. As we walked home, he held my elbow for guidance. I kept pulling for him to walk faster. Just as we approached the top (south side) of the ravine on West Main Street mi Papá asked me to please slow down. Obviously, I had been walking a little too fast for him given that he was carrying a small bag of groceries in one hand and holding his cane in the other, which he also used to grasp my elbow. I was not happy at all that he was slowing me down and I must have said something to the effect that he was a real slowpoke.

Then, as we took the first step down the ravine, mi Papá suggested that we race home. He said that the sun was sufficiently bright to allow him to see well enough to jog the rest of the distance home and that I was free to race on. Incredibly, he also claimed that he was absolutely certain that he would get there before me. I dropped my jaw at the arrogance of this elderly, blind man who thought he could outrun me. I was an impatient eleven-year-old 5th grader and really feeling my oats and so I accepted his challenge. He did ask that I carry the bag of groceries and I arrogantly agreed to do so.

I started a furious run down into the ravine. I looked back and smiled with pity as I saw mi Papá start a very slow jog or as some might call it, a "shuffle." I kept racing as fast as I could confident that there was no way that he could beat me. I even visualized the scene of me waiting for him at home for a long time after the race and even having to come back to help him finish. At about the quarter mile point (halfway down the ravine) he was so far behind that I could barely see him. He was shuffling very slowly but he seemed to be doing it very rhythmically and steadily and kept moving inexorably forward. I also pushed on relentlessly but felt like I was getting nowhere. As I reached the bottom of the ravine, I suddenly felt very tired. I looked back and I saw that he was still a considerable distance behind me but gaining on me steadily. Now it was time for me to start the uphill grind. I could not believe how weak I had suddenly become. My legs were like rubber and totally unresponsive. I may as well have been walking considering how little ground I was gaining. My mouth was parched, my leg muscles ached, I was absolutely out of breath and the bag of groceries suddenly seemed to weigh a ton. Eventually, I was at the halfway point on the uphill side of the ravine. I hurt so much that I actually had to stop. I looked back. He was still gaining on me but I was confident that even if I rested, he could not catch up.

Mi Papá was now on the uphill side of the ravine jogging and shuffling ever so slowly but never letting up. I started running again but all I could feel was exhaustion and pain. My complete lack of training and stamina had caught up with me. I ran as hard as I could to cover the last quarter mile. Yet, he continued gaining on me.

Finally, I reached the top of the ravine. Mi Papá was now no more than 10 or 15 yards behind me. Only another hundred yards or so remained to cover before getting to the front of the store. I was in agony. I shall never forget the physical exhaustion that I felt at that moment nor will I ever forget my amazement at how mi Papá was actually catching up with me. About 50 yards from the finish line mi Papá came even with me. Then he actually passed me. As he passed me, I glanced at him and noticed that he was hardly out of breath. As soon as he passed me, I did what was my prerogative as a young impetuous adolescent: I quit.

He was waiting for me at the front of the store when I finally arrived. As blind as he was, he had a grin on his face that reached from ear to ear. I had all but died traversing the ravine but he appeared hardly bothered. I could not believe what had just happened. I had heard of the story of the tortoise and the hare many times. I always thought that it was a cute fairy tale that made a great cartoon but that it was nothing more than pure fantasy. With mi Papá that fateful afternoon, I learned a huge lesson and I have never forgotten it.

Caddies

During that summer when we lived on West Main Street, mi Papá discovered that the *El Paso Country Club* was just a few miles north and west of where we lived. The *Country Club* was—and still is--the premier and most exclusive golf venue in El Paso where only the rich and famous played. Somehow, he learned that there were employment opportunities there for caddies and he decided that Nachito and I should go there to haul in some of that loose cash and help supplement the family's income.

And so, one fine Saturday morning mi Papá handed Nachito a quarter and told him to take me with him and to go get caddy jobs at the *Country Club*.

After all, how hard could that work possibly be? And so, the caddy odyssey started. Nachito, who was twelve years old and I, who was ten years old, took off with vague directions and 25¢ to try to earn some money.

From our store on West Main Street, we headed directly west on foot. We crossed the railroad tracks that were about 100 yards behind our house, made our way through the ice factory, then walked another hundred yards past Globe Mills to Doniphan Drive. There, Nachito and I took a red bus that headed north on Doniphan Drive.

We left early in the morning right after breakfast and so our bellies were full and our spirits high. Bus rides for us in those days were always an adventure and so even if we did not find these "El Dorado" caddy jobs, we were determined to have a good time. Even though bus fares throughout the city of El Paso were only 5¢ for kids twelve and under, this particular bus line that served El Paso's upper valley, was not run by the city and, therefore, charged 10¢ per kid. Upon boarding, Nachito's quarter was reduced to one nickel. (I suppose we were to pay for our way back with the proceeds of our caddy jobs.) The bus dropped us off at the intersection of Doniphan Drive and Country Club road.

We hiked about a mile from Doniphan Drive on Country Club road to the *Country Club*. I have no idea how Nachito knew how to get there yet, we arrived and Nachito promptly announced to all present that we were available to be caddies. I can only imagine today the smiles that must have covered the faces of the golfers when they heard that. We could see that there were other caddies looking for work but all of them seemed to be much older boys or adult men.

We had arrived at around 9:00 AM and we waited for about two hours for someone to hire us. No one seemed to be interested. It would have been extremely funny if someone had hired us. I suppose we could have carried their golf bags—at least for a little while--but we certainly did not know the first thing about the game of golf.

I recall that by 11:00 AM no one had hired us. Nachito and I had become completely bored and extremely hungry and we needed to take decisive action. Nachito decided that our caddying career had just ended. He ordered me to pick my little butt off the ground and join him as we walked back to catch the bus. He observed at that point that he only had a nickel and no plan.

We walked the mile back to Doniphan Drive and flagged down the red bus heading south. Nachito explained to the bus driver that we only had a nickel.

The bus driver politely told us that we needed 15¢ more. He would not allow us to ride. We deboarded the bus and watched it depart without us.

Nachito noticed a little store near the bus stop and headed toward it. I followed him like a little puppy. When we arrived at the store, we shopped for ten or fifteen minutes looking for something to eat that would not cost more than a nickel. We decided to buy a candy bar. Nachito broke the candy bar in half and handed me a piece. We then started walking south on Doniphan Drive on a long journey back home.

The distance that we had to cover was probably three or four miles and we were hoping that somewhere during the walk we might be able to hitch a ride. We walked and walked and walked and occasionally would raise a thumb at a passing car. No one picked us up. I suppose it took us a couple of hours to complete the walk back to our house. It was midafternoon when we arrived and mi Papá inquired as to our success. We explained what happened and I recall that he showed no emotion at all but rather nodded and indicated to us that we had made a good try.

Like so many other things that I did as a child, I remember only how much fun that experience turned out to be. I never seem to remember anything bad or unpleasant. We were young and apparently fearless. And our parents trusted us and were certain that we and the rest of the world could coexist peacefully. Today, parents could be charged with gross negligence for letting adolescent children do stuff like that. In those days, however, kids did these things all the time. The only thing different about this experience--as opposed to others like it--is that we were not able to actually get a job. So many other times when we embarked on similar adventures, we would come home with a pocketful of change. I'll never forget how important I felt whenever I came home with a pocketful of change.

Patrol Boy

I've always wondered why I have been attracted to the military way of life. I still don't precisely know why but I have always found great comfort in the regimentation and in the uniforms that are so much a part of the military. I apparently was not turned on enough by the military so as to become a career officer, but I have always really liked the model upon which the military is supposed to operate.

Anyway, I can trace my earliest fascination with uniforms to the days of the Cub Scouts. I thought the little blue suits were really nice and so I joined the Cub Scouts at age 8. Soon thereafter, I found great comfort in yet another sort of paramilitary organization. I became a Patrol Boy in the school safety patrol organization.

In the '50s and '60s, the *American Automobile Association (AAA)* supported and operated a school safety program all across the U.S. I believe that it all started back in the 1920's when automobiles entered the scene. I also suspect that there are schools even today that participate in that same program. But in my growing-up years, the safety patrol program was used heavily in elementary and intermediate schools. It was a program whereby actual school students would act as crossing guards in the streets around the schools

Here's how the program worked. At the beginning of each school year, teachers would nominate the best students to become patrol boys or patrol girls. The principal would then make the final selections. Being selected as a patrol boy or patrol girl was quite an honor in those days. Not only did such a selection indicate the high regard teachers had for you, but it also gave you quite a bit of power and authority among your peers.

While the power and authority fascinated me, what I really found intoxicating were the really neat white cloth belts that the safety patrols were required to wear. The belts were about 2 in. wide with one portion circling the waist and another portion going over the left or right shoulder. There was a shiny metal hook that served as the buckle on the waist portion and the shoulder portion had a metal loop that allowed them to be adjusted for length. A real mark of distinction came to those who always maintained their belts in a sparkling clean and white condition. To do that, they had to be washed at least once a week in a strong bleach solution. I honestly believe that, with my Mom's help, I always had the cleanest, whitest belt of all. The teachers and other kids always would tell me so. I remember how proud I was when people noticed that my badge was the shiniest of all and my belt was the cleanest.

When safety patrols were off duty and attending class, we would fold or roll the belt into a tight square bundle and then run our regular belt through one of the loops to enable us to carry the little bundle attached to our waist. We would then take our badge and affix it to the outside of that bundle. It was almost--at least in my eyes--like carrying a weapon on your waist. It gave all of us a great sense of power. So, all day, we would remain identifiable because we were all wearing our belts in a little tight bundle on our waists.

The belts were very neat but even neater were the shiny silver badges that were issued to us. These were about 3 in. high and 2 in. wide with a "AAA" symbol embossed in the middle. School patrol officers, that is, captains and lieutenants, were issued even neater badges. They were more in the traditional form of a policeman's shield except that they were perforated to create a star in the middle and they looked quite official. For my entire career as a safety patrol, I was fixated on being able to be a captain one day and being able to wear one of these badges.

The kids who were selected to be patrol boys or patrol girls would be assigned to work specific crosswalks on a rotating basis. In the mornings, the school safety patrol was deployed beginning 30 minutes before the start of classes. At the end of the day, the patrol would be released from class 10 minutes early so they could assume their posts at the different crosswalks before the rest of the kids arrived.

The actual duties of the school safety patrol were identical to what the school crossing guards do today except that today only adults seem to be hired to do that. The technique was simple. The patrol boy or girl would stand on the curb at a crosswalk and hold both arms out to keep kids on the curb. We did not have little "STOP" signs like those used by crossing guards today. When enough kids were gathered, the patrol boy or girl would hold up a hand to stop traffic. With the traffic stopped, the patrol boy/girl would herd the kids across until they were all safe at the other side. The patrol boy/girl would then return to the opposite side of the street, signal the traffic to continue to move and wait for another bunch of kids to gather.

Being a patrol boy or patrol girl was one of the coolest things that a kid could do in those days. Other kids actually did look up to patrol boys and girls because not only did they look like little mini-cops but they were actually tasked with very real police-like duties. I have a strong personal suspicion, however, that if they had ever discontinued the issuance of the belts and badges, the interest in becoming a school patrol would have evaporated instantly.

My personal experience as a patrol boy started at *Burleson Elementary School* in the fourth grade. I had attended *Guardian Angel* school from Kindergarten through third grade and so when I transferred to *Burleson*, I arrived there as an unknown quantity. The school safety patrol for that year was nominated and selected based on their record in the third grade. I had not been there and so I was not even considered. My exposure to the school patrol, however, got me turned on to it. I felt extremely confident that the end of the fourth-grade year that I would be nominated and selected to next year's safety patrol.

But lo and behold, the following year my family moved to the west side of town where I attended *Vilas Elementary School* to complete my fifth grade. Apparently, for a number of reasons--including a shortage of candidates--I was invited to become a patrol boy at *Vilas* even though I was again, an unknown. I was really thrilled and felt greatly honored when I got my belt and badge. I had a great year doing my patrol boy work. All the kids obeyed my commands and I felt like some kind of military commander with my organization completely under control. I also remember vividly how I admired the captain of the school safety patrol, a kid named Juán Rodriguez. I coveted his captain's badge and somehow, I believed that I would be able to win it away from him when we entered the sixth grade.

My dreams and aspirations in that regard were again shattered at the end of the year when my family moved to the Paisano Projects once again requiring me to move to a different school. I enrolled at *Henderson Intermediate School* for the sixth grade and, to my great dismay, I discovered that they did not have a school safety patrol.

Thus, my career in the school safety patrol ended. Yet, my fascination with authority, uniforms and regimentation not only lived on but flourished.

As an eleven-year-old kid, I actually had a reasonably pleasant time living on West Main Street. I suppose that I have repressed many of the really unpleasant memories of that place, but I remember to this day how I yearned for the old neighborhood that we had left a year earlier. A year after we moved to West Main Street and Mi Papá again failed to make any money operating his new grocery store, he made his announcement that we would be moving to the projects. I could not have felt happier. The prospect of yet another momentous change to the way my family was living was exciting to me once again, but this time the upside was much more palpable. Not only were we moving out of that God-forsaken home behind *Tex-Western Gro.*, and going back to the old neighborhood, but we were actually moving into the house of my dreams in the projects.

Chapter 3-The Paisano Projects

So what exactly are or were the "Projects?" In El Paso, as in many other large cities, local governments undertake to subsidize housing for economically disadvantaged families. Such housing comes in many forms. In El Paso, one of the most extensive ventures in that regard was known as the *El Paso Housing Authority*.

The *El Paso Housing Authority* developed three major housing projects in the 1950's. All of these were located in the south and central parts of the city and all were within 1 mile of the Mexican border. They were predominantly occupied by Mexican-American or African-American families. They each had a particular name followed by the word "Project." The neighborhoods eventually simply became known as "the Projects."

One of these housing projects was the "Paisano Projects." It was located between Hammett and Boone streets and between Delta Drive and Paisano Drive just west of the *El Paso Coliseum*. It consisted of approximately 50 multifamily units. Each unit contained three or four apartments and each apartment had 2, 3 or 4 bedrooms. The units were extremely well-built and very efficient in that they consisted of nothing more than a huge dark-red brick rectangular monolith. The roof of each was perfectly flat and each side of the unit was completely void of decoration. The front and rear doors of each apartment unit had a suspended overhang that projected over each door to provide protection against the elements. The doors were painted brown with the street address and apartment numbers stenciled in dull yellow paint. All windows were made of steel and also trimmed in that dull yellow color. The inside walls of the apartments were made of a very heavy type of wall material that seemed virtually indestructible. The ground floor of each apartment was polished concrete and the second floor was made of golden oak planks. None of the units had air-conditioning although a few of the apartments had been equipped by their tenants with swamp coolers.

The Social Fabric

During the late 50's, most people familiar with the Paisano Projects would probably say that it was not a pleasant place in which to live. The Mexican-American community called that neighborhood "El Diablo" ("The Devil"). Undoubtedly, that name had been earned over the years of its existence. To those who tracked statistics, El Diablo must have offered a mother lode of data regarding how to define a bad neighborhood.

During the years that I lived in El Diablo, I observed the following: The population there was almost 100% Hispanic. Of the 3 generations of folks that I normally interacted with in our neighborhood, the youngest generation—the kids-- were all in elementary, intermediate or high school. It was pretty obvious to all of us that as kids proceeded through the 4 years of high school, the drop-out rate seemed to rise dramatically. The need to earn money would send large numbers of high school students into the job market long before graduation. Some of the older kids had started to face disillusionment and resorted to crime and violence through youth gangs. Those gangs, as well as gangs in other neighborhoods, claimed and defended territories by frequently engaging in battles where knives, guns (real ones and contrived ones called "zip guns" or "scoopets"), brass knuckles and other deadly weapons were used. Some of the disillusioned youth, also in desperation, resorted to drinking alcohol, sniffing glue and to using illegal substances such as marijuana or heroin. Just about all of the young people there spoke Spanish but seemed to be well into the cultural assimilation process. By that I mean that they were born in the US or were moved to the US while still very young, but they also spoke English, and they seemed to aspire to live in and remain in America forever. As kids, no one ever spoke about returning to Mexico. Youngsters in the Paisano Projects were fortunate in that the *El Paso Coliseum* was located nearby. It was the largest indoor entertainment venue in El Paso and it offered job opportunities as popcorn, peanut and soft drink vendors whenever an event was held there. Families with 4 or 5 kids who managed to get jobs there could enjoy a significant increase in household income. For the most part, these kids were my peers when I lived there and our outlook was positive and our dispositions generally happy.

The next generation—the parents—seemed to mostly be Mexican immigrants. A few were US citizens by birth or naturalization, many were resident aliens and a tiny number must have been illegal aliens. The vast majority of the parents had been educated no further than grade school in Mexico. I do not recall hearing of any of my peers' parents who finished high school and I am certain that there were no college graduates among them. Most did not speak English although they could speak, write and read Spanish perfectly. However, some, like mi Papá, who had grown up in the US spoke English well. There were some absentee fathers but most families had a father at home who had a relatively menial job that enabled him to pay for the living essentials. Very few fathers owned a car. The fathers were deeply respected but frequently feared by the younger generation and so communication with them was limited. Most fathers were responsible heads of the household but there were a few who abused alcohol. Although the community was close to 100% Roman Catholic, fathers never went to mass.

Fathers, for the most part, did not get involved in the school activities of their children and never attended school-sponsored sports events, band concerts or other functions where their children performed. They did, however, seem to always be around when one of our neighborhood teams needed a coach or a manager.

The mothers were essentially worshipped and unconditionally adored by their children. Mothers did not hold outside jobs—unless they were single parents—and they maintained the integrity of the household more so than the fathers. Mothers were protected more by the children than by the father. The family unit was of the highest importance and frequently extended to cousins or siblings that also managed to move there or conveniently lived across the river in Juárez, Mexico. Divorces were rare but not unheard of. Mothers went to mass every Sunday but more importantly, they ensured that the children also went. And, mothers were much more likely to attend school functions in which their children performed. If the outlook of parents was at all positive, it was probably due to the promise offered by their children. The parents appreciated the value of an education although they could not know what a college education entailed. They all probably wanted very much for their children to stay in school and even go to college.

Then there were the members of the third generation, the grandparents. Not too many grandparents lived in the Paisano Projects but those who did were respected deeply by all. I suspect that those grandparents had given up on their own dreams of prosperity and assimilation—assuming they even had such dreams. They did not speak English and since living in the Paisano Projects did not require them to speak it, they likely never would. They probably had also given up on seeing their own children become educated, successful and prosperous, but then they had grandchildren who could and did excite them with that prospect all over again. The grandparents probably represented the strongest link to the Catholic faith. It manifested itself through the nightly prayers, the ubiquitous religious icons and the frequent invocations that they would make to God and the Virgin of Guadalupe almost always on behalf of the grandchildren.

Living in the Paisano Projects was essentially the same as living in Mexico. The culture was predominantly Mexican particularly among the adults who resided there. The adults, with very few exceptions, spoke, read and wrote only in Spanish and communicated that way with their children and neighbors. They listened only to Mexican music and Mexican programs on the radio, heard Mass in Spanish at San Javier Church, shopped at grocery stores where advertising was mostly in Spanish and watched only Mexican or Spanish movies at the Colón or Alcázar Theaters in downtown El Paso. But among the kids, the spoken language was very bi-cultural since they were also learning how to speak English at school, were being taught by mostly Anglo teachers, were learning subjects in English that related to American history and American government, were listening to mostly American music on the radio and watching mostly American programming on TV, were occasionally even dating Anglo boys and girls and, for the most part, had accepted the notion that they were Americans.

The Spanish that was spoken in the Projects was considerably different from classical Castilian or even from Mexican Spanish. As is typical in any culture, the language of any given neighborhood evolves into what works for the people of that neighborhood. In the Projects, the language indeed was Mexican Spanish but over time it generated a set of new supplemental words or expressions that were common in Mexican-American barrios but probably unheard of in other areas where Spanish was spoken. Recently, while I was playing a round of golf with an old friend who grew up with me in the Projects, we decided to compile a small list of such words or expressions. Here they are along with their definitions:

1. Apañar- to grab
2. Clavar- to steal
3. Hacer pedo: to make a fuss
4. Camello- work
5. Jaina- girlfriend
6. Madera- lie
7. Simón- yes
8. Pase Braca- give me a break
9. Refín- food
10. Refinar- to eat
11. Tóricas- stories
12. Toriquiar- to chat
13. Cantón- house
14. Talonear- to walk
15. Tolido- toilet
16. Marranear- to overindulge
17. Ponte trucha- be careful
18. Pélate- run
19. Tramados or Tramos- pants
20. Yica- jacket
21. Tandito- hat
22. Calcos- shoes
23. Jale- job
24. Chale or nela- no

25. Alalva- watch out!
26. Bamba or chiripada- lucky shot
27. Escante- a moment
28. Chafa or chafona- cheap
29. Me cais- I like you
30. Cabulear- to tease
31. Aguitado- sad
32. Gacho- to be mean
33. Aracle- show-off
34. Capear- to put out or cooperate
35. Borlotear- to dance
36. Encanicado- smitten
37. Rolando- sleeping
38. Quira- quarter (25 cents)
39. Tolón- half dollar
40. Calo- penny
41. Bola- dollar

I have no actual proof, but I strongly suspect that the words listed above are fairly unique to South El Paso. I know that on those occasions when I have inadvertently used them when conversing with my relatives in Mexico or Spain, the invariable response has been a quizzical look.

I first became exposed to these housing projects in 1956 when I was in the fourth grade and I was utterly fascinated by them. I was attending *Burleson Elementary* which happened to be located right in the midst of another housing project called the Sherman Project. While I was attending *Burleson*, I became good friends with many kids that lived in the Sherman Project. I envied them a lot for having first of all, a home close to the school, and secondly, for living in a nice, neat, brick structure with a lawn. At that time, we were living in the grocery store on Alameda Avenue and I had become somewhat fed up with the store and the house that we were renting immediately behind the store. For some reason that only a fourth grader might be able to explain, I would have gladly traded places with any of my classmates who lived in that project.

And so, in the summer of 1958, we left West Main Street and moved to 405 Webber Way, in the Paisano Projects. Once again, life suddenly began to have real meaning for me as one problem after another that I thought I faced, seemed to get solved.

A real Job for Mi Papá

When we moved to the Paisano Projects, mi Papá's career saw a dramatic change. For reasons relating to his age and his entrepreneurial track record but mostly to his blindness, he took on a job as a door-to-door salesman for the *El Paso Lighthouse for the Blind*. I believe that his new job was what really enabled us to get housing at the projects since one of the qualifications was for the head of the house to have an income-producing job. I remember feeling proud and secure now that our income would not have anything to do with the grocery business.

The *Lighthouse for the Blind* was--and probably still is--a very effective operation. It consisted of a manufacturing facility where some 40-50 blind employees manufactured household goods such as brooms, mops, lint brushes, aprons, dish towels, dish cloths and the like. It also had a field sales team that would sell these items door-to-door throughout El Paso and other nearby towns.

Mi Papá—not surprisingly--landed a job as a salesman. The sales team consisted of one sighted driver and 5 salesmen who suffered varying degrees of blindness. The team chief/driver was a gentleman named Silverio Murillo. He was well-liked and respected by all. He drove a 1954 tan Chevy station wagon with that fake "woody" trim and to it, a trailer was hitched. The Station wagon carried the team (including two Seeing Eye dogs); the trailer carried the household goods that the team sold.

The sales team had some really effective salesmen including Jerry Mitchell who was totally blind and was the lead salesman; Larry Knudsen who was also totally blind and was guided by a beautiful Golden Retriever; Victor Rodriguez who was probably only 80% blind, Hector Luna who was also totally blind and was guided by a German Shepherd named Minks, and mi Papá who was about 90% blind.

The team would go out every day except Sunday (weather permitting) and mi Papá was bringing home $15 to $20 each day. As far as we were concerned, we were suddenly rich. Then to top everything off, on Saturdays, the team would hire kids such as Nachito and me to act as guides for some of the salesmen, and that would guarantee an extra dollar of income for each of us.

6th and 7th Grade

Life for me returned very much to the state of tranquility and happiness that I had known prior to moving to West Main Street. I enrolled at *Henderson*

Intermediate School where most of the kids that I had left behind at *Burleson* were once again my classmates. I also gained a whole bunch of new classmates from the neighborhood around *Henderson*. The only drawback was that *Henderson* was over a mile away from our new home and the daily round trip walk sometimes took its toll, particularly on dusty, windy spring days.

During the first six years of schooling, either I had few impressive teachers or I have simply forgotten who they were. The first teacher that I remember as having impacted me significantly was Mr. Arturo Lightbourn. He was my seventh-grade homeroom teacher at *Henderson*.

When one is 12 years old, it is very easy to be impressed. Mr. Lightbourn impressed me immensely for a number of reasons. First, he was a tall person with a very cool flat-top haircut who simply seemed to be completely in charge of everything. In many respects, he was the younger father figure that I probably subconsciously always longed for. Second, I think he took a liking to me and treated me really well and so I always looked forward to his classes. He genuinely seemed to think that I had above-average potential and so he nurtured all of my skills as any good teacher should have done. Third—and probably most important--he was the older brother of a girl named Lucila who was exactly my age and with whom I had attended class since the fourth grade. I really like Lucila—who was in the other 7th grade homeroom--and I guess I figured that if I impressed her brother (Mr. Lightbourn), word would eventually get to her and maybe, just maybe, she would also like me too. That never happened. I believe that Mr. Lightbourn's seventh grade homeroom class was the closest thing that I've ever experienced to what an ideal school environment should be. The teacher as well as the students seemed to be enthusiastic and genuinely happy about being in school each day. I know I sure was and a classmate from that very class, Manny Marrufo, recently confirmed that he was too. One does not appreciate the value of such an experience until many years later when its true rarity is ascertained.

The Blind Musicians

While we were living in the Paisano Projects, particularly during our second tour there at 3922 East Paisano Drive, (1961 through 1969) mi Papá became extremely absorbed by his music. I suppose that for lack of anything better to do, he started to play his ebony flute with more zeal than ever and to practice his singing more regularly and enthusiastically than before. Even though his flute music as well as his voice left much to be desired, it has always been somewhat impressive to me that he could memorize as many songs as he did, particularly since he had to rely completely on his hearing ability to do so. He seemed to know a really amazing number of songs and poems and other things by heart.

While mi Papá was working at the *Lighthouse for the Blind*, he discovered that Hector Luna, his fellow blind salesman, who was about 25 years old, was actually a somewhat gifted singer and guitarist. Mi Papá and Hector then learned that there was a third blind salesman among them, Victor Rodriguez, who played the accordion. Since the three of them shared an affinity for traditional Mexican music, they decided to form a little band. And so, this trio of salesmen/musicians started getting together frequently to share their love of music.

Somehow, they hooked up with a fourth member, a blind guitarist who lived in Juárez, Mexico. His name was Eugenio. Eugenio was also rather young, probably also around 25 years old. He was a very small person who looked like a child even though he wore a beard. He always wore the same clothes: a well-worn navy-blue suit with a blue and orange sweater underneath. Anyone who saw Eugenio would know immediately that he was blind since his eyes were always closed and he did not wear sunglasses. He was always smiling even when he was alone. He was probably no more than 5 feet tall. Eugenio loved to sing and did so with amazing vigor. His voice was strong but had a nasal quality about it that I found really annoying. When I first heard him sing, I thought he was parodying somebody. It was awful. But, somehow, people found him entertaining. He was married at the time to a woman who, despite her wearing high-heeled shoes, would still be a few inches shorter than Eugenio. She also was blind. As a couple, they were almost doll-like in appearance since they were so tiny and seemingly always so happy. She was always at Eugenio's side.

For some period of time, every weekend on Sunday, the group of blind musicians would gather at our house in the projects for a rehearsal. They would practice for the entire afternoon. Since they were all blind, they could not tell where they were practicing and they probably did not care. Eventually, their music would spill out into our neighborhood and a crowd would gather in front of our house to listen and watch as the strange noises emanated from within. I was horrified. What would my buddies think of me now that they could associate me with that racket?

I truly wish that I could say that they sounded good. But the sad fact is that they did not sound good at all. I believe that each of them thought that he was an accomplished musician and that by merely bringing together a group of accomplished musicians, a successful band would evolve. Each of them would give his own rendition of a song hoping that if all of the others did the same, the resulting song would be even better. In reality, what resulted were separate songs sometimes sung in different keys and at different beats that had little in common.

So, if they sounded so badly, why was it that people always wanted them to perform at their parties? I have my own theories of why they managed to survive and actually attract attention for as long as they did. First, they were all blind with few assets, if any, and people simply felt sorry for them. Everyone was particularly touched by Eugenio and his wife and the sympathy that they could elicit was truly remarkable. Second, they were generally invited to play by close friends or relatives and so there was a much lower expectation level as to the quality of the music the band would be delivering. Third, they were extremely cost effective. After all, they essentially would play for free as long as they could eat and drink and have fun along with the invited guests. Fourth, they were quite a spectacle to behold. I'll elaborate on this in the next few paragraphs. Finally, even though they did not produce great music, they did get the crowds to sing along and dance and in so doing, they significantly enhanced every gathering they attended.

Despite their musical shortcomings, the group kept getting invitations to play at house parties and other small gatherings. The blind musicians certainly did not form the band to make money, although they were happy to receive any kind of remuneration. They formed the band because they loved the music with a passion that I have never again witnessed. They did make a little money occasionally. Sometimes it was equivalent only to bus fare. However, as I mentioned earlier, they would also generally get a free meal and drinks at the event where they were entertaining and given the economic status of each, this benefit was not insignificant.

I will always remember how odd the band must have looked. If the band had to play in our neighborhood, mi Papá would ask me to take them to the site of the event. Picture this: I am at the head of this column of men, each of them holding an instrument in one hand and with the other hand hanging on to another blind man who was walking in front of them. We would also have at least one big dog, and occasionally some spouses also came tagging along. Finally, to further accentuate the bizarre, they were usually dressed funny since they could not see what they wore. Some of the color combinations were pretty dramatic. Sometimes, unbeknownst to the musician, the suit jacket he was wearing would have gravy on the lapel from the last party. Once in a while, again without the knowledge of the wearer, one of them would be wearing pants that were 2 or 3 inches too short. In summary, it was a spectacle to behold when this group of blind musicians moved about.

The column of blind musicians would generally have no other means of transportation other than their feet. And so, whenever they had a gig to perform in our neighborhood, I would lead the column of blind guys down the sidewalk in our neighborhood until we arrived at the party house. The party, which was usually already in full swing, would come to a complete and silent halt as the band slithered in through the front door. The crowd would stare in amazement at the blind musicians as they set up to play. Then, with minimal time spent tuning the instruments or warming up, they would belt out the first of maybe 10 songs. That would be followed by wild cheering, whistling, applause, compliments, drinks, free food and a modest tip to mi Papá for him to split among the rest of the band. The band would stick around for another hour or so and listen to recorded music and have as much fun as they could. Then the caravan would head back to our home.

On a few occasions, the band was hired to play in a different part of town. Getting them there was the same routine except that one or two cars would show up from somewhere to actually carry the band to that neighborhood. I would still accompany them as their guide to assist them in getting from the cars to the actual parties. One time, the blind musicians even went to Juárez. All of us left our house in a walking caravan, boarded the International bus at Hammett Boulevard and went on to Juárez to do the gig.

The blind musicians played only Mexican music and played only before Mexican or Mexican-American audiences. The adults that listened to them loved them. The kids, on the other hand—after listening to one or two songs and gawking at the curious extravaganza--invariably bolted for the nearest door.

Whenever I had anything to do with that band, I recall feeling a combination of embarrassment, humiliation and shock. I never felt any pride or pleasure. I was a teenager after all, in a cultural identity crisis, where my parents and their friends kept clinging to the Mexican way of life while my friends and I were desperately trying to get away from it. Yet, I had no choice but to do as mi Papá asked and to act as their guide. I hated the music and hated even more the way that this band interpreted it. But the musicians and their spouses were so fine and so gentle that even I ended up forming a deep sense of respect and affection toward them that I still feel to this day.

Activities in the Projects before the days of the Boys' Club

My family moved into the Paisano Projects in the summer of 1958. When the *El Paso Boys' Club* opened up a unit in the Paisano Projects a year later in 1959, it offered the neighborhood boys a whole new array of activities to keep us busy and entertained. However, even before the Boys' Club, there were plenty of neighborhood games and pastimes that we used to enjoy as boys then usually did.

Without a doubt, the best thing that happened to me when we moved to the Paisano Projects in 1958 was the formation of my friendship with Sergio "Checo" Reza. My brother, Nachito, and I were avid baseball players from the days we lived on Alameda Avenue. During the year we spent at West Main Street we did not play baseball very often because there was no field or lot nearby on which we could play nor were there any teams we could join. Nevertheless, we were happy to occasionally play catch on the big open space directly in front of *Tex-Western Gro.* Shortly after arriving at the Paisano Projects, we discovered that a huge playground with a baseball diamond existed just across the street from our apartment. One day in the summer of 1958, my brother and I put on our baseball caps, gathered our gloves, a ball and a bat and headed for the playground.

When the playground came into view, we were happy to see two other boys already there playing catch. They were about our age and seemed equally pleased to see us. They were Jesús "Chuy" Reza who was about the same age as my brother, and his brother, Checo, who was about my age. We introduced ourselves to them, learned that they lived in an apartment whose rear door faced the fence along the 3d base line of the baseball diamond, loved baseball as much as we did and had a father who once played professional baseball. We instantly decided that we had just found the best baseball playmates we would ever have.

Baseball essentially consumed us in those days. It seemed that all of the boys in the neighborhood loved to play sandlot—or in this case, playground—baseball. And, there were plenty of boys of all ages available to set up a quick game after school on weekdays or to organize bigger, longer games on weekends. The playground was large enough to accommodate games for older boys as well as games for younger boys without significantly interfering with each other. In addition, it seemed that there were plenty of dads who were also interested in baseball and who would always be around to act as coaches and sometimes even as players.

Our baseball equipment also seemed plentiful. Each of us had a genuine leather baseball glove that probably had been purchased in a sporting goods store in Juárez for a few dollars. Somewhere, we learned that the glove needed to be regularly coated with *3-in-1* oil so that it remained pliable and, that it should always be stored with a baseball in the palm of the glove so that it could retain its shape. I recall how on rainy days or when I otherwise could not be on the baseball field, I would stare lovingly at my glove as I snapped a ball into the palm over and over and smelled the intoxicating aroma of oiled leather.

We also never seemed to lack for any baseballs. It's not as if we had a huge supply of them. We really only needed one ball and we each seemed to somehow have acquired one that we could produce when a ball was needed. If the baseball had its original stitched leather cover, then the owner's name would have been written on it with a ball-point pen. If the cover had fallen off, it would have been re-covered with black electrical tape. The tape-job itself would be sufficient for the owner to be able to identify it. We never purchased a baseball but rather would have come upon it at the nearby professional baseball park, *Dudley Field*, or found it at the high school baseball field where it had been inadvertently lost.

Then, of course, there was the baseball bat. We did not normally have more than one bat at a game and usually it was cracked and repaired also with black electrical tape. One bat even had a nail or two driven in to repair a break near the handle before it got wrapped with black electrical tape. For us, a roll of black electrical tape was one of the most precious and useful commodities of the day. I remember that for a few years, we only used the cloth variety of black electrical tape since that was all that we had ever seen. Then one day, someone showed up with a roll of black, electrical *plastic* tape. We all seemed to agree that this new technology was a miracle of the times.

But there were other extremely pleasurable games we played besides baseball. "La Quemada" (pronounced "la keh-MAH-tha") is a Spanish term meaning "the burning" or "the bruise." It was also the name of a wonderful childhood game that we used to play in the Paisano Projects. The year was 1958. It was a game very suitable for twelve-year olds for many reasons that you will understand as you read on. It was also economically extremely appropriate for life in the Projects because the only thing you needed to play the game was a tennis ball.

No specific number of players was required to play La Quemada. Normally between four and seven boys played. In order to play, we would find a patch of bare earth that would abut against a brick wall of one of the many two-story housing units in the neighborhood. The walls between each housing unit were perfect since they had absolutely no windows or doors. They consisted simply of two stories of solid red brick each wall being about 30 feet wide and 20 feet high. We would find a small spot in the center of any such wall and each player would dig a hole about 4 inches in diameter and 2 inches deep (to accommodate a tennis ball) right against the wall leaving one or two inches between each hole. This would be his hole. Once the holes were dug, we would step back approximately 6 feet away from the wall and draw a line in the dirt parallel to the wall. Then two more lines would be drawn from each end of that line to the wall to form a square that we called "home."

Here's the way the game was played. All players would stand outside of the line opposite the wall. One player would roll the tennis ball from the line toward the row of holes. The ball would find its way into one of the holes. The player who owned that hole would then dash to his hole to recover the ball. As he did that, the other players would immediately sprint to a pole or tree about 50 to 60 yards away across an open area. That was the "base."

The player with the ball would immediately start chasing the other players as they ran toward base. The object was for the player with the ball to throw the ball at any one of the players running and to hit one of them. If the pack of runners was out of range and arrived safely to base, the player with the ball would simply hang onto it and wait until the pack tried to return to home. While he waited, he would throw the ball high into the air repeatedly until the other players--one at a time or as a group--would attempt to run back to home. They would wait until the player throwing the ball would mishandle it momentarily and then the sprint for home would begin. As soon as the fumbling ball-thrower recovered the ball, he would start chasing the pack again trying to throw the ball at one of the running players hoping to strike him.

If, during the run to base or during the run to home, the player with the ball succeeded in throwing the ball and hitting one of the runners with it, the cycle would end. The player who got hit by the ball would get one pebble placed in his hole and then that player would get to roll the ball at the row of holes to start another cycle. If, however, during the run to base or during the run to home, the player with the ball missed all the runners and thereby allowed all of them to arrive back home safely, the cycle would end and the player with the ball would get a pebble in his hole. He then would get to roll the ball at the row of holes to start another cycle.

The first player to accumulate five pebbles in his hole would be declared the loser. Since he was the loser, the rest of the players then got to punish him. The loser would stand in front of the brick wall--facing the wall--and every other player got to throw the tennis ball at him, as hard as possible, three times. The distance between the thrower and the target was normally not much more than 30 or 40ft. Therefore, a direct hit would sting and sometimes even leave a burning welt. That's precisely why the game was called "La Quemada." By the way, the punishment phase of this game was also used in other games that we used to play. The punishment phase actually had its own name: "La Fusilada" which means "the fusillade."

It may sound as if "La Quemada" was a nasty game but I assure you that it was not. The fear of a Fusilada kept the adrenalin flowing in torrents but the fun and the exhilaration of running and throwing were so great that they more than compensated for the risk of becoming the loser. As in any game, there were some boys who were more skilled than others. Even though I believed that I was among the more skilled players--there was always the overweight, clumsier or much younger scapegoat that we all took advantage of--I did manage to lose on various occasions and I distinctly remember receiving at least one direct shot on the back of my thigh (I was wearing shorts). Although it never happened to me, it was not uncommon for the loser to take such a pounding that he would end up running home in tears. But we loved the game and there were collateral benefits: For the short term, the game allowed us to keep our throwing and running skills honed in preparation for the upcoming baseball season. For the long term, the game taught us about how life can be competitive and how sometimes, despite our best efforts at winning, the results can be painful.

Another pastime for kids in the Projects--and for that matter—for kids everywhere was what we called "canicas" (pronounced "cah-NEE-cus") which is the Spanish word for "marbles." During my childhood at Alameda Avenue as well as in the Projects and in the school playgrounds, we played canicas a lot.

Marbles came in a variety of sizes and colors. They were almost always made of glass. The most popular were probably those that looked like a cat's eye. There were also large marbles called "jumbos" and there were marbles made out of stainless steel. The steel marbles were, in reality, ball bearings but they functioned reasonably well as indestructible marbles. We used to carry all of our marbles in Bull Durham tobacco bags. We would sort marbles in different bags and then carry the bags in our pant pockets.

If one of the glass marbles happened to have a chip on the surface, that chip seemed to give incredible destructive power to that marble. Whenever the chipped marble impacted with another marble, and if the impact occurred right on the chip, it was not uncommon for the impacted (target) marble to break. Of course, the chipped marble would occasionally break as well. This was a rare event, almost like a grand slam home run in baseball. When anyone pulled it off, the story would spread around the neighborhood like a gasoline-fed fire.

Here, more or less, are the rules/protocols of the game of canicas that we used to play in our neighborhood. You first had to find a nice, smooth and clean patch of dirt. You would then draw a circle in the dirt about 3 feet in diameter. If two players were playing, each player would place the same number of marbles (usually five) in two lines forming a cross at the center of the circle. If more than two were playing, there would be as many lines of marbles intersecting at the center of the circle. The first shooter would then place the index-finger knuckle of his shooting hand on the circle and thumb-flick his shooter-marble at the cluster of marbles trying to knock as many of them out of the circle. The energy required to cause a marble to travel 18 inches in the dirt after impact was substantial. The good players could fire off marbles at amazing speeds and, upon impact, marbles would fly all over the place. The shooter would get to keep any marbles that he knocked out of the circle. Obviously, the shooter would aim at the choice marbles. A shooter keeps shooting as long as he is knocking marbles out of the circle or until his own marble goes out of the circle. If a shooter hits the target marble but does not knock it out of the circle and if his own shooter-marble stays in the circle then the next kid would get his turn. The next kid could target the previous shooter's marble (now in the circle) and if he knocked it out, he would get to keep it as well as any other marbles he shot out of the circle. The owner of a shooter-marble that gets shot out of the circle is thereby eliminated from the game. Whoever succeeds in knocking out the final remaining other shooter-marble wins and gets to keep the rest of the marbles in the circle.

As in any other playground sport, there were friends of mine who were incredibly accurate in how they shot their marbles. Those who played often would develop huge calluses at the base of their thumbnail in the shooter hand and on their knuckles as well. Those armed with thick calluses could play for hours and some of them seemed to be unbeatable.

One of the funny things that I remember about playing marbles was the language. As in most playground activities, the kids will invent words that they use in particular games. In marbles, one word that I remember originating in the playground was "safis" (pronounced "SAH-fees.") It is derived from the Spanish verb "safar" which is also slang but means "to slip" or "to slip away." Safis was the expression that one would utter after shooting a marble that missed the target. By saying "safis" you would be telling everyone that the miss was not your fault, it just "slipped" away from you.

Aside from the "thrill of victory" as well as the "agony of defeat" that any sport or game produces, marbles also offered a distinct but noteworthy additional pleasure. That pleasure was derived from gazing at the beauty of certain marbles. I remember taking particularly colorful examples of cat's eyes and holding them up to the lamp light as I lay in my bed at night and staring at them as I rotated them slowly in profound amazement of their beauty.

The last I remember of my collection of marbles was looking at them sometime in the mid-sixties as I stored them in separate little bags in a cigar box that I put in my foot locker. I was immensely proud of the collection not only because of their intrinsic beauty but also because of the pleasure that they had brought me over the years. That footlocker was the same one that disappeared in the warehouse fire while my brother, Nacho, was in Vietnam and I was at West Point.

Another game that I know I enjoyed immensely was called "Balero." The Balero consisted of two pieces of wood and a 12-inch string that linked them. One piece of wood was barrel-shaped, 3 or 4 inches in length and maybe 2-3 inches in diameter. The top of the barrel had a small eye-screw to which one end of the string was attached. The bottom of the barrel had a hole drilled in it about ½ inch in diameter. The other end of the string was tied to a small stick with a handle carved at the bottom and a 1-inch dowel tip at the top. The tip was designed to fit in the hole at the bottom of the barrel. Baleros were inexpensive and ubiquitous in market places in Juarez, Mexico, and therefore were a common possession of just about every boy in the Projects.

The game was played as follows: Player 1 would take the Balero and while grasping the handle would allow the barrel to hang vertically. Then he would swing the barrel forward attempting to make it flip over and land the hole on the dowel end of the handle. The object of the game was to catch the barrel with the dowel. If the barrel missed the dowel, it would become Player 2's turn to make the same attempt. If, however, the barrel landed on the dowel, then Player 1 would get 5 points and continue with his turn by attempting to make the barrel do a 360-degree flip *from the dowel* and once again land it on the dowel. If this 360-degree flip again landed on the dowel, Player 1 would get an additional 10 points. If the 360-degree flip failed to land on the dowel,

Player 1 continued with his turn and once again would try to land the barrel on the dowel from the vertical hanging position. The first player to reach 100 points was the winner. Frequently, there would be 3 or 4 players competing in a single game.

Most probably, I became familiar with this game when I was in elementary school. We played Balero mostly to kill time while we waited for a baseball game to start or on the grass under a tree when it was too hot to do anything else. As with every skill game, some of my friends were extremely good at this game and could get the 100 points without ever giving the second player a chance to play. When these experts played, they would achieve unbelievable rhythm and a beat as the barrel made a "clack" each time it landed on the dowel. The beat would be accompanied by the player's voice as with each successive "clack' he said: "five; fifteen; twenty-five; thirty-five; forty-five; fifty-five; sixty-five; seventy-five; eighty-five; ninety-five; game over!"

Then there were those games that we had been playing for years and which are familiar to most boys who grew up in the 1950's regardless of ethnicity. The first of these is the spinning top or the "trompo" as we used to call it.

Although I cannot place the exact age during which I played with trompos the most, I would imagine that it was between the ages of 10 and 15. I remember that we used to sell them at mi Papá's grocery stores and that I used to have a small trompo collection including one that I considered my favorite. Why would I consider it my favorite? Because it was the one with which I used to win the most games.

Anyone who has ever spun a trompo probably remembers how it is done. It is much easier to do it than to describe how it is done. Nevertheless, I will try to describe how a trompo is spun based on a relatively recent experience that I had with a trompo in 2001, just after I turned 54. My brother, Nacho, had recently given me 3 vintage trompos with strings as gifts for my two sons and me. They were identical to the trompos (and strings) that we used to play with when we were young boys. One nice day in the fall of 2001, while in Tucson, AZ, I went outside with a trompo and string, found a patch of bare earth, closed my eyes, and let my instinct and memory take over. Sure enough, my right hand placed the trompo in my left hand with the top of the trompo facing the sky. My right hand took one knotted end of the string and placed it under my left thumb at the ridge of the top of the trompo. I then ran the string counterclockwise around the top and over the knot held by my left thumb. At the same instant, I rotated the trompo so that the top was now facing to my left, the puya (the steel tip) facing right and I continued to wind the string--this time clockwise--beginning at the puya until only six inches of string remained. Using my right thumb and middle finger, I wrapped the remaining six inches of string until it gripped my middle finger. The puya was now pointing to the sky. I opened my eyes. I was ready to throw the trompo to the ground and make it spin.

A conflict then occurred: Should I throw it to the ground like a baseball so I can give it maximum spin speed and destructive momentum but less accuracy; or should I throw it and whip the string back so that it spins more slowly with much less likelihood of giving a good puyaso (a direct strike with the tip of my trompo) but with a greater degree of accuracy.

I did what every young boy would have done. I threw it like a baseball. Two things happened; First, the trompo smashed into the ground on its side and bounced against the wall of the house and then furiously spun on its side kicking up all sorts of dust and dirt. Second, I felt a stabbing pain in my right shoulder much like I imagine a torn rotator cuff to feel.

My first conservative thought was to pick up the trompo, go inside for some *Aspercreme* and let my childhood stay comfortably in the back of my mind. My second thought was to do what any young kid would have done: Rub the shoulder for a few seconds and try it again.

After five or six baseball throws--all with the same result and with more intense shoulder pains--I decided to try the whip throw. I know for a fact that in the Projects only girls used to do the whip throw so I looked around to see if anybody was watching. No one was... so I did the next attempt with a whip throw. The trompo landed gently on its puya but spun swiftly. Instinctively, I reached down with my right hand and slid it so that the trompo came onto my hand between the index and middle finger. The trompo spun on my hand for 8-9 seconds and I was the happiest I had been in a long, long time.

Let's go back to the Projects and the past so I can tell you what a trompo game used to be like. I would find an opponent who would also have a trompo and before starting a match we would exchange trompos so that each of us could inspect each other's trompo. The reason you would inspect each other's trompo was so that we could determine afterward whether either trompo had inflicted any damage on the other trompo. Having noted the damage that existed on each other's trompo, we would then put a bottle cap in the middle of a patch of bare ground to start the game. Each of us would spin our trompo by throwing it to the ground aiming at the bottle cap. Whoever landed his trompo closest to the bottle cap would win this initial round, provided that the trompo remained spinning in a stable manner. That would mean that the loser now had to place his trompo on the ground to be the target.

This is where the fun would begin. The object of the game now was to take your trompo and to spin it while at the same time making contact with your opponent's target trompo. I honestly do not remember how we would keep score, but I believe that whoever first made contact with the opponent three times would win.

There were various ways that you could make contact. If you aimed your trompo to the ground and your trompo directly struck the target trompo and stayed upright and stable while spinning, then you scored one point. If you struck the opponent's trompo with the metal tip of your trompo, you would be declared the winner instantly. If you only struck with the body of your trompo you would only get one point. If you threw your trompo to the ground and missed your opponent's target trompo, then you would have to pick up your spinning trompo in your hand —while it was still spinning--and throw it gently on the target trompo so that it could make contact. If you threw your trompo and completely missed your opponent's, and never made contact or if the trompo didn't spin upright at all, then you became the target and your opponent would start to throw his trompo at yours.

I remember on many occasions picking up a target trompo to examine it to see whether the contact had been made by the puya or by the body. And I'll never forget the one time when either my brother or I succeeded in hitting the opponent's top directly with the puya and causing the opponent's trompo to split in half. But I also can still remember the times when the puya of an opponent's trompo would strike mine and how I would flinch as if I had been stabbed in the gut.

The Playground

The playground was really important to all of the kids who lived in the projects. It was a relatively huge and fascinating complex. Let me try to take you on an imaginary tour of that wondrous place.

The entire playground was about 100 yards by 150 yards located at the southwest corner of Paisano Drive and Boone Street. Directly across Boone Street from the playground was the *El Paso Coliseum*. Directly south of the playground was where in 1959 the *El Paso Boys' Club* opened its Unit 2 facility. And directly west from the playground were several of the housing project buildings where most of us lived. North of the playground across Paisano Drive was a giant parking lot where fans would park who came to watch baseball games at the biggest ball park in the city, *Dudley Field*, which was just north of that parking lot.

There was a set of bleachers at the southwest corner of the playground. These bleachers were a key part of life in the neighborhood. There were maybe eight rows of seats where about 125 people could sit to watch a baseball game. Try to imagine standing in the middle of the top row of the bleachers. From there, facing to the northeast you had a great view of the baseball diamond directly in front of the bleachers as well as of the entire playground.

The baseball diamond (the area between the three bases and home plate)—like most baseball diamonds--was void of grass. It was actually covered in reddish dirt and had a pitcher's mound including a pitching rubber. The rest of the ball park was fairly lush Bermuda grass. (In El Paso in those days, such grass on a ball park was pretty rare and we were extremely fortunate to have it.) There was a white chalk line that ran from home plate down the *first* base line about 175 feet all the way to the chain link fence in right field. Another chalk line ran from home plate down the *third* base line for maybe 300 feet up to where the grass ended. There was no fence along left field since that's where the playground equipment was located.

If, from that spot on the top and back of the bleachers, you looked east down the *first* base line beyond the baseball diamond, there was nothing but grass all the way to the chain link fence that paralleled Boone Street. That chain link fence constituted the right field home run fence of the baseball field. If, from that same spot on the bleachers, you looked north down the *third* base line beyond the baseball diamond, there was that same grass. However, about 50 yards down, the grass turned to dirt and gravel and constituted the *playground*. There was no fence there and that transition from grass to dirt merely represented deep left field. No left field over-the-fence home runs were possible because the distance was simply too great. The ball remained in play even when it sailed or rolled into that area covered in dirt and gravel.

That baseball field in the playground was actually one of the nicest and best maintained in the entire southern part of El Paso. Not only did it have thick, green grass but it also had a full complement of lights so that we could play sports at night. And, they were some of the best lights in any of the parks in the city at the time. The *El Paso Boys' Club* used this field extensively and the Housing Authority ensured that it was kept well-maintained. That same baseball field would be converted into a touch-football field during the fall and winter each year. I personally have countless memories--every one of them pleasant--about experiences that I had in that grassy area.

From that spot on the top row on the bleachers, while looking toward the north down the *third* base line, you reach a point where a rectangular portion of the playground was cut away. The cutout area measured about 25 by 50 yards. They actually built a 3-family housing project building in that space but it didn't take away any space from the playground.

The dirt-and-gravel area north of the baseball field had some amazing playground equipment. If someone were to hit a ball toward left field close to the foul line into the dirt-and-gravel area the ball would probably end up right under one of the biggest playground swing sets ever built. I remember one time chasing such a ball and frantically trying to pick it up from beneath a toddler who was playing in the swing area. By the time I threw the ball back into play, the hitter had crossed home plate (and probably had also read a few comic books while waiting for my throw).

The swing set had four swings made of the absolute highest quality materials including galvanized steel and 25,000 lb.-capacity chains. The swing set was the conventional A-frame type. The cross bar at the top of the A which supported the swings probably was at least 12 ft. high. The swing had been built to last and it really did. The swing seats were thick planks of hardwood framed in steel and suspended by those huge chains. One of the greatest pleasures that I had when I first moved into the projects was swinging on that swing set and jumping off at the highest point of the up-swing. Sergio Reza (Checo), Daniel Miranda (Pelusa) and I used to compete all the time to see who could swing the highest before leaving the swing seat and falling back to earth like a parachutist without a parachute. The earth beneath the swing sets had become sandy and soft over time due to heavy use. That allowed for safe, soft landings whenever we played the parachute game.

In that same dirt-and-gravel area, just east of the swing set--and in the farthest northeast corner of the playground--was a teeter-totter set with four teeter-totters. The teeter-totters were a favorite place to bring a female friend. They were as far away from the projects as you could be without actually leaving the projects. Next to the teeter-totter was a monkey bar set with three monkey bars, two of which were 5 ft. high and the third being 6 ft. high for the bigger kids. We used to do chin-ups there whenever we were close to them.

Between the teeter-totters and the grass of the baseball field, still in the northern part of the playground, was an apparatus I had never seen and have never seen since. It consisted of a single galvanized steel pole embedded in concrete. The pole was about 12 ft. high with a perforated disk secured to the top of it but that could rotate freely. Then there was a heavy 6 foot chain attached to the disk. It had a wooden handle at the other end. The object of this apparatus was for a kid to hang on to the handle and then for someone to propel the kid around the pole so that as long as the kid would hold on, he or she would rotate around the pole at the highest velocities and greatest heights possible. That particular apparatus was extremely entertaining and fun to watch as well as to play on. Occasionally, one of the younger kids would accidentally let go of the handle and fly off into the distance crashing into Earth causing a major commotion. I do not recall, however, that anyone ever got seriously hurt on it.

Right next to this rotating pole was a complex structure of 1-½ inch galvanized steel pipes that was also extremely entertaining. I don't know what these are called but they're nothing more than adjacent squares formed by steel tubing. The entire structure rises to a height of maybe 10 ft. on a base that's also about 10 feet square. It actually forms a house consisting of cubes bounded by the galvanized steel tubing. We used to climb all over this structure having lots of fun playing tag on it. We outgrew this one early as it was really meant for the younger kids.

Then there was the smaller slide for the kiddies. It was maybe 8 ft. tall. Not too far from that slide and closer to the chain-link fence along Boone Street was a bigger slide for older kids. The top of the bigger slide was at least 14 ft. tall with a slide that seemingly went forever. The ladder portion of the slide--which one had to climb in order to use the slide--was just a few feet away from the chain link fence. When someone climbed it and slid down the slide they would actually be heading west as they came back to earth. Again, the slides were made of absolutely the highest quality materials available. The slides were always shiny and slippery, and the galvanized steel seemed indestructible. In the entire time that we lived there I never saw any part of the playground equipment that required maintenance.

By the way, this big slide was also in a relatively remote part of the playground and afforded a bit of privacy. I remember sitting at the bottom of the slide with a girl on a number of occasions. And, in 1959, I remember using that stainless-steel bottom of the slide (which was so smooth and shiny that it actually resembled a surgical table) to perform surgery on a frog. I experimented freely on frogs at that time using cinnamon juice as a type of anesthesia. In those days, you could buy cinnamon juice in a tiny bottle. The idea for that was to stick 5 or 6 toothpicks in the bottle and let them soak the juice. Then you could stick the toothpick in your mouth and taste cinnamon while you picked your teeth. I discovered that, contrary to my expectations, cinnamon juice does not put a frog to sleep. In fact, I had enormous difficulty keeping the critter on the operating table once I injected the juice into its tummy. I wonder why?

I also recall on at least two occasions watching the annual July 4th fireworks display from the top of the bigger slide all by myself. The fireworks were set off from *Hugo Meyer Field* in Washington Park which was less than a half-mile northeast of the playground. It was a heck of a thrill to watch the fireworks from there.

Coming back to the bleachers for one last time, imagine that you are sitting at the far-left side of the 5th row of the bleachers. That bleacher row actually touches the top of the chain-link fence which surrounds the playground. Right where the bleacher seat touches the chain-link fence there happened to be a 4-inch steel fence pole. As was customary in those days, the galvanized steel fence pole had a galvanized steel cap on it that normally did not require being secured to the poll since it would sit so high that no one ever attempted to remove it. However, at this point where the bleacher row touched the fence, the fence pole was very accessible and one could remove the cap very easily.

One day, somebody rolled a *Playboy* magazine and stuffed it down the top of the fence pole. Apparently, there was a steel bolt that ran through the fence pole about a foot down from the top and thus prevented the magazine from falling to the bottom. The pole cap kept the magazine dry and secure. For about two weeks the hiding place of the *Playboy* was one of the best kept secrets among 13 and 14-year olds of the neighborhood. At any given time, there would be a group of kids sitting on the bleachers perusing that magazine. Needless to say, eventually somebody snitched it. There was great disappointment and anger on the part of my peers upon discovering that one of us, to whom the secret had been disclosed, violated the sacred trust of the group and caused the magazine to disappear. Also, whenever one of us had dirty pictures to share with the others, the best place to do that was at the top of the bleachers.

I personally liked the playground for all of the obvious reasons but also because it was so large and open. If you stood in the middle of it, you could see others coming for quite a distance. It gave one a sense of privacy and no one could ever surprise you there. One July, probably in the early 1960's, I heard that my friend Zekie, who was one of the best-liked kids in the neighborhood, was having a birthday. I had noticed earlier when we were playing baseball that his socks were full holes. And so, I had purchased a pair of socks, gift wrapped them and then asked Zekie to walk with me to the middle of left field on the playground. There, where no one else could see me do it, I pulled the present out of my pocket and handed it to him wishing him a happy birthday. He was very touched by my gesture and I was happy to have found a place in the neighborhood where I could engage in that type of activity without having to explain to my peers what I was doing. To this day, Zekie remains a close friend even though he is wheel-chair bound.

San Xavier

The Catholic Church that served the neighborhood of my youth—particularly the Paisano Projects--was *San Francisco Xavier*. It was located on the north side of Paisano Drive just two blocks west of Hammett Blvd. We lived on the south side of Paisano Drive one block east of Hammett.

This was the third Catholic Church that we became associated with during our lives in El Paso. The first was *Guardian Angel* when we lived on Alameda Avenue, and the second was *Holy Family Church* in Sunset Heights during the year when mi Papá tried to operate *Tex-Western Gro*. I was never particularly interested or enthusiastic about church or religion but instead participated because mi Mamá insisted that I do so. On the other hand, my brother Nacho did have and still has a genuine interest and, as a kid, was even an altar boy.

So, like it or not, *San Xavier* was my church. I remember the routine of every Sunday morning. While I was young enough to still be dependent on mi Mamá, I would always attend church with her and my little sister Hilda Luz. Later, as I became more independent--and more unwilling to be seen in public with either of my parents--I would attend church alone or with my brother.

Services were mostly in Spanish, although the 9:00 AM mass every Sunday was designed for a youthful congregation and normally celebrated in English. Either way, I always wanted to be somewhere else. Mi Mamá would always give me either a dime or a quarter to place in the collection basket and I was tempted countless times to keep the money instead. Similarly, I was tempted many times to simply skip church and go do something else during that hour. But I had a genuine fear of God and of the punishment that I believed he would mete out for such transgressions and so, I always toed the line.

Mi Mamá used the power of God and religion very effectively. She would always tell me to do the right thing or to not do evil things lest God punish me. Since I had been hearing this from my days as a toddler, I believed strongly that God would punish me if I wasn't good. And, since God was everywhere and could see you at all times, I always did the right thing and obeyed my parents because I simply wanted to live long and without pain. Mi Mamá told me when I was very young that if I ever raised my hand in anger against my parents, that God would permanently freeze it in the upraised position and that I would forever therefore be identified as a bad child. It wasn't until recently that I concluded that her warning really wasn't anything more than a religious scare tactic.

But even though my body was at church every Sunday, my heart and soul were elsewhere. It was usually my objective to be the last person to enter the church before the celebrating priest entered, and to be the first person to leave the church after the priest's closing benediction. It was amusing how many of my peers shared that objective. Even before the priest would say the last word of the benediction, the three sets of doors of the church would be flung open by me and other kids like me, who looked as if they were being released from an environment that had no air to breathe.

In those days, the priest did not conclude the service by walking to the back of the church to talk to people as they left. Instead, he simply would disappear into the vestibule and no one would see the priest again until the following Sunday. We certainly did not hang around the church after the benediction. What we did do, however, was to head straight for the little candy concessionaire store named *El Popo* at the northeast corner of Paisano Drive and Hammett. There, we would spend the first chunk of our weekly allowance by buying a snow cone or a candy bar to celebrate having survived yet another mass.

The only times that I recall sitting in a pew at *San Xavier* was when I attended with mi Mamá. Mi Papá never attended mass for reasons that will always remain a mystery to me. Even though I had suggested to her many times that I would prefer to stand in the back with the rest of my friends, she would insist that I sit with her and Hilda Luz as close to the front as she could get us.

It was embarrassing to sit so close to the altar together with my family because kids my age simply did not do that. It was a clear signal of total dependence and of being completely uncool when a kid did that. It was also embarrassing because I never really learned when I was supposed to stand, kneel or sit during the celebration of a mass. I suppose if I had applied myself minimally, I could have learned all that, but I did not. Instead, I always waited for some lady in front of me to make the first move and then I would imitate her in hopes that we both got it right. If I ever had any doubt, I would simply move very slowly until I felt certain what position I should be in and then I would assume it.

When mi Mamá was unable to go to church due to her illness, she would simply ask me to go alone. How could I refuse? And so, I would go alone and, on those occasions, I would not only remain in the back of the church but also, I would never sit in a pew even if one was empty. Interestingly, most services were jammed to capacity with some people actually standing on the steps outside the church as the mass was conducted. The steps outside the church were, in fact, my favorite place for attending mass. If I got there late enough, and all the pews and standing room inside were filled, I would position myself on one of those steps and spend the next hour turning my head constantly and looking at the traffic pass by since I couldn't hear anything that was going on inside. Yet, I felt safe since God would be able to see that I could not get in but should still be given credit for attending.

I also felt very comfortable using this technical loophole since so many of my peers were also using it. As I would stand on the steps, I would not only see eight or nine of my buddies there doing the same thing, but there were also some full-scale adults watching the traffic with us. I suppose I figured that God would not punish all of us since we were just too many.

By the time I was in high school, I had learned every trick in the book on how to go to church and at the same time not go to church. By that time another factor entered the equation that started to draw me into the church itself more frequently. That factor was girls. It became apparent to me that the only ones attending church by standing in the steps outside were boys and young men. For some strange reason, girls did not do that. And so, as my need to look at and associate with girls grew, so did my willingness to actually attend a mass *inside* the church. Fortunately, my peers were experiencing the same pressures and they too were finding themselves more willing to go inside rather than stand on the steps outside like idiots.

In those days, even though parents were extremely effective advocates for God, the best crusaders had to be the priests. Priests were feared because they were direct agents of God and we all believed that their job was to ensure that the will of God was done. The way I saw it, if God can punish me at will then so can any priest. In those days, priests came into our lives basically in two ways: at mass and during catechism classes as we prepared for confirmation. I do not recall ever being fond of any of the priests at *San Xavier*. In fact, I did not like them at all. Yet, none of them ever did anything to me directly that would offend or scare me. I did, however, hear many stories that circulated among my buddies of trouble that they had had with a priest.

One such story related to a priest who in the middle of a mass berated all of those men and boys standing on the steps outside who he claimed were obviously afraid to enter. It cleared the steps for that one mass but the following week the men and boys were at it again.

There was another story about a priest who chastised a boy who was standing in the back of the church during mass but who was apparently standing inappropriately close to a girl right in front of him. I was not there when it happened but the boy who was chastised was an acquaintance of mine and he was extremely humiliated by the event. Apparently, every mother present at mass that day reported the incident to the boy's mother. That was a heck of a pickle to be in during those times.

I also remember vividly how, while in high school, boys my age felt obligated to attend midnight mass on Christmas Eve. Again, our parents would insist that we complete that obligation and so, as we would on any given Sunday, we grudgingly would do so. But midnight mass on Christmas Eve invariably would get complicated by yet another factor of the times: alcohol. It seems to me that every young man who attended midnight mass on Christmas Eve at *San Xavier* was drunk. It was a ritual that was honored like few others. The men would go to a party, get stinking drunk and then leave so as to attend mass. I remember seeing many of my buddies arrive at midnight mass and become loud and boisterous. Then they would conclude their appearance by falling down or throwing up or doing both. Their ever-faithful buddies--who were in just a slightly better state of inebriation--would assist them in getting out of the church before the priest could catch them. To this day, my buddies from the projects like to tell stories like these with great pride. While I myself did consume varying amounts of beer before going to midnight mass, I never did anything untoward while there.

The Catholic Church is a very interesting institution. I am very happy to report that during the many years that I participated in church activities as a boy, not once did I ever encounter a priest who acted in any way like a child molester. Many were arrogant and many were mean, but not one of them ever did anything inappropriate to me or, as far as I know, to any of my buddies.

Being a Chauffer

For Christmas of 1957, our uncle Sal gave Nachito and me a brand-new *Huffy* bicycle. Yes, it was one bicycle for the two of us. This made sense mainly for two reasons. First, we could not afford even one bike. Second, even if we could have afforded a second bike, our living quarters behind the store were much too small to store two bikes. As one might imagine, the only time I got to ride the bike was when Nachito did not want to. Still, I don't remember being disappointed about the arrangement. In fact, like most kids, I really liked enjoyed riding that bike and did so as often as I possibly could.

In the spring of the following year, after we moved to the Paisano Projects and when Hilda Luz was still five years old and not old enough yet for first grade, mi Mamá enrolled her in a preschool that was operated by a nun named Madre Mercedes ("Mother Mercedes"). This preschool operated out of a modest home in a neighborhood that was not exactly nearby. It had a small front yard enclosed by a chain link fence. That yard was the school's playground. Madre Mercedes was the principal operator but she had one or two young assistants that would help her. Every day, Madre Mercedes would be charged with the care of ten or twelve preschool children. It was not a terribly sophisticated operation but it was inexpensive and, ostensibly, it was of the right religious orientation. After all, mi Mamá had sent both Nachito and me to preschool programs at *Guardian Angel* catholic school and probably paid a pretty penny to do that. But times and economics had changed. There was simply no money to permit such an extravagance with Hilda Luz. Mi Mamá probably felt guilty that she could not provide the same quality preschool education for Hilda Luz, but she felt good about the fact that the pre-school was operated by catholic nun.

During that period, mi Mamá was suffering those occasional seizures that required her to always stay home. Mi Papá was selling household goods door-to-door with the *Lighthouse for the Blind*. Nachito was an eighth grader at *Jefferson Intermediate School* and I was in the sixth grade at *Henderson Intermediate*. It would have been nice if this preschool had been located within walking distance of our home. However, it was not. It was actually located about two or three miles away. It would've been nice if we had a car on which to take Hilda Luz to her preschool sessions; however, we did not have a car. It would've been nice if someone in our family had a driver's license so that we could borrow a car to take Hilda Luz to her preschool sessions; however, none of us had a license.

And so, the way that Hilda Luz would normally get to school was by city bus accompanied by mi Mamá. Our apartment at 405 Webber Way was on the south side of Paisano Drive, a six-lane thoroughfare that in those days was one of the main east-west arteries of El Paso. The bus stop from which they would take the bus to the preschool was on the north side of Paisano. Once in a while, when mi Mamá could not take her, Nachito or I would walk Hilda Luz to the bus stop and then wait with her for the next west-bound bus. We would place her in the bus and she would ride alone on Paisano Drive until she got to the bus stop at Eucalyptus Street. Right after we placed her on the bus, we would telephone Madre Mercedes and tell her that we had just sent her Hilda Luz. Madre Mercedes would then dispatch one of her assistants to walk a half a mile to the bus stop at Eucalyptus Street to meet Hilda Luz as she got off the bus.

Hilda Luz's daily return trip from school was usually handled by Nachito. After school, he would take a city bus to Hilda Luz's school, pick her up and bring her home. When Nachito was unavailable, mi Mamá would arrange to have one of Madre Mercedes' assistants walk Hilda Luz to Paisano Drive, help her get across the treacherous Paisano Drive to the bus stop, and then put her on the bus that was heading east toward our apartment. One of us would then wait at the bus stop on Paisano Drive near our apartment until the bus arrived with Hilda Luz.

The above routine was followed probably four times a week. However, about once a week we had to be creative. On those occasions when Nachito was unavailable to bring Hilda Luz home and when Madre Mercedes did not have an assistant to take Hilda Luz to the bus stop, the job of getting Hilda Luz home would fall on my shoulders. Since I had no money to spend on bus fare and since I had no time to waste, I--with mi Mamá's blessing--would go pick her up on my *Huffy* bike.

On those occasions when I had to do this, I would be notified immediately upon my arrival home from school at about 4PM. Once I got the word, time was of the essence. I had no time to argue or to make excuses. I simply and immediately had to get on my bike and start pedaling toward the preschool. On the way there, since I was alone and unsupervised, I would usually take advantage of the straight shot provided by Paisano Drive even though it was extremely dangerous to do so. I would pedal straight west for two or three miles on Paisano Drive to Eucalyptus Street and then turn right (north) on Eucalyptus for another half mile until I got to the preschool.

Hilda Luz would be waiting for me patiently sitting on a small bench in the yard in front of the house and, if I recall correctly, with some degree of excitement and anticipation about the upcoming bike ride. I would take her little book satchel and pass one of the handle-bars through the satchel handle so it could just hang there. Hilda Luz would then sit sideways on the frame immediately behind the handlebars. I would then push off from the curb heading east to get back home.

I was no dummy and so, on the return trip, I would never take the highly dangerous Paisano Drive route. Instead, I would always use the side streets and other avenues through which little or no traffic would be encountered. I would pedal for 30 minutes or so and eventually we would get home.

Even though traffic was lighter on the side streets and other avenues, it still had to be a fairly risky proposition to have two kids riding home on a bike. Due to my age and inexperience, I never considered the matter to be risky. And I suspect that Hilda Luz did not think so either. I'm certain that mi Mamá and mi Papá would have preferred to have used a less risky method of getting Hilda Luz back home on those occasions, but they simply had no choice. I wish I could say that traffic conditions back then were somewhat safer than they are today, but I honestly do not believe that to be the case. I think that the speeds at which cars traveled then is no different than today and I believe that the likelihood of having a problem while riding on the bike was as great then as ever. Yet, we had to do what we had to do. But in all honesty, I do remember being somewhat annoyed at having to waste an hour of my precious playtime on those occasions when I had to go pick up Hilda Luz. Eventually, I accepted this job as a routine--although annoying— matter. Despite the annoyance, I really did enjoy the thrill of that treacherous ride.

When I asked Hilda Luz about those bike-rides recently, she told me that she remembered very little about them. What she did remember was that one occasion when apparently no one told her what to do and after waiting for some time while nothing happened, she walked by herself from the preschool across Paisano Drive to the bus stop and then, after borrowing a nickel from a stranger, took the bus home. To everyone's surprise, she showed up at home safe and sound. She just vividly remembers growing impatient while waiting for people to help her get home.

Chapter 4-Time to Move Again

And so, beginning in the summer of 1958 and continuing for two years, as life in the projects was stabilizing beautifully for me and my family, a nasty curve ball was hurled at us. Even though he was doing well as a salesman for the *Lighthouse for the Blind*, mi Papá could not help but to always be on the lookout for new business opportunities, particularly those involving retail sales. Early in the summer of 1960 he entered into a partnership with a couple whom he had recently met. Somehow, mi Papá found out that a small restaurant with a home attached was available for lease. It was on Evergreen Street just on the edge of El Paso's largest park, *Washington Park*, and no more than a mile from our house in the Projects. He partnered with that couple whereby he would pay the monthly rent, the couple would live in and operate the restaurant and they would split the profit. I suppose that mi Papá had accumulated enough cash to pay for the rent for at least 2 or 3 months after which, the restaurant would presumably start generating sufficient revenue to pay the rent.

In June, 1960, mi Papá made the first rental payment and the couple moved in and prepared to open the restaurant. Within a few days, mi Papá gathered the family and delivered the bad news: the couple had absconded and we, as a family, would have to move into the restaurant and operate it. We were stunned. By the end of June, we were going to be living in that restaurant and none of us, including mi Papá, seemed to be very excited about that prospect.

I remember very well how distressing the news was to me. I had for many years looked forward to living in the Projects and when the dream finally came true, I never even considered the possibility of having to leave them. In 1959, a year after we had moved into the Projects, the *El Paso Boys' Club* had opened a Club right there just a block from our apartment and my brother and I had become heavily involved in Club activities and sports and moving away would mean having to give all that up as well. I also did not look forward to once again seeing mi Papá trying to earn a living by running a business. Nevertheless, on or about the first of July of 1960, right after my 13th birthday, we left the Paisano Projects and moved into the restaurant/home that mi Papá had leased.

In fairness, there were many positive things about the restaurant. It was actually a relatively new building, and it was fairly well-equipped to be a successful restaurant. And unlike any home that we had ever lived in before, this restaurant/home had an evaporative air cooler mounted on the roof. It was a one- story structure, with the restaurant occupying the front half of the structure and the home occupying the rear half. The quality of the house and restaurant was actually quite good. The doors and windows did not let air leak out or water in and the walls and floors seemed to be intact. Except for the Projects, which were actually extremely well maintained, every other home that I remember living in was in pretty shabby shape. This house and restaurant were really quite nice. There was a tiny backyard that was as wide as the house but only about 10 ft. deep. The restaurant was located on Evergreen Street about one block south of Alameda Avenue just one block outside of the gates of *Washington Park*. I seem to recall being somewhat impressed when I first walked into the building. I was not happy about leaving the Projects but I think I felt a little optimistic about what was about to happen.

But there were also a few negative things about the restaurant. First of all, while I always enjoyed the food that mi Mamá used to make, I never thought that she was a professional cook. I believed that customers who would eat her food would probably think that while it was OK, it was certainly not worth the $1 or $2 that we were going to be charging for a meal. Secondly, I did not think that mi Papá would be much of a waiter. After all, he was old and blind. Thirdly, I feared that my brother and I and even my little sister were going to end up being the dish-washers, griddle-scrapers and floor-moppers of this operation and I did not like that.

Nevertheless, I guess I was somewhat enthusiastic about it in some respects because I do recall once again being in charge of the advertising signs and window lettering that ultimately were placed in the restaurant. There I was, a 13-year-old boy using a sliver of soap to do the outlines of the letters of the restaurant's name on the front picture window of the restaurant. The window was 5 ft. by 8 ft. and I painted the name of the restaurant, *Las Cazuelas,* on the window pane from the inside in an arching pattern from one end of the window to the other in letters that were around 12 inches high.

I also remember using fine brushes and oil paint to prepare a sign for the front of the restaurant. It consisted of two plywood slabs each around 3 ft. by 6 ft. hinged together at the top with a chain holding the two sides so that they would form an "A" figure. Using the fine brushes, I hand-lettered the menu for the restaurant on each side along with other pertinent information such as the hours of operation. I do remember having an enormous sense of fun and gratification when I finished both of those paint projects.

All that hard work turned out to be the easy part. My recollection is that from the early morning until late at night, very few customers ever came in. For that reason, we could not afford to have a very extensive stock of food. That meant that whenever a customer came in, the waiter--whether it was mi Papá, my brother or I--would try to sweet talk the customer into buying what we *had* rather than what was listed on the menu. We had lots of hamburgers, hot dogs and chili beans and that was about it. The two-ounce patties of hamburger meat were really only one ounce of beef and one ounce of bread and egg, which had always been the way mi Mamá made burgers. Nevertheless, they weren't that bad, actually.

This restaurant had a fairly impressive jukebox. I assume that we got it from a vending machine operator who installed it and who would receive the bulk of the coins that were put into it by customers. In consideration, mi Papá would receive a portion of that. Thankfully, there was a switch in the back of the jukebox that allowed one to play a song without paying. That switch allowed us "insiders" to play the jukebox constantly. Some of the songs that were in the jukebox included *It's Now or Never* by Elvis Presley, *Cathy's Clown* and *Let it be Me* by the Everly Brothers, *Only the Lonely* by Roy Orbison, *Puppy Love* by Paul Anka, *I'm Sorry* by Brenda Lee, *Walking to New Orleans* by Fats Domino and *North to Alaska* by Johnny Horton. I remember playing those songs over and over and over as we waited for customers to show up. I also remember feeling extremely lucky for having that jukebox. Every time I hear those songs today, I am immediately transported back in time to *Las Cazuelas*.

At that time, I had just completed the seventh grade and Nachito the ninth grade. That fall, I attended *Jefferson Intermediate School*, and Nachito attended *Jefferson High School*. I must not have been terribly busy in school, but my brother and I had lots to do at home and in the restaurant. He and I would sweep and mop the asphalt tile floors every day. We would also take the pumice stone and clean the huge griddle every evening. We also did the dishes, however, when a restaurant does not have more than two or three paying customers per day, the dishwashing workload is not likely to be very heavy. We also kept the front sidewalk clean and the many windows sparkling.

One of the most gratifying memories of my days in that restaurant revolved around the dog that I had at the time. Unfortunately, I don't remember the name of the dog. I do remember, however, that he was medium-sized with a German shepherd body, black-and-white color and really smart. He lived in our backyard and even though the yard was small I remember having lots of fun with him there. I don't remember at all how I came to acquire the dog nor do I remember what ever happened to the dog. What I do know is that we could not have a dog in the Projects and therefore he did not come with us when we moved into the restaurant. Furthermore, since we moved back to the Projects after a year in the restaurant, I know for a fact that we did not bring him with us. So, I had fun with the dog for one year but then I could not have a dog again.

It was around this same time that I experienced my first and only mugging. The time was the spring of 1961. I was 13 years old and Nachito was 15.

The mugging occurred on a Sunday morning. In those days, I still enjoyed playing with toys. One of my favorites was a little 3-panel trick card that I must have purchased at the dime store. This was not a little-boy toy but one for a more mature kid who had discovered the fun of magic tricks. It consisted of three individual cardboard panels, each panel about the size of a baseball card but a little bit thicker. Imagine if you can, the three panels laying side-by-side but held together by small cloth straps about a quarter inch in width that, through pure magic, permitted the panels to be flipped on top of or under each other without ever being separated from each other. I thought it was an incredibly interesting toy and I carried it with me everywhere I went. When all three panels were stacked together, the toy would fit perfectly into any kid's shirt pocket. I happened to be carrying that toy in my shirt pocket when Nacho and I went to church together that particular Sunday.

The church that we attended in those days was still *San Xavier*. On that particular Sunday, as we did on most Sundays, Nachito and I would ride to church on the one bike that we shared. Nachito would steer and pedal and I would be the passenger on the frame between the seat and the handlebars. After the Mass, we headed for home. As we passed in front of *Dudley Field*-- the city's only professional baseball park which was situated between our home and the church--we saw three older boys approaching us. As we passed each other, the biggest of the three boys latched on to the handlebars of our bike. He then stood directly in front of the bike straddling the front tire between his legs. His snake eyes were no more than 5 or 6 inches from mine as he stood there with a snarling smile.

I did not know his name but I recognized the guy as the neighborhood bully. He was probably one year older than Nachito (that making him sixteen) but he was big and lanky for his age. He actually had very broad shoulders and long arms that dangled from them so that he walked like Frankenstein, the monster. He was also notoriously vicious. The way he looked and dressed that day fit perfectly within the juvenile delinquent profile that prevailed in those days. He wore starched khaki pants, a neatly pressed shirt with razor-sharp creases up and down the front and back and shiny, black shoes with pointy toes. His shirt was unbuttoned revealing a clean white undershirt. His two friends were younger but similarly dressed. There was no question in my brother's and in my mind that these were bad kids and we were scared.

As they held us and our bike captives, the big guy proceeded to make fun of us. He made fun of the bike, of our clothes, of our haircuts and he called us "sissies." After a few minutes of this, as Nachito and I trembled in fear, he cut to the chase: he said he wanted our bike and our money.

Nachito then took charge. He observed that we were clearly outnumbered, that they probably were armed with switchblades and that we had, in fact, invaded their territory. We had two choices: Fight them (and get whupped) or beg for mercy. Well, since we probably were sissies, he decided to plead for mercy.

I remember Nachito's response. He told the big guy that we only had one bike between us and that we simply could not lose it since we used it to go to school. He also pointed out that when we left our house earlier, we each had 10¢ but that we had given that to the church moments earlier.

The big guy must have realized that he could not squeeze blood out of a rock. As he was pondering what next to do, I saw his eyes affix themselves upon my shirt pocket. Suddenly, he reached into it and pulled out my 3-panel trick card toy. He tinkered with it once or twice, thought it was cool and proclaimed it as his. I was furious but I also knew that I was going to have to let him keep it. The big guy and his buddies then fired off a few more insults at us--in the style of El Guapo and El Jefe from the movie *The Three Amigos*--but then backed away laughing at us. By taking my toy they avoided walking away empty-handed and thus losing face. I'm sure that in their minds they had declared victory and were now free to leave as victors.

Nachito and I were very angry but we had never felt such terror. We were extremely fortunate that we had not gotten beaten up. As we assessed what could have happened versus what did happen, we also declared victory (to ourselves) and headed for home.

But good things also happened while we lived at that restaurant. During that year while I attended *Jefferson Intermediate School*, I was privileged to have been a student of Mr. Joseph Putera, a math teacher who had a significant impact on me. He was not a popular teacher. In fact, most students did not like him. But he was the most dedicated mathematician that I ever met. He also seemed to recognize in me a little bit more potential than he saw in my peers and so he seemed to dedicate a bit more attention to me than to others. I remember experiencing an amazing transformation that started with me hating math at the beginning of the year and really liking it by the end of the year. Another memorable thing about Mr. Putera was his ghastly style of dress. Although he always wore a tie, it seemed to be the same tie and it seemed to be dirty all the time. He always wore suspenders which caused his pants to ride high and expose his ever-present white socks. Except for his laughable demeanor attributable primarily to his clothing, he was an excellent teacher who left a huge mark on me.

For the remainder of that 1-year lease at the restaurant, we struggled to make it work out for us. But it was not meant to be. By June of 1961, mi Papá had used up all of his savings running the restaurant and had made no profit at all. When the lease expired, we all knew what we had to do. We were forced once again to return to the Paisano Projects. Once again, I was elated.

Chapter 5-Jobs I got as a Kid

Like most kids growing up in the 50's, I was always looking for a way to make a little money. Up until 1958, the grocery stores that mi Papá operated kept my brother and me busy but we never got paid for that. The same thing happened in 1960-1961 when mi Papá operated *Las Cazuelas*. However, when mi Papá's businesses did not occupy me, I managed to find any number of ways to earn a little cash.

Newspaper Boy

Up until the advent of the internet, one of the most memorable rites of passage that young boys used to experience was managing a paper route. In previous generations, newspaper delivery was a domain exclusively operated by young kids and, almost without exception, by young boys.

The newspaper delivery concept in El Paso in the 60's was the following: Newspapers were generally published daily with one newspaper publishing a morning edition (*The El Paso Times*) and another competing newspaper (*The El Paso Herald Post*) publishing the afternoon edition. Only the *Times* would publish a Sunday edition. In the early '50s and '60s, the price for the daily and Saturday editions was 5¢ and the Sunday edition was 10¢. Even though there were some other outlets through which newspapers were made available to the public, the most common method was home delivery.

Home delivery accounted for the bulk of the newspaper sales. Each newspaper boy would get a real neat customer or "route" book. The best way to imagine what these looked like is to picture one of those black, metal binder clips that are used these days to keep large stacks of paper together. In order to open the spring-loaded clip, you must press the two little handles together. By doing so, the spring opens and you can slip papers inside. When the spring is released, the papers remain safely clamped. The route book was 4 inches wide (top/bottom) and maybe seven inches long with a spring clip at the top. The covers and spring clip were covered with cloth or black vinyl. The two book covers were attached to the spring at one end and the spring would be opened by using the two covers to gain leverage. The two covers would open and close the spring so you could stick any number of sheets of customer records in it. Each sheet had perforations that, in effect, created twelve little postage-sized stamps that would serve as payment receipts. Each stamp had a calendar week printed on it. The perforations would allow the newspaper boy to remove one stamp and give it to a customer as a receipt once the customer paid the 35¢ for a full week of delivery. That was a saving to the customer of 5¢ per week over retail. The twelve stamps per sheet meant that each sheet contained three months' worth of individual weekly stamps. Each sheet was pink and therefore a successful newspaper boy who had 30 to 40 customers would have a half-inch stack of pink sheets in his route book. A wildly successful newspaper boy with 80 to 100 customers would have all of these sheets jammed into the book and it would appear to be extremely overstuffed. An overstuffed route book was the trademark of a successful newspaper delivery boy. I remember occasionally seeing some kid in high school with an overstuffed route book in his back pocket and envying him for the enormous amounts of money he had to be making from his route. Anyway, the cost to each boy for papers was 3¢ for dailies and 7¢ for the Sunday edition. Thus, for each daily customer, the delivery boy would make 10¢ profit per week and if that customer also took the Sunday paper, the profit was a total of was 13¢. With 30-40 customers, that means $4 to $5 per week profit. It was not a bad deal at all in those days.

Home delivery was accomplished as follows. A van from the newspaper company would deliver bundles of newspapers to central locations in every neighborhood in just about every city. Each morning and each afternoon at the specific locations one could find 20 or 30 wire-bound bundles of newspapers each with a number identifying the pertinent route. Shortly after the delivery of the bundles, a small army of young boys on their bicycles would converge to the area of the bundles. Each boy would find the bundle with his identifying number, he would drag it to a spot that he had claimed based on seniority (very junior kids had to drag the bundles way across the street), he would snap the bundling wire, and then he would fold each individual paper into a nice square about 6 in. on each side. By the way, every bundle would usually include at least one, maybe two, extra copies ("Extras") that the delivery boys could sell at full price and pocket the entire amount. In our case, the sale of an Extra would enable us to get a cherry-coke before heading home after the deliveries were done,

The folding of the newspapers was an art and was very competitive. Since time was of the essence, whoever could fold newspapers quickly had the advantage. The boy would position himself on his knees with the bundle of newspapers in front of him with the folded edge closest to him. He would then stick his thumbs under the folded edge and then fold the bottom forward toward the top. He would line up the bottom edge with the top edge of the paper and at the same time tuck the bottom right hand corner into the newspaper which is now folded into quarters and run his palm along the new fold to make sure it stays folded. In a swift and continuing motion, he would pick up the entire paper, flip it and slap it hard again along the folds so they would stay. Then he would rotate the paper clockwise, fold the left side to the middle and take the right side of the paper and tuck it into the left side.

Then he would give it one last powerful slap to flatten it and then he would flip it to the stack of folded papers. I remember how we used to admire those boys who could fold newspapers as if they were machines. I actually became pretty fast but probably never fast enough to draw the admiration of others.

Once the newspapers were all folded, they were neatly placed inside canvas bags that were originally designed to be placed over the shoulders of newspaper boys. The bags therefore had pouches on the front and on the back with a head-size hole in the middle where the boy would poke his head through. When the bags were originally designed, the delivery boys apparently used to walk their paper groups. That's why they had those head-sized holes. Later, when all the boys had bicycles, the bags would be placed on the handlebars of the bikes with only the front pouch being utilized to carry newspapers whereas the back pouch was used to secure the bag to the bike. Once the bag was filled with folded newspapers it would be secured on to the bike handle bars and the delivery boy would start his delivery. Those bags started out white but, invariably, because of the newspaper ink, they soon would turn black and dirty.

The real fun of being a newspaper boy would occur when the actual home delivery of the paper was made. Speed and accuracy were again very important but now balance and coordination mattered too. The idea was to go down the street of your designated paper route and, without ever slowing down, fling a folded paper onto the porch or front stoop of every house on that route. I remember having immense fun as I would pedal the bike furiously while reaching into the bag in front of me and taking a folded newspaper and flinging it to its destination. On a good day, I would be able to strike my target 100 percent of the time.

A paper route consisted of as many delivery customers as one could enlist on specifically designated streets. One route might consist of three streets. The number of customers however, would vary. Sometimes, three streets could generate 30 customers; other times, three streets could only generate 3 or 4. The newspaper boy was motivated to enlist new customers. If a newspaper boy suddenly found himself with such success that he was having to deliver 70 or 80 papers, he would then hire a friend or little brother to help. Eventually, the odds were that the friend or little brother would take over the entire route.

I don't believe that too many newspaper boys kept their routes for more than one or two years before handing it off to a successor. For that reason, it didn't take a lot of effort to find a paper route. It was always a memorable occasion when the incumbent delivery boy would ceremoniously hand off to his successor the route book indicating that he had completed his tour of duty and was now solemnly entrusting it to the new kid.

My first recollection of selling newspapers goes back to perhaps age 5. I don't know or remember this for a fact but I'm told that I would accompany my seven-year-old brother on the bus to downtown El Paso where we would go to the newspaper office and purchase 10 or 12 newspapers for 3¢ apiece. We would then take those papers and sell them in the downtown El Paso area on foot for 5¢ apiece. I understand (from my brother) that we used to frequent all the bars and commercial establishments in the downtown El Paso area (same places where we used to hustle shoe shines) and after an hour's work come home with five or 10¢ profit even after paying the bus fare.

My first experience with home delivery of newspapers occurred in 1957 when we lived on West Main Street in El Paso. My brother, Nachito had hooked himself up with an older kid whose name was Richard something-or-other, who had a paper route in *Sunset Heights*. Richard's route got so big that he had to hire Nachito as his helper. Eventually, they required still another helper. Nachito put in the good word for me and soon I was one of the guys in the team. Within a few weeks, Nachito took over the entire route and together he and I made real good money from it for a few months until we moved away.

When we lived in the Paisano Projects in 1959, I suppose I was too busy in the Boys' Club to think about a paper route. However, in 1960, when we moved to Evergreen Street where mi Papá was trying to run a restaurant, I recall that the newspaper delivery opportunity came up again. A few blocks away near a flower shop on Alameda and Linden, we used to receive the bundles and—again after being a "helper" to one of the kids that had a route--I was given my own route with 40 or 50 customers. It was at that point that I achieved the peak of my folding and throwing ability with respect to newspapers. I was 13 years old at the time and I enjoyed that experience for one year.

I'll always remember the smell of the fresh newspaper ink that would engulf us as we folded the papers. And, I'll always remember how our hands would get blackened as we folded. But the best memory of all was--as I pedaled and threw one--the sight of a folded newspaper flying through the air apparently heading toward the yard off to one side of the house but magically getting caught in the draft and being redirected to the front door of the house where it landed with a "whoof" right on target. You could not do that with any accuracy unless you had honed your skills after having thrown a whole bunch of them.

Ball Chaser

In 1961, I was 14 years old and in the ninth grade. A professional farm team of the *San Francisco Giants* was organized in El Paso. They were called the *El Paso Sun Kings* and they played at *Dudley Field*. *Dudley Field* was the best baseball park in El Paso at the time. It was located directly across Paisano Drive about a quarter mile north of the Paisano Projects and literally across the street from my home. *Dudley Field* had been the home of the *El Paso Texans*, a minor league team that played in the Southwestern or Arizona-Texas leagues from 1930 until 1957. From 1958 until 1960, professional baseball disappeared from El Paso until the *Sun Kings* arrived in 1961. *Dudley Field* and the *Sun Kings* introduced at least two new elements of life for the boys of the Projects. First of all, it brought us the opportunity to see and even meet some baseball players who eventually became stars in the majors. Secondly, once in a while, we were able to find employment at these games.

Jobs for young kids at *Dudley Field* were laid out in the following hierarchy: The youngest kids--and therefore the most inexperienced--could be hired to sell popcorn and peanuts at the ball games. Over the course of the years such kids could rise in the hierarchy to sell soft drinks, then hot dogs and eventually, if they were of proper age, they could sell beer. The hierarchy, however, had another more interesting branch to it. A few select kids could get jobs at *Dudley Field* doing non-selling activities. For example, during every ball game, young kids were hired to operate the manual scoreboard, chase fly balls that were hit over the fence or foul balls that would land in the parking lot or on the roof of the grandstand, or guard entrances to locker rooms, press boxes or even entry gates to the park. This set of jobs had its own hierarchy. Kids would start by chasing balls, progress to operating the scoreboard, and then reach the crest of the opportunities by becoming a park guard.

I started out as a popcorn vendor. I did that for an entire season. I would not sell popcorn at every game but once a week at least, I would go there and I would probably earn around a dollar for my work. At the beginning of the second season, after my pal Checo put in a good word, I was "discovered" by the other park talent-hunter, the groundskeeper. He offered me the job of chasing Home Run balls. This job also paid a dollar but it was a much more prestigious job than selling popcorn. My post was behind the fence at center field. I and a fellow Home Run ball chaser would be posted there and our job was to wait until someone hit a Home Run. When the ball sailed out of the park, we would give chase. We would recover the ball and run it back to a certain point where the ball would eventually find its way onto the playing field again. There was an irrigation canal that ran behind center field almost the entire length of the ball park fence. Probably one out of every three or four home runs would actually fall into the canal and those balls were lost. Other home runs, however, would land in the dirt outside of the fence and we could recover those.

Midway through that second season, I was promoted. The groundskeeper, whose name was Joe Manago, asked my pal Checo and me to become foul ball-chasers. We started by just positioning ourselves at different points near the entrances to the ballpark. Our job was to watch for foul balls and to try to recover them. Sometimes, the foul balls would be caught by fans and they were allowed to keep them. However, if the ball landed on the pavement, in the area of seats in the ballpark or in the parking lots just outside the ballpark, our job was to chase them down and bring them back.

This job was somewhat risky. Even though we were supposed to find these errant balls, there were always other kids from the neighborhood trying to get a free baseball that had been fouled. Once in a while, there would be a confrontation at the parking lot between one of those kids who had caught a ball and did not want to give it up and an authorized foul ball chaser such as Checo or me. Most of those times, a policeman would actually appear to ensure that we recovered the ball.

After being a chaser of foul balls for a good portion of the season, I once again was "promoted." My job now was to recover foul balls that had landed on the roof of the grandstand. The grandstand was a seating area directly behind home plate. It had a net in front of it to protect spectators who were sitting in it from foul balls or tipped balls that went from the batter's box into the grandstand. The grandstand had a roof that was probably 50 or 60 ft. above the seating area. It was made of corrugated tin sitting on a metal frame pitched from the front to the back so that rainfall (and balls) would gather at the back of the roof. Shortly before the start of a game, two of us (Checo and I) would climb a little catwalk-type metal ladder to the back of the grandstand roof and then we would walk to the front edge of the roof so that we could actually see the ball game from there. Most of the time, the two foul ball catchers would be lying on their stomachs next to each other peering over the top of the roof down onto the infield. Sometimes the two catchers would be on opposite sides of the roof. Nevertheless, whenever a foul ball landed on the corrugated metal roof it did so with a loud bang and the ball would bounce once or twice but generally would end up rolling to the back of the roof and sitting there until someone recovered it. Our job was to recover and return that ball. Returning the ball generally only required that we throw the ball back into the playing field or, placing it at the top of the net and releasing it to slide/roll down to someone waiting below to catch it.

As one might imagine, of all of these jobs afforded us with lots of opportunities to shake hands and chat with the ballplayers. Three whose names I remember were Jesús Alou, Manny Mota and Charlie Dees. There were many more but I simply do not remember their names. I do remember, however, that every year any number of them would become major league players and once in a while they would become huge stars. Jose Cardenal probably was the biggest player to move up from the *Sun Kings*.

I can't recall specifically when this happened, but there were times when I was not working as a ball chaser and, in fact, was just another kid in the parking lot trying to catch a free ball. Therefore, on one or two occasions, I found myself on the wrong side of a confrontation where I had found a ball and was trying to keep it but I was being challenged by a legitimate foul ball chaser who wanted to take it away for me. All I remember is that I did catch and actually keep a few balls of the *El Paso Sun Kings*.

Concession Vendor

The *El Paso Coliseum* was--and remains so today--an entertainment venue that hosts all sorts of programs. It is a huge red-brick structure that can accommodate 6,500 people. Back in the 60's the *Coliseum* was the principal site for world famous entertainers to play before El Paso audiences. The *Coliseum* was located on Paisano Drive at the intersection of Boone Street. It was on the northeast corner of my neighborhood, the Paisano Projects.

The *Coliseum*, like most entertainment venues, routinely would grant the right to sell food, drinks and other commodities to certain providers for a fee. Such arrangements are often referred to as a concession and the business of selling those items to event attendees became known as the concession operation. Beginning around 1961, when I was around 14 years old, I started working as a concession vendor at *Coliseum* events. Since our neighborhood was so close to the *Coliseum*, it was natural that my friends and I would go there on event nights to try to make a little money. Whether it was the circus, the *Ice Capades*, the rodeo, a wrestling match or a top 40 pop singer, something was always going on at the *Coliseum* and the operator who had the food and beverage concession business always needed vendors.

About two hours before an event was to begin, the concession manager would open the main door and let all of the prospective vendors come in. The vendors—including myself—ranged in age from 14 to over 21. There were basically five vendor job categories: The popcorn and peanut vendors (ages 14-15); the soft-drink vendors (ages 16-18); the cotton-candy or balloon or cushion vendors (ages 19-20); the beer/hot dog vendors (over 21); and the behind-the-counter vendors (also over 21). The concession manager knew how many vendors he would need for a given event and he would gather the crowd of prospects around him and simply start pointing at the lucky ones who would get a job that night.

I would always show up looking for a vendor job with my brother Nacho who was 2 years older and my pal Checo and his brother Chuy. More often than not, we all got selected to work. Checo and I would sell popcorn and peanuts and Nacho and Chuy would sell soft drinks. The average take-home pay those days for a popcorn and peanut vendor was $1-$2 and for a soft drink vendor $2-$3. The cash that we would bring to our households each night made a huge difference to our families.

I will never forget the time in the early 60's when comedian Jerry Lewis came to town and did a series of shows at the *Coliseum*. Jerry Lewis was in his prime in the late 1950s and early 1960s. Not only was he making all sorts of money in motion pictures, but he was also hauling it in doing records and in appearances throughout the country. Somehow, El Paso became one of those cities where his show would make a stop every year during that period.

His show was fairly typical of the type of entertainment that could be done at the *Coliseum*. A huge stage would be set up on the main floor of the *Coliseum*. The rest of the floor would be populated with wooden or metal folding chairs to accommodate the audience. The rest of the seating at the *Coliseum* (box seats and bleachers on two sides of the main floor) was also made available so that on shows such as these, it was not uncommon to fill the house with all available space utilized for seating except for the stage.

Jerry Lewis' show consisted of two hours' worth of jokes, songs, funny stories and antics as only Jerry Lewis could do them. He would fill the *Coliseum* each time he appeared.

As far as the guys of the Projects were concerned, the Jerry Lewis show was just another opportunity to get a concession job at the Coliseum. I was a rookie vendor that particular year, and because of that, I was relegated to selling popcorn and peanuts. My friend, Checo, however, who had a very good relationship with the owner of the vending concession, had been promoted early on to sell soda pops.

And so, in 1961, the Jerry Lewis show came to town. On the day of the first show, Checo and I were both lucky enough to get hired by the *Coliseum* concessionaire. As was customary, we were out there, peddling popcorn, peanuts and sodas hours before the show actually started. Slowly but surely the audience would arrive and fill all the seats. Then the show would begin.

At around the halfway point of the show there would be a short intermission. A few minutes before intermission on that first day, Jerry Lewis stepped forward on the stage right to the front edge and signaled to the first soda pop vendor that passed by. It just happened to be Checo. Jerry looked tired and sweaty and wiped his brow with a hanky. He asked Checo for a *Coca Cola*. Checo popped the cap from the bottle of *Coke*, poured it into a Dixie cup and handed it to the famous entertainer. Jerry took it and handed Checo a crisp dollar bill to pay for the 15¢ Coke and while holding the microphone close to his mouth so that everyone could hear, Jerry told Checo to "keep the change." The crowd roared its approval. Checo beamed. In that 10 second exchange, not only had Checo doubled the usual take-home pay that he earned, but also participated in a truly memorable and totally unexpected life-moment.

I observed all of this from a vantage point very close to the nosebleed seats of the *Coliseum* where I had been trying to peddle popcorn and peanuts. As soon as the Jerry Lewis-Checo sale was completed, I was able to take advantage of the significantly increased interest of customers in buying anything from any vendor in the wake of what Jerry Lewis had just done. And so, whereas I would normally sell at most two trays of popcorn and peanuts on any given day, on this occasion, I must have sold an additional tray simply because Checo and Jerry had created such a favorable and generous buying environment for all vendors.

I remember telling customers as they purchased popcorn or peanuts that the guy down on the floor who just got that dollar from Jerry Lewis was my best friend. Almost invariably, whoever was buying from me at that moment would also utter the magic words "Keep the change." It was a great moment for all vendors.

As you might well imagine, Checo was the hero of the night among the vendor corps. Everybody shook his hand, patted him on the back, acknowledged the good fortune that he had brought to the other vendors... and they got to take a peek at the Jerry Lewis dollar. It was a truly exciting evening for all of us.

Because Jerry Lewis was well-liked by the entire world--including Mexican-American mothers of popcorn, peanut and soda pop vendors--the celebration over Checo's notable achievement continued even after we went home that evening. I told the story to mi Mamá and she excitedly telephoned Checo's Mom to congratulate her and Checo. The story traveled rapidly through our high school the following day and eventually was noted in the high school newspaper too.

But the story does not end there. Jerry Lewis was scheduled to do a second show at the *Coliseum* on the day after he gave Checo that dollar bill. Once again, Checo and I were among the 20 or so young vendors that were hired to work during that performance. Everything proceeded as usual from the start. Long before the crowd arrived, the vendors started their sales operations. All went normally during the show until about a few minutes before the intermission. At around the same time that Jerry Lewis had bought the Coke from Checo the previous day, every single one of the 20 or so vendors hired that day, in his own separate and sneaky way, converged so that just about all of the vendors were loitering immediately in front of the stage as the intermission approached. Even though I suspected--as all the others did--that Jerry Lewis was likely to repeat his purchase on this day, I chose to stay up near the nosebleed seats again. I'll never forget the sight of the swarm of 20 or so vendors that cluttered the main aisle immediately in front of the stage each hoping he would be the lucky one that day.

Jerry Lewis was no dummy and he also noticed what was happening. He decided to exploit it a bit. He told the crowd of what had happened during the earlier show and explained why all these vendors had once again gathered in front of the stage. The crowd laughed heartily, and so did the vendors. Eventually, Jerry Lewis picked one of the vendors and repeated the purchase that he had made with Checo again telling the lucky kid to "keep the change."

On this second occasion, I did not benefit anywhere near as much as I had the day before. The vendor that got the dollar this time was no longer a hero as Checo had been but was now looked upon by the rest of us as an opportunist, a back-stabber, a vulture and a fraud. He was not hailed by his fellow vendors and the story was no longer remarkable. I have even forgotten who that vendor was. However, I shall never forget the moment that Checo had his encounter with fame, fortune and Jerry Lewis.

Another vendor experience that sticks out in my mind is the time that I got my first real taste of gambling. As soon as a vendor was selected to work during an event, he was given a $2 roll of nickels for use in giving change to customers. Each vendor would, of course, have to pay back the $2 at the end of the evening when he was doing final check-out. One night, after being selected to work as a popcorn and peanut vendor, I put my $2 worth of nickels in my apron pocket and hung around with fellow vendors waiting for the signal to pick up our popcorn and peanut trays and start selling.

As we waited, I learned about a game called pitching nickels. I had never heard of or seen that game played. A few kids slipped away into a dark corridor and proceeded to play. I could see them. The three players selected a wall, then lined up about 5-6 feet away from it and each pitched a nickel, presumably from his $2 roll of nickels, to see which one landed closest to the wall. The one whose nickel landed closest then walked up to the wall and picked up all of the nickels. They repeated this process three or four times. Then they all came out from the dark corridor. One kid asked me if I wanted to play. I said, "Sure." A couple of other kids joined us and we all then went into that same dark corridor and started to pitch nickels. The game did not take long. By the time we got the signal to pick up our trays and start selling, I had lost my entire $2 worth of nickels.

I distinctly remember the feeling of fear and despair that overwhelmed me as I realized what I had done. It had all taken place so quickly and I had been so helpless in trying to prevent it. Yet, there I was, $2 in the hole with only the prospect of selling a lot of popcorn and peanuts in order to pay back the $2.

I found my brother, Nacho, who was already busy selling soft drinks and I told him everything. I was embarrassed and felt humiliated but he did not judge me. He simply handed me ten nickels so I could give change and told me not to do it again. By the end of the evening, I managed to sell enough popcorn and peanuts to pay back my brother and the $2 I had been advanced but I got home with maybe a dime or two and a commitment never to gamble again.

Balloon-Boy

There were a number of events that would take place at the *Coliseum* each year that were oriented specifically toward children. The *Ringling Brothers/Barnum & Bailey* and the *Shrine* circuses were examples. Whenever the circus came to town, school would actually be let out early one afternoon to allow the children to attend. The same thing happened for the annual rodeo and the *Ice Capades*.

These children-oriented programs had a particular impact on the concession business at the *Coliseum*. These shows would require the concessions operator to bring out the helium balloon vending program. This was clearly one of the most profitable of the concession operations. It was profitable because balloons would cost the vendor maybe a penny each, the helium that would go into each balloon would also not cost much more than a penny since it was purchased by the tankful, and the string that allowed a child to hang on to the balloon to keep it from floating to the ceiling was cheap kite string and also could not have cost much. Yet each balloon would sell for 25 cents. Even if the individual vendor got a nickel for each balloon sold, the concessions manager still made 16 or 17 cents profit on each. It was one huge cash cow!

Since the balloon vending operation was so profitable, the individual vendor who got to sell them normally was a very seasoned and older man and not a young kid like me. A few hours before any show, this individual would start inflating the balloons. Here's what the process looked like. Somewhere in a room in the concession area he would take a balloon, stretch it a bit to prevent it from bursting, place the opening of the balloon on the helium tank valve and open the spigot. In about two seconds the balloon would be about 18 in. in diameter and filled with helium. He would then wrap the opening of a balloon around his finger and roll it back off of his finger thereby causing a knot to form and to seal in the helium. Then he would take a 5 ft. length of string and tie it to the balloon and then let the balloon float upwards to join the other balloons that he had previously filled. He would then tie the string of that balloon to the strings of all the others. After about 20-30 minutes, he would have a cluster of 40-50 colorful balloons all ready to dazzle the children. Then he would secure the room, take the entire bundle of balloons and proceed to sell them. As he entered the seating area of the *Coliseum*, he would be assaulted by the young kids and their parents who wanted to buy the balloons and he would not get relief until every one of them was sold. Generally, the entire bundle would get sold within 10 or 15 minutes. The vendor would then go back to where the tank was and repeat the process three or four times before the show even started. He would make a ton of money every time.

I was never experienced enough or old enough to get the balloon vending job. However, I discovered--as many other young vendors did--that there was still a way to make money selling balloons. And here's the way that worked.

The shows where balloons were popular generally would have at least two performances during the day. There would be a matinee in the afternoon and then an evening performance. At the conclusion of the matinee performance, it was very common to find that 20-30 balloons had somehow escaped from the grasp of the child that had bought it and then floated to the ceiling of the *Coliseum*. So, if at those moments you looked up to the ceiling, it was not uncommon to see a large number of escaped balloons bobbing and swaying gently in the breeze maybe 50-60 feet high up there in the semi-domed ceiling and each with the string still attached.

One day, I decided to attempt to retrieve some of those balloons. I started by retrieving one of those escaped balloons that was easy to reach. In the cheap-seat area where the ceiling was no more than ten feet above the seats, if you were quick and clever, you could actually reach up with your extended arm and grab one of those escaped balloons. Once I had a balloon (the captive balloon), I would take some kite string that I had brought from home and attach enough of it to permit that one balloon to rise to the highest points of the ceiling of the *Coliseum* while still remaining tethered to me on the floor. I could only do this between the matinee and evening performances when the *Coliseum* was fairly empty.

The captive balloon then acted as a shepherd dog to help me retrieve some of those escaped balloons bouncing around up in the ceiling. Here's how: Once my captive balloon reached the top of the ceiling and found its way close to another balloon, I would start rotating my arm in circles above me. This would cause the string that I was holding to create a corkscrew motion that went all the way to the ceiling. Eventually the corkscrew pattern of the string attached to my captive balloon would start to get closer and closer to the dangling string of one of the escaped balloons until the two strings would become ensnared with each other. If I continued to rotate my arm for a few more seconds, the corkscrew effect would cause the two strings to become one. At that point, I would stop rotating my arm and gently but steadily start to bring back down my captive balloon. As I did this, the escaped balloon would also start to come down. A few seconds later, at about the time that the string of the escaped balloon was becoming untangled from the string of the captive balloon, they would both be within my grasp and the retrieval process was completed. I would do this routine five or six times in about an hour and eventually I would have five or six balloons. I would hang on to them until the start of the evening performance and before anyone got wind of what I was doing, I would be able to sell them to the evening audience for 25¢ apiece. I remember engaging in this activity two or three times during one particular season and thereby making an additional profit of about $1.00 to $1.50 or more each time. Then it became too much of a hassle trying to avoid getting caught or too many other kids had started doing the retrieval thing and so I quit doing that. I also got physically tired of doing it. After all, between performances--during which I normally would sell popcorn and peanuts--I really did not feel like continuing to work to retrieve those balloons and then to try to sell them while doing everything necessary to avoid getting caught.

Some of the very vivid recollections in my mind about those moments are the following: First, since the distance between the ground and the ceiling where the escaped balloons would end up was probably around 60 feet or so, and given that the average time it took me to retrieve each of the six balloons was 5–10 minutes, all during which I was looking up, I invariably would wind up with a very stiff and sore neck. Secondly, I remember how incredibly bright the lights were up in the ceiling of the *Coliseum*. Even though the lights did not contain the modern technology of today, they were still bright enough to cause discomfort if you were looking even indirectly at them for any period of time. Finally, I remember the frustration that I felt after working diligently for a few minutes and thinking that I had snared a balloon only to lose it just as I would reach up to grab it just inches above my head. As that retrieved balloon was getting closer to me, I could see that the string was becoming untangled from the string of the captive balloon. I dared not bring it down faster for fear that the dis-entangling would proceed even more quickly. So, many times, just as the retrieved balloon was about to come within reach, it would slip away and float right back up to the ceiling requiring me to spend another agonizing 10 minutes trying to retrieve it again.

As more and more young kids showed up between performances to try to retrieve those balloons, they brought more and more attention to what we were doing. Eventually we were told never to do it again. And so, I stopped. But I'll never forget how much fun I had coming up with this methodology of retrieving the escaped balloons. More importantly, I'll never forget the incremental profit that I gained from selling them off.

Cushion-Boy

As everyone knows, all spectator events require the audience to sit for hours at a time. At the *Coliseum* and at *Kidd Field* (the Texas Western College football stadium) the seats were made of wood, concrete or metal. None of the seats in those days had any padding whatsoever. Hence, the cushion concession was born. This was nothing more than offering to spectators a cushion about 18 inches by 18 inches square and 2 or 3 inches thick and filled with feathers so that they could place them between their butts and the hard seat surface. The price per cushion was 25¢. The spectator would be permitted to use it during that performance but they had to leave it behind.

The cushions were covered in the classic cotton mattress fabric that was colored white with ¼ inch black stripes. It's was the same fabric that was commonly used in mattresses of the past.

Those cushions inevitably would get dirty over time and they couldn't be cleaned regularly or replaced due to cost considerations. One day, after complaints were mounting about how filthy the cushions had become, someone got the bright idea to simply paint them. Imagine that: some 2000 cushions were hauled into a paint shop and each cushion was individually spray-painted, top and bottom, in a sky-blue color. Some of those cushions took the paint well and remained soft and pliable. Others did not take to the paint and became stiff. However, whether pliable or stiff, they were still a good thing to place between a butt and a hard surface.

Here's how the cushion concession worked. At every spectator event, underneath each of the seating areas on either side of the building or stadium--and near the conventional concession stand (where they sold popcorn, soda, etc.)--there was a huge wooden cage where all the cushions were stored. It remained padlocked until about two hours before the start of any performance. One of the older (i.e. adult) vendors would get the job to handle the cushion concession. Unlike other vending jobs that paid by the number of units sold, cushions were a fixed-payment arrangement where the man in charge would get a flat $25 and his two or three assistants would get $5 each. Eventually, the man in charge would also get paid based on the units sold. These were coveted positions since there was little chance that anyone could make that much money on unit sales of soft drinks or popcorn and peanuts unless they really worked their tails off.

I sold popcorn and peanuts for a year and then got promoted to soft drinks the next year. During my third year, due to my selling prowess, my reliability and the fact that I was a close friend and classmate of Gene Almanzán, Jr., one of the sons of the cushion concessionaire, I nailed one of the cushion assistant jobs. The two sons of the concessionaire got the other two jobs.

Eugene Almanzán, Sr. was a seasoned vendor who worked his way up from beer and hot dogs to cushions. He was a very hard worker who sold his products very aggressively and therefore usually made lots of money. His two sons were Gene, Jr. (my classmate) and Charlie, who was two years younger. I'll never forget Gene, Jr. and his dad for giving me that shot at making more money.

If the reader will pardon the pun, I have to admit that it was indeed a cushy job. The cushions sold themselves. Spectators would get in line before each performance in order to buy three or four cushions at a time. By the start of the performance, all the cushions would usually be sold. On those rare occasions when things did get slow, we, the assistant vendors, would be required to promote sales by yelling out: "Cushions!! Nice soft cushions!!"

I got a kick one time when Charlie, started yelling "COLCHONS" instead of "Cushions." I immediately figured out why. In Spanish, a mattress is a "colchón" pronounced "col-CHON." The cushions we were selling were mini-mattresses and so this guy started calling them "COL-chons" which, when said rapidly, sounds like "Cushions," but with a huge Mexican accent. The Mexican-Americans who heard him thought he was very clever and funny. This was just another example of the strange and funny things that happen to language in a bi-cultural situation such as the one we lived in.

Here's more of why the job was cushy. After all the cushions were sold--and that happened just about every time--the concessionaire and his assistants would lock up the wooden cage and go up into the stands to simply watch the performance for free. All the other vendors had to continue to sell their products. And so, as they worked their butts off, the cushion team was relaxing and even buying stuff from the other vendors. For those reasons, the cushion team enjoyed an enviable status.

At the end of the performance, the cushion team went back to work collecting the cushions. Collecting the cushions was a two-step process. First, all of the cushions needed to be brought down from the seats to the main aisle below. Second, they had to be carried in bundles of 10 to 15 from there back to the wooden cage.

Getting them down from the seats was easy since there were always lots of other kids willing to help. After all, they got to launch these cushions like Frisbees from as high up as the nosebleed-seat areas down to the main aisle. The cushions would rain down for a few seconds and most of them were thrown to the main aisle by the other kids saving me and the rest of the cushion team a lot of work. Occasionally, a small cushion war would break out between factions situated high up in the seats attacking other factions down below. It was a thrill to watch a cushion spinning and flying down from high up that would smack some kid down below. No one ever got hurt since, after all, they being struck with CUSHIONS!

The hauling of the cushions to the wooden cage was real work and so that's where the cushion assistants (such as me) did their hardest work. My friend, Zekie Chavira, would always stick around and help me collect the cushions. Eventually, about an hour after the performance had ended and long after the other vendors had gotten paid and gone home, the cushion team would lock up the wooden cage and go collect their pay.

It was always a great pleasure to go home after working as a cushion assistant. I would always have at least two and sometimes three times more money than the average vendor took home and, I would not be wiped out from having had to lug the case of soft drinks or popcorn up and down the aisles for four or five hours. Mi Mamá always gave me a special hug and kiss on those nights since that additional money would definitely make a positive impact on our family finances. Life was indeed good on those occasions.

Car Watcher

Before I established myself as a competent vendor of concessions, there were many times when I simply did not make the cut when vendors for specific events were being selected. That meant that I would not be able to work on a given evening and, therefore, had to go back home empty-handed. Even after I did establish myself as a vendor, sometimes, due to a low expected audience turnout for a given event, or for other reasons, they would hire only a few vendors, and once in a while, at those times, I would not get a job.

On those occasions when I was not able to work at the *Coliseum*, I managed to nevertheless make a little money by falling back on opportunities involving parking lot security.

Right at the intersection of Paisano Drive and Webber Way, where the business offices of the *El Paso Housing Authority* were located, there was a parking lot that could accommodate approximately 30 automobiles. It was intended for use by Housing Authority employees and by prospective housing tenants who had cars and could drive there to apply for housing. The parking lot was not used very much during the day because, in reality, if you were seeking subsidized housing, you probably could not afford to own a car. Furthermore, there weren't that many employees who worked there. More importantly, it was normally completely vacant after hours, except for Mr. Manuel Miranda's monster-finned *Plymouth* (or *Dodge*) and Leo Sotomayor's 1958 light green *Plymouth* that he had named *Nomad.* Our apartment was located to the west of the lot directly across Webber Way no more than 30 yards away. If we had owned a car at that time, we would have parked it in that lot. In fact, when my brother Nacho finally got his first car-- a Triumph GT 4+ in 1966--he used to park it there.

As will happen in any entertainment venue of any size, parking spaces can become scarce. Over time, the Housing Authority lot became a regular site for overflow parking from the *Coliseum*. So, for the hour that preceded most *Coliseum* events, a steady stream of cars would start trickling into the housing authority parking lot looking for a space. The event-attendees would park their cars there and then walk across a patch of grass maybe 75 yards long to the *Coliseum*.

I did not discover the parking lot security income opportunity myself but rather capitalized on it after other kids had shown me how to do it. Here's the way it worked. I would know whether or not I was going to have a vendor job at the *Coliseum* about an hour before the start of a performance. Once I knew that I was not going to be hired to sell concessions, I would run home and would put on the set of clothes to distinguish me from the juvenile delinquents that were known to live in the Paisano Projects. In other words, I would dress neatly. I would then take my metal, olive-green *Boy Scout* flashlight and proceed to the Housing Authority parking lot.

I would try to get to the lot just as cars would be pulling in that were arriving obviously to attend a *Coliseum* event. I would take my flashlight and guide as many as I could into a parking space much as a traffic cop would. Once parked, as the driver and passengers exited, I would ask whether they would like for me to watch their car. Normally, there would be no inquiry as to terms or conditions but merely a "yes" or "no." If one of the passengers was a mother, there was a very high probability that she would say "yes." I would make a mental note that that particular car was one of my responsibilities for the evening and then I would go after the next car that was coming into the parking lot and repeat the process.

On a normal night, I might have assisted as many as 20 cars in finding a space in the Housing Authority lot and nearby streets and the vast majority of them would have indicated that they would like for me to watch the car. So, for the next two or three hours, while the occupants of the vehicles that were under my care went to watch the event at the *Coliseum*, I took a seat on the low, red brick wall that surrounded the Housing Authority office and started my vigilant tour of duty for the night. Unlike some of the other kids who claimed to watch cars, I would actually stay there and watch the cars. Those other kids would usually go home, watch TV for a few hours, then come back and demand compensation from the car owners who had no idea whether their cars had been watched or not.

I remember very fondly that brick wall on which I would sit as I watched those cars. The height and width of the wall made it a perfect, albeit somewhat long, bench for sitting. The dark red bricks were not of the smooth variety but rather of the scalloped kind that made the surfaces quite rough. The entire length of the wall was probably 60 ft. and every bit of it was suitable for sitting. The wall had been built some two feet away from the exterior wall of the building itself and the space between was filled with dirt to hold landscaping and plants that had been set around the Housing Authority office. Most of the plants were cactus type plants including those huge barrel cacti that stood 2-3 ft. tall, 2 ft. in diameter and were covered with thorns shaped like hooks, each one about 2 in. long. As long as one did not attempt to sit too close to a cactus, it was actually a very pleasant experience to sit on that wall particularly on a warm, dry summer evening. It was on that very wall that I once filled a small brown cylindrical plastic pill bottle with gun powder that I removed from .22 caliber bullets, whittled a cap for the pill bottle from a piece of cork to look like a rocket nose cone, inserted three straight pins in the bottom panel to keep it off the ground, and put a wick through a hole in the bottom in order to ignite the gun powder. I actually believed that once the powder ignited, the pill bottle would lift off at least a few feet. It didn't. The pill bottle started to melt and then the gun powder flashed and smoked and burned itself out. I went back to the drawing board.

My responsibilities as a car watcher were simple. If anyone tried to get near any of the cars in the lot that were under my care, I would become suspicious and take whatever action necessary to ensure that none of the cars were broken into or damaged. I don't recall ever having to talk to anyone or do anything for fear that security was being breached. All I remember is sitting peacefully on that wall watching traffic zoom by on Paisano Drive while I passed the time away.

Frequently, while I sat performing my guard duties, some of my buddies would wander by and we would sit together and talk. Usually, in the course of the conversation, I would invite them to partner with me in the job that I was performing. If they stuck around for the remainder of the evening, and, if they acted with the sense of professional demeanor that I felt was required, we would split the proceeds of the evening evenly. One of my usual partners was Zekie Chavira. Since he was a few years younger than me, I would not split the proceeds evenly with him but maybe just give him 10 or 20 percent. He was such a nice kid and so easily pleased that he always seemed grateful and as thrilled about his smaller share as I was about mine.

There was one occasion, when I sat for two or three hours doing my guard duties while at the same time visiting with one of the cute girls that lived in the neighborhood. She happened to be walking by while I sat on the brick wall and we got to talking. Before long, I had to tell her that I had to get back to work since the car owners were starting to return to their cars. She waited for me and I recall wondering whether I should share the proceeds with her. I decided that since she really had done nothing, I did not need to share any of my income with her.

When the event at the *Coliseum* was concluded, the spectators would pour out and the drivers and occupants of the cars parked at the Housing Authority lot would start returning to their cars. As they did, I would make my presence known to them by turning on my flashlight and otherwise looking very official by acting like a traffic cop. I would quietly and without ever asking for compensation, begin assisting departing cars in exiting safely from the lot. Without ever demanding payment, I would appear to be so efficient and so concerned about the security of their automobiles that the drivers would normally lower their windows as they passed me and simply hand me a tip. The amount of the tip varied dramatically ($1 was the most I ever got) but usually it was a quarter. Of the 20 or so cars that had parked in the parking lot I would normally get a tip from it least half of them. And so, on average, I would make $2 or $3 from watching cars.

Recall that on a good night at the *Coliseum* selling popcorn and peanuts, I would only make between $1 and $2. So, the parking lot gig was not bad at all. Needless to say, there were occasions when the tips were few and far between. But even then, I would still manage to get 50¢ or a dollar by the end of the evening.

As much as I appreciated the money that I could make watching cars, I never got over the feeling that I was begging for money. It was very different from lugging the soft drink and the popcorn and peanut boxes, while wearing an official white hat and apron, and simply selling those goods. That just felt a lot more like real work than those security services that I was offering. So, after doing it maybe a total of 5-6 times, I forever gave it up. Of course, by then, I was beginning to get involved in much bigger and better things.

Soda Jerk

During the spring of my junior year at Jefferson High I had the opportunity to earn a little money working as a soda jerk at a nearby drug store. The *Del Camino* shopping center was a strip mall located about a quarter mile west of Jefferson High on Alameda Avenue. At the east end of the strip was a *Gunning-Casteel* drug store. *Gunning-Casteel* was probably the biggest chain of drug stores in El Paso at the time.

One of my best friends in the neighborhood around the projects was Hector "Diablo" Lopez. We were the same age but he was a year behind me in school. We played in the same Boys' Club team for many years and I always thought of him as one of the friendliest kids I ever met. In addition, he always struck me as one of the most industrious since he always seemed to have a regular after-school job.

One day, while we were playing softball at the Boys' Club, we were discussing his latest job. He was the soda jerk at that *Gunning-Casteel* drug store and for reasons that I cannot recall, he had decided to leave the job. He described the job as extremely easy since it rarely had any customers, yet the few customers who did order anything seemed to always be generous tippers. The hours were perfect in that he went directly to work right after school, attended to his duties from 4PM until 7PM and then was able to get home in time for dinner. But the best part of the job, according to Hector, was the fact that he was able to help himself to a sandwich and a *Coke* every day while working. He pointed out carefully that he was not supposed to do that and could get fired if caught, but he had been doing just that for months and had never gotten into trouble. I was fascinated by all that and when he offered me the job, I gladly accepted. He was certain I would get the job since he would recommend me to his boss Mr. Carlos Aguilar.

A few days later, after a brief interview and an hour of on-the-job training from Hector, I took over as the soda jerk. Hector had been right. Very few customers came into the drug store and fewer to the soda counter. I spent most of my time polishing the counter top, sweeping the floor and making the place shine but, mostly, I was just waiting for a customer. Mr. Aguilar was a nice enough guy and even though he patrolled the aisles of the drug store regularly, he spent most of his time at the opposite end of the store near the pharmacy. Hector had told me that it was at times like these that he would make himself that perk of a sandwich. I decided not to do that on my first day. I felt extremely uneasy about it.

The next afternoon was very much like the previous one although I recall that I did prepare a grilled-cheese sandwich and a *Coke* for at least one customer. Then everything again turned monotonous. At that point, I decided that I would make a ham and cheese sandwich on the sly for myself.

The process of making that snack turned out to be extremely stressful. I worked in the back kitchen behind swinging metal doors, hidden from the counter, yet I was very fearful that Mr. Aguilar would walk in any second and catch me in the act. To cover what I was doing, I made the sandwich in the range oven which was shut off at the time. I assembled it one ingredient at a time: A slice of bread, the mayo, a slice of ham, a slice of cheese, a lettuce leaf, a slice of tomato and the second slice of bread. I would take each ingredient from the refrigerator to the oven and stack it up and then close the oven door. When the sandwich was done, I put ice in a glass, filled it with *Coke* and also stashed it away in the oven. I was ready to partake of my unauthorized meal just as my friend and mentor, Hector claimed he had done so many times before.

I remember having a very difficult time taking the first bite. I would spend a few minutes cleaning something out front near the counter then go back to the oven, open it and hold the sandwich. But, for some reason, I simply could not take the bite. Then I would put the sandwich back down and go out to the front again to make sure the "coast was really clear." After another few minutes of making work and of total customer inactivity, I would head back to the oven to take that first bite. Again, I recall feeling "gripped" by an overwhelming sense of guilt which rendered me completely helpless in consuming the sandwich. I did, however, take a sip of the *Coke* to sooth my parched palate but ended up heading back out to the front in case someone had showed up. I repeated this drill another time or two and I remember thinking that no stinking sandwich was worth the hassle that I was feeling. But I did not give up. After about my fourth trip to the oven in the back, I picked up the sandwich and took a huge bite.

As soon as I had started to chew the bite of sandwich, I heard the voice of Mr. Aguilar from a spot that could not have been farther away than the counter saying, "Willie, where are you?" I thought to myself, after so much care and cunning, how could this have happened? I had been busted! I would surely get fired for trying to steal from my employer and when all this became public, my nomination for *Boy of the Year 1964*—submitted just weeks earlier—would certainly get pulled.

I chewed no more but instead swallowed that first bite of sandwich whole and at the same time replaced the rest of the sandwich in the oven as I hurriedly walked out from the kitchen toward the counter. Mr. Aguilar met me as I got to the counter and I could see that he was looking behind me for who knows what. But after noticing how composed I was with a dish towel in my hand, he must have concluded that I had indeed been doing something useful in the back. I cannot recall what it was that he needed me for but minutes later, I had taken care of it and he had returned to where he came from. That pricey sandwich did get eaten that day after all but I never tried the same stunt again.

Chapter 6-The El Paso Boys' Club

My family lived in the Paisano Projects from the summer of 1958 until the summer of 1960 and again—after mi Papá's failed restaurant venture--from the summer of 1961 until the summer of 1968. A few years later, around the mid 1970's, the apartments of the Paisano Projects were converted into assisted living units for seniors. The external appearance of each unit was changed dramatically to make them appear more contemporary. Then, in the late 1990's, the growth of the city of El Paso and the need to build new highways resulted in the destruction of most of the Paisano Projects. If you drive by that area today you will find that the site of the Projects is now nothing more than access roads and rights-of-way for a new highway that connects El Paso to Juárez. A few of the assisted living units remain and are surrounded by chain link fences. Despite all that, whenever I go to El Paso, I can still get a good sense of the past by going to the Sherman Projects which still stand today. In just about every respect, the Sherman Projects were a mirror image of the Paisano Projects and whenever I see them, they evoke similar beautiful memories of my childhood.

In the preceding chapters I've tried to describe how life was in the Paisano Projects in the late 50's and early 60's. However, as I mentioned earlier, something really significant occurred in those Projects in the summer of 1959. Up until that point in time, each boy that grew up in the Projects and who was between say 8 and 12 years old was essentially an individual who may have had one or two close friends who lived nearby or siblings with whom they spent the majority of their after-school time. We would play baseball or La Quemada or canicas or other such activities with this tight circle of peers and sunset would invariably find all of us in our respective homes with our families. There was widespread fear in the neighborhood that it was downright dangerous to wander too far away from your home and so we simply never did. The only exceptions to that were Boy Scouts and Little League baseball which were well-established and always supervised by adults. We, as kids, and our parents felt safe in those particular activities but they generally required that the kids be transported to and from parks or churches that were in other neighborhoods and since most families in the Projects did not own cars, we generally did not engage in those activities. All that changed dramatically when the Boys' Club came to our neighborhood in June, 1959.

Before describing the arrival of the Boys' Club at the Paisano Projects, it's useful to look first at a little bit of Boys' Club history and some of its facts and figures. The *El Paso Boys' Club* (now the *Boys and Girls Clubs of El Paso*) traces its origin all the way back to 1929. Mr. Harry A. Markham, then the manager of the *Mutual Building & Loan Association of El Paso*, and Mr. J.P. Mestrazat, then the Executive Director of the *Boy Scouts*, became aware that a troubling cycle seemed to exist in the south part of the city. Juvenile delinquents from that part of town—who happened to be almost exclusively of Mexican descent--regularly were being sent to reform school. They noticed that a great percent of the delinquency within the entire state of Texas seemed to be coming from South El Paso. And many of the boys sent to reform school appeared to be repeat offenders. The cycle seemed to be one where upon completing their time at reform school, these boys became social outcasts when they returned home to El Paso. Once back home they had nowhere to go but to roam the streets and get in trouble all over again. The vision that these two gentlemen had was to open a facility in the middle of the troubled south side of El Paso where all boys, including reform school returnees, could find a social sanctuary complete with salutary activities to help them stay out of trouble. And thus, the *El Paso Boys' Club* came into being.

What exactly was the *El Paso Boys' Club* during the 1950's and early 1960's? While I can speak with some authority about life in the Paisano Projects in those years and certainly about the effect of the Boys' Club in that particular east-central neighborhood of El Paso, the domain of the *El Paso Boys' Club* was much larger than just the Paisano Projects. In fact, in those days, the main branch (Unit 1) of the Club was located in South El Paso at 801 S. Florence St. in an area known as Second Ward and the impact that it was having in that area was quite significant.

The *El Paso Boys' Club* in the late 1950's and early 1960's, under the direction of Mr. O. D. Hightower, used to periodically publish a newsletter, *News and Views*. In the March 4, 1960, edition, Hightower addresses the specific issue of how the Club helped combat juvenile delinquency. In covering that subject, he prefaced his response by providing the following glimpse of what life was like in the Second Ward.

> South El Paso is the very heart of the Mexican Colony in the City and it has many characteristics of the slum sections of old Mexico. Most of South El Paso is in the "Chamizal Zone," which is disputed territory with both Mexico and the United States claiming it. However, it is under the jurisdiction of the United States and there seems to be little chance of this area ever going over to Mexico. [In fact, the Chamizal was turned over to Mexico a few years later.] Two room flats housing families of from six to fourteen people are common, with as many as sixteen families sharing four outdoor toilets and two cold water taps.

Each teenage gang in this area has a "territory" which they call their own, and a rival gang member or an outsider enters this territory at the risk of being thoroughly beaten. Gang warfare between rival teenage gangs is common, with zip guns, switch blade knives, ice picks and other equally dangerous weapons being used in these gang fights. The Boys' Club recently called Police to break up a gang fight on the street in front of the Boys' Club where a thirteen-year old boy was stabbed in the back with an ice pick, the weapon missing his vertebra by only one eighth inch. About a year ago a teenage boy was fatally stabbed in a Youth Center located only two blocks from the Boys' Club, and there have been several fatal stabbings on the street of South El Paso since that time.

The *El Paso Boys' Club Annual Report* for 1961 provides useful information in understanding why the Club existed. It states that the purpose of the *El Paso Boys' Club* is "to promote the health, social, educational, vocational and character development of boys throughout El Paso." It also enumerates the unique characteristics of a Boys' Club:

1. A club for boys. It satisfies the age-old desire of boys to have a club of their own. It attracts and can serve large numbers of boys because all of its facilities are reserved for that purpose.
2. Strategically located. The El Paso Boys' Club is located in the most crowded area of our city. The method of joining is so simple that any boy can easily do so. Hence, all of the privileges of the club are available to all members and each boy is on an equal basis with the other.
3. Full-time operation. The El Paso Boys' Club is open every weekday afternoon and evening. It is also open every Saturday and on most holidays. There is always something to do at the Boys' Club.
4. Varied program. The program is varied to attract boys of different inclinations and to meet their varying needs. It is the policy of our club to try to have a program so broad that every boy who joins can find an activity in which he can be interested.
5. Guidance. It is the purpose of the staff of our Boys' Club to provide guidance for the individuals and groups through a friendly, informal, every day relationship. The ultimate purpose is the development of character and the building of good citizens.
6. Nonsectarian. The El Paso Boys' Club is completely nonsectarian in its management and staff as well as in its membership.

It is certainly appropriate to recognize the community leaders that provided direction to the *El Paso Boys' Club* during the early 1960s. The annual report for 1961 lists the following as the members of the board of directors:

1. James F. Elliott, President
2. Henry Horwitz, Vice President
3. Dr. Philip Segall, Vice President
4. Mrs. Chris Aranda, Vice President
5. Mrs. Harry A. Markham, Treasure
6. Mrs. Edwin D. Vickers, Secretary
7. Louis Daeuble
8. Arthur Gale
9. Robert Hampton
10. Freeman Harris
11. Mrs. George Hervey
12. L. H. Koogle
13. William Latham
14. Dr. Francisco Licon
15. John Mason
16. George McCarty
17. Raymond Pitts
18. Frank Pollitt
19. George C. Staten
20. George Stauning
21. H. R. Street
22. Fred T. Wagner
23. Claude Williamson and
24. G. E. Wing

Funding for the operation of the *El Paso Boys' Club* in those days came primarily from the *United Fund of El Paso* and El Paso County. Fully 75% of its $40,000 operating budget in 1961 came from the United Fund. The remainder came from donations, memorials and loans. It is interesting to note that the Club did not rely on membership fees very much to sustain itself. That year the total amount received for membership fees came to $160.45.

And so, for some time prior to the days when I joined, the sole Boys' Club unit located on South Florence Street existed as an alternative environment to the unforgiving streets and the flourishing youth gangs. The Club building was formidable and imposing in contrast to its surroundings. It covered the whole square block west of Florence St., east of Campbell St., between Eighth and Ninth Avenues. The building in those days was painted mostly sky-blue in color. Above the main entrance to the building was the following inscription: *Through these doors pass the leaders of tomorrow.*

As a member entered the building, he would be greeted by a fellow-member door monitor who was actually employed part-time by the Boys' Club to check-in each boy as he entered. Upon joining, each member was given a military dog tag with a unique member number and before entry could be granted the member had to recite his member number to the door monitor who would then circle that member's number on the preprinted sheet that was filled-in each day to track attendance. Once in, the member was free to participate in any of the many activities that the Club offered.

The facilities that comprised Unit 1 of the *El Paso Boys' Club* during those days included a modest but fairly complete library where members could find peace and quiet to read. The library was also used for club meetings and was the venue where the Jr. Toastmasters Club met each week. (Jr. Toastmasters will be covered in much more detail later.) Adjacent to the library was a large game room wherein were located a billiards table, Ping Pong tables, bumper pool tables and other games. Beige *Samsonite* chairs were located along the walls in the vicinity of each of these games. The boys would queue themselves up on these chairs as they awaited their turn to play on any given game. On one side of the game room was the doorway that led to a substantial kitchen. The kitchen was staffed by mothers of members who volunteered their services in order for there to be a fairly limitless supply of bean burritos and Kool-Aid for the boys. The cost for a burrito and drink was five cents. If the kid didn't have the money, a staff member would ensure that he got it for free. By the way, the flour used to make the tortillas as well as the beans and cheddar cheese used to stuff the burritos were government surplus supplies delivered regularly to the Club without cost.

Toward the back of the building was the gymnasium. It was regulation-size with basketball goals on each end and also along the sides. The floor was made of highly polished vinyl tiles. It was brightly lit with electric lights and large windows set high along the West wall. Along the south side of the facility were two large rooms where arts and crafts were taught. Finally, immediately outside of the facility was a large playground for a variety of outdoor sports and activities offered by the Club.

So how specifically did the *El Paso Boys' Club* fight juvenile delinquency? In the days when Mr. Hightower ran the Boys' Club, he made it a point to directly engage those infamous youth gangs. He and his staff members would go to the hangouts of these gangs and invite them to the Boys' Club for a friendly game of basketball with a Club team in their age group or to be guests at the weekly teen dance. Once the gang was inside the Boys' Club, they were shown how the entire program worked including the extremely diverse and competitive sports teams, the opportunities in arts and crafts, the recreational activities of the game room, the kitchen where inexpensive burritos could be purchased, the peace and quiet of the library and the commitment of the Club personnel to the welfare of the boys. This introduction was normally all that was needed to convert the gang into a sports team or club within the Boys' Club where their energy could be channeled into more productive activities.

The Boys' Club also maintained a close relationship with other social agencies in the community such as the police department, the juvenile detention home, churches and schools. These organizations would often refer boys suspected of being delinquents or pre-delinquents to the Boys' Club. Eventually, the Boys' Club established a remarkably high level of credibility and effectiveness thereby becoming a very attractive alternative to gangs.

The Boys' Club Comes to the Paisano Projects

In early 1959, the *El Paso Boys' Club* Board of Directors was very fortunate to have as one of its members, Mr. Raymond Pitts. Mr. Pitts was the Executive Director of the *El Paso Housing Authority* and was also the Chairman of the *El Paso Boys' Club's* Extension Committee. The main office of the *El Paso Housing Authority* was located in the Paisano Projects directly across the street from the home-apartment on Webber Way in which my family and I lived.

Apparently, when mi Papá applied for housing at the projects in the spring of 1958, he met and befriended Mr. Pitts. I believe that friendship was pivotal in how the *El Paso Boys' Club* opened a Unit in our neighborhood. Mi Papá was acutely aware of the reputation associated with the Paisano Projects with respect to juvenile delinquency. He must have wanted to ensure that his two teenage boys steered clear of gang trouble so he advocated to Mr. Pitts that some kind of youth recreation center should be established within the Paisano Projects. Mr. Pitts must have been intrigued by the idea primarily because he was a member of the Board of Directors of the *El Paso Boys' Club*. As they talked, they determined that a youth recreation center could easily be established there within the Projects under the auspices of the *El Paso Boys' Club*. The dialogue that developed between mi Papá and Mr. Pitts was facilitated enormously by the fact that our apartment just happened to be directly across the street from the Housing Authority offices where Mr. Pitts worked. So, mi Papá—despite his visual handicap--could walk across the street anytime he wished and drop in on Mr. Pitts to talk about how best to pursue this idea of an activity center for boys right there in the neighborhood.

Years earlier, when the Paisano Projects were originally built, a large hall was also constructed on Caufield Place between Webber Way and Boone Street right in the middle of the Projects where the community could use it as a meeting or socializing venue. The large playground facility and ball field that I described earlier were also built adjacent to this hall. During the first year and a half that we lived in the Paisano Projects, I don't recall ever seeing this recreation center being used for anything and the playground was nothing more than a huge vacant lot although the playground apparatuses did get used quite a lot by the kids in the neighborhood.

In the spring of 1959, Mr. Pitts worked with Mr. O. D. Hightower, the Executive Director of the *El Paso Boys' Club* and the founding of a Boys' Club in the Paisano Projects began in earnest. Mr. Hightower then became the driving force. His peers called him "OD"; we (the boys) called him "Mr. Hightower." Once Mr. Hightower got involved with setting up a Boys' Club in the Paisano Projects, things started to move with lightning speed. Since the facilities were all there and for the most part, unused, all that was needed was a program and a staff to implement it. Mr. Hightower hired Manuel De la Rosa ("Mr. D") as the first Director of the new club. He would be assisted in running the new unit by three high school student staff members Luis Nava, Freddie Cortinas and Albert Ruiz. Until that time, the *El Paso Boys' Club* had operated from its only location at 801 South Florence Street in South El Paso. The Florence Street Boys' Club became known thereafter as Unit 1; the Boys' Club at the Paisano Projects became known as Unit 2.

The Boys Club Staff - Unit 1- 800 S. Florence St.

In 1959, as life took flight for all of us in the Unit 2 area, we realized that we were the smaller branch of the *El Paso Boys' Club* system. As members of Unit 2, we could see that the real action—and resources—were at Unit 1. Unit 1 had been founded many years earlier and had gone through a succession of professional staff members that had conducted a largely ineffective campaign in South El Paso against juvenile delinquency. A few years before its expansion into my neighborhood in the Paisano Projects, however, the Boys' Club started to make significant inroads in combatting the gangs and violence that had flourished there for so long. This turnaround was the fruit of the labor and commitment of many individuals who dedicated their lives to the kids of South El Paso. The person most prominent among them was the Executive Director, Mr. O. D. Hightower.

Mr. O. D. Hightower

Mr. Hightower was born and raised on a farm near Adona, Arkansas. He attended schools in Adona and in Clarksville, Arkansas, and during this time became an outstanding boxer laying claim to seven Golden Glove championships. After high school, during World War II, he served overseas with the Army Signal Corps. After his discharge, he received a bachelor's degree from *College of the Ozarks* in Clarksville and later a master's degree from the *University of Arkansas*. While in college, he found time to win five more state championships in boxing and qualified for the US Olympic boxing team.

Right after graduation from college, Mr. Hightower started his work at the Boys' Club in Clarksville. In 1956, he moved his family to El Paso and became the Executive Director of the *El Paso Boys' Club*. He remained in that position until his death in 1964. He was a thin fellow with an extremely receded hairline, weighing probably 170 lbs. and standing about 6 ft. tall. In my mind and certainly in the minds of many other boys who had the privilege of knowing him, Mr. Hightower was the best thing that ever happened to the *El Paso Boys' Club*.

Mr. Hightower was the very first and the most enduring image that I have ever had of a business executive. He took his role as executive director quite seriously and recognized that he had to appear credible to the power brokers of El Paso and also had to appear as the leader and real driving force of the institution called the Boys' Club. He always wore a dark suit and conservative tie, his shoes were always highly polished, he always seemed to have a briefcase hanging by his side and, invariably, he acted in the most professional way imaginable. He was the top guy in the *El Paso Boys' Club* and reported to the board of directors which was made up of prominent members of the El Paso Community. I remember that Mr. Hightower seemed to have their complete trust and confidence.

Although he always dressed like an executive, he never required his staff to dress in any way other than as needed to do their jobs. Their jobs were to work and play with the boys of the different neighborhoods and, therefore, jeans and sneakers were appropriate. As for Mr. Hightower, however, no one ever saw him in jeans or sneakers around the Club.

I did not have too much insight as to Mr. Hightower's job-related benefits but I do know that he got a car as a perk. The one I remember was a white, 1956 *Chevy* four-door sedan with blue vinyl interior. The car was no nonsense, simple, modest and frugal just like the Boys' Club should be. I believe that Mr. Hightower's work hours were from noon to 9:00 p.m. daily and then from 10 to 3 on Saturdays. From my perspective, he managed to get the job done like no one else ever did or probably has been able to do since then.

Somehow, everybody recognized that he was an amazingly effective executive director. Without jumping in and actually playing in sports or engaging in other activities, he maintained a very high level of interaction with members of the Boys' Club. Kids respected him yet never hesitated to talk with him. Mr. Hightower was always trying to engage kids in conversation and the kids were always responsive. I think that the members of the Boys' Club--almost without exception--admired, respected and emulated him. He was very soft spoken, very gentle and he made all kids feel important.

The vision which Mr. Hightower brought with him to the Boys' Club and to South El Paso was essentially that while you probably cannot eliminate the need for juvenile gangs, you can indeed channel the energy of gangs into more beneficial activities. I remember well that prior to 1959 in the Paisano Projects, there were plenty of notorious teenage gangs. Their crimes and violence were regularly reported in the local papers and our parents constantly warned us to be careful lest we end up as a member or even worse, a victim, of one of those gangs.

Then a Boys' Club unit was opened in the neighborhood and the gangs as we had known them disappeared and with them went the associated violence. However, the "gangs" really never went away. Many of them just got renamed as teams or clubs that competed with each other in the sports leagues operated by the Boys' Club. Mr. Hightower spent very little time trying to eliminate the gangs. Instead he would seek out the leaders and challenge them and their followers to prove their prowess in the friendlier fields of strife such as the baseball diamond or the basketball court.

Mr. Hightower's son, Danny, once told me a story of how his dad put his vision into practice. Shortly after becoming Executive Director, Mr. Hightower took a walk around the South El Paso neighborhood surrounding Unit 1. The gangs that had been operating there for the longest time hung out openly in the streets and did not try to be invisible. On that afternoon, one gang with a particularly nasty reputation was loitering around in the street where they lived, leaning against parked cars, smoking, drinking and killing time. Mr. Hightower walked directly into their midst and engaged the apparent leader. Mr. Hightower tried in various ways to get the leader and the other gang members to come to the Boys' Club and to give it a try. They all declined. Then, Mr. Hightower proposed to that leader that the two of them engage in a boxing match and if Mr. Hightower came out the winner, the leader and the rest of the gang would come by and check out the Boys' Club. The young leader, who probably had achieved that position by being tough, immediately agreed to the proposition believing that no lanky, middle-aged Anglo like Mr. Hightower could possibly be a threat.

A few hours later, the boxing match was arranged and carried out right in the street where the whole neighborhood could see it. It was no contest. Mr. Hightower quickly showed his skills as a former Golden Gloves champ and convincingly won the bout and the bet. Soon, the gang and the leader were touring the Boys' Club and eventually they joined and formed a team that competed vigorously in the many sports leagues offered at the Club.

I had many occasions to visit with Mr. Hightower in private. That was because even as a kid, after benefitting greatly from Boys' Club activities such as the Jr. Toastmasters, I became a frequent invitee to speak at breakfasts or luncheons of the board of directors or for local civic clubs such as the *Lions Club*, the *Optimist Club* or the *Rotary Club*. Mr. Hightower would always pick me up at home or school, take me to these engagements and then drive me back afterward. He was a smooth and polished individual and it was a great pleasure to chat with him. He was so easy to talk to and he effortlessly managed to fit in so nicely regardless of the type of gathering. Everybody seemed to trust and like him completely. Other Boys' Club members like my brother, Nacho Chavez and Joe Renteria also recall riding in the car with Mr. Hightower as they drove to some Boys' Club engagement and how gently powerful a figure he was.

I remember the day in late 1963 when we were told that Mr. Hightower had been diagnosed with leukemia. For a while thereafter, Mr. Hightower did not look or act any differently to me. However, after a few months, he did start to look extremely thin and became almost totally bald. After a few more months, he quit coming to work and so we did not even see him. Then it was announced that he had died. I was 17, a junior in high school and am sure that I went to his funeral along with many other club kids, but I don't recall very much about it. Mr. Hightower was 41 years old when he died on January 30, 1964.

Mr. Hightower for sure dedicated his life to the kids of the *El Paso Boys' Club*. But, perhaps more importantly, he also provided a compelling image of exactly what a really fine man is all about. His death was the first direct assault on my faith since I simply could not understand how God could allow such a great person to die at such a young age and while doing such an amazing job developing boys. The influence he had on me was substantial and he will always remain in my mind as one of the most outstanding men I ever knew.

As good as Mr. Hightower was, he certainly could not have been successful without a strong staff. While the newly opened Unit 2 was being operated by its Unit Director, Mr. D, his counterpart at Unit 1 had already firmly established his skills and ability as a youth leader.

El Huevo

The Unit 1 Director in those days was Mr. Salvador Ramirez. I knew Sal Ramirez from around 1960 until 1965. He was the organizational equivalent to Mr. D but because of seniority, he probably outranked him. Sal also carried the title of Assistant Executive Director.

It is customary in the Mexican-American culture to assign interesting nicknames to practically everyone. Sal's nickname was "Huevo." Huevo is Spanish for "egg." He was called Huevo because he was 5 feet 7 inches tall and shaped exactly like a perfect egg. Throughout my life, I have known and seen many shapes of men but no one was shaped more like an egg than Sal Ramirez. Given that Mr. Hightower was the Executive Director and that Huevo was the Assistant Executive Director, it seems proper that both should have been addressed as "Mister." Even the Unit 2 Director, Manuel De La Rosa, was accorded the title of "Mister" ("Mr. D"). Yet, few if any of the older kids of the Boys' Club ever called Sal Ramirez "Mister Ramirez." We all called him "Huevo." I truly believe that he always preferred that the boys call him by that name over any other.

Huevo was born in 1933 and grew up in South El Paso near the corner of Florence and St. Vrain Streets. Even when Huevo was a kid, South El Paso was considered the slum of the city and the source of most of its juvenile delinquency problems. But he was not going to become a victim of his surroundings. He became a standout high school baseball and football player at *Cathedral High School* and later went on to play football for two years (1951 and 1952) at Texas Western College (now UTEP) there in El Paso on a full scholarship. He discontinued his studies in 1952 and became a salesman at *Al's Shop for Men* until 1953. From 1954 until 1956, he served in the *United States Marine Corps* where he became a Drill Instructor in less than 6 months. He joined the *El Paso Boys' Club* upon receiving his Honorable Discharge from the Marines in 1956.

When Huevo first got a job at the Boys' Club in 1956, he was actually doing janitorial work which included sweeping and mopping the building every day. He clearly did not see any future in that position so without giving up his job at the Club, he re-enrolled at *Texas Western College*. In late 1956—five months after Huevo started working--Mr. Hightower joined the Boys' Club as Executive Director. Mr. Hightower apparently was impressed with Huevo's work and almost immediately promoted him to Athletic Director at Unit 1. For the next two years, Huevo somehow balanced his workload at the Boys' Club with his academic requirements and in January, 1958, graduated with a Bachelor's degree in Business Administration. Mr. Hightower once again acknowledged Huevo's worth and promoted him to Assistant Executive Director, the position he held for the entire time that I knew and worked with him. To me, Huevo was pretty unique because he excelled in college sports, eventually completed his requirements for a degree and then dedicated his life to the youth of the community from which he came. I always deeply respected Huevo for that.

When I think about why the Boys' Club was extraordinarily effective in the years when I was a member, I have to believe that one of the biggest reasons behind that success was the teamwork of Mr. Hightower and Huevo. Mr. Hightower correctly envisioned that in order to reach the boys in the community—particularly the ones prone to getting into trouble—the Club staff needed to go to the streets and somehow make those boys trust the Club and want to go into the facility. Huevo described that philosophy as follows: "To work with the boys you must start where the boys are and not where you would like them to be." With all due respect to Mr. Hightower, he alone was not likely to be welcomed every time with open arms at the hangouts of the many gangs in South El Paso that the Boys' Club was trying to reach. That's where Huevo came in. As a Mexican-American and as a product of South El Paso, Huevo had enormous credibility among those gangs and they not only gave him access to their hangouts but also even to their homes. As a result, the agenda for reaching South El Paso bad boys-- envisioned and articulated by Mr. Hightower-- was able to get implemented primarily because of the efforts of Huevo.

Huevo was an amazing person but, above all, he had a tremendous sense of humor. He had a unique and sometimes very funny way of talking, canting his head to one side as he said something and using his hands generously to gesticulate. When you add all of that to his unique shape and his very closely cropped hair which covered a head that was also perfectly egg-shaped, he was quite amusing to look at. Huevo knew that he was an amusing person and he used that attribute to his advantage frequently.

Huevo was universally well-liked and respected. For a few years, he was the all-important single bridge between the Mexican-American constituency at the Boys' Club and the predominantly Anglo staff. His success in that role catapulted him to a more comprehensive role throughout the city where he provided a useful bridge between the Mexican-American and Anglo cultures that comprised El Paso.

Huevo became prominent when Unit 1 produced the first El Paso boy to be selected as the National Boy of the Year by the *Boys' Clubs of America* in 1961. His stature was reinforced when Unit 2 produced the second National Boy of the Year two years later. The executives at the Boys' Club during those years, including Mr. Hightower, Huevo and Mr. D, could rightfully take credit for the achievements of those two boys and many others who followed in their footsteps.

I liked Huevo almost as much as Mr. D but I knew that Huevo was much more ambitious and aggressive and, in many ways, resented Mr. D. Huevo was always competing, like a salesman wanting to achieve more and more sometimes even if it meant bending the rules. For example, if Mr. D wanted a kid to do something or to participate in a Club activity, he would normally try to persuade the kid to do so by objectively discussing the pros and cons. On the other hand, when Huevo wanted a kid to do something or to participate in an activity, very often he would simply threaten the kid in a way a father would threaten a son. Both methods were effective, but clearly, Huevo's was perhaps scarier.

Huevo grew up in an environment where physical strength and force were important. Kids and adults seemed to get into fights all the time. He achieved success in football due in large part to his physical prowess and athletic skills. One time, when he was Unit 1 director, he got in trouble when he tried to protect the mother of a Boys' Club kid from the father of that kid who had beaten her up. Huevo confronted the father who promptly assaulted him sending him to the hospital. I have always given Huevo lots of credit for having the guts to physically act on behalf of that mother.

In 1961, I remember that Huevo bought a brand-new white Buick with a light blue vinyl interior. One summer day, he invited me to go with him in that car to Carlsbad, New Mexico, where he had some Boys' Club business to conduct. This would be an overnight trip for just the two of us. The idea of an adult staying with a young boy in a hotel room today sounds extremely precarious. But not in those days. The trip was an extremely pleasant experience for me and I believe for him as well. He treated me like his own son and my parents trusted him completely.

During that trip, he demonstrated to me the leading-edge technology speedometer on his car. The driver would set an indicator at a given speed and, when the car reached that speed, a buzzer on the dashboard would alert the driver. I remember how he set it for 65 miles per hour in a 60 mile stretch of U.S. 180. I suppose that Huevo believed that a 5-mile buffer would not be risky. We lazily cruised along that highway for about an hour and I started to doze off. Suddenly, I was awakened by the buzz of the speedometer. Within seconds, a state trooper car appeared behind us with sirens blaring and lights blazing. We were pulled over and Huevo tried to defend himself by showing the trooper his new speedometer and how it certainly must have malfunctioned. The trooper was not impressed; Huevo got a ticket for going 65 in a 60 MPH zone.

My respect and admiration for Huevo really grew during the summer of 1963. That's when he was appointed director of the *Crossroads of the Americas* project that traveled to Parral, Mexico. *Crossroads of the Americas* was the brainchild of Dr. Cleofas Calleros. It started in 1962 and involved the selection of some of the best and brightest high school juniors in the city of El Paso who would spend a month in a small town in Mexico engaged in humanitarian and educational service for the people of that town. [More on *Crossroads of the Americas* in Chapter 10 below.] Huevo was the Director of the Program in 1963. I was fortunate to have been one of the 18 boys who participated. It was a wildly successful project that was repeated the following year in the town of Chihuahua, Mexico, with an equal degree of success.

Huevo was a very colorful person who in some very significant ways served as an adult role model for me. However, in some other ways he represented things that I did not ever want to be. In my eyes, he was overweight and despite his collegiate sports background, he did not act athletic. I also never liked his extremely physical approach to everything in life. But, generally, he was a very good influence on me and just about every other kid whose life he touched.

Interestingly, when Mr. Hightower died in 1964, Huevo did not take over as Executive Director. I believe he was passed over probably because he was Mexican-American. In those days, for many different reasons, it was politically necessary that the Executive Director be Anglo-American. Thus, a certain Mr. Bob Lottridge was brought in from outside to become the Executive Director. About a year later, Mr. Lottridge ended up leaving. Lane Smith, who worked under Mr. Lottridge as Director of Unit 2 at the time remembers Mr. Lottridge as "a square peg trying to fit into a round hole."

Finally, in 1966, due to cultural activism and emerging forces pushing for diversity and because he was clearly the right man for the job, Sal Ramirez became Executive Director.

Luis Peña

During those exciting years at the beginning of the 60's, the *El Paso Boys' Club* seemed to be unusually stacked with very talented staff. I will never forget one in particular, the staff member in charge of Arts and Crafts, Luis Peña, or as we used to call him, "Louie".

Louie was a gifted artist who specialized in art and drawings. His drawings in a variety of media were prominently posted all over the walls of Unit 1. Probably his best work was a portrait of President John F. Kennedy that depicted him wearing a Mexican sombrero. That portrait traveled to Washington, DC in 1963 and was presented to the President himself by the National Boy of the Year, my brother, Nacho (Lefty) Chavez, as a gift from the *El Paso Boys' Club*. In 1961, when Richard Lopez, the first National Boy of the Year met President Kennedy, he also presented the President with a picture drawn by Louie Peña.

Louie Peña left an enduring impression on me in in a very specific way. It turns out that when I won my first prize in a speech contest in 1961, I was awarded a 5"x7" plaque on which was inscribed the *Boys' Club Creed*. My name had been hand-painted on at the very bottom of the plaque in tiny, perfectly configured letters. Louie Peña was the artist who did that.

More significantly, however, Louie Peña possessed an uncanny ability to communicate and work with kids. That combination enabled dozens of club members to spend many pleasant hours working under Louie to create all sorts of art objects. While those objects may have had little or no intrinsic or artistic value, they certainly allowed the kids to express and otherwise occupy themselves under the guidance of a most gentle and inspiring teacher.

The tough neighborhoods of South El Paso seemed to place a premium on physical strength and generous size as well as aggressiveness. Those characteristics really did give a person an advantage albeit based on fear and intimidation. Many staff members of the Boys' Club were effective because they possessed these characteristics. Louie Peña had none of them. He was diminutive, soft spoken and almost always bore a contagious smile. When I would arrive at Unit 1–which was after all in a neighborhood other than my own--and he happened to be on duty, he would personally greet me with his beaming countenance (as he would greet everyone else) and make me feel as if I had entered my own home and was greeted by my own dad.

I remember well how Louie always seemed to be available to do other tasks outside of Arts and Crafts. When any sports competition required officiating and the regular official was not available, he would appear and get the job done. He would also frequently show up as the staff member in charge of field trips and on many occasions supervised meetings and training sessions of the Jr. Toastmasters. I do not believe that any other staff member was as respected, admired and appreciated as much as Louie Peña.

Randy DeShazo

If anyone perfectly embodied the notion of what a Boys' Club staff member should be, it had to be Randy DeShazo. Perhaps he had the necessary attributes because, at that time, his father was the Executive Director of the Boys' Club of Carlsbad, New Mexico. But regardless, Randy was a tall, gangling young man in his early twenties who just was excellent at leading and inspiring boys. He was attending *Texas Western College* and worked part-time at Unit 1. What made him the ideal staff member was his quiet, friendly demeanor that all of the boys could relate to. He could instruct the boys on all sorts of sports activities and never caused anyone to be intimidated. Thus, even the most reticent kid would join a team if Randy was the sponsor. He was always able to pacify kids when conflicts broke out because he was respected by everyone and he had a very effective way of diffusing hostilities and there were always hostilities all over the place.

Maria Isabel Martinez

The *El Paso Boys' Club* seems to me now to have been replete with operationally talented staff and leadership in the 1960's. But someone had to be responsible for maintaining administrative order. On those few occasions when I got a glimpse of how the Boys' Club was administered, the common denominator was the Membership Secretary, Maria (Mary) Isabel Martinez.

Mary had her office on the right side of the main entrance to Unit 1. It was a small cubicle with a counter and a glass partition that separated her from the building foyer through which flowed on most days a steady stream of boys. Mary was usually the first staff-person that club members would see as they entered the building. Mary usually had a member-assistant who would be posted in the cubicle to take and record the member's number (for attendance tracking purposes). But Mary always seemed to be close by to oversee who and what came in and who and what went out.

Probably the most important responsibility of Mary was to serve as Mr. Hightower's secretary (now she would be called his "Executive Assistant"). In that role she would answer the phones, greet visitors, prepare correspondence, administratively support the rest of the staff at all units, maintain all Club records and otherwise ensure that the inevitable administrative requirements of running the Club were performed.

I was impressed by Mary because she appeared to be everywhere at all times and because she seemed to be able to do every administrative chore effortlessly and very efficiently. Despite the frenetic nature of her job duties, she was perpetually in a happy mood with a sweet greeting and a ready smile for everyone, particularly for the Club members. She was the first "secretary" that I ever knew and, in my mind, she created a benchmark that I would carry for the rest of my life for what secretaries should be.

The *El Paso Boys' Club* had other staff members that undoubtedly contributed to the success of the institution during those amazing years. These included Doug Cooper, Neto Madrid, Eddie Haddon, Ben Rodriguez, Victor Peñaloza, Al Velarde, John Maddox, Danny Hightower (son of O. D. Hightower), Jay Lofton, Ruben Bustillos, Ronald Hutchison, Russell Ingraham, Robert Ochoa, Lorenzo Candelaria and Joe Hernandez. Almost without exception, each offered to the Club members an image that they could and often did emulate. They were energetic, dedicated to helping the community and, above all, in hot pursuit of a college degree. They were the young adults that chose to be right there on the spot as the Club members evolved. They frequently found themselves embroiled in the conflicts that arose in the Club neighborhood and occasionally got roughed up as they strove to make peace among the disputants. Conversely, these same staff members frequently found themselves basking in the good-news happenings that touched down in the neighborhood such as weddings, birthday parties, high-school sporting events, weekend dances, field trips, *etc*. In summary, the staff members were almost like family members and perhaps for the first time ever, gave the neighborhood a striking symbol of what a college student was. That symbol must have propelled many of the kids of the neighborhood to not only get a high school diploma but also to go on and do what few other members of their families had ever done before: go to college.

Chapter 7-Unit 2 takes off

In order to paint the most accurate and detailed picture of what life was like in the Paisano Projects around the time that the *El Paso Boys' Club* arrived in 1959, I would like to offer the reader a series of personal memories that collectively should convey what was happening then. These memories relate to people, events, places, activities and simple experiences that comprised the lives that defined me and many of my friends during that period of time that I hold so dear to my heart.

In those days, the Projects in El Paso--as in most other cities--were places where very little good happened. They were all infamous for the gangs that roamed within, for the crime that seemed to flourish and for the social and economic despair that acted like quicksand to its inhabitants. I suppose I was a bit too young to see or understand the risks associated with living in the Projects. I preferred instead to bask in the comfort of living in a sturdy and comfortable home.

But then in June, 1959, in the Paisano Projects, Unit 2 of the *El Paso Boys' Club* opened its doors. The Club, with ample support from the many interested parents, recruited every boy in the area who was between the ages of 8 and 18. The membership was parceled into four age groups: Midgets were ages 8-10; Juniors were ages 11-13; Intermediates were ages 14-16; and Seniors were ages 17-18. Initially, just about every boy in those age groups joined, including groups of boys who were previously associated with each other by common gang membership.

The Club—formerly the Recreation Center of the Projects--would open its doors every weekday from 4 to 6PM; close from 6-7PM so the kids could go home for dinner; then re-open from 7 to 9PM. On Saturdays it would open at 10AM and close at 6PM. It would remain closed on Sundays.

The huge paved parking lot that served the needs of the former Recreation Center was partitioned so that a lighted basketball court could be set up within it. The adjacent ball park, complete with lights, bleachers, a backstop, and thick, green Bermuda grass in the outfield, became available just about every single night for baseball, softball and touch football leagues administered by the Club. [The ball park is the same one described earlier in Chapter 3 as part of the Playground.]

In order to enhance the effectiveness of Unit 2, a Parents Club was formed to assist the new Director, Mr. D. Mi Papá, who was considered by many parents in the neighborhood as the driving force behind the founding of Unit

2, was elected as the first President of the Parents Club. He and Mr. D presided over monthly meetings where a highly productive dialogue was established to ensure that Unit 2 flourished. One of the first actions initiated by the Parents' Club was to open a food program for the members. As alluded to earlier, The *El Paso Boys' Club* was eligible to receive surplus food from the US government. These foods included flour, lard, cheese and Pinto beans. The former Recreation Center had a fully equipped kitchen that essentially had remained unused since it was first constructed. The Parents Club of the Boys' Club started a project whereby they would take government surplus food stuffs that were being delivered to the Boys' Club and use them to prepare food for the members of the Club and that they could consume while at the Club. And so, using the government surplus food stuffs, the mothers of the Parents Club on Saturday afternoons would prepare some of the best bean burritos on earth. However, they did not give them away for free. Instead, the burritos were sold to the membership for a nickel apiece. That money would then be used to fund other Boys' Club activities. Later on, the Parents Club was permitted to use the hall for dances and other social events for the parents themselves.

The Boys' Club Unit 2 quickly became the center of most of the community's social life. Many of the parents became involved with Club activities of their sons. For example, Mr. Manuel Miranda, father of three members (Filiberto (Porky), Daniel (Pelusa) and Manuel, Jr. (Múcura)) became the coach of the Little League team sponsored by *H. Welch & Co.*, and whose players were almost without exception Club members. Mr. Jesús (La Borrachita) Reza, a former major leaguer and father of Club members Jesús, Jr. (Chuy); Sergio (Checo) and Homer (Chacho) became the coach of the Pony League team sponsored by the Club.

It did not take long for Unit 2 to become the hub of youth activities for families in the immediate neighborhood and even beyond. The Club provided a place for boys to spend their free time doing something, which if not constructive, at least was not destructive. Like boys everywhere, if they are given too much free and unsupervised time, they will probably get into some trouble. Unit 2 was a haven where lots of boy-energy could be dissipated in entertaining and developmental activities. The Club installed a regulation-sized billiards table, a Ping-Pong table and two smaller pool tables in the main room which probably only measured 20 feet by 30 feet. The walls of the room were lined with beige *Samsonite* metal chairs on which the boys would queue up waiting for their turn to play. At the west end of the main room was an elevated stage on which sat a stereo Hi-Fi radio-phonograph that played rock and roll music from radio station KELP during most operating hours.

Each day, for a few minutes before the doors of the Club would actually open, the boys would already be lined up to check in and start playing pool or Ping Pong. As I mentioned earlier, each boy was issued a military dog tag upon joining. It displayed the boy's name and his membership number. Membership was paid for on an annual basis and varied according to age. Annual dues were: Midgets: $.50; Juniors: $1.00; Intermediates: $1.50; and Seniors: $2.00. If any prospective member did not have the fee, he would be given small jobs around the Club so he could earn enough to cover it.

The Club also hired "Jr. Staff members" to perform minor functions such as "Door Monitors" who would sit on an old oak school desk by the main door and ask each boy for his member number as he entered. As in Unit 1, the number would then be circled on the standard daily attendance form for purposes of tracking facility utilization. As "Door Monitors" they frequently were called upon, even at their ripe ages, to supervise their peers and to maintain order in the main room if a Sr. Staff Member happened to step away momentarily. These Jr. Staff Members would also sweep and mop the floor of the Club each night, clean the restrooms, control and secure the sporting equipment and table games (*Monopoly, Chinese checkers, etc.*) made available for use in the Club or on the courts and grounds, turn off the lights on fields after use and lock up at closing time. Only two such positions were available: One during the afternoon shift; the other during the evening shift. Just about every kid aspired to one day hold one of these jobs. Those lucky enough to land these Jr. Staff Member jobs immediately secured for themselves a position of considerable respect and power among their peers. In addition, they were actually placed on the Boys' Club payroll and received $15 a month for their services. They also were given the awesome power to hire cleaning assistants who would receive compensation for their labor in the form of surplus government food, donuts or "irregular" blue jeans given to the Boys' Club by local manufacturers.

Probably the most valuable aspect of the Club was the sports program. The Club conducted a year-round program that kept most of the boys in the neighborhood challenged, entertained, physically fit and exhausted. The program also provided priceless lessons in sportsmanship, winning, losing and team work. Not every boy participated in this program but there is no question that many a youth and fellow members of what were previously known as street gangs, joined the Club's sport program and channeled their energies into sports competition rather than into unsavory activities they otherwise may have gotten into.

In the spring and summer, teams were organized to play in intramural softball leagues as well as in city-wide baseball competition. The intramural softball league was organized according to age and the different age groups played on specified nights so that all teams could play at least once a week. I was a member of the *Gladiators* and we competed in this league against 5 or 6 other teams in the Junior age division. My older brother Nacho (Lefty) played with the *Lancers* in the Intermediate age division. Other teams that I recall playing were the *Rebels* (Intermediate age division) and the *Aristocrats* (Senior age division). The Club would provide the bases for the field, the catcher's equipment, the bats and the balls. Each boy had to provide his own glove. Fortunately, most boys had one which they had purchased for around $2 across the border in Juárez, Mexico, during a bi-weekly trip taken with their fathers to get a haircut. Those gloves were treasured, bore the owners' name or initials in large black letters, were well-cared for and rarely got lost or stolen.

The same boys could also play in Little League, Pony League and Babe Ruth League teams that would compete all over the city. Boys' Club league games were played in the Unit 2 ball park where the bleachers would typically get filled each night by families of the players.

In the fall, the Club organized touch football leagues that also played at night on the same Unit 2 ball park. These were also organized into age divisions and the teams were generally the same teams that played in the softball league but now competed in an entirely different sport. As in the softball leagues, the organization and competitiveness of teams in touch football was pretty rigorous. Kids would look forward with great anticipation to the upcoming game each week and the excitement provided by the games never disappointed anyone.

I have many fond memories of the evenings in the fall when we played touch football. I once again played in the league for boys in the Junior age group. I was again a member of the team called the *Gladiators*. We competed with probably five other teams in our age group. The teams were pretty much evenly balanced in terms of skill and so the games tended to be very competitive, exciting and enormously pleasurable.

During one game that lingers in my memory, an opposing player happened to be wearing football shoes with cleats. Since we were playing on grass, the cleats could give a runner a huge advantage. This particular player was literally running circles around us as we unsuccessfully tried to keep up with him in our slick-soled tennis shoes. We simply could not keep up with him and, therefore, we could not defense their team. We were soundly defeated.

I remember being extremely impressed by the advantage generated by cleats. Cleats in those days were not cheap. All of us who did not have cleats assumed that those who did had either stolen them or were borrowing them from the high-school teams they played on. In any event, no one in my team had cleats and, therefore, we were not as competitive as the teams who had one or two players who wore cleats. I put my mind to work and decided that I might be able to find a pair of shoes with cleats at a local army surplus store where I recalled seeing athletic gear previously. The local army surplus store was actually located in downtown El Paso. Getting to it was no simple proposition. But I was obsessed with obtaining cleats and so one Saturday I caught the bus and went shopping.

The Army surplus store indeed had used sporting equipment. They had a bin that was pretty much full of used football shoes. These shoes were the type used in high-school, college, and professional football. The cleats were at least an inch long and made of rubber or nylon and each shoe had seven cleats. Upon seeing the bin full of shoes, I became ecstatic. I rummaged through the 20 or 30 pairs but couldn't find anything smaller than the size 12. At that time, I recall that I was around the size 10, at most.

Since I was desperate, I purchased one of those pairs of shoes and decided that I could wear them if I wore sufficient pairs of socks. At the next game, I had at least three pairs of thick sweat socks on to make the shoes fit. To make a long story short, I became somewhat of the laughingstock of that particular game. I did have extremely good traction; however, the shoes and the socks simply weighed me down too much and caused me to lose what little speed I had to begin with. We lost again.

I decided to return the shoes to the Army surplus store and did so a few days later. As I returned them, I looked in the bin and spotted a pair of black leather *Puma* soccer shoes. These were almost in perfect condition except for one thing: they were a size 9. I tried them on. My foot was barely able to fit but it did. They were feather light. They had 12 cleats per shoe. And they looked extremely cool. And so, I bought them. I recall paying $2 for them.

At the next game I showed up wearing my size 9 *Puma* soccer shoes. Everyone was duly impressed. This time, I not only had traction but I had extremely light feet and therefore I was fast. I remember out-running everyone and scoring a whole bunch of touchdowns. I also remember being the kicker and with those soccer shoes I was able to kick the football extremely far and therefore once again gain a huge advantage.

Early on during the game, I sensed that the bunching up of my toes into these extremely tight shoes was somewhat painful. The pleasure of running so fast and of scoring, however, caused me to ignore that pain and to just enjoy the thrill of winning. But toward the end of the game, the pain became unbearable. Even though I slowed down at that point because of the pain, we were so far ahead that the opposing team would never catch up. We won that game. Immediately after the game I removed my shoes because I simply could not walk on them anymore. I shall never forget what I saw. Upon removing my socks, I discovered that my two fat toes were swollen and purple. The next two toes on each foot were not swollen but they were purple too. And they hurt like hell. I was hobbled for at least a week and I could hardly stand the pain. Eventually, the six affected toenails fell off. I never wore that pair of soccer shoes again. And we went on to complete the season in a fairly forgettable way. Nevertheless, I will never forget how great I felt as I was running and scoring at will for the first half of that game. It could easily have been my greatest moment of athletic glory.

As the cooler weather came to El Paso each winter, the sports program at the Club would turn to basketball. The teams would take off their football sneakers and then put them on again as they magically became basketball sneakers to play on the paved basketball court. It was a single court but on any given day, the league could play 3 or four games in the afternoon and 4 or 5 games in the evening under the lights.

As the basketball teams of Unit 2 became better, the leagues would extend the competition to include games with teams from Unit 1 on their home court. This was a special treat for two reasons: First, the Unit 2 teams would get to "travel" to South Florence Street in the 1956 sky-blue, retired military ambulance that served as the official vehicle of Unit 2. Second, the Unit 1 basketball court was an indoor court that made players feel as if they had taken a giant step up from the playground.

Incidentally, in my view, the *Aristocrats* and the other Senior teams actually comprised the true beneficiaries of the Boys' Club. That's because they were in that age group (17-18) that was most at risk of failing to survive the Projects. If they could reach age 18 without getting into real trouble, they would probably do well beyond that. I, for one, really respected and admired those older boys particularly the *Aristocrats*. Among those who I still remember as friendly leaders and role models are Abel Orona, Pete Medina, Danny Montez, Benito Ruiz, Ruben Felix, Cruz Saucedo and Jesús Perea.

Summertime in the Projects

Everyone knows that summertime is the best time for young people and it doesn't matter whether you live on the lap of luxury or in the puddle of poverty. Living in the projects in El Paso was certainly not the lap of luxury; yet, I never thought that it comprised a puddle of poverty either. I always thought that life in the projects--particularly during the summers--was actually rather amazingly pleasant. And once the summer started, all of us kids found ourselves with lots of time to spare. Whereas, during the school year, we didn't get home from school until 4PM, and thus could not start having fun until then, in the summer we were ready to have fun as early as 8AM every day. The Boys' Club also changed its operating hours on summer weekdays by opening up at 1PM every day except Sunday.

Summer days in the projects were great for many reasons. First of all, school was out. What kid does not enjoy the sensation of not having to worry about school? But there were other reasons why summer was so pleasant. Even though most of us were too young to have economically meaningful jobs, we all were able to compete on a daily basis for two helper's jobs at the nearby *Washington Park* swimming pool, if we were willing to get up early to be there at 8AM on any given morning. There were probably four or five kids who were regular competitors for those jobs. We did not compete for those jobs every single day of the week, and so, if one spreads the 2 jobs over five days among five kids you can almost guarantee each kid to get that job two or three times during any given week. So, what was the job? Basically, the job was to clean the public swimming pool as well as the men's and ladies' locker rooms. The supervisor who selected the two helpers each day was the lifeguard who would be on duty for that day. One of those lifeguards, Leo Sotomayor, was partial to my buddy Checo and me and so when he was on duty, we generally got the jobs. We would arrive at 8AM and be selected moments later and then complete the work by 9AM when the pool would open. As compensation for our work, we would receive a free pass to swim for the rest of the day. It was absolutely delightful and it saved each of us 15¢ every time we worked.

First Dive

When a child takes his or her first dive into a large body of water, it may or may not constitute a significant or memorable event. In my case, it did.

It was the summer of 1958 and it happened at the *Washington Park* swimming pool. We had moved from 1900 West Main Street to 405 Webber Way in the Paisano Projects. I was 12 years old and it was summertime. The *El Paso Boys' Club* had not yet opened in our neighborhood. That would still take another year. What young kids did during the summer was mainly to partake of recreational activities at high-school gyms (such as *Jefferson High School*) where kids could spend most of any summer day in a variety of activities. I started to do that at the beginning of the summer and on the way back each day I made it a habit to stop at the pool at *Washington Park*.

The *Washington Park* pool was the nicest public pool in El Paso at the time. It was a huge structure. It was a perfect rectangle approximately 50 feet by 150 feet; the depth was 3 feet at the shallow end and 12 feet at the deep end; there was a low and a high diving board at the deep end; there was a nylon rope suspended by about 20 foam ovals that separated the shallow portion from the deep portion; the life-guard stand was just above that rope on the west side of the pool; there were stainless steel entry ladders at the 3 and the 5 ft. depths on both sides of the pool; and since the pool was used for racing, there were 10 black stripes, each about 12 inches wide painted on the bottom of the pool that ran the entire length of the pool.

The pool was completely surrounded by a 3 ft. high cinderblock wall that was painted light green. A four-foot chain-link fence had been erected on top of the wall. At around noon, as I was returning from the gym, I would make it a point to stop by the pool. I even had my own viewing spot on the west side of the pool at the point where the nylon rope separated the shallow from the deep parts. I would stand with the fingers of both hands hooked into the chain link fence and would press my face against the openings to get a better view of what was happening inside the pool.

I liked going to that spot because a few good-looking girls were always there. They included the niece of the head football coach at *Jefferson High School* (who was the pool manager during the summers) and some of her friends. I would simply stand by the fence and, from a safe distance, gawk at these beautiful girls.

Up until that point in my life I had never learned how to swim. At the pool, I watched every day as kids younger than me enjoyed seemingly endless fun swimming, diving, laughing and retrieving objects from the bottom. I honestly believed that few things at that time could be more fun.

After a few weeks of heavy imagining, I somehow convinced myself that I could swim and that I had nothing to fear at the *Washington Park* pool. And so, all by myself, one day I got 15 cents and went swimming for the first time. I went alone because I still had not made friends from the Projects nor from school.

For some unknown reason I had made up my mind to simply dive into the pool at the four-foot depth. I had never swum nor dived before yet I felt completely comfortable simply diving in since I had seen so many other kids to it. I also knew that I could lose my nerve if I hesitated and, therefore, I swore not to even think about hesitating. I had a simple plan: First, take the mandatory pre-swim shower, then immediately walk to the part that was 4 feet deep, get a 3-step running start and then simply dive head-first into the pool.

I executed the plan perfectly. It was a typical July day in El Paso. The sun was bright, the smell of chlorine was strong and there were no clouds, and even though the usual noontime crowd of swimmers was present, most of them were in the very shallow part.

I took my pre-swim shower and confidently stepped onto the wide concrete deck at the shallow end. I notice that the 4 ft. level of the east side of the pool was practically deserted. I sucked in my gut, inhaled and stepped off sharply in that direction. I reached the designated point and as planned, stepped off three paces away from the edge, turned around and without any hesitation whatsoever, initiated my dive sequence.

All was fine as I flew through the air. I remember tightly closing my eyes and entering the water and a split second later touching the bottom with my hands. Then everything got weird. It started when I attempted to find some footing at the pool bottom to propel myself to the surface.

I was crouched in a ball at the bottom as I tried to regain my footing. With my eyes closed tightly, I searched for the pool bottom with my feet and found it. But as I extended my legs forcefully to send myself to the surface, both feet slipped on the slick bottom and I felt myself tumble backward, my feet above my head. I stayed underwater instead of rising to the surface. Only then did I open my eyes. To my horror, I couldn't see the surface at all. I could only see bubbles and a large expanse of white with a broad black stripe. At that point my lungs started clamoring for air. I desperately tried to touch the bottom with my feet again but it was simply too far away. I found myself flailing away underwater with no control whatsoever. As I flailed away, believe it or not, my life played itself out in my mind. I had heard sometime in the past that that was supposed to happen when one is about to die. I even asked my parents to forgive me for all the bad things that I had done. For that brief period of time, I truly felt that I was a goner.

Eventually, my feet felt the bottom and this time I got the traction that I had been searching for. I thrust myself upward. I broke through to the surface and as I took in a breath of fresh air, it became one of the happiest moments of my life. Then, I stood upright and realized that the water barely came to my shoulders. I knew then for sure that I was going to live.

I got out of the pool and sat on the concrete deck for long time thinking about what had just happened. No one--including the lifeguard--even suspected that a near-drowning event had just occurred. Even I started to laugh quietly at myself at how silly my first dive experience had really been. I suppose that I quickly became convinced that maybe what happened wasn't such a big deal after all. Within a few minutes, I was back in the pool trying hard not to be bothered by that dive.

Over time, that incident did indeed turn out to be insignificant. But to this day, I remain convinced that on that July afternoon in 1958, in my mind, I truly had come face-to-face with death.

Summer Gymnasium

As I mentioned earlier, another fantastic summertime activity venue available to the kids of the Paisano Projects was the gymnasium at *Jefferson High School*. The gym would be open from 10AM until 4PM every weekday and they would have a huge variety of activities available for kids at no charge. I remember participating in tumbling, basketball, volleyball, and badminton. They also had table games that we could play. But most importantly, it was coeducational. I always looked forward to seeing at the gym the many girls that would also show up for a bit of exercise.

Summer Activities at the Boys' Club

And so, Unit 2 of the Boys' Club opened in the summer of 1959. Because summer days in El Paso tend to get very hot, the best feature of the Club was simply the fact that it was air-conditioned. Even though the air-conditioner was really just a so-called "swamp cooler" or evaporative cooler and did not involve refrigerated air, it worked fine due to the generally low humidity levels found in El Paso. I would go in the hall and spend as much time as I could shooting pool or playing Ping-Pong or listening to the radio in air-conditioned comfort. In the afternoons and evenings, we would suck up the heat and go outside to play organized sports such as baseball and basketball.

In the summer, even though there was an abundance of organized play available at the Boys' Club for the kids in the projects, it did not begin until 1PM. During the mornings, however, there was one activity that sticks out in my mind as being as enjoyable as anything offered at the Boys' Club. At around 10 AM on any given summer day, a group of us would gather on the surprisingly well-maintained lawns on the north side of the playground (at the southwest corner of Paisano Drive and Boone St.) and we would play *Monopoly*. There would always be four or five of us available and the games would last a few hours. I simply remember how pleasant it was to be sitting on the thick Bermuda grass in the shade of Cottonwood trees protected from the overbearing heat having lots of fun with my buddies.

Later on, during Boys' Club operating hours, there were many more opportunities for pleasure. On any given day of the week, one of the staff members at the Boys' Club would announce that the Boys' Club van would be going to a drive-in movie that evening and that anyone interested could sign up, pay 10¢ and be able to go. I—and a few of my buddies--therefore would go to the drive-in movies once or twice each week. 9 or 10 kids would be packed into the back of the Boys' Club van (that converted sky-blue 1952 *Chevy* military ambulance) and we would bring along a folding *Samsonite* tan-colored metal chair for each of us. Then we would be driven by a Sr. staff member to the *North Loop Drive-In Theater* which charged 99 cents per carload. Once there, we could either move the chairs to the very front of the parking area or grab an adjacent parking space on which to set up the chairs, and watch the movies from there. Some truly fond memories remain in my mind about these drive-in movie experiences.

For those kids in the neighborhood who did not have a dime for drive-ins, the Boys' Club would set up a huge screen in the parking lot next to the outdoor basketball court and they would project feature-length movies that the club was able to borrow from Fort Bliss, the huge military installation there in El Paso. Once again, as many as a hundred *Samsonite* chairs would be set up in front of the screen and anyone--including parents, grandparents, siblings on parole, visiting relatives and grandchildren--could attend these movies for free.

One of main attractions of the week occurred on Friday evenings when the Boys' Club would sponsor a Friday night dance. For a few years I was actually the disc jockey for these dances. Before I took that disc jockey job, I was just another kid there, chasing girls and trying to learn how to dance. I would stand next to my best friend, Checo, by the edge of the dance floor, and carefully look at all of the girls who had arrived. I remember vividly having a crush on one particular girl named Celia Valenzuela who I thought was as pretty as any girl I've never seen. Unfortunately, she happened to be dating some other guy at that time and I was never able to persuade her to leave the guy for me. I remember dancing with her many times and feeling the excitement and passion that only slow-dancing teenagers feel.

Also, on any number of evenings during the summer, as I have described in an earlier part of this book, I, along with some of my buddies, would work at the *El Paso Coliseum* selling popcorn, peanuts, cold drinks or anything else at any of the events that took place there. I recall that during the summer, some event would take place at least two or three nights per week at the *Coliseum* where just about every kid in the neighborhood could get a job.

Home Run Derby

Home Run Derby was a televised program that was very popular in 1960. Each week, two prominent major league baseball players would meet in a neutral field in a home run hitting contest for nine innings. Whoever hit the most home runs would win. Anything that wasn't a home run (i.e. a pop fly, grounder, strike or foul ball) was an "out." The winner would receive $2,000 and would come back the next week. The loser would get $1,000. Also, anybody who hit three home runs in a row would get a $500 bonus, another $500 for a fourth consecutive homerun, and $1,000 for each consecutive homer after that. This show featured some of the best hitters of the day like Hank Aaron, Mickey Mantle, Ernie Banks, Rocky Colavito, Harmon Killebrew, Willie Mays, Duke Snyder and Frank Robinson. We used to watch it religiously.

As I stated earlier, most of the kids in my neighborhood--including myself--were baseball fanatics. After seeing this television program, we immediately instituted a version of the game that we could play in our own neighborhood playground. I recall having some of the best memories of my youth while playing *Home Run Derby* with my buddies.

The way we played in the playground was similar in concept to the game played by the pros. The idea was for a pitcher to send hittable balls to the batter. The batter would then simply try to hit the ball over the fence and thus claim it as a home run. If you hit anything else or if you simply got a strike on the pitch, that was called an "out." When the batter had three outs, he traded places with the pitcher, who now became the batter and he then got a chance to hit home runs until he got three outs. When that cycle was completed (six outs) that was called an inning. We probably only played five or six innings but at the end of any such game, the players would invariably have hit a few balls over the fence and had a whole heck of a lot of fun doing it.

As I described earlier, the playground that was located in the Paisano Projects had a very nice baseball diamond within it. We played hundreds of games in that baseball diamond during that era. That baseball diamond, however, was not really suitable for playing *Home Run Derby* because the diamond had been set in one corner of the playground and therefore it only had a chain link fence along right field. The left field side of the diamond had no fence. It just had more space where swings and merry-go-rounds and other playground devices sat. Thus, a long ball hit into left field just rolled on and on past the devices until it hit the chain link fence that ran along Paisano Drive.

And so, in order to compensate for this design deficiency, we set up home plate on a spot along the left-field or third base line facing Boone Street which paralleled the right field fence. What that did was to create a dead centerfield distance equivalent to the distance of right field on the regular diamond. And so, in order to get the most efficient home run whenever we played *Home Run Derby*, the idea was to knock it straight over the pitcher into dead centerfield. As you hit farther left or farther right from dead center you simply ended up increasing the distance that you had to cover before the ball could get over the fence

I seem to remember that the probability for a 12-year-old to knock the ball over that fence was relatively low. And so, after a four or five innings game, a kid like myself might have gotten one or two home runs. However, the 14, 15- and 16-year-old kids enjoyed a much higher probability. At the end of a four or five inning game one of those kids could well have knocked 8 or 9 balls over the fence.

The fact that there was no dirt infield in this re-designed layout was irrelevant since the game only counted those balls that flew over the fence. You really didn't need too many players either since you only needed the batter and the pitcher (as long as the pitcher did not mind chasing the ball each time it was hit). However, there normally were a few other kids available to chase balls, and eventually, they too would get their turn to play the *Derby* themselves. In addition, there were also non-playing, younger siblings who were always available to chase those balls.

The tools of the game were a baseball bat, at least one ball and the glove for the pitcher in case he had to do any fielding of non-home runs. In those days, baseballs were a lot scarcer than they are today. Therefore, I don't recall ever playing with more than one ball. If my playing partner happened to have another ball, then we would play with two. Imagine how much running around we had to do when we played with such few balls. And there's no doubt that none of those balls had its original cover and stitching.

Most of the time the balls were well-used and often re-covered by the owner with black, electrical (cloth or plastic) tape to keep it from unraveling.

In those days, since I was only 12 or 13 years old, it was difficult for me to compete with bigger boys such as my brother. A few years of age difference created significant advantages for the older, bigger boys. Just as they played in a more senior baseball league, they also had no business playing *Home Run Derby* with the younger boys. But for me, there was never a lack of peers. Since we were out of school during the summer, we used to play *Home Run Derby* for hours just about every day during its heyday.

Whenever the bigger or older boys were playing *Home Run Derby*, the younger boys such as me could play the position of fielder so we could practice catching balls that were hit but that did not fly over the fence. In those situations, whenever a home run was hit, it was the job of the younger kids to climb over the chain link fence into Boone Street and to recover the ball.

The advantage in *Home Run Derby* went to the bigger boys. And so, even when I played against my peers, if I was playing a smaller guy who was my age, I normally could beat him. But whenever I was playing the huskier guys I generally would lose.

And so, what were the rewards of winning? Nothing...other than bragging rights. But these were really special bragging rights because they involved one's ability to hit a home run. Whether one hit a home run at an actual ballgame--and of course, this was reserved for the really gifted athletes--or whether one hit a home run in a game of *Home Run Derby*, that act entitled you to a whole lot of respect around the neighborhood.

My recollection was that there was one of my peers who stood well-above all the others in this game. That was George Leon. He probably was the most gifted athlete in our neighborhood. There may have been better baseball players such as Neto Madrid, or faster runners such as Robert Rangel, but George really dominated his peers in many different sports. I could never compete against George. Other peers that were around my same size and with whom I could compete nicely included, Sam Saldaña, Hector Lopez, George and Peter Mares and Roger Felix. There were other peers of mine who were smaller with whom I could compete better. These included Daniel and Filiberto Miranda, Sal and Rodolfo Garcia and, of course, Checo.

Guides for the Lighthouse for the Blind

But Boys' Club activities were not the only things for a kid to do during the summer. One of the most pleasant things that I did was actually a job that mi Papá and other blind salesman from the *Lighthouse for the Blind* would offer to young kids. [The door-to-door sales operation that created these opportunities for boys like me is described in detail in Chapter 3 above.] The blind salesmen would hire a boy to act as his guide as he went door-to-door selling household good. During the school year, these jobs were available only on Saturdays, but during the summer they became available on a daily basis. One of the biggest reasons why these jobs were enjoyable was the fact that it included a free lunch at the local *Oasis* drive-in restaurant where we would get a hamburger, fries and a coke. The job also paid a dollar a day. One of the fringe benefits that I shall never forget about these jobs was the incredibly amazing sense of humor that each of the salesmen seemed to have. The jokes and the pranks that these blind adult men told and engaged in were simply amazing. In addition, a few of them were musically inclined and during moments when we were just driving around, they would start singing and I always enjoyed that quite a bit.

All of these activities were tremendous fun in and of themselves. But what made them even better was the fact that I participated in all these with some really good buddies including Checo. He and I always did these things together. Occasionally, we would be joined by Daniel "Pelusa" Miranda and Salvador E. "Chichi" Garcia. Parents were simply not a part of anything that was happening. We were just extremely fortunate to have all these activities--organized by others--that could consume all or at least the better part of every single summer day.

Attire

As is typical during any period of time, the kids in the projects liked to dress in certain ways. As always, it was very important to dress in conformity with peers. That tendency has not changed very much and probably never will.

My recollection as to attire during the 1950's is relatively simple. In the early 50's, I was too young to care very much and so mi Mamá basically dictated what I wore. Even though I attended a parochial school from kindergarten through the third grade, we were not required to wear any particular uniform. What I do remember wearing were simple inexpensive blue jeans along with custom tailored shirts made by mi Mamá. She would make shirts for my brother and for me and we were generally indifferent as to what they looked like and so we wore them. One shirt in particular stands out in my mind. It was basically a white shirt with a pattern on it of tiny marine-related flags. It attracted a lot of attention and so I remember receiving many comments about it. I think I wore that while I was in the third grade. I also remember that I used to play on my knees a lot and wear holes right through on my jeans. Mi Mamá periodically would sew matching patches to cover up those holes. Since just about every other kid wore similarly patched jeans, it was absolutely common to see these everywhere and therefore it was not embarrassing for any of us. Nevertheless, I remember getting comments from my teachers as to how professional my knee-patches in particular looked. I would proudly point out that mi Mamá was a "professional" seamstress.

The mid to late 50's--my elementary and intermediate school years--were a time when peer pressure regarding clothes--and other matters of course--became more considerable. Even though mi Mamá continued to sew customized shirts for me, I was not very eager to wear them simply because they looked *different* from what other boys were wearing. Since mi Papá was not earning very much money in those days, the option of shopping for shirts simply did not exist. Furthermore, being the second son meant that I was the heir to the shirts passed down by my brother, Nachito. I do recall feeling a tremendous amount of peer pressure in those days as to what clothing kids my age should wear. It was very likely "self-inflicted" pressure because in reality, no peer ever made fun of my clothes. I just imagined that they would.

I continued to wear inexpensive blue jeans during that period as did most of my peers from the Projects. I attended *Henderson Intermediate School* for the sixth and seventh grades. That school was located in the relatively affluent neighborhood known as *Clardy-Fox* and so it included children of well-to-do parents as well as children like me from the Projects. I used to play lots of sandlot games with the well-off kids and they all seemed to be wearing genuine *Levi's* blue jeans and *US Keds* or *Converse All-Star* white, low-top sneakers. The kids from my neighborhood would also wear blue jeans but they were not *Levi's*. They were an inferior brand available at *J.C. Penney*. We also wore white, low-top sneakers but they were not *US Keds* or *Converse*. They were from a budget shoe store called *Karl's* and they were only $2.99 whereas the *Keds* were normally $4.99 and the *Converse* $5.99. I was always envious of the kids who wore *Keds* or *Converse*. I would daydream in class about one day being able to afford them. Even though I knew mine were of the cheap variety, I was very proud to wear my sneakers because I took time every so often to throw them in the washing machine and keep them looking nice and white.

At about that time, I discovered the *J.C. Penney* basic, crew-neck, white T-shirt. It was customary in those days to wear such a T-shirt underneath your shirt and then leave the shirt unbuttoned. To this day I enjoy wearing those T-shirts because they hug the collar very nicely and because they are made of a very heavy weight of cotton.

Then, in the early 60's, I entered high school. Blue jeans remained appropriate attire as did the white T-shirts under shirts. But there's no question that I quit wearing any shirts that were sewed by mi Mamá. First of all, she was ill a lot and therefore could not produce anything on her sewing machine. Secondly, the peer pressure to wear nice button-down stylish shirts was too great. I remember during this time that mi Mamá taught me how to sew. Because I was a very skinny kid, I used to take whatever shirts I had and I would tailor the sides so that they would look more fitted on me. Most of the time, the customization worked just fine. Occasionally however, I took in too much and as a result, I could hardly button the shirt in front. That was an irreparable error. Yet, because I had no shirts to spare, I would wear them to school anyway and become the object of some snickering for the ridiculously tight shirt I was wearing. However, it was still a button-down shirt and therefore very much in style.

Only in high school did I endeavor to save enough money to buy discounted but genuine *Levi's* blue jeans. It seems like everyone in my high school that had any fashion sense at all would buy these *Levi's* blue jeans. When I was a junior in high school, mi Mamá and I went shopping for some jeans. It seems that during those days, corduroy--particularly in dark olive--had become very fashionable. But they were very expensive. Mi Mamá and I found a set of tan-colored corduroy *Levi's* that were heavily discounted. I decided that I would buy them and also buy a package of dark olive fabric dye for 25 cents and just dye them. I believed that plan to simply be economic genius. Unfortunately, they did not have dark olive dye. The closest that I could find was a bright, almost emerald-green color. But I became obsessive and decided to go with that color anyway. Somehow the difference did not seem that great to me as I paid for the dye. That evening, I dyed the pants. A few days later I wore them to school and was ridiculed seemingly by everyone. After that one wearing, those bright, almost emerald-green corduroy jeans never saw the light of day again.

Except for Physical Education (PE) class, no one wore sneakers in high school. Instead, we wore inexpensive but stylish shoes. I recall paying between $15 and $20 for a pair of nice shoes at a shoe store called *Thom McAn*. By the time I was senior, I had elevated my fashion sense regarding shoes to buying $20 and $30 shoes at the *Florsheim* shoe store.

While in high school, as far as boys' attire went, there existed a very clean split. There was on one side, a whole bunch of boys who fell in the clean-cut, all-American, straight arrow category. On the other side, there was a bunch of not-so-nice, less law-abiding kids that were called "Pachucos" or "hoodlums."

There were many distinguishing dress characteristics of the Pachucos. First of all, the Pachucos had very elaborate hairdos. Their hair was generally very long compared to the clean-cut kids and it was always laden with hairdressing. They also wore white, crew neck T-shirts but the shirts that they wore over them were invariably expensive and meticulously pressed with military creases running down the chest and back. These shirts were never meant to be tucked in and they never were. As for pants, the Pachucos wore wide-legged khaki pants that were also meticulously starched and pressed. The pants were held up by very thin leather belts that in many cases were quite nice. Finally, the Pachucos would wear some really extravagant shoes that were called "Tablitas." "Tablitas" is the plural diminutive of the Spanish term "tabla" which means "board: as in "a wooden board." The "Tablitas" were extra-long (like a board), were pointy, highly polished and in many cases the stitching on the welt was maintained in a clean, white condition. Even though I never had any interest in dressing like a Pachuco for social reasons, I have to admit that some of them looked really cool in those outfits.

While in high school around 1964-65, we occasionally needed to wear a suit. I remember one suit in particular that I owned. It was extremely popular because of the British rock-and-roll invasion. It was fundamentally a very tight suit with no collar or lapels and with a little strap around the waist only in the back. I wore that suit for my "All-Jefferson High School Boy" picture in my 1965 class yearbook. There was a slightly more conservative version of a suit that was also worn in those days. It had a lapel and was baggier. I inherited such a suit from my big brother, Nacho. He wore that suit in 1963 when he met President John F. Kennedy. I used it for a few years until eventually I outgrew it. I then stored it for many years until, in 2014, I returned it to my brother in pristine freshly dry-cleaned condition so he could, in turn, pass it on as an heirloom to one of his grandchildren.

Mindset

In the summer of 1959, I turned 12. I was a relatively happy kid and even though my parents were earning very little, I did not really lack for anything material. Somehow, with the money I made from the different jobs that I had,

I was able to buy enough kid-stuff so as to not feel any different from my peers.

However, life was not perfect. There were a few things that always seemed to bother me and most of these things were not likely to ever go away. I was still troubled a lot by the age and blindness of mi Papá. Thoughts about the awful seizures that mi Mamá was still experiencing never left my mind even when I was playing ball at the playground. Those two issues weighed heavily on my mind.

But there were other issues as well which, as I recall, drew my attention more than I wanted. I was acutely aware of the color of my skin and frequently found myself wishing that it be fairer. I was envious of my friends who happened to have lighter-colored skin and thankful that my skin was not as dark as that of other friends. As I was growing up, I had been taking inventory of all those things that I thought would make it more difficult for me to be like everyone else in this country and this society that I wanted so much to join. From very early on, I knew that skin color was one of those things. It was a childish concern and one that I never mentioned to anyone but I remember how it often weighed heavily on my mind. Then there were the other three perennial problems that I shared with other kids that were my age: Pimples, buck teeth and stick-out ears. I was bothered by these three burdens but I took some comfort knowing that most of my peers were no better off in having to deal with them

I remember also being troubled frequently by my name: Guillermo Chavez. At home and in my community, my name was not a problem. However, I resented that people could not pronounce it whenever I found myself in an Anglo environment. One teacher in the 6th grade, despite good intentions, always made it sound like *"gwee-larry-more"* and that always caused the class to snicker. But I did not blame those who could not pronounce my name. After all, I was in their country and I just happened to have a name that was unpronounceable to most Anglos. In those days I remember being very grateful that mi Papá had nick-named me "Willie" at an early age. Everyone seemed to be able to say Willie without any difficulty.

Issues with my name continued for the rest of my life, but fortunately, I outgrew them at about the time I finished high school. Many years later, however, I had one more name issue that laid all name issues to rest forever. It was one of those perfect days in early May of 1978 in upstate New York which just happened to be one of the nicest and prettiest times imaginable. And I felt really good too. My first-born son was almost three months old and doing great. I had just completed three years of law school and I was about to begin my first job in the law department at IBM's corporate headquarters. I actually was not going to get my law degree for another week, yet I was going to start working at IBM as a law clerk on that day. My spirits had never soared higher.

I arrived at the lobby of the corporate headquarters and was met by my official guide for the day, a gentleman named Wyman Procter, who was a veteran lawyer at IBM. Mr. Procter was probably in his early-sixties at the time and as far as I could tell, he had it made. After all, he had been with IBM for over 30 years as an attorney and if I could ever say that about my career, I think I would be pretty happy and grateful. Mr. Proctor was the quintessential Northeasterner. He was a white male that had spent his entire career in the corporate law department of IBM in and around Westchester County, New York, and Connecticut. He had a full head of silver hair and an exceptionally charming personality. But apparently, he really didn't know much about ethnic minorities, particularly those that had confined themselves to the southwestern US. He seemed fascinated by my Mexican-American background.

The mid and late seventies were a time in American society when ethnic and cultural minorities started to really assert themselves. While attending law school, I personally had also found a renewed sense of identity in my Mexican origins and had decided that I would exploit them rather than minimize them as had previously been popular. As I transitioned from student to professional and from humble Mexican to proud Chicano, I decided that I would never again be embarrassed by my name and henceforth I would thrust that name proudly into the face of anyone whenever I got the chance. Thus, the résumé that I had originally submitted to IBM proudly bore my complete name "GUILLERMO DANIEL CHAVEZ." Even though I had been known as Willie throughout my entire life--including my four years at West Point, five years in the US Army and three years at law school--I decided that when I started looking for a job, I would be known as "GUILLERMO" and that "Willie" would henceforth be locked forever in the footlocker of my youth.

When Mr. Procter greeted me at the lobby and introduced himself, he seemed genuinely pleased to meet me. That is, until I introduced myself. I announced for him (and all others within hearing range) that my name was Guillermo Chavez. I distinctly recall how his face went from a beaming smile to an agonized and disoriented look as he desperately tried to digest what I had just said. He said something like "I'm pleased to meet you, Gooey-ler-mo," and quickly moved to a new subject. I could see that he was troubled by the fact that he could not pronounce my first name.

The hallways of the corporate headquarters at that particular moment were largely abandoned. We basically ran into no one as we walked for what seemed like tens of hundreds of yards until we finally reached the law department. As we entered the main corridor of the law department, Mr. Procter spotted someone who knew him so he politely proceeded to introduce me to that person. I was delighted to make the acquaintance of this member of the law department and I picked up his name ("Chet") easily. However, once again, I sensed that this new person was also struggling mightily with my first name. We chatted amiably for a few seconds and then continued on our march toward the interviews that had been set up for my arrival.

A few seconds later, Mr. Procter was surprised by someone we met on that hallway. Mr. Procter, again politely attempted to introduce us as well. He could not say "Guillermo" and anyone could tell that he was deeply troubled by that. He became nervous and actually seemed to be sweating. But we got through that second introduction as well and continued walking.

Mr. Proctor then took advantage of the empty hallway and decided to talk to me privately. He placed his left hand on my right shoulder and asked me to please help him learn how to say my name. I said "Guillermo" slowly and clearly three, four, maybe five times, each time exaggerating the "Y" sound of the two LL's and of the rolling "r" and he carefully but painfully repeated "Guillermo" each time. But also, each time, he knew that he was simply not saying it right. And you could tell that he felt awful. As he struggled with it, I privately felt a strange sense of relief and perhaps even revenge for the countless times my teachers in grade school had butchered "Guillermo."

We finally made the turn into the hallway where my first interviewer had his office. I could tell that Mr. Procter felt good since soon the ordeal of having to say my name would soon come to an end. However, before we reached that interviewer's office, three other IBM attorneys suddenly entered the hallway from nowhere. I saw Mr. Procter frown and slouch has he contemplated the need to have to say my name at least one more time.

He reluctantly looked at the three attorneys and said "John, Gus, and Bob, I'd like for you to meet the newest member of the law department..." But then Mr. Procter paused, decided that he couldn't pronounce my name without help and resorted to reading my resume where he once again stumbled badly as he read my name. In fact, he attempted to say "Guillermo" three or four different times and each time would butcher it even more. Mr. Procter's face was now beet red and I could again see the drops of perspiration forming on his brow. I felt like I was living through a Manifest Destiny in reverse. Then

Mr. Procter said, "I am really having a devil of the time saying your name. Can you tell me what your name means or what it is in English?" I thought that Mr. Procter had suffered enough and I wanted to help him out of his agony. So, I told him, "Guillermo is William in Spanish." Mr. Procter's face showed immense relief. He smiled broadly, turned to the three lawyers and said "John, Gus and Bob, I'd like to introduce you to "Bill" Chavez." And that became my moniker for the next 30 years during my entire corporate legal career.

Anyway, back in 1959, I believed I was a fairly typical adolescent of Mexican extraction, living reasonably comfortably in a barrio within the "land of opportunity." I also believed strongly that I truly belonged there and would eventually assimilate successfully even though I was burdened by a name that Anglos could barely pronounce and a skin color that would always set me apart from most other Americans. Little did I know that when Unit 2 of the *El Paso Boys' Club* opened its doors in the Paisano Projects that summer, my life and the lives of so many of my peers would change so dramatically.

The Staff at Unit 2

I know for a fact that beginning in the summer of 1959 and continuing until I finished high school in 1965, the *El Paso Boys' Club* Unit 2 was operated by a remarkable team of men. They came from a variety of backgrounds and they brought different skills to the jobs they had to do and each brought with him a unique way of dealing with young boys. Most of them made deep impressions on me and, I'm sure, on the rest of the Club members. And by being there to supervise and coach us, each of them undoubtedly kept us on the straight and narrow path to avoiding youthful trouble.

Mr. D

Mr. Hightower could not have picked a better person to run Unit 2. Manuel De La Rosa ("Mr. D") was born in El Paso but moved with his family to Chicago as a young kid. He received a Bachelor of Science degree in engineering and played football at *Purdue University*. He also obtained a Bachelor of Arts degree from *Roosevelt University*. His prior studies also included a year of ministerial courses at *McCormick Seminary* and a year of Social Work classes at the *University of Illinois*. I recall Mr. D as a deeply religious man who came very close to becoming a man of the cloth but instead became a man of the kids. Prior to taking the Boys' Club job, Mr. D was Director of Youth Activities at *Divine Savior Presbyterian Church* in El Paso. Previously, he had been Youth Director at the *Fourth Presbyterian*

Church in Chicago. He became the Director of Unit 2 in 1959 and remained there until 1964.

Being the Unit Director of a Boy's Club branch was--and probably still is--an example of one of the most extreme combinations of employment frustration and gratification. It is extremely difficult and frustrating to keep young boys busy or entertained and out of trouble when you have very scarce resources and little or no money. The Boys' Club in the late '50s and early 60's had precious few resources and little money. Nevertheless, Mr. D was hired and, during his tenure, I truly believe that he produced incredibly good results in all respects and, I'm sure, derived for himself the most extreme professional and personal gratification possible.

When I think about what it was that made Mr. D a remarkably effective director, I tend to conclude that one big factor had to be his great affection for sports. Everybody knew that he was a former collegiate football player. He certainly looked like one. But he was also very enthusiastic about the other sports programs offered at the Boys' Club such as baseball, softball, volleyball, and touch/flag football. He was always on the field or court either coaching or officiating and sometimes even playing. He seemed so happy and at ease in the midst of the competition and he also seemed so naturally skilled. As a kid playing those sports, it was unavoidable for me to be impressed by his presence. And, it was impossible to not see how much he enjoyed being there. We were drawn like iron filings to a magnet when Mr. D was around. And, when he was present, we always seemed to be having fun and things always felt under control. We loved to be close to him and to hear him tell stories about sports and, once he gained our respect and attention, there was nothing that we would not have done for him if he had asked.

Mr. D had a very special relationship with all of my family. Even though he always made me believe that I was very capable and could accomplish anything, Mr. D thought that my brother Nacho (or Lefty, as he called him) was really, really exceptional. Mr. D also thought very highly of mi Papá. Despite mi Papá's age and his blindness, Mr. D recognized that he had a certain ability to lead and inspire others. Therefore, he supported mi Papá unconditionally as the leader of the Unit 2 Parents' Club. I recall that both my parents leaped into their Parents' Club roles with enthusiasm and vigor such as they had never shown me before. I distinctly remember how happy and fulfilled they both seemed to be during those first few years of the '60s. The bond between Mr. D and my parents was truly wonderful.

On various occasions, Mr. D observed me acting like a jerk and he took the time to correct me. For example, one time I decided to make one of the young girls of the neighborhood the butt of some jokes that I was telling. As some buddies and I were chatting, I made jokes portraying that girl as ugly and stupid. In doing so, my buddies roared with laughter. From a distance and unbeknownst to me, Mr. D saw this and later, in private, told me that this was a not a nice thing to do. He was absolutely correct and he taught me an extremely valuable lesson not only on the importance of not being hurtful but also on how to counsel impressionable kids.

Mr. D was of Mexican-American descent. All of us in the neighborhood could not help but notice that most staff members at Boys' Clubs in El Paso tended to be Anglo. In our eyes, even though Mr. D was not an Anglo, he was qualified to be a Unit Director simply because he had a college degree. We strongly believed that he was even more qualified because he was one of us. The kids in the neighborhood admired, respected and loved him. And the parents in the neighborhood thought of him as an incredibly capable leader and role model. It was a tremendous deal for all concerned.

My brother Nacho recently told me that he was particularly impressed by Mr. D's determination to help the kids of the Boys' Club speak good English. He told me this story: Mr. D knew that at home, practically all of the Boys' Club kids spoke only Spanish because one or both of the parents did not speak English. He felt that practicing English was important and, since it was likely that the kids would not practice it at home, he would encourage them to speak only English at the Boys' Club. If a kid asked him a question in Spanish, Mr. D would reply in English. If the kid continued in Spanish, Mr. D would still use only English. Mr. D would never demand that the kid speak English; he would simply and gently encourage him to do so by example.

I remember being extremely impressed at the way that Mr. D interacted with parents who did not speak any English. He would speak to them in Spanish to ensure that they were communicating but if their child became engaged in the conversation, Mr. D. would speak to the child only in English. Thus, by communicating this way with the kids, Mr. D would incidentally give them confidence and make them better communicators. It's important to note that it was during this same period that kids could get in real trouble in school if they were caught by a teacher speaking Spanish.

Eloiso De Avila was a kid in Mr. D's Unit back in the 60's and he recently recalled a lesson he learned from Mr. D on the softball field. One of the teams of 12-year-old boys, the *Gladiators,* was about to play and they seemed disorganized. They lacked a leader, so Mr. D appointed Eloiso to be the Captain and told him to fill all of the positions and have them take the field. When one position was left to be filled, Eloiso looked to the bench and saw the two remaining bodies. One was a long-time member of the *Gladiators* whose attendance at games was sporadic because he also worked part-time as a Jr. Staff member. The other was a brand-new kid that had never played before. Eloiso picked the new-comer. As the dejected-rejected player left the bench to do something else, he walked by Mr. D and told him what had just taken place. Mr. D immediately called out to Eloiso so all could hear: "Menso! Menso! (Rough translation: "Dumb-ass!" "Dumb-ass!") Then, Mr. D approached Eloiso and explained why he had so harshly drawn his attention: "I called you "Menso" so you will never forget this lesson: Always maintain the integrity of your team and *never* ignore your veteran players." Eloiso told me he never has forgotten the lesson he learned from Mr. D that day.

Douglas Cooper

Sometime in 1960, Mr. D hired Douglas "Doug" Cooper as the first staff member (Assistant Unit Director) not from the projects. It was a truly unique experience for most of the Club kids to now interact and be influenced in their own neighborhood by an "Anglo."

When Doug Cooper came to Unit 2, he was probably in his early twenties and a student at *Texas Western College*. He was lean and athletic and sported the most precise flat-top haircut that I had ever seen. At the beginning of his days as a staff member, many of the kids at Unit 2 were naturally suspicious and distrusting of the new Anglo. However, his friendly, easy and helpful manner and attitude quickly enabled him to gain the respect of just about everybody. The impact Doug made in the neighborhood was significant because he may have been the first blond male who had dared not only to enter it but to actually be making a living from helping its youth. The Paisano Projects in those days were inhabited almost exclusively by Mexican-Americans and Anglos simply had no reason to ever go there.

But Doug appeared at Unit 2 one day and during the course of the year or so that he spent there, he left a deep impression on many of the boys with whom he worked. I was one of those boys and I was profoundly impressed by two characteristics possessed by Doug and that were previously virtually unknown to me. The first was his commitment to a college education. I was thirteen years old and had no appreciation for what college was. He was the first to show me how one's schooling can continue beyond high school. And he convinced me that there was significant value in in such additional education. The second characteristic that impressed me was his commitment to a career in social work. Doug really wanted to help society and apparently was then in the final year of his quest to receive a degree in Social Work. Even at that tender age, I recall feeling a sense of gratitude that people like Doug were willing to help kids like me. It further amazed me that guys like Doug seemed to be genuinely happy doing that for a living.

Eloiso De Avila, the previously mentioned "Menso," remembers Doug as a great baseball coach who taught him how to be a pretty good second-baseman. I know he was pretty good because he always was the guy against whom I competed for that position in the Pony League baseball team and he always managed to beat me. He also remembers Doug as a model of respect and courtesy. One day, when the coach of Eloiso's team—a resident of the Projects and father of a teammate—showed up late and drunk for a game, Doug took over as Coach. When it was Eloiso's turn to bat, the drunken coach showed up, stood behind the backstop and without knowing what was happening on the field, instructed Eloiso to bunt. Eloiso did as instructed and was promptly put out at first base and the game was lost. Immediately afterward, Doug summoned Eloiso over and gave him another lesson that Eloiso would never forget. Without denigrating the drunken coach, Doug told Eloiso that he should always listen to whatever his coach tells him but that he should not have listened to him that night. Doug had every right to lambast the drunken coach but he did not. Doug was simply too respectful to ever do any such thing.

Sal "Chichi" Garcia, another Club member during Doug's tenure, was deeply inspired by Doug who caused him to test the limits of his abilities like no one else had done before. Doug took a group of boys to a trampoline center one afternoon to teach them how to do mid-air somersaults. Doug was a gymnast and he taught by example. He would demonstrate how to do a single somersault and a double somersault and would then ask each boy to do the same. Eventually, Doug had taught them all to do a single somersault but only Sal could do a double. Then Doug challenged Sal to do a triple. He wanted Sal to be the very best. Sal hesitated but Doug assured him he could do it. Finally, Sal took the jump. Unfortunately, he was not able to stay centered on the trampoline and as he came out of his third somersault in mid-air, his feet went through the springs that held the trampoline to the frame. As his skinny legs passed through the springs, they tore the flesh off of one of his shins and when he finally came to rest, he saw that his flesh was all gathered near his knee like "the rolled lid of a sardine can." The injury eventually healed but Sal will never forget this particular test of his skills or the coach who encouraged and assured him that he could do it.

Doug Cooper's tour of duty at Unit 2 came to an end in the summer of 1962. To his credit, the success of Unit 2 was remarkable and he clearly laid the foundation for more successes in the individual boys he mentored.

Alfonso Velarde

Mr. D was very ably assisted at Unit 2 by a staff member named Alfonso (Al) Velarde. The neighborhood—in the usual enigmatic way--assigned him the nickname of "Pelón" which can mean "baldie" or "hairy." In his case, it could not have meant "baldie" since he had a full head of hair.

Al Velarde was also somewhat of a rarity since he too was on the verge then of completing the requirements for a degree from *Texas Western College*. Al quickly gained the trust and friendship of the members as well as of the parents. Under the supervision of Mr. D and Al Velarde, Unit 2 became a beehive of boy-related activities.

John Maddox

John Maddox was another staff member at Unit 2 who had been brought in by Mr. D. He had previously been a close friend of Mr. D and was somewhat older than most other staff members. Unlike other staff members, John was not a college student, was relatively small in stature, was pale blue-eyed and his face seemed to always be suffering from a nasty sun burn.

John also happened to be disabled. He walked with a pronounced limp and his left arm was permanently bent at the wrist and elbow so that his left fist was always pressed against his left breast. His left arm was almost completely useless. Despite all that, John was an avid softball player. He played on teams and he coached baseball as well as softball teams at the Club. His favorite position was pitcher. He would jam his baseball glove under his disabled left arm and pitch the ball with his perfectly normal right arm. As the ball reached the batter, John would insert his right hand into the baseball glove and wait for the batter to swing the bat. He was always ready to field any ball hit back in his direction. When that happened, he would catch the ball with his glove, place the glove and ball under his left arm, remove the ball from the glove with his good right arm and then throw it to first base to put the runner out. I saw him do that effectively many times.

When it came time to bat, John would do that with one arm. He obviously was not a power hitter but could regularly hit hot grounders. Because of that nasty limp in one of his legs, he could not reach base in a great hurry. But despite all of that, his batting average was no worse than that of most of the other players. I will never forget how muscular and hairy his good arm was. It had obviously served him well over many years.

As a staff member, he would occasionally have to spend time supervising activities inside the main room of the Club where the pool tables and ping pong tables were in constant use by members. Every staff member had to go through a rite of passage whereby he would have to show everyone present that he could play any of those games as well as or better than the next guy. It was an interesting sight to see him playing ping pong but he was quite a good player despite his handicap. He was an even better billiards player. He would stretch his disabled left arm so that his permanently clenched left fist would rest on the edge of the table. Then he would align his shots by aiming the cue stick as it rested on the table alongside his left fist. John was as competitive as most and it was always inspiring to see him playing all of the different games offered at the Club.

John Maddox was also extremely quiet. I do not think he ever initiated conversations with anyone. But he had the perfect temperament for the position that he held. He and Mr. D got along beautifully and, eventually, John too gained the respect of all Club kids as well as the parents.

Lane Windsor Smith

I had greatly admired and respected Doug Cooper and believed strongly that his contributions had been of a level of significance that seemed to me unlikely to ever be matched. Yet, a few years after Doug left, Lane Smith came along and proceeded to leave an even greater impression.

Lane was born in Atlanta, Georgia, on April 27, 1937. His father's job got the family transferred temporarily to El Paso while Lane was very young. But when his father and family moved on, Lane stayed to live in El Paso with his grandmother until he graduated from Austin High School in 1955. As he grew up, he managed to become extremely proficient in Spanish. Following his graduation, he enrolled at *Texas Western College* majoring in Inter-American Studies with a minor in Spanish.

While studying at *Texas Western College* in 1958, a friend, Clark Knowlton, introduced Lane to Sal Ramirez, the Assistant Director of the *El Paso Boys' Club*. Sal, who Lane remembers as a "master manipulator," saw in Lane a huge opportunity for the Club. Sal knew that Lane was the nephew of a wealthy and prominent El Paso businessman, R. B. Price of *Price's Dairy*, who could bring pecuniary value to the Club. Sal also could see that Lane's fluency in Spanish could be a great communications tool for working with

Club boys. So, Sal hired Lane as an Assistant Director at the main unit, Unit 1. His main work project at the time was to assist with a Juvenile Delinquency Study that involved corroboration between *Texas Western College* and the Boys' Club.

Lane continued as an Assistant Director at Unit 1 until the summer of 1964 when the new Executive Director, Mr. Lothridge, appointed him Unit 2 Director to succeed Mr. D. Apparently, some friction developed between Mr. D and Sal Ramirez and Mr. D decided to leave. Lane had just completed his requirements for his BA.

Lane was a very fair-complexioned person with platinum blond hair and blue eyes who also, because of his appearance, stuck out in the neighborhood like a pearl in a bed of coal. He was occasionally called "Güero" which is a common and generally inoffensive Spanish nickname for a person with a fair complexion. Simply because of his physical characteristics, he seemed to attract a lot of attention. I remember him also having a receding hairline even though at the time he had to be in his mid to late-20s. He seemed destined to be totally bald by the time he was 30 and, for that reason, I remember feeling sorry for him.

More importantly, the Spanish that Lane learned to speak while growing up was perfect barrio Spanish without any trace of an Anglo accent. As likable as Lane was, we the kids feared that simply because of his "extreme" Anglo appearance, he did not have a prayer in ever establishing credibility in the Projects. However, because of his excellent Spanish, he managed to completely overcome the disadvantage of his appearance. In fact, his ability to very comfortably be multi-cultural gained him enormous respect because in those days, people with that ability were extremely rare.

Lane had the perfect personality for being a Boys' Club professional. He was a very cool, calm and collected individual. Even though the Boys' Club afforded an inordinately high number of opportunities to do so, I never saw him lose his temper. On the contrary; he always seemed to be in a good mood. He had a great sense of humor and his laughter was loud and contagious.

Lane was an excellent counselor because he was patient and very deliberate in everything that he did. He never panicked in a crisis and always had time to smile and relax. The thing I probably liked the most about Lane was his genuineness. He was blunt and honest in his dealings with everyone even though sometimes he told you things you really didn't want to hear. I learned a lot from him about life, relationships with girls, getting along with peers, and perseverance. He also taught me a lot about respecting and admiring my own Dad. I always wanted to be as genuine and consistent as Lane was.

At the time that he worked at the Club, Lane was a married man. I can't recall his wife's name but I do recall that she was extremely attractive. One time, Lane invited me and a few of the other members of the Club to come to his home for barbecued burgers, or "hangabers" as his kids called them. I was very impressed with the house that he had in the foothills of Mount Franklin but I was most impressed by his family. They could have been the subjects of the cover of *Family Life* magazine. His two kids were probably five and six years old at the time and they looked like little "mini-Lanes." Both were as blond and blue-eyed as Lane and, interestingly, they had names similar to his: Laney Jr. and Lee Ann. I remember looking at his family and his overall situation and wishing that I should ever be so lucky.

There are a few specific memories that I have that involve Lane. The first memory is of his first day at Unit 2. As soon as he arrived, he went to the main room of the Club where a pool game was going on. The pool players and all the others present seemed to stare uncontrollably at Lane's extreme Caucasian-ness. The two guys playing offered to let Lane play with them. As Lane was lining up his cue stick to take a shot, one of them made a slightly disparaging remark in barrio Spanish about Lane. The other guys watching the game softly chuckled at the remark. Lane did not react at all but proceeded to make his shot. In the course of the game, other similarly condescending or even offensive remarks were made by some of the guys also in barrio Spanish and, as with the first such remark, Lane did not react at all. Lane proceeded to run all the balls in and never gave the other guys a chance to take even one more shot. The other players and everyone else watching were clearly impressed with Lane's pool-playing ability, but they were even more impressed when at the end of the game *in absolutely perfect barrio Spanish* he thanked his opponents for giving him a chance to play and told them that he looked forward to working with them there at the Club.

Another memory that I have of Lane involves the car that he used to own. On his first day of work at Unit 2 he arrived in one of the coolest looking *Volkswagen* beetles that I've ever seen. What made it unusual was the striking metallic emerald green paint job on the car. It was simply beautiful. On many Saturday mornings thereafter, he would wash and wax his car as it was parked in the shade of some trees right in front of the Boys' Club. He did it in such a caring and meticulous way that eventually I felt a strong desire to learn how to do that. Eventually, I found myself washing and waxing his car. It was a mutually satisfying arrangement since I enjoyed doing the work and he always would pay me for doing it.

The final memory that lingers in my mind about Lane revolves around a touch football game. One Saturday morning in the fall when the smell of pigskin was permeating the air, we gathered a small group of guys and started to play touch football at the playground. We were short one player and so we invited Lane to join our team. The team consisted of three players. On one particular set of plays I was the quarterback. I gathered the other two players in front of me as I had my back to the scrimmage line and, in a soft voice, I told one of them to run long and deep for a pass. I then told Lane to hike the ball and to remain "stationary." For some reason, Lane found it humorous to hear the word "stationary" come out of my mouth on the football field. He couldn't stop laughing for the remainder of the game. And for the remainder of my life I have never stopped recalling how he kidded me about my vocabulary while at the same time complimenting me for having it.

Lane eventually moved to the Dallas, Texas, area but we were able to stay in touch with one another throughout the years. He split up with his first wife some years ago and remarried. His current wife, Pam, is a church minister who actually presided over my brother Nacho's and his second bride Athena's wedding. A few years ago, Lane and his wife moved to Port Townsend, Washington, where she was assigned a new congregation. Lane is currently in the business of buying and recycling obsolete technology and continues to be at the very top of my list of most admired people and closest friends. Incidentally, his receding hairline really didn't move back very much in the ensuing 40 odd years that I have known him.

Eddie Haddon

Eddie Haddon was hired by Lane Smith as a staff member at Unit 2 shortly after Lane became the Director. Eddie was the first African-American staff member at the Boys' Club and the first African-American that I and the rest of the Club members ever associated with in any significant way. He also was a student at *Texas Western College*.

Even though Eddie was a quiet and extremely friendly person, some of the older Club members found reasons to dislike him. Lane Smith recalled for me one occasion when a scary confrontation occurred on the playground. He distinctly remembers that it was a racially motivated issue. As was true in the rest of the US, some of the kids at the Club somehow learned to be hostile to African-Americans for no reason other than the color of their skin. Lane managed to diffuse the situation and over time, Eddie was able to establish himself as an effective staff member. I know that I really liked and respected Eddie as did most of the other kids.

Lorenzo Candelaria

Lorenzo Candelaria is a name that would have to appear in a list of the top five people to have had a profound influence in my life. The year was 1961. I was a freshman in high school. I was working evenings at the *El Paso Boys' Club* Unit 2. My main responsibility was to record the member number of each person who entered the club in the evening from 7:00 until 9:00 PM. I, in turn, was supervised by staff members who were either professional social workers or college students working part time. Lorenzo was one of those part time college students.

Lorenzo was in the *Reserve Officer's Training Corps* (ROTC) organization at *Texas Western College*. For that reason, once a week he would actually have to wear his ROTC uniform while he attended classes. Since he went immediately to work at the Boys' Club after his classes, he would have to wear his uniform as he was acting as a supervisor at the Club. Lorenzo's military uniform was the most impeccable that I had ever seen. And the most impressive aspect of his uniform was his spit-shined shoes. He had achieved a shine on those shoes that was the closest thing to glass that I had ever seen.

I had joined high school ROTC that same year. I also had to wear a uniform to school once a week as part of my high school ROTC program. When I saw Lorenzo in his uniform, I knew then that I had to learn from him all of the secrets that were manifested in his military appearance. And so, one day I asked him to teach me how to spit-shine my shoes. He was more than happy to oblige.

His secret was really no secret. He showed me how to take a soft cloth, wrap it tightly around my right index finger, touch the tip of that cloth-wrapped finger to my tongue (to coat it with my saliva (spit)), and then to rub it gently in a can of shoe wax before finally applying it to the shoe in small areas in a tiny circular pattern. This method of spit-shining shoes is not a great secret. He did tell me, however, that the reason most people do not succeed in achieving the glass-like results, is because most people do not have the patience required. He taught me then--and through 30+ years of experience I can now confirm--that in order for shoes to really shine like the sun, you must diligently go through the process described above over and over and over at least for one hour.

It was not long thereafter, that I started to impress everyone in my school with my spit-shined shoes. I was asked repeatedly to teach my classmates how to spit-shine shoes. And I did. But no one seemed willing to invest the required time, and therefore their results never compared to mine. Pretty soon, the promotions started to come my way. Eventually, after participating in the ROTC program for four years, and for excelling in various aspects of the program--not the least important of which is properly shined shoes--I rose to the number two spot in the Jr. ROTC program in the City of El Paso. Whenever I appeared in uniform, people were not likely to comment about my extremely short haircut, or my crisply pressed uniform, or my highly polished decorations; but invariably, people would ask me how I got my shoes to shine so much.

In September of 1965, I started my freshman year at *Texas A&M University*. I joined the Corps of Cadets and shortly after my arrival, I could sense that the ability to spit-shine shoes would carry me far in that environment as well.

You must remember that in those days, patent leather shoes were practically unheard of. Nevertheless, it was expected that your military shoes, particularly if you were a freshman, had to look better than patent leather. Mine did.

One of the traditions at Texas A&M was that upperclassmen had the right to delegate punishment to freshman ("fish") whenever a freshman committed an infraction. The two most popular forms of punishment were push-ups and having to spit-shine that upperclassmen's shoes. Apparently, some enterprising freshman had earlier devised a method of cheating on spit-shining of shoes. He concocted a solution of sugar and water that, if applied to a pair of shoes and permitted to dry properly, would give the appearance of a very good spit shine. The biggest advantage of this--assuming that you could get away with it--was that you could spit-shine someone's shoes with sugar water in ten or fifteen minutes, whereas, if you did it the proper way, it would take you one to two hours.

One day, I got in trouble with an upperclassman. I don't recall what I did wrong, but he took me to his room found a very dirty pair of military shoes and handed them to me for a spit-shine. I took them and—despite having lots of homework to complete--worked diligently for two hours to apply an authentic glass-like, spit-shine finish to them. I took them back to him and presented them proudly. He looked at them, concluded that no one could have possibly done a legitimate spit-shine in so little time, then declared that I had cheated by using sugar water, and made me do 100 pushups on the spot. I had no choice but to comply. I have never in my life been more disappointed with the reception that I got for my work.

Eventually, I got my revenge. At the end of my freshman year at A&M, I was selected as the "Best Drilled Fish" in my company. This was and probably still is a coveted honor. The guy that had won it the year before was none other than Henry Cisneros. (Henry went on to become US Secretary of Housing and Urban Development under President Bill Clinton.) The upperclassman who had questioned my ability to spit-shine shoes came to me then and congratulated me for having been selected as "Best Drilled Fish." He then apologized saying that he realized now that that job that I had done on his shoes months earlier had been, in fact, a legitimate spit-shine. I smiled graciously, tightened my butt and suggested to him that maybe he should now give *me* 100 push-ups. He smiled back and told me to go to hell.

In July of 1966, I was enrolled as a Plebe (first year cadet) at West Point. Because of my skills at spit-shining shoes, I immediately made a huge impression on my classmates, who generally had not the foggiest idea of how to shine shoes, let alone how to spit-shine them. I spent lots of time teaching my classmates and when the time came to recognize leadership skills, many of them paid me back by saying that I was indeed a gifted leader of men. If you think about it, there are very few ways that you can distinguish yourself as a leader of men when you're just starting out as a Plebe. Knowing how to spit-shine shoes has got to be one of the best ways.

I regret having to admit it, but I no longer spit-shine my shoes. It seems that the casual look has taken hold not only in society in general, but even in corporate America. It's a shame that this wonderful tradition has also come to pass in the military. It seems to me that everyone who needs to have glass-like shoes in the military--including West Point-- is now permitted to wear patent leather shoes. What a shame.

One of these days, I want to look up Lorenzo Candelaria and thank him for what he did for me. I'll never be able to fully assess the real value of anything in my life, but I believe that the ability to spit-shine shoes helped me immensely during my years in high school, college and in the military.

Ben Rodríguez

As mentioned earlier, Unit 1 of the Boys' Club was located in South El Paso where all of the kids who lived there aspired to go--and indeed went--to *Bowie High School*. The neighborhoods there were fiercely loyal to and supportive of Bowie High. Unit 2, however, was in the Paisano Projects which was the territory of *Jefferson High School*. Over the years, an intense rivalry evolved between those two schools and those two neighborhoods.

Ben Rodriguez had to be the most courageous staff member to ever work at the El Paso Boys' Club. He was a graduate of Bowie High and a celebrated football player there, but somehow, he ended up getting assigned to work at Unit 2. He was a student at *Texas Western College* during the day and, every afternoon or evening after classes, he would report to work to develop, inspire and train Boys' Clubbers. Working at Unit 2, he was a Bowie High "Bear" in the land of the Jefferson High "Foxes." He was also the 1960's version of an "in your face" young man. When he came to work at Unit 2, every day he would wear his navy-blue and white Bowie High letterman's' jacket that he earned playing football and he would strut around defying anyone to do something about that.

Ben was not huge but he was extremely strong, quick and athletic. In the 60's, whenever we went to a barber shop, we would see hanging on the wall, an artist's renditions of the popular haircuts. One in particular that stands out in my mind was the image of the "flat top with fenders." Ben's head was shaped perfectly for that cut and he wore it proudly. And usually he simply wore a crew neck white T shirt under his letterman jacket. Whenever there was a commotion on the playground or in the game room, he would jump into the fray to restore order. He was not well-liked but was universally feared and respected. All of the sports-oriented boys at the Club could not get enough of his aggressive and competitive techniques. For all these reasons he was incredibly valuable to Unit 2 and probably an excellent staff member. But I knew that he was very different from me and so I did not get a lot of inspiration from him. He clearly was a very successful young man but probably had achieved his success through the force and violence of football. I knew even then that my preferred approach was through reason and gentility. But I respected how he had used his athletic skills to advance his education and, in that regard, he set a fine example for me and I'm sure for many of the other kids of Unit 2.

Mr. Jesús Reza

Mr. Jesús Reza was not actually a staff member of the Boys' Club but was the father of 3 Reza boys who were members of Unit 2 between 1959 and 1966 (Jesús "Chuy" Reza, Jr., Sergio "Checo" Reza and Homer "Chacho" Reza). Mr. Reza, in my mind, is the greatest symbol of how a large number of forces converged in our neighborhood in those days to create the perfect environment for the development of boys.

Mr. Reza brought his family from Mexico to El Paso in the mid 1950's. Because he immigrated in search of a better life for his family, he was in many ways just like most of the dads that lived in our neighborhood. But he was very different in one particular way: Mr. Reza, until recently, had been a professional baseball player. How fortunate were we? At a time when baseball essentially consumed us, we were incredibly lucky to have as a neighbor someone who played the sport at the same level that Willie Mays, Mickey Mantle and Yogi Berra played.

Mr. Reza played 7 seasons of professional baseball as a 3d baseman or shortstop between 1940 and 1949. He played in the Mexican League each of those years except in 1947 when he played for the *El Paso Texans* in the Arizona-Texas League. He maintained a .281 batting average during his short career. Mr. Reza's greatest professional accomplishment came in 1944 when he played for *La Esperanza* who won the National Championship in Mexico.

During his baseball career and afterward, Mr. Reza's nickname was "La Borrachita." It was a moniker given him by his older brother, Francisco, although no one seems to know why in particular he got that nickname.

Mr. Reza was employed in a variety of jobs while he and his family lived in the Paisano Projects, including concession vending at entertainment venues such as the *El Paso Coliseum*, the *Washington Park Zoo* and *Kidd Field*, the *Texas Western College* football stadium. Nevertheless, he made time to take on the role of manager of many baseball teams that were formed at the Boys' Club Unit 2. A generation of boys there played Little League, Pony League and Babe Ruth League baseball under the guidance of Mr. Reza and learned to love the game. During various summers in the early 1960's, he coordinated games between the Boys' Club teams and teams that he knew of from across the border in Juárez, Mexico. The games were played in Juárez or at the modest Boys' Club playground and when they played at the Boys' Club, it seemed that the entire population of the Paisano Projects would turn out to support the local team. These events were huge. I remember playing in one such game and facing Juárez pitchers who seemed to be older and bigger than us. Yet we competed well and learned to play the game at a substantially higher level than we otherwise would have. Mr. Reza's contribution to the development of the boys of Unit 2 was profound because he influenced us in so many ways. He was a world class ball player, a beloved father, a fine neighbor and a great coach. It was truly fortuitous for us to have had him around when we were growing up.

Mi Papá and Mr. Reza happened to be great friends as were Mrs. Reza and mi Mamá. My best chum in those days was Checo Reza and the best chum of my older brother, Nacho, happened to be Chuy Reza. The connection between our two families was deep and strong and despite the many years that have passed, it remains that way even now. Mr. Reza died tragically in a car accident in 1968 at the age of 52. His role as a father and coach is remembered even today by his children, grandchildren and their friends through a yearly golf outing that began in 2009 and is called "La Borrachita."

And so, from the summer of 1959 until the summer of 1960, life was quite alright for me. The Boys' Club had become firmly established under Mr. D and the exceptional members of his staff. The Boys' Club, with all of its programs, was proving to be a fantastic place to hang out. During those years, I formed friendships that even now remain strong and meaningful. I felt lucky beyond words to be a part of all that was happening there. Only the wildest optimists could have predicted that the benefits of opening Unit 2 would have been as great as they turned out to be during that nascent period. From the perspective of a kid who lived through that beginning, life in the Projects had become almost dreamlike. I—like most of my peers—could not understand how living there could in any way be termed "disadvantaged." We were having the time of our lives.

Time to Move Again-Return to the Paisano Project

And so, in the summer of 1961, my family ended the year-long failed restaurant-effort, *Las Cazuelas*, which I mentioned in an earlier chapter, and moved back to the Paisano Projects. This time our address was 3922 East Paisano Drive, Apartment 3. This apartment actually faced Paisano Drive which was a six-lane highway. We had a nice, two-bedroom apartment once again with a little grassy park directly in front of the apartment that provided a buffer against the traffic noise. I firmly believe that my entire family was delighted to be back in the Projects again.

During the year that we lived in the restaurant, Nacho and I continued as members of the Boys' Club Unit 2 but certainly not as actively as during the previous year. As soon as we were moved into our new apartment on Paisano Drive, Nacho and I--and even mi Papá and mi Mamá--resumed the very high level of participation in Club activities that we had enjoyed before moving away. Mi Papá also returned to his sales job at the Lighthouse.

Unit 3

The early 1960's were, without doubt, a time of great prosperity for the *El Paso Boys' Club*. Unit 1, in the heart of El Paso's Second Ward had become a firmly established venue for developing productive boys and could proudly claim that it was home to 1961's *Boys' Clubs of America* National Boy of the Year, Richard Lopez. Unit 2, in the Paisano Projects, was also in full operation and was also providing pretty solid guidance in moving boys away from delinquency. Mr. O. D. Hightower and his staff had somehow cracked the code on how to bring out the best in South El Paso boys, and the results of their work had thus far been good enough to attract national attention. It became logical and extremely desirable for the Boys' Club to expand to still other neighborhoods in town that could benefit from what it offered.

Once again, the *El Paso Housing Authority,* through its Executive Director, Raymond Pitts--who was also still a member of *El Paso Boys' Club* Board of Directors--proposed that another Unit of the Boys' Club could be opened in another of the city's housing projects. The approach had been tried and proven successful when Unit 2 was opened in the Paisano Projects so why not duplicate it at the Tays Housing Project also located in South El Paso roughly between the locations of Unit 1 and Unit 2.

Thus, in June, 1962—exactly 3 years after Unit 2 was opened—Unit 3 opened its doors at 2035 Cypress Ave. The Unit was staffed by John Jimerson, James Harrison and Ralph Fierro, and by October of that year had enrolled 238 boys.

I recall when the announcement was made that a new Unit had opened and I even recall going to it a few times for ball games but aside from that, neither I nor any of my friends at Unit 2 had any contact with that Unit.

In 1963, Danny Hightower, son of Mr. O. D. Hightower, became the Unit 3 Director and I started to notice that boys from Unit 3 were joining the rest of us from Units 1 and 2 in activities such as the Jr. Toastmasters. Eventually, Unit 3 started to function very much like the rest of the *El Paso Boys' Club* and even began to produce its own nominees for the *Boys' Clubs of America* "Boy of the Year" competition. And so, as the *El Paso Boys' Club* moved into what I believe was the zenith of its operational years, it was organized into 3 fine units located in some of the most troubled sections of the city and led by an incredibly dedicated staff under the extraordinarily insightful guidance of Mr. O. D. Hightower.

Chapter 8- My Years as a Club Member

Once again, as I attempt to describe what it was like to be a member of the *El Paso Boys' Club* in the early sixties, I am fortunate to be able to do so from first-hand experience. I was a member of the *El Paso Boys' Club* from the summer of 1959--just before I entered the seventh grade--until I graduated from high school in May, 1965. Those six years encompassed the most formative period of my life. I did not think then that there was anything terribly unpleasant or even unusual about growing up in the Projects and hanging out at the Boys' Club with the kids in my neighborhood and about going to the different schools there. Yet, there was no doubt in my mind that this was not paradise. Good things could indeed happen to those that called the Projects their home but lots of bad things could also happen. I have to believe that I was extremely lucky not because I survived the experience but because those years and what happened to me and many others like me, energized, strengthened and ultimately propelled us to safe and productive lives.

The experiences that I will recount below are unique because they happened to me. But most of them involved institutions or organizations or simply activities where other boys like me probably did very similar things. I look back and have to conclude that, one way or another, all of these experiences molded me to some degree and made me a better person. I feel compelled to write about them for many reasons, not the least significant of which is to acknowledge the roles played by all those men, women and other kids and to express my gratitude to them. In recalling those days, I will start with the amazing friendships that I was so fortunate to make then and to still enjoy even to this day.

Sergio Rolando Reza

This chapter about the Boys' Club has to begin with Sergio Rolando Reza, affectionately known to all as "Checo." Checo is the one guy who has been a constant "best friend" from 1958 until the present. In 1958, when I was 11 and he was 12, we became friends because we both lived on Webber Way in the Paisano Projects.

Checo was--and still is--an incredibly likable person. As a kid, everybody seemed to get along with him and wanted to associate with him. He was a funny kid with an almost professional ability and talent to entertain others. He could impersonate contemporary singers in both English and Spanish but would add a comedic dimension as he mimicked their moves that sometimes made him better to watch than the figure he was impersonating. He had a very fine sense of timing and rhythm that enabled him to dance the latest steps as well as anyone in the neighborhood. As a result, he never had any trouble finding a partner to dance with at the Friday night dances. He has, even today, an amazing ability to not only talk like certain famous people but also to walk like them and to recreate their moves instantly and incredibly faithfully. If you give a microphone to Checo, you are guaranteed to be laughing raucously soon thereafter from the antics and sounds that he will be only too happy to generate.

Around 1959, when the Boys' Club opened in the Paisano Projects, he was one of the kids that the adult staff members looked to when they needed to bring other boys to the Club. Eventually, he even got a job at the Club as a junior staff member. Once he had that salaried position ($1 for 3 hours of work per day) and because he and I were best friends, he hired me as one of his two assistants. And so, at one time, I actually worked *for* him. We had a ball during that era because even though the pay was low (my pay was fifty cents a day for 3 hours work) we got lots of substantial fringe benefits that were really quite valuable. For instance, as his assistant, I got preferential treatment when he was passing out government surplus food to club members. Then, when the local blue jean factories would donate overages or seconds to the Club, Checo would arrange so that I and his other assistants could get first pick.

The work-related experiences that Checo and I had at the Boys' Club were positive and priceless. For at least a year, he and the two assistants that he hired, were responsible for keeping track of all the boys who entered the Club and also for keeping the Club clean. I was one of those assistants; Ramon ("Mon") Gonzales was the other. The chain-link swinging gate that surrounded the Club and the huge double doors of the recreation hall would open at 4PM on weekdays and 1PM on Saturdays. On weekdays it would close for an hour at 6PM then re-open at 7PM and close at 9PM. My job was the one I described earlier: to sit at the entrance on a little wooden school desk and circle on a form the dog tag (membership) number of each kid that walked in during the 7-9PM shift. Other responsibilities included maintaining order and discipline in the game room (where pool, billiards and Ping-Pong tables were set up), answering the phone and assisting the senior staff members. Immediately after the Club closed at 9PM each night, the junior staff--which included Checo, Zekie Chavira, Guadalupe Saldaña, Jr. and me--would fold all of the tan-colored *Samsonite* metal chairs in the game room and stack them on the billiards table which had been covered with a protective furniture pad. Then Checo would sweep the entire building with a huge 3-foot-wide dust mop. I would then wet mop the entire place while Zekie and the others cleaned the toilets. We would be completely finished by

9:30PM. It was an incredibly efficient team effort and a whole lot of fun as well.

Checo's Dad, the former professional baseball player, became active in organizing youth baseball teams at the Boys' Club and in the neighborhood. Because of our common ages, Checo and I were always in the same teams. Sometimes, his Dad was our coach and we always had a great time in those leagues. Checo and I were never the best players on those teams but we were good enough to feel like real players most of the time and not just like bench warmers.

As the seasons changed, he and I together would move to different sports such as basketball and touch football but still end up in the same team. Our most memorable team was *The Gladiators*. From the time that we were 12 until we were 14, we played various sports as *Gladiators*. Other members of that team included Rodolfo ("Popo") Garcia, Sammy ("Bala") Saldaña, Daniel ("Pelusa") Miranda, and others whose names escape me for now. But Checo and I were constants in those teams and together, we learned a lot, won our share of games and trophies and had tons of fun.

One event that stands out in my mind is when Checo may have saved the life of his infant little brother, Tony. It occurred on a warm summer night in 1960. The baseball field bleachers in the playground were jammed to capacity to watch the Boys' Club baseball team play a team from Juárez. Lots of neighborhood families had come out to support the local boys. On the lowest bleacher row at the extreme first base side of that row, Mrs. Reza (Checo's Mom) sat with the rest of her younger kids. She had even brought her new baby, Tony, who lay sleeping in a carriage right next to the bleacher seat occupied by Mrs. Reza. Checo and I were in the Boys' Club team but we both happened to be on the bench, which was in a covered ground-level dugout along the first base line. In the middle of the game, since he was not likely to see any action, Checo left the dugout to go chat with his Mom. While he was chatting, a ball was fouled back and high toward the bleachers. Checo was not watching the game at that moment but as soon as he realized that a foul ball was high up in the air and potentially could hurt someone in the bleachers, he instinctively got up and stooped his body over Tony's carriage. We all watched the foul ball go up and then start to come down. Checo remained in his protective crouched position over Tony and waited for the ball to land never really thinking that it would land close to him. The ball came down very hard and just happened to land squarely and very forcefully right in the middle of Checo's back. It knocked the wind out of him and gave him a huge welt but he kept that ball from hitting Tony. This act was pure

Checo. He always thought of others first and he always felt protective of others, particularly younger kids and especially his brothers.

In addition to athletics teams, Checo and I joined all of the same clubs and activities within the Boys' Club, such as the Jr. Toastmasters, Arts and Crafts, Talent Shows and boxing. We were always together and we never had any disagreements about anything.

Since Checo's parents and my parents were also very good friends, I was frequently at Checo's house--or he was at mine--and my parents always trusted his family whenever I was with them. Checo also was there with his dad's green 1958 Ford station wagon whenever I needed a ride or whenever I needed to borrow it.

Our friendship grew even stronger from the jobs that he and I took as ball chasers for the *El Paso Sun Kings,* that minor league baseball team that played at *Dudley Field,* and as popcorn and peanut vendors at the *El Paso Coliseum* or at *Kidd Field.* Again, the disadvantage of living in the Projects with all of these public entertainment and sports venues almost in our back yards, became a positive setting for the neighborhood boys to learn responsibility and to make a few bucks.

At school, Checo was one year behind me even though he was one year older. That happened because his family immigrated when he was in grade school and, as was customary, he was set back two years in school. Nevertheless, because we were such pals in high school, we joined the same extracurricular activities whenever we could. One of those activities was the *Jefferson High School* band. He and I would be partners whenever we did anything with the band. He was extremely well-liked among students in general but he was by far the most popular boy in the band. He also played in the B-Team (Jr. Varsity football team) where he excelled as a linebacker. That was one of the few activities that we did not take up together. I was simply not willing to risk getting hurt playing football (i.e. I was too scared!) He, however, was fearless and, in fact, ended up breaking his leg one season while playing and therefore had to sit it out.

Then of course, there are the many experiences that we had as we transformed ourselves from boys to men. Everything that I knew about girls and sex during those formative years came from close friends like Checo. He provided me with tons of information about how to form a relationship with a girl and because he was so successful at doing that, I listened carefully. He was fortunate in that he was a good-looking young man and girls naturally were attracted to him. In addition, his personality was extremely charming and so friends, particularly girls, flocked to him. He never had any trouble finding dates and so when I needed advice regarding girls, I would go to him. The playground at the Paisano Projects--particularly at night--was the site where either through war stories or girly magazines or other communications between us or through actual interaction (Spin the Bottle) with our young female friends of the neighborhood, Checo and I together took great strides forward toward manhood.

The reason why Checo ranks as my closest lifetime friend is simple: He was there and shared with me the most exciting adventures during the most impressionable times of our lives. Not only did he share them with me, but he personally enhanced them to such a degree as to make them priceless memories. I will now try to share some of them.

Clearly the most memorable shared event was when he took a knife in the belly as we were serenading mothers on Mothers' Day in 1963. Anytime that someone experiences an event during which a close friend narrowly escapes with his life, the experience is bound to always remain vivid and will greatly strengthen any bond.

The great service provided by the Boys' Club thus far had started to give members of our community a sense of comfort and security that previously had never been felt. Juvenile decency seemed to be the rule rather than the exception and everyone's expectations for the future were decidedly bright. Nevertheless, every so often, something would happen in the neighborhood that would remind everyone that juvenile delinquency had not disappeared altogether.

This particular incident occurred at dawn on Mother's Day, May 3, 1963. It involved a number of Boys' Club members including myself. We were in high school having relatively pleasant and successful times. The reason we were out that fateful morning was fund-raising. We were all members of the *Linguistic Jr. Toastmasters Club*, an activity within the Boys' Club dedicated to teaching boys how to speak in public. [In a subsequent chapter I go into more detail about what the *Jr. Toastmasters Club* was all about.] At any rate, the *Jr. Toastmasters* had competed earlier in the spring in Optimist Club Oratorical contests and had been very successful. One of us had made the regional finals in San Francisco and the *Jr. Toastmasters* decided to raise enough money so that all of us could go. Since many of us were also members of our school bands, someone proposed that we form a small band and serenade Mothers in our neighborhood on Mothers' Day for a small fee.

There is a Mother's Day tradition in Mexico by which sons, daughters and/or husbands express their love for their mother/wife by hiring a professional musical group to sing to (or serenade) her on this special day. By tradition, the songs are sung outside at the front door or beneath the bedroom window of the woman-honoree right at the crack of dawn to awaken her to beautiful sounds of love. The song that is traditionally sung is called "Las Mañanitas" (or "the Little Mornings"). As kids growing up in the Mexican culture, all of the boys in the band were certainly familiar with this tradition although I honestly don't think any of us had actually seen it performed except in Mexican musical western movies of that era.

From the *Jr. Toastmasters Club,* we put together a group of around 8 of us to carry out this task. They included Checo, Ben Garcia, Julio Pellicano, Joe Renteria, Bernie Del Hierro, Manny and Javier Alvarez and me. Manny Alvarez and his brother Javier provided a medium-sized flatbed truck from their father's produce business to transport the group from house to house as we did the serenading. The plan was to load all the musicians on the truck at 4:45AM, drive to the first house, park the truck in front, unload the musicians, scramble to the front door or bedroom window, play "Las Mañanitas" for no more than 3 minutes, retreat to the truck, load back up and drive to the next house.

For weeks in advance of Mother's Day, we had approached sons, daughters and fathers in the neighborhood and offered to do the serenade for $5. We had figured that we could only do the serenading from around 5AM until 7AM. After 7AM, surely no mother would still be asleep. We calculated that by properly planning the route so that we minimized travel time, we could probably do at least twelve 3-minute serenades for a grand haul of $60. That was not a bad deal.

Everything started out exactly as planned. We did probably three or four houses in the dark and made a bunch of mothers really happy. I suspect those mothers had also never seen a real serenade except in the movies. Then the dawn came. We left one neighborhood and went to the other neighborhood nearby, the Paisano Projects, where Checo's and my family lived. As mentioned earlier, the neighborhood was called "El Diablo" ("The Devil") because it had a history of some violence. The projects were a collection of maybe 30 or 40 two-story flat roofed red brick buildings scattered within 5 or 6 city blocks. Each building had 6 apartments with 2, 3 or 4 bedrooms each. The buildings were set about 30 feet apart from each other. These spaces between buildings were called "callejones" or "alleys."

The sun was starting to peek at us over the horizon. The truck pulled into a parking lot very close to our target houses. We figured we would leave the truck there while we went on foot from house to house doing the serenading. We may have started with mi Mamá and it went well. Then we walked to two or three other homes and everything went well at those homes too.

We moved through an alley en route to the next gig. In that alley, there were two young thugs. One was nick-named "Meneo"; I have forgotten the name of the other. These guys were notorious troublemakers. They were school drop-outs; they smoked pot; they drank beer; they had been to juvenile detention homes; they had older brothers that had been in prison; etc. As the band passed through the alley, the thugs were squatted and leaning against the brick wall on one side. They each held a quart of beer. They saw us, stood up and walked to block our path. We must have looked very weird to them: we were carrying brass instruments, guitars, drums and we had put on a weak attempt at a uniform (white shirts and jeans). They were confrontational but we tried to ignore them and continued moving through the alley.

Once out of the alley, Meneo became more belligerent. He did not like the fact that we were squarely in his turf and worse than that, ignoring him. He caught up with the group and passed it and placed himself in front of us to block our path. Meneo still had the quart of beer in his hand. As he confronted our group, Meneo tried to snatch one of the musical instruments. Checo—who was admired and respected by everyone in the neighborhood-- immediately stepped up to him. Checo knew Meneo as well as any of us did and tried to tell Meneo to settle down and to quit messing with us. In less than ten seconds, more words were exchanged and Meneo suddenly dropped his beer bottle and with a small paring knife that instantly appeared in his hand, he jabbed Checo in the belly with it.

Meneo then wiped the blade between the thumb and forefinger of the other hand. He was ready to stab again. As soon as I and the other band guys saw the knife, we spread apart. Checo put his hand to his belly and then looked at his fingers. Sure enough, they were bloody. He staggered a little. One of the other band guys and I each grabbed one of Checo's arms and suspended him. We feared that Meneo--and maybe his buddy--would stab someone else so we started to back away as quickly as we could. Meneo and his bud then ran off back into the projects through the alley.

While still holding Checo up, we started to shuffle back to the parking lot where we had parked the truck. It was about a quarter mile away. The guy who had been driving the truck (Manny) saw that Checo was bleeding and so he sprinted ahead to start the truck and maybe bring it closer. There was no way to bring the truck closer, so we hauled Checo all the way there. Once we got to the truck, we put Checo on his back on the flatbed and loaded the rest of us. Manny then sped all the way to *Thomason General Hospital* which was less than two miles away.

Checo was taken in at the emergency room. We told the attendant what had happened. While we hung around waiting for news the police arrived. I told them what happened. They asked me to accompany them in the squad car right then so we could go apprehend the thugs. I asked myself whether I really wanted to be any hero in this. Given that it had been Checo who had been knifed I answered "YES" without hesitation. We went off in the squad car in search of the thugs.

By 8:30AM the cops and I were cruising the Paisano Projects. We drove slowly past one alley after another. We were concentrating in the units where I believed Meneo lived. Then we came to one alley where the two thugs and a third much younger kid were again squatting against the wall. They turned and saw the squad car and immediately broke in a run in three different directions. The squad car screeched to a halt; the cops and I jumped out and one of them told me to go after the youngest one. They took off after the other two.

I ran after the youngest one. I recognized him as a member of the Boys' Club. I caught up and while I ran even with him spoke to him. I could've jumped on him and tackled him like cops did on television but instead, I convinced him to stop. We then walked back to the squad car where the cops now had the other thugs in handcuffs. Meneo was bent over the hood. He saw me approaching and said in Spanish "They may send me up for a long time, but I'll get you when I get out." I remember feeling really bad when I heard that. All three were placed in the back of the squad car. They sped away. I stayed behind. I was very close to my house. I walked home.

Well, Meneo never got me and, of course, Checo recovered. I do remember being very scared for a few weeks because Meneo was released shortly after the incident. Eventually, time--and Mr. D--took care of everything. Mr. D, the Director of the Boys' Club Unit 2, knew all about what had happened, including that Meneo had threatened me, and, according to another staff member, Mr. D told Meneo that he would kill him if anything ever happened to me. So, I lived.

On a lighter note, one of the most pleasant memories that I have involves a prank that Salvador E. Garcia (Chichi) and I played on Checo. Chichi's stepfather, Alfonso Castillo, worked as a security guard at the local bank. Apparently, one of the employee perks that Mr. Castillo received was the use of the bank car on weeknights and weekends. At the end of each working day, when the bank car was brought to the parking lot, Mr. Castillo was able to drive it home and then back to work the next morning. After Chichi got his driver's license, his stepfather actually permitted him to borrow the car once in a while.

There was a movie theater in El Paso called the *Cactus Drive-in*. The theater-front had a spectacular--though non-moving-- neon sign of a cactus in the desert. It specialized in showing adult movies only, the type that parents did not want us watching at our age. It also charged by the person rather than by the carload. One day, Chichi was feeling daring and so he invited Checo and me to go the *Cactus Drive-in* with him in his stepfather's company car to catch an adult movie. Chichi was 17 years old, Checo was 16 and I was 15.

Chichi and I decided that we would play a prank on Checo. Prior to leaving for the movies, I got a miniature tape recorder and recorded my best impression of the voice that we occasionally used to hear at other drive-in theaters in those days. We became familiar with that voice because with great regularity, that voice would alert all movie-goers to the fact that the snack bar would close in 15 minutes. I had memorized the tone and accent of that voice and before heading out for the drive-in that day, I recorded the following statement mimicking that same voice: "Would Sergio Reza please come to the snack bar."

That night, with the miniature tape recorder in my hand, I went directly to Chichi's house and with his knowledge and participation, I hid the tape recorder under the front seat. Then we went to pick up Checo. We then drove to the *Cactus Drive-in* theater. It was way out of town. About a mile before we got there, Chichi pulled over so Checo and I could get into the trunk and thereby avoid paying. Then we proceeded to go in. Chichi paid his $1 admission and drove in slowly. Moments later, after Chichi found a parking spot, Checo and I sneaked out of the trunk. Checo took a seat in the back alone while I sat in the front next to Chichi. Then we watched the movie.

About an hour into the movie--and still about a half-hour before the snack bar was supposed to close, I reached under the seat and quietly pushed the "play" button on the tape recorder. A voice crackled out saying: "Would Sergio Reza please come to the snack bar?" Checo, lying comfortably and spaciously in the back seat jumped ever so suddenly and almost did poo-poo in his pants. He became extremely nervous that anyone might have known that he was at an adult movie theatre. After a few minutes he became absolutely convinced that something bad had happened at his home and that his mother was trying to contact him. He started to accuse Chichi and me of telling his mother that we had planned to go--of all places—to the *Cactus Drive-in.* Chichi and I, of course, denied it. Checo was extremely agitated and worried. For 30 minutes, he could not make up his mind whether to go to the snack bar or not.

Finally, he decided to go to the snack bar and find out why he had been summoned over the intercom. I went with him. By that time, the snack bar was indeed closed. So, he proceeded to start knocking on windows and doors of the snack bar until he alerted somebody inside. A man came out--apparently the projectionist--and asked what he wanted. Checo told him that he had been paged through the intercom. The projectionist laughed and told him that he was crazy. Checo started to argue with him insisting that he had been called. I remained quiet. The projectionist then said that if he didn't get out of there, he would call the cops. So, we returned to the car. I tried to reassure Checo but at the same time could barely contain my laughter. We got back into the car and proceeded to continue to watch the movies.

Half-hour later, I reached under my seat and pushed the "play" button one more time. The same announcement for Checo crackled out again. Instantly, Checo leaped over the back of the front seat looking to see if I was operating any devices and, sure enough, he found the tape recorder. We all laughed our asses off for the next hour. To this day, Checo assures me that he continues to plan on how to get even with me and Chichi for what we did to him that night.

Fernando Arturo Casas Aguirre

The impact that Checo had on my life in the early 60's was profound given all that we did together. Yet, nothing that he ever did for me was as significant as when he introduced me to his friend Fernando Casas. Fernando and Checo were classmates in the eighth grade at the time and they were essentially inseparable on the school grounds. Checo and I were best friends in the Paisano Projects where we both lived, and because of activities that we shared in the Boys' Club, we seemed to do together everything that was important to us in those days. Given that Fernando and I were such good friends with Checo, it became inevitable that eventually we would become a trio.

I met Fernando in 1961. I was in the ninth grade at the time and simply on the basis of school experience, I was the senior member of the trio. In terms of age, however, all three of us were less than a year apart. My first impression of Fernando was that for a kid growing up in the US, he was a bit too Mexican. He gave the impression--even as a teenager--that sooner or later, the entire United States and possibly the world would inevitably become part of Mexico. He was passionate about all things Mexican. Whenever he was asked to state his name, he proudly would state "Fernando Arturo Casas Aguirre" including his second surname (his mother's surname) as is customary in Mexico. Like most teenagers, he listened to rock and roll music but definitely preferred Mexican music. Because of his insistence on listening to it, he actually got me to gain a much greater appreciation of Mexican music than I probably would ever have gotten. Fernando could dance to rock-and-roll but he preferred to dance to Mexican songs called "danzones" (pronounced "dahn-SO-nes"). He actually taught me how to dance them. He was so enthralled by the Mexican culture that as a teenager, he even wore glasses that were distinctively of the Mexican style. They were so because they had rectangular shaped frames with the lenses slightly tinted on the top half. In those days you only saw those on people who lived in Mexico. In addition, he only smoked Mexican cigarettes. His favorite brand was *Raleigh*. Eventually, Checo and I took to smoking *Raleighs* also. Finally, even as an adolescent, he sported a moustache that made him look considerably more Mexican than the rest of us. I seem to remember that it was Fernando who later caused the administrative staff of our high school to look for the first time ever into the legality of a student wearing a mustache to class.

His enthusiasm for the Mexican culture inevitably rubbed off on me. I suppose that as teenagers growing up in a bi-cultural context, we all needed somehow to reaffirm our Mexican identity and, while his way of doing it was somewhat extreme, I consider his model to have prompted me to be a lot more Mexican than I had been before. Fernando's approach was quite daring at that time since the message from the Anglo society always seemed to be "Assimilate!" He really wanted no part of assimilation. One had to be supremely confident and self-assured to take the approach he took. I've never known anyone more confident and self-assured.

Fernando was an extremely intelligent person. He was not only clever and full of common sense but he also received extremely high grades in school. Everyone in school recognized and appreciated exactly how smart he was. It later came as no surprise that he graduated as Valedictorian of his high school class.

He also acquired a reputation for being quite arrogant, conceited and impatient. He did not put up with any nonsense from anyone. When we were young, I always feared that he would lose patience with me or with Checo because we simply did not have the same serious outlook on life that Fernando had. However, we all came to find out that Checo and I desperately needed a mature friend like Fernando and so the three of us then became great and inseparable friends.

In 1962, during my sophomore year in high school (Fernando's freshman year) the three of us got involved with the activities of Dr. Cleofas Calleros. It all began one afternoon when the *Pan-American Club* of Jefferson High invited Dr. Calleros to speak. The three of us attended and were impressed by Dr. Calleros as he spoke about the history of northern Mexico and his own personal experiences as an immigrant. He also managed to get us somewhat excited about the *Crossroads of the Americas* Project which, at that time was in its second year. Our exploits in *Crossroads* are chronicled more fully in a subsequent part of this book.

That same year, we all became drivers and, therefore, expanded considerably our roaming range as teenagers by frequently crossing the border to Juárez for entertainment and excitement. The adventures that we had in Juárez were absolutely defining moments in all of our lives. We got involved in risky activities by going to bars and nightclubs there that featured adult entertainment. We were 14 or 15 years old at the time. Juárez was the place where most--if not all--of the boys from the Projects learned all the specific facts that relate to sex. We went there and, as very young men, we saw a very harsh version of adult oriented entertainment. At the Juárez nightclubs, as long as we had enough money to pay, we would be treated as adults--stupid and immature adults, but dollar-bearing adults in any case. All of that provided us with quite a sex education that, while not sophisticated, it certainly has become an indelible memory. And through all of that, Checo and Fernando were always my faithful companions and partners in crime.

Juárez also facilitated the introduction of alcohol to young boys from my neighborhood and for that matter from all over El Paso. In the first place, liquor was available in Juárez regardless of your age. Secondly, it was available very cheaply. And so, we did what just about all young men our age did: we went to Juárez and learned all about liquor. It was during those trips to Juárez that we experienced some of the most hilarious events of our youth.

We managed on one of those trips to get stopped by a Juárez motorcycle cop who claimed we were speeding. He offered to let us go if we gave him money for "sodas." Fernando dropped a few names of powerful local officials (including a former famous baseball player) suggesting that he had close ties with them. That somehow convinced the cop to apologize and leave empty-handed. That turned out well since we had no money left at that point and would not have been able to bribe the cop.

We also got involved in less risky yet dramatically enriching cultural experiences in Juárez as well. The three of us went to at least one bullfight one Sunday afternoon in Juárez. We were amazed and thrilled to see the mayor of Juárez enter the seating area of the bullring with none other than the most notorious madam in Juárez clinging onto his arm. The crowd almost went crazy. How did we know who she was? Well Fernando told us. He happened to know of her.

On some Sundays the three of us would go to the late afternoon dances ("Tardeadas", pronounced: "Tar-deh-AH-das") held in very fashionable Juárez hotel ballrooms. We would get into our best (and probably "only") suits and pretend that we were in our 20s as we met, danced and tried to form relationships with young and beautiful women from Juárez.

On Saturdays and sometimes on Fridays in the evenings, we would go to the drive-in bars of Juárez where, unlike El Paso, we 15-year-olds could get alcoholic beverages. We would sit in the car with the windows rolled down sipping 10-cent bottles of beer and listening to live music. Occasionally, we would convince girls to sit with us in the car.

In addition to those activities that we partook in Juárez, we also did lot of stuff together in El Paso. Because of three of us were so close (and had limited use of a car), we frequently triple-dated. One such occasion stands out in my mind. We were in Checo's 1958 *Ford* station wagon and we had somehow managed to pick up three girls. Since we had no money Fernando suggested that we go explore the ruins of a dairy farm in his neighborhood that had been shut down some years back. And so, we did. The three couples took off in different directions among the rubble of the old dairy and each of us in our own way entertained our dates. I will leave the rest to your imaginations.

We also attended all sorts of Friday night parties, dances at the local *Golden Key Club* (a dance club for teens covered in more detail in a subsequent chapter), assorted weddings, and occasional Quinceañeras (traditional Mexican and Spanish 15th Birthday parties for girls). We also spent lots of time together at the *Oasis* drive-in where lots of high school classmates and students from other schools hung out. For the two or three years that the three of us hung around, we spent a huge amount of time growing up together.

Fernando seemed to be a more natural fit with respect to the pure Mexican culture than Checo or I. Fernando could honestly pass for a genuine Mexican from Mexico. He had much greater knowledge about the Mexican culture, geography and lifestyle than either Checo or me. He definitely looked more Mexican then we did and his speech was decidedly a much better Spanish than Checo or I could speak. And, to make an even stronger Mexican statement in El Paso, on those frequent occasions when his relatives from Mexico City were visiting his family, Fernando would get to drive his uncle's *Mercedes Benz* which happened to have license plates from the Federal District of Mexico or the nearby state of Puebla. By merely hanging around with Fernando in those days, Checo and I would also have some of the Mexican look rub off on us. And we all were very proud of it. After all, we were Mexican, weren't we?

It was during those days that our high school buddies, both male and female, liked to gather in a place called the "*Oasis.*" It was a drive-in restaurant located on North Loop Drive on the near east side of El Paso. Every Friday and Saturday night during the school year--and much more frequently during summers--all those students from Jefferson and other nearby high schools who happened to have a car would hang out at the *Oasis*. You could sit in your car, play your radio loudly and sip on a 10-cent cherry *Coke* and kill hours socializing. It was perhaps the most popular teenage hangout in El Paso in those days.

During those days also, Checo, Fernando and I were always on the hunt for girls. I'd have to admit now that we were not very successful in that respect. Nevertheless, whenever we got the chance, we invested a lot of time and most of our money into that hunt.

One day, we went to the *Oasis* in Fernando's uncle's *Mercedes*, the one with Mexico City license plates. As we were approaching the *Oasis,* we came up with a scheme whereby we would pretend that we were rich Mexican students visiting El Paso. In those days, rich Mexican students were considered very cool by El Paso girls. Plain old ordinary Mexican-American students, on the other hand, were a dime a dozen. Since in reality we fell in the latter category, we thought it might be interesting to see what life was like for those in the former category, even if for just one night. From that moment on for the rest of the evening, we would speak only Spanish, pretend to know no English at all and assume the identities of college students visiting from Mexico. Like hungry wolves, we circled the *Oasis* once or twice, spotted one particular car that appeared to have three single girls in it, and, with our hearts racing with excitement, proceeded to pull in right next to it.

Within minutes we had started a conversation with the three girls. Relying on Fernando's excellent Spanish and superior ability to fake being classy, we succeeded in convincing the three girls that we were, in fact, three bored students visiting from Mexico City who spoke no English and who knew nobody in El Paso other than our boring relatives.

The girls were a bit older than us. They were students at the *University of Texas at El Paso*, whereas, in reality, I was a junior in high school and Fernando and Checo were sophomores. Of course, we didn't tell them that. We told them that we were seniors at the *University of Mexico* in Mexico City. Fernando had just enough real knowledge about all that to fully convince them.

The girls started falling for the scam. They seemed very interested in us and promptly invited us to sit with them in their car. I recall that we even managed to get them to buy the cherry *Cokes* by showing that all we had was Mexican currency (which Fernando always carried) and the *Oasis* only accepted U.S. currency. Before long, each of us had snuggled up to one of the girls and we were well on the way to becoming best of friends with them.

We then raised the stakes. We mentioned to them that we had heard from our local boring relatives that there was a cool place on the big mountain called "Simi" drive or "Skinny" drive and they quickly corrected us saying it was called "Scenic Drive." We told them we were just wondering what it was all about. As we had hoped for, the girls offered to take us there so we could see it for real. Scenic Drive was the "lover's lane" of El Paso and our plan all along had been to somehow get them there so we could better take advantage of them.

And so, the girls drove us to Scenic Drive. We got there, found the perfect spot and parked. Fernando, Checo and I felt certain that we were about to score. Although Checo and Fernando will probably deny it, none of us was able to succeed in putting the moves on the girls after all. I don't know why we failed. Perhaps we were real rookies, or they were too clever. Or maybe the car was too crowded. Nevertheless, we established enough of a relationship with them to convince them to meet the three of us at the *Oasis* again the following evening. Later on, they dropped us off at the *Oasis* and left us with nothing to show for a whole night's worth of deception other than the hope of gaining better results the next day.

As we drove home afterward and again the following day in school, Fernando, Checo and I congratulated ourselves profusely for what we had done and anticipated eagerly how we would conquer these three hapless beauties the following day. At school the next day, we told everyone who would listen about how we had scammed these three college girls into thinking that we were rich Mexican students and how we planned to seduce them later that evening.

And so, the next evening, we once again met the three girls at the *Oasis*. We arrived a bit early and cruised around a little before parking. We noticed that our classmate and good buddy Robert "Peanut" Rayas was there. Peanut almost seemed to "live" at the *Oasis*. He had a really nice 1953 *Chevy* painted sky-blue with chrome baby moon wheel covers. It was one of the nicest cars in the school. He was a relatively popular guy who seemed to know everyone at the *Oasis*. Unlike us, he never seemed to have trouble picking up girls. We saw him there but since we had assumed our "fake-Mexican" identities, we ignored him. He didn't recognize us because we were in that strange *Mercedes* again. We would later come to regret how earlier that day, we had shared our story with him at school and so he knew about our plan to meet these three unsuspecting college girls.

After sitting in the *Mercedes* for a few minutes, the girls arrived right on schedule and pulled up next to us in their car. We got out of the Mercedes and climbed into their car. From a distance, Peanut saw us. Inspired by either extreme mischief or jealousy, Peanut raced over to the car we were all in and announced to the girls that the three of us were a bunch of imposters. We, of course, pretended that we did not know Peanut. We told the girls that we had no idea what he was talking about since we did not speak English, and we tried to talk them into leaving the *Oasis* with us quickly before we were forced to get out and teach this punk a lesson.

But Peanut persisted. He simply had too many facts on us. He even suggested that we settle everything by producing our driver's licenses. We continued to deny everything in perfect Spanish not really knowing how we were going to extricate ourselves from this situation. In my mind, I knew that our plan to put the moves on these three girls had suddenly come to a complete stop. I was trying to think of a way to end the matter. Maybe they would understand if we called it a joke. Since no damage had been done, maybe we could still get away with some dignity.

But things only got worse. One of the girls, the one who had been sitting with Checo the previous evening, then decided to accuse Checo of having kept a ring that she showed him the previous night. Checo expressed great surprise at the accusation and vehemently denied having taken the ring. The girl was insistent. The accusations and denials got louder and louder. A crowd started to gather. Peanut smiled broadly as if to say "I told you so." Then, in the worst case ever of poor timing, a police cruiser entered the parking area of the *Oasis*. As it passed us by, the accusing girl flagged the cruiser down.

Now I started to worry. I knew we were about to be forced to confess that we were indeed merely dumb Mexican-American high school students but I became very concerned that the accusations of theft would get us in real trouble. Eventually, we told the policeman and the girls who we really were. But we continued to deny that we had taken anything from them. Thankfully, the girl was not 100 percent sure that she had given the ring to Checo after all and so she started to backpedal a little bit on her version of the story. The police decided that nothing unlawful happened and so they ordered us back into our car and they departed.

We sat in the *Mercedes* for a few minutes wondering how so much could go so wrong so quickly. We considered for a moment that maybe lies and deceit were not a good means of attracting girls but concluded that we had simply not executed the plan as well as we could have. So, we each lit up a *Raleigh*, turned up the radio (it was playing *Nave Del Olvido*--a really popular Mexican song) and drove off into the night in search of more gullible college girls.

Needless to say, as Fernando and I became better friends, I became very close to Fernando's family. His mother and dad were extremely affectionate and cordial to me at all times. I shall never forget them (Don Rito and Doña Estér) may they both rest in peace. I also was a very good chum to Fernando's little brother Carlos, and his little sister Estelita.

Fernando had access to two automobiles during that period and that was the real key that enabled us to get around and do all the things that we wanted to do. His dad owned a 1957 green *Plymouth* that was completely rundown yet it always enabled us to get anywhere we needed to go. We called it the "Green Dragon." Fernando's mother had a nice, clean 1960 *Plymouth Valiant*. Whenever we needed good-looking transportation, we would use the *Valiant*.

Among the three of us, Fernando was clearly the most industrious. Whereas Checo and I got goof-off jobs at the Boys' Club earning low wages and getting bonuses of government surplus food, Fernando landed a serious after-school job as a busboy at the *Del Camino Hotel*, one of the nicest hotels in El Paso. It happened to be very close to his house. And he was extremely diligent. He never let our fun activities interfere with his work schedule.

A few months before my graduation from high school Fernando ran for student body president. He invited Checo to join his ticket and run for Assembly Manager. Fernando asked me to be his campaign manager. We fought a tough interesting campaign but, at the end, our entire ticket was defeated. But we had a great time during the campaign.

As I finished my high school years, my friendship with Fernando and Checo was at its absolute peak. We had done all sorts of things together for three or four years and we were as close as we have ever been. We were like young bulls looking for matadors to gore and heifers to adore. We all enjoyed strong reputations in our communities and at school and we were just champing at the bit to get on with the rest of our lives. We had participated in the international exchange program called *Crossroads of the Americas* the previous year; we had campaigned together for student body offices--and although we had lost, had bonded immensely as a result; we could date just about any girl in the entire city; we eventually all got real jobs and we all were seriously planning to attend college in the very near future. And, even though none of us owned a car, we were able to enjoy almost unlimited use of someone else's automobile for whatever purposes we desired, simply because everyone trusted us so much. We were on a roll!

And so, around January 15, 1965, we were living high and with great confidence. I was a senior and they were juniors at *Jefferson High School*. We were so cocky that every so often, we would play hooky. On that particular day, Fernando had again somehow obtained the use of a late model *Mercedes Benz* from one of his uncles who was visiting from Mexico City. Fernando suggested that we leave school at around eleven that morning and that we drive to Juárez, Mexico, in the *Mercedes* for a leisurely macho-type lunch.

With respect to crossing the international border in those days, here's the way it worked. If a person had applied for and received permanent residence status, meaning that even though they were not US citizens, they could still live in the US, the Immigration and Naturalization Service (INS) would issue that person a laminated green wallet-sized card called a "green card." With that card, that person could enter and leave the United States without any complication at all. If on the other hand, a person was an American citizen, the process was incredibly simple. An American citizen who was returning from Mexico into the United States simply had to "declare" his or her citizenship. For example, when the INS officer would inquire as to one's citizenship, one would simply state "American" or "United States" and the INS officer would permit entry. Of the three of us at that particular point in our lives, only one, yours truly, was a U.S. citizen. Checo and Fernando were permanent resident green card holders.

Fernando always carried his green card in his wallet. However, since he made the suggestion that morning without adequate prior notice, at least one complication arose. Checo normally left his green card at home unless he anticipated needing it. Since he had not planned to cross the border that morning, he had not brought his green card to school. We contemplated the risks for a split second or two and naturally decided that we would nevertheless go to Juárez because we felt confident that Checo could fake his way through the American immigration screeners on our way back.

Our plan was to go to Juárez, have a leisurely lunch and upon re-entry to the US, all three of us would declare in our most Mexican-accent-free English that we were U.S. citizens. Since we were all perfectly fluent in English and since we did not otherwise precisely fit the then-current profile of illegal aliens, we thought that the odds were almost 100 percent in our favor that we would succeed in getting through. And so, we got into the car and drove into Mexico for a well-deserved break.

After consuming generous portions of Mexican food and beer, we headed back to El Paso. It was too late to go back to class and so our objective was just to go back home. As we approached the border crossing from Mexico, we discussed the situation one more time just to make sure everyone knew what to do. The three of us agreed that there would be no difficulty except possibly with Checo. He was extremely nervous. And so, we coached him carefully and repeatedly. We told him to remain absolutely quiet except when he was asked to declare his citizenship. He was to reply "American," and then say absolutely nothing afterward. Our expectation was that we would be treated as totally ordinary American citizens returning from Mexico. We even rehearsed the process three or four times as we approached the border.

As has always been the case, there was a long line of cars waiting to cross from Mexico to the US. From a distance, we could see that each inspection by the INS officer was taking a little bit longer than normal. We weren't sure why but we could see that the INS officer was engaging in a little bit more dialogue with the cars that were immediately in front of us than was normal. We also noticed that the officer had a pack of letter-sized white cards in his hands. We noticed all that but we did not become concerned since we were confident that we could get through without incident.

Finally, Fernando drove the *Mercedes* into the portal and the INS officer looked into the car and noted the three of us through the fully opened windows. He then asked us to declare our citizenship. Fernando responded by crisply saying, "American." I was riding shotgun. I responded by saying, "American, sir!" (I was a member of the El Paso ROTC high command). Finally, the inspector turned to the back seat where Checo was sitting immediately behind me. Checo responded in perfect accord with the plan by saying, "American." I stared directly ahead. A tiny smile formed in my lips because I sensed that we had once again established the benefits of proper prior planning and had just about completed the deception.

The INS officer took a step backward, nodded, fingered the deck of white cards in his hands and waved us through. Just as Fernando's foot moved from the brake and settled cautiously on the accelerator, Checo suddenly leaned toward the window next to the INS officer and blurted out "Excuse me but what are those cards you are holding?" The officer replied, "These are Alien Registration cards. All aliens must fill one out every January. Do you need one?" At that moment, the *Mercedes* again came to a full stop. The tiny smile vanished from my face and beads of sweat started to form on my brow. Nevertheless, I remained cool; I stared straight ahead wondering how Checo would respond.

Checo, now flush and flying high with confidence cheerfully responded "I sure do." Whereupon the officer tilted his chin quizzically to his right, frowned at Checo and asked, "Didn't you say you were an American citizen?" Instantly, all of Checo's confidence departed and he turned white. He hesitated, leaned back away from the window and stuttered something unintelligible but thickly Mexican-accented. The officer then stuck his head into the back window and said "I beg your pardon?" In a stunning recapture of control and momentum, Checo calmly and confidently said: "I said it's for my mother".

The inspector played a little bit more with the cards in his hands then looked from side to side momentarily. He finally looked directly at Fernando and said "Please pull over to the side. We need to talk to you a bit more." I felt totally crushed. I was not worried about myself (a US citizen), nor about Fernando who could pull out his green card. I was worried about Checo. I knew that if they gave him enough opportunity, he would effectively paint himself into a corner, be positively identified as an illegal alien and get deported to Mexico forever.

Once we were pulled off to the side, another INS officer came to us and asked us to please step out of the car. We did as we were told. When we were all outside the car the officer asked Fernando to open the trunk of the *Mercedes*. Fernando promptly complied or at least attempted to do so. He put the key into the trunk key-slot and turned it but the trunk did not open. Then I noticed that Fernando's brow was now all sweaty too. He attempted over and over to turn the key and he simply could not get it to work. As he was doing this, the officer turned to Checo and asked him a bunch of questions. Fortunately, Checo had fully regained his old form and confidence and coolly responded to all the questions in ways that satisfied the officer. Eventually, the officer appeared convinced with Checo's explanation and handed him one of the white Alien Registration cards "for his mother." The inspector then turned his attention to Fernando. The trunk still would not open. We also then realized that we had no idea what was in the trunk. What if Fernando's uncle had left a gun there or some marijuana or a case of liquor? I was standing off to one side watching all this and I started to rehearse in my mind the story I would begin to tell if they decided to handcuff Fernando and detain him. I decided that I would defend Fernando and Checo if necessary, by vouching for their reputations, for their integrity, for their honor and patriotism and for their academic status. I would tell the officer that I was intimately familiar with the families of both of those men and that they were all upstanding respectable members of the El Paso community. I would explain to the officer how Fernando had just run for student body president, and that Checo had run for Assembly Manager, and how I had been the campaign manager for their campaigns. I would also explain how we had participated in the *Crossroads of the Americas* program the previous summer which had done much to promote friendly relations between Mexico and the United States. As I continued my private rehearsal as to what I was going to tell the officer in order to free my friends, the trunk of the *Mercedes* popped open.

Inside the trunk was nothing more than a spare tire and jack. The officer looked at Fernando, directed him to close the trunk and told us to wait a few minutes. He then departed. We sat in the car and waited. We could see the officer was engaged in doing nothing that seem to be related to our situation yet he didn't come back to see us for at least an hour. In the meantime, we sat in the car not knowing for sure what was going to happen.

Finally, well into the afternoon, after we watched literally hundreds of cars pass through the border back into the United States, the officer came back to our car. He told us two things: First he said we were free to go into the United States. Second, he said, "Don't let me catch you playing hooky again!"

The three of us enthusiastically nodded our acknowledgement of his warning and slowly pulled away from the inspection portal heading back home in the good old US of A. The last thing I remember about that little experience was how hard we laughed as we drove home. Laughter is one of the best ways to release pent up tension. We all knew that we had dodged a bullet and we—especially Checo--felt very good about it.

Fernando paid me a huge tribute in 1967. While I was in my second year at West Point, he also pursued and obtained an appointment to the *United States Military Academy*. I always felt very proud that he followed my footsteps. Once at West Point, he excelled in every respect including managing to rise to the top 5% of his entire class academically. However, at the end of the first year, he concluded that the military was not for him and he resigned. Knowing Fernando as I did, I was quite frankly surprised that he even spent one year there. But it turned out to be a good year for both of us.

Interestingly, a few years later, I paid a similar tribute back to Fernando by following his footsteps and going to work for IBM where he had been working for some six years. Checo--perhaps not coincidentally—also started working for IBM shortly before I did.

Once our careers took off, the likelihood of getting together did not seem promising. Yet, the three of us had the great fortune of receiving assignments from IBM to work in Dallas at the same time in the early 1980's. The three years that I spent in Dallas were perhaps the most enjoyable of my career primarily because I was able to spend lots of time with both Checo and Fernando in a professional as well as in a social context.

Salvador Estorga Garcia

Salvador Estorga Garcia has always been and will always be known to me—and to the other kids with whom we grew up--as "Chichi." Of all of the kids that I have known from our days in the neighborhoods of the Paisano Projects, no one has maintained a longer, continuous relationship with me than Chichi. He and I go back to September, 1956, when both of us were classmates at *Burleson Elementary School*. He and I were in Mrs. Florence Deyoe's 4th grade class. He lived in the Paisano Projects at the time and I lived on Alameda Avenue where mi Papá was struggling to operate his first grocery store. Chichi was one of those kids that I envied so much because his family was privileged to be able to live in a nice dark-red brick building. I did not know that these buildings were the Projects and that they were for the economically disadvantaged members of the community. I just thought those multi-family buildings were really cool and everybody in school seemed to live in them except me.

Chichi was two years older than the rest of us in the class because he enrolled in the first grade late due to a bout he had with the measles. As far as I recall, that age difference never really meant anything in the many activities and experiences we shared in our lives.

My family moved to the west side of El Paso for my 5th grade school year and so I lost track of my Burleson classmates until we moved to the Paisano Projects in the summer of 1958. From that moment until we graduated from Jefferson High in 1965, Chichi was one of my best friends and my most formidable competitor in just about every single aspect of life that touched us.

Academically, he killed me. He was simply one of the most intelligent kids I ever knew. He got all A's and he gained lots of respect for that. He was the Valedictorian of my graduating class and he just swept all of the awards available for academics. I was jealous of his academic abilities for a few years but eventually I decided he was simply much smarter than me. I then just gave up trying to compete with him academically. I just went after other prizes that were more winnable for someone like me.

During a recent conversation, Chichi reminisced about what life was like for kids like us in the 60's. He recalled an experience he had during our junior year in high school. Since he was a member of our high school Student Council, he joined a group of El Paso students invited to attend the Texas Student Council Convention held in Austin, Texas, that spring. The El Paso delegation, however, decided to boycott the convention because African-American students had experienced discrimination the previous year when they were excluded from some hotels in Austin on account of their race. The El Paso delegation, therefore, decided to instead attend the New Mexico Student Council convention in Farmington, NM. When the delegation bus arrived in Farmington it pulled into the parking lot of a hotel where they had planned to stay. The adult sponsor was unable to get rooms for the delegation and so they went to a second hotel. There, the delegation was able to stay. When Chichi inquired of the adult sponsor as to why they did not stay at the first hotel, the sponsor initially balked, but eventually disclosed that it was because he had been told that there had been too many Mexicans on the bus.

The Boys' Club experience was as big a factor in Chichi's life as it was in mine. He acknowledges today that the people he met there and the experiences he had—particularly the Jr. Toastmasters—made a huge impact in his life. He believes that the Boys' Club exposed us to the Anglo-American community as we had never been exposed to it before and that it took us beyond the 5-mile radius that had previously bound us. In fact, he believes that the Boys' Club, through many of its activities, took us outside the city and even the state. Chichi considered the Boys' Club to be "his entire world." He remembers spending more time at the Boys' Club than he did at home.

The main reason why the Boys' Club had such an impact on Chichi was the staff. Chichi recalls that the staff seemed to always be there to point us in the right direction and to correct us whenever we needed it. Chichi considers Mr. D (Manuel De La Rosa), the Unit 2 Director from 1959 until 1964, to have been the "greatest influence" of his life. Chichi believed then that Mr. D was so dedicated that he probably spent more time with the boys of the Boys' Club than with his own children. He also believes that staff members, Douglas Cooper and Lane Smith—who eventually succeeded Mr. D as Unit 2 Director--were very impressive and affected him profoundly as he navigated his adolescent years. Then there were the volunteers who gave so freely of their time and skills to help the boys to be better. Chichi recalled that one of his mentors in the Jr. Toastmasters was Mr. Edward Marquez, an attorney. I'll write more about Mr. Marquez later on, but until that point in his life, Chichi had never even met a lawyer. Suddenly, he had one as a friend and coach all because of the Boys' Club. Like so many of us, Chichi today regrets deeply that he never thanked these staff members and volunteers as much as he should have.

During our high school careers Chichi and I competed viciously in the political arena. Once again, I have to admit that he beat me soundly. In the one school campaign that would define the final conqueror.... he took me. It was the spring of 1964. We were both juniors in high school at the time and we locked horns in a hotly contested race for Student Body President (President of the Student Council).

Chichi's main advantage was that he was an extremely intelligent guy and everyone seemed to know that. But I thought I had the advantage as far as popularity went. I remember that he was a few inches shorter than me and skinnier and had a skin condition that seemed to cause his lips to be perpetually chapped. I, on the other hand, was enjoying great press from exploits that I was having in the senior band, the Jr. Toastmaster's and the Boys' Club generally. But I certainly did not have a reputation for being anywhere near as intelligent as Chichi.

The campaign ran for two months. We each had very effective and popular campaign managers and there was no question that the campaigns were run very well. We had banners, speeches, rallies, dances, car washes and many other activities to try to get the vote. From what I could tell toward the end of the campaign, I had a slight lead. I was smitten with optimism.

Even though Chichi and I were running for President, we were also each heading a slate of other candidates for the other offices in the Student Council. My slate of candidates was the "United Student Ticket." Today, I honestly do not remember for sure who the other candidates were. But I do remember vividly that we felt very strongly that we wanted to win as a *complete* team and that any individual wins were certainly not desirable. Our belief was so strong in this regard that I remember spending one evening at home painting a banner that read, "United we stand; United we fall." I thought I was being really clever with that play on Abraham Lincoln's words from the Civil War era. Mr. James Burton, a revered counselor and teacher at Jefferson High, saw the banner, shook his head and told me that except for that banner, my campaign had been brilliant. He warned me that the banner might cause the whole ticket to crash in defeat and suggested that I take it down. I was too confident and stubborn to back off and so I left the banner up.

On the day of the election, the two competing slates were doing everything possible to get every vote cast on its behalf. I had even asked the five or six members of the band who sat near me every morning in band class to please go out on the day of the election and to encourage anyone that they ran into to please vote for Willie Chavez and the United Student Ticket. Every one of them enthusiastically told me that they would do exactly that.

On election day, all of the votes were tallied at the end of the school day. The results were going to be announced the following day during the morning bulletin. The morning bulletin was the daily ritual during which the school principal (or his representative) gets on the school-wide intercom and announces the latest important information for the benefit of all.

On the day following the election, during the morning bulletin, the principal announced that Chichi had won the student body presidency election. I was sitting with all of my band classmates when that announcement was made. I was devastated and assumed that all of my band classmates were similarly devastated—although they did not seem to show outwardly what I was feeling inside. The principal went on to say during the bulletin that the election had been the closest ever. He said that a total of five votes defined the margin between the winner and loser. I felt even worse. We had worked hard and to lose by such a close margin was really difficult to accept.

At the conclusion of the bulletin, many of my band classmates came by and patted me on the back and expressed sympathy. As the band class proceeded that morning, I leaned over to my left and I asked my very close friend Luis Fernandez, who had sat next to me in the band for three years, whether he had gone out and encouraged others to vote for me. He said, "Of course." I then asked him "What about you? Did you vote?" He admitted that he had been so busy encouraging others to vote that he himself had not had time to vote. Bummer!

I then turned to my right and looked at another faithful friend, Armando Perez (Nickname: El Batuta). I asked him the same questions. He also indicated that while he had encouraged others to vote for me, he had run out of time at the end of the day and he himself did not get to vote. I again turned toward my left side and asked Joe Soltero, the guy sitting next to Luis Fernandez, the same questions. I got essentially the same answers. In a few minutes I had spoken to at least five of my closest friends, classmates, and election supporters and made the determination that not a one of them had actually voted for me.

To this day, I feel badly about what happened that day. At the time, it seemed like a huge event. In life and over time, that election was, of course, really insignificant. Yet, it's funny how it continues to bother me to this day although nowhere near as much as it bothered me then. I think I am now remembering this event primarily because of its humorous aspects. But unless you ever had a rival like Chichi, you probably will never know what it's like to lose to such a rival. And I suppose that's what makes it difficult to forget.

I nevertheless managed to win a few other honors and leadership positions in competition with Chichi and so I never really felt that he beat me. I was selected over him as the All-Jefferson boy; I was selected over him as the highest-ranking ROTC cadet in our school; and I beat him in the race for Senior Class President.

As our class Valedictorian, he was traditionally supposed to give the main speech (*The Welcome Address*) at our graduation. However, the faculty member that oversaw that speech, Mr. James Burton, decided that I and not Chichi would get that honor. Chichi never forgot that miscarriage of justice and on various occasions—usually when we are recalling the good old days--he has reminded me of how I had unfairly been chosen to give that speech.

Until he reminded me, I had actually forgotten that I had given that speech. I do remember smiling broadly when he reminded me of it for the first time some 30 years after the fact. In reality, the damage that he suffered on our graduation day could not have been that great since he nevertheless did address the gathering. There were only three seniors who had speaking roles during the graduation program and he was one of them. He delivered the *Benediction*.

This is probably a good time to delve deeper into the personality of Mr. Burton, who had a profound influence on me, Chichi and many, many other kids at *Jefferson High School*. James Burton taught at Jefferson from the late 50's to the late 60's. His two principal subjects were Government and Speech X. He was my Government teacher as well as my Speech X teacher. I believe that most students who were pupils of Mr. Burton would agree with me in saying that the impact he had on us was immense. No other teacher taught me more about succeeding in life and no other teacher--or person, for that matter--influenced me then and even later more than Mr. Burton.

The effect of what he taught in Speech X was stunning. When my brother, Nacho, was a student in Mr. Burton's Speech X class (two years before I became Mr. Burton's student) he would often tell me all about what he learned in Speech X that day. Right before we went to sleep in the bedroom we shared, Nacho would pull out his Speech X notebook, flip to the notes he took that day and then show me how he and the other students that day had figured out how to say certain English words properly (without a Spanish accent). Using the phonetic alphabet, he would show me what he and I were doing wrong and how to correct it. It was an amazing revelation when he would demonstrate how a subtle difference--such as running a sound through one's vocal chords--could remove the improper tone or sound of a word instantly converting it to correctly-sounding English. I could not wait until the day I would also be so fortunate as to be Mr. Burton's student.

Mr. Burton's Speech X class was one of the most interesting and impactful experiences that I ever had. I think the single most important objective of Speech X was to help students get rid of any "Spanish accent" in their speech. A Spanish accent is that peculiar language inflection and tonal quality that distorts the English spoken by people whose first language is Spanish and who learn English later in life. Mr. Burton believed—as American society in general believed—that a Spanish accent was unattractive and that it impaired one's ability to communicate and to assimilate. He taught the class so that his students might be able to learn how to get rid of that accent and thus enjoy a better life in America. I absolutely saw the merit in his view.

Mr. Burton's technique in Speech X was simple and yet very effective. It was entirely based on the International Phonetic Alphabet (IPA) which is a standardized representation of the sounds of oral language. The IPA uses over 100 symbols to represent just about every sound that comprises all spoken languages. Mr. Burton's technique required his students to learn the IPA, identify the phonetics (sounds) in their speech pattern that cause the "Spanish accent," and then eliminate them. For example, the word *"much"* when pronounced correctly ends with a harsh sound resembling *"tch."* However, a student struggling with a strong Spanish accent commonly would pronounce the word and end it with a soft *"sh"* sound. Using phonetic symbols, Mr. Burton would teach us the correct way to pronounce "much," then show us the incorrect heavily accented way that sounded like *"mush"* and finally, through seemingly endless repetition and correction, managed to teach us how to always say it in the way that it was meant to be pronounced in mainstream America.

I remember being amazed one day in his class when he demonstrated that English and Spanish have two completely distinct ways of making the sounds that relate to the letter "z." To illustrate this he showed us how the correct English pronunciation of the "z" in *zebra* has a strong reliance on the use of the vocal cords. Unless the vocal cords are engaged, the initial sound becomes simply the sound of an "s." In correctly pronounced Spanish, however, words that contain a "z" *never* engage the vocal cords and therefore *always* end up sounding like the sound of "s." To further illustrate that, he used my own surname: *Chavez*. He pointed out that in Spanish, my surname is pronounced as if it ended in "s." Until that point in time, I had not realized that. Engaging the vocal cords to pronounce a "z" simply does not happen in Spanish. That's why people who speak Spanish as a first language almost invariably sound funny when they pronounce a "z" in English. A sufficient number of such speech variations is what is collectively termed "speaking English with a Spanish accent." He was telling us, in essence, that in order to learn to speak correct English, and he certainly believed that we needed to, we must learn to always engage our vocal cords whenever we spoke English words that contained the letter "z."

In a fascinating and extremely effective way, he graphically showed us how to recognize and eliminate those incredibly subtle sounds in our speech that he believed impeded our ability to communicate in English, to assimilate and, ultimately, to succeed in realizing the American dream.

Another big part of Mr. Burton's technique was to teach his students how successful speakers speak English. His teaching technique was to again relate that success to the phonetic patterns of those speakers and then to get the students to emulate those patterns. I remember that Mr. Burton would introduce his students to voice recordings of significant literary pieces such as poems by Robert Frost and Rudyard Kipling, plays by William Shakespeare and great speeches by Abraham Lincoln and John F. Kennedy. He would then have the students analyze the phonetic patterns of those works. Finally, he would have some of the students actually recite these in class often recording them in order to dramatically show the differences between our Spanish-accented English and the more proper English of these recordings. Frequently, Mr. Burton would also focus on the actual *content* of these works as a means of better understanding American values and mores.

In order to "sell" his students on the value of his Speech X program, Mr. Burton frequently would bash certain aspects or elements of the Mexican-American culture of the times. He advocated that we should assimilate as quickly as possible. I believe he defined Chicanos as recently immigrated Americans of Mexican descent who were caught between two compelling sets of forces. First, there were those forces linked to their Mexican origins such as "machismo," pride in "la Raza" and family-centric life. Then there were those forces inherent to their new American society where one had to live in an environment that required you to speak unaccented English, to convert your Spanish name to its English counterpart so you could melt more readily into American society, and to otherwise cut off any ties to the Mexican culture. He was particularly critical of those whom he called "professional Mexicans." These were Chicanos who, rather than blend into the American mainstream, preferred to cling to their culture and distinguish themselves not by the substance of their work but by calling attention to the shabby way that they and other Mexicans were treated. He believed that Chicanos would be more successful in every endeavor by adopting the "American" values. I think the Chicano-bashing was a necessary by-product of his teaching technique. I ended up fully subscribing to his view and I would look scornfully upon those Chicanos who thought El Paso was the center of all civilization or who spoke with a thick Spanish accent or who strove to educate themselves only in El Paso, Los Angeles or San Antonio. There were a few students in Speech X who found this bashing too much to take and ended up leaving the class. While now, as an adult, I feel guilty and am apologetic of the scorn that I felt then against "professional Mexicans," there is no doubt in my mind about the correctness of Mr. Burton's assimilation theory. Now that I have matured a bit, I--and I'm sure many others--have found that the right answer lies in a combination of full assimilation while at the same time remaining in close contact with one's ethnic culture.

I think that Mr. Burton had a whole lot of courage. He dared to get in the faces of young, ambitious Chicano students and tell them to disconnect themselves from everything in the Mexican culture that is likely to drag them down and to hitch themselves instead to the American dream through a proper command of the English language. It was extremely presumptuous of Mr. Burton to believe that he knew what was good and what was not good about the Mexican culture, but I think that his "assimilate at all costs' message was correct for the times. Assimilation was indeed the fastest way to attain the American dream. What he did not--and probably could not--anticipate was the cultural activism and even fanaticism that swept the country a few years later which became known as the Chicano Movement. One of the premises of that movement was that one did not have to abandon the language and the customs of the old country in order to assimilate. Assimilation has properly given way to diversification as the better objective in what America should be.

Getting back again to my friend, Chichi, despite all of that competition that we engaged in while in school, we really always remained good friends because of the Boys' Club. We played in the same teams at times and we played against each other at other times. We were in the same activities and basically did everything together. Even though he was smaller than his peers he was a really good athlete. I remember particularly his ability to play basketball and how accurately he could shoot baskets. For that reason, I always wanted to be in his basketball teams. We were in the Jr. Toastmasters together for many years and we also held down vendor jobs together at the *Coliseum* and at *Kidd Field* where again we frequently found ourselves competing for the jobs as well as for customers.

I always believed that Chichi certainly had the right personality to succeed. He was smart, funny, athletic and quite likable. But, by far, the most notable of Chichi's characteristics was his arrogance. As a kid, he was as conceited as anyone I had ever met. If anyone had the superior skills and intellect to get away with arrogance, it was Chichi. His cockiness emerged frequently in school when he would challenge the knowledge even of the teachers. Only he had the ability to make such challenges. Unfortunately, there was no way for him to win. His teachers would resent his assertiveness which frequently bordered on disrespect. Chichi recently recalled how even though Mr. Burton's Speech X class was a huge part of his life, he frequently clashed with Mr. Burton about the subject matter. Chichi would merely assert his dissenting opinion to Mr. Burton but be so persistent that Mr. Burton would lose his patience and send him out of the classroom. Chichi believes that his assertiveness is probably why Mr. Burton did not allow him to deliver the graduation *Welcome Address* and instead selected me.

I once related my story to Chichi about how various trusted teachers (including Mr. Burton) and counselors in high school had advised me to not go directly to West Point from high school. They were all of the opinion that an education from *Jefferson High School* was inadequate for such a challenge. Chichi was surprised that I had relationships with teachers and counselors that were conducive to such discussions. He said that no teacher or counselor at Jefferson High ever talked to him about college. I, on the other hand, could not understand how a superior student such as Chichi—the *Student Body President* and *the class Valedictorian*--was never approached by his teachers or counselors to discuss his future.

Chichi also remembers how students from Mr. Burton's Speech X class would frequently be selected to read the daily Morning Bulletin over the school's public address system. Their renditions of what was going on were heard by the entire student body. Later in the day, in his Speech X class, Mr. Burton would critique that day's Morning Bulletin reader. I remember those critiques as mostly substantive but occasionally with some poking of fun at the reader. Chichi, however, remembers that whenever he was the reader, Mr. Burton was always unnecessarily harsh in his criticisms.

When Chichi displayed his arrogance among his peers we merely saw him as a show-off. I believe it was the consensus of the barrio that for a guy with Chichi's diminutive physique, he sure was one cocky son-of-a-gun.

But Chichi could dance and he could sing better than just about anyone else in the neighborhood. We would form singing groups like those that were popular at the time (e. g. *The Platters, The Four Seasons,* and *The Tymes*) and he would always sing the lead and the rest of us would give him backup harmony. At school and neighborhood dances, he clearly had the most skill and rhythm and never had any trouble getting the girls to dance with him. I never did learn how to dance and so I used to just watch him with deep envy.

I guess that Chichi and I would also have competed vigorously for the affection of the many girls that were our mutual friends, except for the fact that he and I formed steady and exclusive relationships and we never even talked with each other about our girlfriends. I think his relationship was much more serious than the one I had. He recently confirmed that the reason why he dropped out of college (and lost his full-ride *Stevens* scholarship at UTEP) was because his girlfriend had broken his heart in a very big way. One has to admire his sensitivity and vulnerability and be sympathetic for the loss and pain that he suffered. I, on the other hand, in those days would never have permitted a girl to affect my blind and relentless drive toward a college degree. Now, as a man who's been around for more than 7 decades, I believe that sometimes it might be better not to be so blind and relentless about anything.

Today, more than 60 years after we first met, I thoroughly enjoy Chichi's company whenever I can have it. We have played on the same foursome at *El Paso Boys' and Girls' Club Alumni* charity golf tournaments, worked together on a high school reunion and I'll never forget that he honored me deeply in 2002 by attending my surprise 55th birthday party.

Armando Gallego

Armando Gallego, who everyone called "Mando," was another of my very best high school buds. Mando was a classmate in my high school class of 1965. My friendship with Mando evolved primarily during our junior and senior years in high school. At that time, he was just about as close a friend of mine as Fernando and Checo were.

He moved to El Paso from California in his freshman year. For reasons that I cannot recall, he left his family in California to live with his grandparents in a small and modest home located near another El Paso housing project. His grandfather was a retired elderly gentleman who was extremely likable because he was so gentle and soft-spoken. His grandmother was also very sweet but I did not get to know her well since she died shortly after Mando moved in with them. I recall that whenever I came to Mando's house, his grandfather was always there and he seemed to love to watch television. Mando was in many respects his grandfather's caretaker although legally, the grandfather was Mando's guardian.

I got to know Mando in the *Jefferson High School* band. He was a drummer and happened to be one of the best. He also was a very popular person and seemed to get along well with everyone. He had a great sense of humor and played jokes and pranks on lots of people including me whenever he could. In his spare time, he played drums for one of the local rock-and-roll bands.

During the spring of our sophomore year, he and I and a few others competed for the job of band drum major. I won the competition and had the job during our entire junior year. During the spring of our junior year, the band director, Mr. Berne Glover, decided to split the band into two units in order to create even more spectacular halftime shows for the upcoming football season. With two bands, we could cover the entire field at halftime and almost have two separate shows going on at the same time. And so, since there would be two bands, there would be two drum majors. In the spring, tryouts were held for the two drum major positions. Mando and I won that competition and we became co-drum majors. When Mando became a co-drum major, we had a small issue figuring out what to do about our uniforms. The entire band had been issued brand new uniforms the previous year and I, as the sole drum major at the time, had also gotten a new one. The old drum major uniform had been left in a storage room to await disposition. Then, Mando and I got named as co-drum majors and I wondered who would end up wearing the old uniform. When he and I went into the storage room and retrieved the old uniform to decide that question he immediately offered to wear it so I could keep the newer one. I was deeply touched by his unselfishness and I knew then that our friendship was a strong one. I also got a sense at that moment that we would make a really good drum major duo.

Mando and I worked very hard to be good drum majors. In addition to practicing with the band for two hours every day, we spent lots of additional time developing innovative drum major moves including some that required us to throw our 4-foot-long, chrome batons at each other through the air over significant distances. The crowds at football games loved those stunts and would roar whenever we did them. I confess that we did not always catch the flying batons like we were supposed to. At the end of the marching season in November of our senior year, when we competed at the annual city-wide marching band competition, the *Jefferson High School* band received the highest rating and Mando and I were selected as the outstanding drum majors and given a trophy,. I can't recall what became of that trophy but I do recall the moment when the announcement was made. All of the drum majors from the 10 competing schools formed a circle in the middle of the football field and waited for the decision of the judges. When our names were announced, Mando grabbed me in a big hug and he spun around like a top with me hanging on. Next thing I remember, we are both holding the trophy up in the air and posing for the photographers. This was one of my proudest accomplishments and I was thrilled to share the moment with Mando.

He and I were fortunate to have had our picture taken by the *El Paso Herald Post* at the beginning of the *Sun Carnival* New Year's Day parade on January 1, 1965. The band was lined up and getting ready to march. He and I were adjusting each other's uniforms when the photographer snapped the picture. It was unique because when it appeared in the paper the next day it was one of the first times that a newspaper printed a picture in full color. Needless to say, Mando and I were extremely proud and lucky to have ended up in that picture.

Mando was one of those few fortunate guys in my high school who happened to own his own car. Actually, it was a station wagon but he had managed to make it look really cool. It was a 1955 *Chevy* painted slate blue with wide, always freshly cleaned white-wall tires and Baby Moon hubcaps. It had a standard transmission and nothing else but he kept it looking clean and smooth-running at all times. I remember getting countless rides from Mando in his station wagon to and from many band events and to other activities and also to parties on Friday nights.

We hung out together during all of our band activities and had a particularly good time during our band trip to Mexico in the spring of 1965. This trip was arranged by Dr. Cleofas Calleros as part of his *Crossroads of the Americas* program. The band traveled by bus caravan from El Paso to Chihuahua City and then to the town of Parral a few hours farther south. In both towns, the band paraded through the center of the city in the afternoon and then in the evening performed a concert for the townsfolk.

Mando dated a girl from another high school during his freshman, sophomore and junior years. During his senior year, he got hooked up with a really cute sophomore named Mary Ontiveros. Mando and Mary dated steadily and eventually got married while I was at West Point. When they had their first child, a son who they named Armando Jr., Mando and Mary honored me by asking me to be the baby's godfather.

Mando finished college and became a teacher and counselor in a local high school. He went on to get a master's degree and to work on a doctorate. During the two most memorable and exciting years of my youth, Mando was literally--as well as figuratively--marching lock-step at my side. To our friends in high school and to the part of the El Paso and northern Mexico community that followed the adventures of the *Jefferson High School* band, he and I comprised a unit that worked extremely well. I was very fortunate to have had him as a partner during those heady moments.

The Miranda Brothers

The Miranda brothers were Filiberto and Daniel Miranda. Their barrio nicknames were "Porky" and "Pelusa" respectively. I was very close to both of them from around 1959, when the Boy's Club opened its doors in the Paisano Projects, until I graduated from high school in 1965. Porky was in my high school class although he was a year older than me. Pelusa was exactly my age but was two years behind me and Porky in school. That two-year set-back was once again due to the fact that their family immigrated after they were eligible to start in elementary school and because they spoke no English when they finally did get started.

In high school and in the projects, Porky was my class peer and so I got to know him really well in those contexts. In Boy's Club activities and in sports and other activities where age was the grouping factor, Pelusa was my peer and I was really close to him there.

The Miranda family was typically large in number but small in physical stature. Mr. Manuel Miranda, their father, was the quintessential Mexican-American father. He was of medium stature (around 5 feet 7 inches tall), was extremely well-liked by the neighborhood kids (he was our little league coach) and acted and dressed like a Pachuco of the forties. That is, he wore his hair very carefully combed and dressed very neatly. I don't recall what he did for a living but he had a penchant for new cars with huge tail fins. I specifically recall that at one time he had a very late model—maybe even brand new—*Plymouth* similar to Stephen King's *Christine*. He also owned, at a different time, a similarly flamboyant *Dodge*. He kept them meticulously detailed and never let his children drive them. He thrilled me immensely a number of times by inviting me to join his family on trips to drive-in movies in those cars.

Mrs. Miranda was a tiny woman (around 4 feet 9 inches tall) who was perhaps the nicest and sweetest mother in the neighborhood. All but one of the six Miranda children were diminutive like their mother. Porky and Pelusa just barely passed the 5-foot mark and it seems that the other kids in the neighborhood always towered over them.

Despite their small size, the Miranda brothers were superb athletes. Regardless of the sport, they excelled. I was always competing with Pelusa for spots in baseball, basketball and touch football teams and he invariably got selected over me. Pelusa was the Pete Rose (or Charlie Hustle) of the Projects. He was extremely competitive and when that attribute was combined with his athleticism and confidence, he became every coach's dream-come-true. Pelusa was my teammate in a Little League baseball team sponsored by the *H. Welch Co.* His dad was the coach. We did not win any championships but every game was a showcase for Pelusa who would regularly go 4 for 4 at bat, snuff out opponents with his defensive play at second base and, with his incredible speed, would stretch routine doubles into triples and even into inside-the-park home runs. Pelusa represented the gold standard of sports performance while we were members of the Boys' Club. On many occasions, a win by the team he was in would be due entirely to his production. I always wanted to be in his team.

Porky was equally dominant as an athlete in all of the sports he played. Since he was 2 years older than Pelusa and me, Porky was in the leagues and teams of the older boys. Porky was one of the best high school wrestlers in El Paso in 1964-5. I seem to recall that he won the District title in his weight class one or both of those years.

In keeping with the aggressive Miranda style of living, they had a penchant for risk-taking that sometimes went off the charts. I once got involved with them in a stunt that almost got me in trouble with the law. What kid has ever grown up without feeling an urge to shoplift? I am no exception. The time was 1959 or 1960. Both of our families lived in the Paisano Projects and I was attending *Henderson Intermediate School* in the seventh grade. We had lived there for a year or so and The Boys' Club was flourishing. At that particular time, Pelusa was in the fifth grade and Porky was my classmate in the seventh grade. They and I participated together in just about every Boys' Club activity. We were also teammates in Little League and we all were sales kids at the concession operation at the *El Paso Coliseum* and *Dudley Field* baseball park nearby. These two guys were really good friends of mine.

One day, in the playground in our neighborhood, where we would gather daily to engage in some sport or other play activity, Pelusa showed me a brand-new yo-yo. I admired it greatly and would have really been happy to own it or one just like it. Then he proceeded to pull other neat stuff from his pocket. I remember things such as shiny *Matchbox* cars, brightly colored water pistols, ballpoint pens, pencils, and erasers. He was wearing a jacket and his jacket pockets were filled with all of these goodies.

As I was admiring all of this, his brother Porky approached us and proceeded to show me all the neat stuff that he had in his pockets. He also had a comprehensive collection of little toys and trinkets that caused me to experience overwhelming feelings of envy.

The first thing I asked them was, "Where did you get all the stuff?" They both grinned and explained that they had gotten it the *Woolworth* department store at the *Fox Plaza* shopping strip. Without explicitly saying so, they communicated to me that they had shoplifted everything. They had all this stuff, did not pay a dime *and* did not get in trouble. My initial reaction was revulsion. That was theft and my parents, my big brother, my teachers and my priests had always taught me that theft was wrong and punishable by all sorts of nasty consequences. But within two or three seconds my revulsion was replaced with greed. I really wanted to be like Pelusa and Porky and have all of those things myself.

Pelusa and Porky felt really cocky and, having previously been so successful, they clearly were now yearning for more. They told me that they planned to return the next day to that *Woolworth* store and to pick up a few more items. They considered me a good friend and so they asked whether I would like to join them. We agreed to meet at the front of the *Woolworth* store right after school the next day.

The *Fox Plaza* shopping center/strip was not exactly on our route to school. We needed to do about a quarter-mile detour to get to it. Yet, it was not so far out of the way so as to delay us too much from our normal scheduled arrival at home after school. Adhering to schedules was important. Otherwise, parents would ask questions.

So, as agreed, the three of us were standing in front of the *Woolworth* store at about 3:30PM the next afternoon. All three of us were wearing jackets not only because it was cold but because we all expected to fill the jacket pockets with loot. We went into the store as a team. It wasn't long before Pelusa and Porky started to lift small objects and put them in their jacket pockets. I was extremely nervous. Even though I saw them do it--and they were doing it with such ease-- I could not do it; at least not then.

The three of us wandered throughout the store. I could see from a distance that Pelusa and Porky were picking up small toys and small school items without any hesitation whatsoever. Finally, I too crossed the line: I put a yo-yo in my pocket. We went around the store one more time to see if there was anything we missed. By then Pelusa and Porky had picked up some 10 items each. I only had that yo-yo.

Then I had a change of heart. I decided that the overwhelming feelings of guilt and betrayal—not to mention a racing heart that absolutely would not slow down—that were crushing me were simply not worth the price of the yo-yo. So, I left the two of them momentarily and walked back to the counter where the yo-yos were on display. I stood there for what seemed an eternity. I was truly conflicted. I did not know whether to leave it in my pocket or put it back. I pondered and pondered. Then, I put the yo-yo back. I slowly started to walk back to rejoin Pelusa and Porky. But I could not see them anywhere. Suddenly, out of nowhere, a gentleman wearing a coat and tie appeared, grabbed my jacket at the shoulder and told me to come with him.

He led me to the back of the store where we entered a huge room through large, white, swinging doors each with a circular glass window on it. My heart was now racing even faster--I was as scared as I had ever been. There was no doubt in my mind as to why he wanted to talk to me. As we walked to the back of the room, I saw another gentleman--also wearing a coat and tie--standing there between Pelusa and Porky. There was a table in front of them and on the table was all of the loot that Pelusa and Porky had picked up in the last few minutes.

I was asked to stand next to the table and to empty my pockets. I did. Everything that I produced was mine and--because I had returned that yo-yo--there was no shoplifted loot to put there. The man next to me proceeded to search me and acknowledged to the other man that I had nothing else. The man next to me then told me that Pelusa and Porky were thieves and were in big trouble for shoplifting and that I should not hang around with them. He then ordered me to go home and to tell my father what had just happened.

I walked out of the *Woolworth* store still shaking but feeling completely relieved, happy and very reassured about the notion that crime does not pay. I--like most kids--had experienced the temptation to shoplift many times in the past and had never yielded to it. This time, even though I did yield, I had the presence of mind to undo the deed. I view what happened that day as one of the truly momentous decisions and actions of my life. Clearly, someone earlier in my life had taught me what to do and, despite the temptation, the lesson of the past prevailed.

Later that same day, after supper, I went to the playground and sure enough, Pelusa and Porky were there. They were playing catch and killing time as if absolutely nothing had happened. I ask them about what had happened earlier that day. They told me that the store manager had called their father who had come to the *Woolworth* to pick them up and then did nothing more to them as punishment than to give them a lecture. By the way, I did NOT tell my father about the incident as the guy at the *Woolworth* store asked me to do. I was a good kid but not that good.

The good times continued. In the summer of 1960, Pelusa and I received one-week summer camp scholarships to attend *Skyline Ranch* in Cloudcroft, New Mexico. Cloudcroft is about 2 hours north of El Paso but is within the Lincoln National Forest. Despite being located in an otherwise arid region, its extremely high elevation (8,600 feet) allows for a relatively mild summer. That, coupled with the lush, mountainous forest, makes Cloudcroft a perfect setting for a summer camp. The camps actually ran for two weeks and sessions were held 4 or 5 times during the summer, each session accommodating around 50 kids. The Boys' Club would receive maybe a dozen scholarships each summer but instead of sending 12 kids there for two weeks, they would send 24 kids for one-week camps.

At *Skyline,* Pelusa and I were cabin-mates and we did everything together. He did extremely well at all of the camp activities (most were sports) and, because of his athletic prowess, he was the most popular kid there. At the end of our week, he was awarded the "Outstanding Camper" award. I was envious but he really did earn it and I always respected him greatly for what he did that summer.

As much as I admired the Miranda brothers, we did not always get along. One time, the three of us were in the main recreation room of the Boys' Club along with 10-15 other kids. It was a hot summer afternoon and we were all seeking the cooled air of the large game room where we could pass the time away playing pool (billiards) on a huge 8x4 foot table. We all patiently waited in line seated on the tan, metal *Samsonite* chairs that lined the entire hall. The kid at the end of the row of chairs was the next to play and he would play against the winner of the last match. The winner of a match would continue to play as long as he kept winning.

Pelusa was good at everything that required coordination and so was very good at pool. He had strung together 5 or 6 wins when my turn came up. He racked up the balls and took his first shot. One ball went into a pocket and then he kept sinking balls until only the 8 ball was left. While attempting to sink the 8 ball, he scratched. That meant that he had lost. He was not happy at all about that. After all, I had just defeated him—and broken his impressive string of wins—without my having to shoot even once.

I laughed when he scratched and he did not like that either. Then he called me *"pinchi culero"* or something like that and so I replied with a *"chinga tu madre"* even though I rarely used any profanity. He decided that my verbal response was an overreaction in light of his remark and so he took the dispute up one notch. Standing on the opposite side of the table from where I was standing, he picked up the green-striped 14 ball and did a full pitcher's windup and fired it at me. I never thought he would actually let the ball go and so I was slow in reacting. But there the ball came at probably 50–60 mph right for my chest. I managed to turn my back toward the missile and took the ball directly below my left scapula.

The billiard ball momentarily knocked the wind out of me but in the blink of an eye, I decided to rush him. I had not taken the first step toward Pelusa when suddenly, I had Porky on my back and he had a full Nelson stranglehold on me. At the same time, Pelusa rushed to attack me from the front.

Before Pelusa could reach me and before Porky could make me pass out, Mr. D, the Director of the unit, somehow appeared and stopped Pelusa in his tracks and removed Porky's arms from around my neck. He took all three of us to his office and counseled us. He also said he would kill any of the three of us who dared to carry this matter forward. On the spot, I entered into a truce with the Miranda brothers that lasted for the rest of our lives.

Upon graduation from high school in 1965, I went off to Texas A&M and Porky was drafted into the Army. He is the closest friend I ever had who got killed in Vietnam. Here's what a recent Google search revealed about him:

The 35th Infantry Regiment Association salutes our fallen brother, SP4 Filiberto G. Miranda, who died in the service of his country on March 12th, 1967 in Kontum Province, Vietnam. The cause of death was listed as Multi-Frag. At the time of his death Filiberto was 20 years of age. He was from El Paso, Texas. Filiberto is honored on the Vietnam Veterans Memorial at Panel 16E, Line 71.

The decorations earned by SP4 Filiberto G. Miranda include: the Combat Infantryman Badge, the Bronze Star, the Purple Heart, the National Defense Service Medal, the Vietnam Service Medal, the Vietnam Campaign Medal and the Vietnam Cross of Gallantry with Palm Unit Citation.

When I found this information on the web, for the first time ever, I realized that Filiberto's middle name was the same as my first name: *Guillermo*.

Pelusa graduated high school in 1967 (after Porky died) and joined the Air Force. He retired 30 years later. Unfortunately, he died a few years ago.

There should be no doubt that as I and my buddies grew up in the Projects, our friendships with each other were of supreme importance. Nevertheless, it would be an unforgivable omission and mistake to ignore the role that the girls of the neighborhood played.

Maria Luisa Velarde

Without a doubt, the best female friend that I had while growing up was Maria Luisa Velarde, known to all as "Tita." I got to know Tita because my mother and her mother had been very good friends and neighbors since the days when Tita and I were toddlers. Tita's mother, Graciela Velarde, had divorced her husband and was one of the few, true single mothers that I knew about while growing up. Graciela was a strikingly beautiful woman with the prettiest blue eyes. She looked a lot like Grace Kelly, in fact, and she was also a very assertive woman.

Graciela had three children. The oldest was Tita, who was the same age as me but a year behind me in school. Then there was Sophia, who was 3 or 4 years younger than Tita and then there was Armando, who was a year younger than Sofia. Graciela was the prototype single mom who worked tirelessly during the day at low-paying jobs such as in clothing factories, and yet maintained a very disciplined household despite the absence of a husband-father figure.

For some strange reason, Graciela always seemed to be kidding mi Papá. She was a very outspoken woman and would become extremely loud whenever she got into serious arguments. She would start relatively quiet discussions with mi Papá about how hard mi Mamá worked around the house or about how little recognition or gratitude mi Mamá received from mi Papá and the discussions would turn into arguments. The volume of these arguments between mi Papá and Graciela would invariably reach the shouting level. Mi Mamá would usually join the fray on Graciela's side and eventually mi Papá would have to give up in defeat. At the end of these arguments, after Graciela and mi Mamá had ridiculed and laughed at all of mi Papá's responses, mi Papá would simply walk away knowing that he had once again been out-talked by a couple of women. There was never any serious animosity in these discussions and while all argued loudly, there always seem to also be lots of fun and laughter.

In 1958, when mi Papá moved my family to the Paisano Projects, by pure coincidence—and because of our comparable economic status—we ended up in a housing unit that was no more than a block away from where Tita's family lived. So, the friendship between our mothers continued to thrive. When Graciela would come to visit mi Mamá, she would usually bring her kids. Because Tita was a girl and since we were both 11 or 12 years old, I did not like her very much. I seem to recall believing then that most girls were annoying and obnoxious but Tita had to be the worst in the world. Tita was very much like her mother in that she was very assertive, vocal, and could also become very loud. She also laughed a lot and had a very loud and boisterous laughter. Not surprisingly, I believe strongly that, at that time, Tita hated me as much as I hated her.

I have only had one fight with a girl in my entire life. Perhaps that's one too many. After all, I had always been taught that it is completely unbecoming for a man/boy to fight with a woman/girl. Nevertheless, I did have that fight and here's how it came about. The year was 1958. We lived at 405 Webber

Way in the Paisano Projects. I was either 11 or 12 years old and in the sixth grade. One Saturday morning, I was in the kitchen with mi Mamá having breakfast. I remember enjoying Saturday morning breakfasts because we would get pancakes or some other special treat no matter what time we got up. In any event, I was comfortably enjoying my breakfast when Graciela showed up accompanied by Tita. They entered our home through the kitchen and I remember feeling annoyed by their intrusion into my special moment. At the time that they arrived only mi Mamá and I were in the kitchen.

I recall that Graciela and Tita stood by the dining table and, as they watched me eat, they entered into a three-way boisterous conversation with mi Mamá. I tried to ignore them since I wanted only to finish my breakfast.

As Graciela and Tita were hovering over me, Tita said something about me being skinny and therefore having to eat a whole lot to stay alive. I ignored her and quietly continued to eat. Tita then said that skinny kids tend to be weak. I slowed my chewing a bit but continued to ignore her comments. Then Tita said something about me not being able to fight. With my mouth full of pancakes, I told her that while that may be true, I could beat *her* up any time.

Tita glared at me and then smiled as she thought of the next dart she would fire at me. I decided to leave before she said anything else. I pushed the chair back and stood up by the table, turned in her direction and started to walk away. As I walked by her, she put her face in my face and challenged me to a fight. Tita was not a small girl. She was as tall as I was and probably outweighed me by 10-15 lbs. She had correctly observed earlier that I was skinny but at that point she had simply not yet gotten rid of her baby fat. I recall that both of our mothers seemed to be enjoying the dialogue that was running between Tita and me.

Even though her face was only inches from mine when she issued the challenge, I continued to walk on into her face. As I turned abruptly at the last second and passed by her, she shoved me. It wasn't a forceful shove but because I was between steps and off-balance, the next thing I knew, I was on my back on the floor looking up as she stood over me in what seemed to be a position to deliver a *coup de grace*. This could not possibly have looked good for me.

I instinctively sprang back to my feet. Once again, we were confronting each other and she again tried to shove me with both hands using her palms to push on my chest. As she did, I caught her palms on my palms and somehow, we immediately interlocked fingers. So, there we were, palms glued against each other pushing at each other and engaged in a sort of Indian wrestling match.

As we wrestled, we careened all over the kitchen knocking against the dining table and bouncing off walls. At about that point our mothers tried to break us apart but our hands remained locked together as we each tried to shove or wrestle the other into submission.

As the encounter continued with neither of us wanting to let go, I noticed that Tita's face had become red and contorted in anger. I, on the other hand, was trying to keep a look of non-exertion and mild nuisance but inside I remember thinking how amazingly strong this girl was.

The dance of death between us continued for what seemed a very long time until in some strange and inexplicable way we both ended up on the floor again. This time, however, I was on top, straddling her between my legs and pinning her hands down with mine. I had almost immobilized her. She kicked her legs violently slamming my back repeatedly but I did not release her for one second. Eventually, she stopped trying to escape and seemed to concede defeat.

At just about that time, the two mothers interceded and pulled me off of Tita. As we were each restrained by our respective mothers, we continued to hurl insults and denigrations at each other for a few seconds more.

When everything was once again calm, I turned away to leave making sure I did not get even close to Tita as I walked away. With my back turned to her, I kept waiting for her to pounce on me and to once again try to prove how weak I was and how strong a person she was and how much of a fight she could put up. With each step that I took I felt more relief at not feeling her pounding on my back. I exited our kitchen into our backyard where I finally felt secure.

So that was it. It was a very violent fight although there was no blood and no one was injured. The experience is etched permanently in my mind and comprises one of the most distinct memories that I have of growing up.

During a conversation that I had with Tita recently, she told me that she did not remember that particular fight but she reminded me that we almost came to blows again a few years later. The encounter she remembers occurred in the fall of 1962. I was a sophomore in high school and she was a freshman. We had moved from our apartment on Webber Way to another apartment less than 100 feet away on Paisano Drive. She still lived nearby with her mother and siblings in the same neighborhood, although in a different apartment. I guess I was immersed in my quest to one day become a Boys' Club "Boy of the Year" and at that particular time, I was campaigning vigorously for the position of Sophomore Commissioner in the Student Council.

As Tita recalled during our recent conversation, one day that fall, I was just being industrious painting a Sophomore Commissioner election poster on the kitchen table in our apartment, when once again, she showed up at our back door. I saw her and proceeded to ignore her but mi Mamá invited her to come in and visit with us. Soon, she was *criticizing* the work I was doing and eventually, I got fed up with her meddling and the strong words started to fly between us. Apparently, however, on this occasion, I restrained myself and a re-match was somehow miraculously avoided.

Our families continued to live in close proximity as Tita and I progressed through high school. As with most adolescent relationships, this contentiousness eventually subsided and, by the time I was a senior and she a junior, it was completely replaced by friendship and real affection. I could not help but notice that she was developing into a very pretty girl and into an extremely smart student as well. In addition, she became a varsity cheerleader and a musician and her popularity started to soar.

Tita and I remained friends after high school and in 1968, while Tita was a student at the *University of Texas at El Paso*, she was selected to be a Duchess in the court of the *Sun Carnival* Queen. The *Sun Carnival* is an El Paso tradition and celebration that started in 1936 and includes a New Year's college football game (the *Sun Bowl*). Tita and I permanently "buried the hatchet" when she asked me to be her escort during the entire week of the *Sun Carnival* that year.

Tita later became Mrs. Victor Yanar and went on to receive a Bachelor of Science degree and a Master of Education degree from the *University of Texas at El Paso* in 1971 and 1975 respectively. She retired in 2017 after working for 22 years as Director of the *Upward Bound* program at UTEP. *Upward Bound* is a college preparatory program for low-income first-generation high school students and is sponsored by the *US Department of Education*. Her daughter, Soraya, earned a Bachelor's degree and a Juris Doctor degree from *Stanford University* and is now practicing law in El Paso, Texas. Her son, Omar, received a Bachelor's degree and a Master's degree from *Stanford University* and then another Master's degree from *Harvard's Kennedy School of Government*. He currently is the founder and CEO of the *El Paso Leadership Academy*.

Elizabeth Varela

The Boys' Club and high school essentially consumed me from 1961 until 1965, but fortunately, nature did not forsake me. During those amazing years I managed to have my first real relationship with a girl. The year was 1963. It was the spring of that year and I was in the 10th grade at *Jefferson High School*. This was right about the time that my brother, Nacho, was achieving national fame having been selected as National Boy of the Year of the *Boys' Clubs of America*. I fortunately became the beneficiary of some of that fame simply because I was his little brother. Right around April of that year the *El Paso Boys' Club* sponsored a "Walk Against Leukemia." In essence, the idea was for a whole bunch of people to gather at the Boys' Club in our neighborhood and to spread out throughout the city gathering donations to fund efforts to eradicate leukemia.

I was a junior staff member at the Boys' Club Unit 2 and I was assigned some responsibilities organizing the teams of participants that were to canvass the city. As I was doing so, I met a young girl named Elizabeth "Lizzie" Varela who was in the eighth grade and who was attending this event along with her older sister Martha. Martha was a classmate and fairly good friend of my brother, Nacho, and she knew that Nacho had a little brother. So, as I found out later, she had brought Lizzie along to try to hook her up with me.

After we were introduced and as I was diligently performing organizational duties, Lizzie seemed to be constantly shadowing me. She was very cute and, therefore, I was flattered by the attention she was showering upon me. The entire day was spent walking around town and even though I did not see her for most of the day, we did see each other again later that afternoon when the campaign ended and everyone gathered once again at the Boys' Club. The organizers of the campaign announced then that in recognition of the work done by all the volunteers, a dance would be held in the next few weeks at the *El Paso Coliseum* for the exclusive benefit and pleasure of the volunteers.

I recall vividly during the few weeks preceding the dance my many attempts at picking up the phone and calling Lizzie to invite her to be my date for that dance. It was just like in the movies. I rehearsed over and over the lines that I would use to reintroduce myself (since I assumed she had forgotten who I was) and to inquire as to whether she would be my date. I also remember picking up the phone many, many times and starting to dial but then hanging up as panic flooded me in anticipation of a rejection. I had heard from friends and from my brother that she was going steady with some guy so I was fully prepared to go down in flames during that call. When I finally made the call and popped the question, she told me that she was in the process of breaking up with her boyfriend and that she would be delighted to go with me to the dance. I was alone at home when I made that call and so when I hung up, I jumped up and down for a good while whooping and hollering about my good fortune.

That's how a steady relationship started that ran for the next fifteen months through the end of my junior year. During the fall of 1963, when I was fully wrapped up in dating Lizzie, I actually attempted to see her every single night of the week. My daily routine was as follows: I would participate in after-school activities until 5:00PM; then I would walk home to have dinner; then at 6:30 I would start the 20-minute walk to Lizzie's house; I would stay until 9:00; I would be home by 9:30; then I would do homework until 11. Occasionally, I would get a ride from someone in my neighborhood--such as Checo Reza or his brother, Chuy--to Lizzie's house and, occasionally Lizzie's sister, Martha, would drive me home. But 95 percent of the time I simply walked.

During that period, there is one incident that stands out in my mind. One pleasant autumn evening, as Lizzie and I were sitting on a bench in the porch in front of her house, her ex-boyfriend pulled up in front of her house. He and one of his friends--who happened to be a member of our high school football team--stepped out of the car and walked up to the front gate of the rock wall that surrounded Lizzie's house. Lizzie suspected trouble and so she immediately went inside and brought out both of her parents.

The ex-boyfriend, who had obviously been drinking, then started to shout obscenities at me from outside the gate. He basically told me that my days were numbered and that he was going to get me. As he said all this, Lizzie's parents had reached the front porch and were hearing everything. Then they told her ex-boyfriend to shut up and to go home. He became quiet but refused to leave. Lizzie's mother then told him that if he did not leave immediately, she would call *his* mom, whom she apparently knew well. The ex-boyfriend then turned around, signaled to his buddy and then both got into the car and left. I stood silently in mild shock during the entire episode.

I was never an aggressive person and so after having experienced this confrontation I was scared. I knew that the ex-boyfriend had enough rowdy buddies and resources to catch me alone sometime and to put significant dents on my not-so-flawless complexion. As I walked home that evening, I conjured up a plan through which I would deliver to her ex-boyfriend an absolutely devastating, lightning-like pre-emptive strike to ensure that he would not bother us again.

She had been dating this other guy since they were in grade school. He had been one year ahead of her and, for as long as anyone remembered, the two of them had been an item. Then, suddenly, for no apparent reason, in the spring of 1963, she broke it off and started dating me. Her ex-boyfriend was widely recognized as one of the most spoiled brats in our school. He was the youngest of a set of kids that had gone through *Jefferson High School* before him and who had been outstanding students. When he came along, he simply did not measure up to his older brothers and sisters. He happened to have a car and that distinguished him from among his peers since very few of us had cars. That car--a souped-up 1952 pale green *Hudson* or *Mercury*--enabled him to command the attention not only of prospective girlfriends but also of guys who thought that anyone with a car was cool. I recall seeing her ex-boyfriend at the local teen hangout, the *Oasis*, in his car with two or three of his buddies always raising hell and being obnoxious. He really owned the perfect personality if one was casting the bad guy in a high-school drama. I never spoke to her ex-boyfriend yet I did not like him because I knew that he had been Lizzie's boyfriend previously. So, at school, as my relationship with Lizzie was developing, he and I would run into each other in the hallway, look at each other silently and pass on by. Even though he knew I was Lizzie's new boyfriend, he simply never said anything to me.

Anyway, the day after the ex-boyfriend—armed with a football player--confronted me at Lizzie's house, I called her and told her that I could not come see her that evening. And so, instead of following my usual pattern, I went to my very best friend Checo's house to tell him that I needed two things from him that night. First, I would need him to give me a ride in his green 1958 *Ford* station wagon to the home of the ex-boyfriend. I intended to stand up to this jerk once and for all and to get him out of my life. Second, I would need him to provide backup for me in case the ex-boyfriend was not alone.

As I stood in front of Checo's house and hollered out his name--as I customarily did--his brother Chuy came out the front door and explained that Checo would not be home until late that night. When I heard all this, I was disappointed since now my plan for that evening was in jeopardy. Chuy then asked me what was happening. I explained my plan and my need for back-up and without one second of hesitation or reluctance, Chuy said that he himself would drive me there and also cover my back.

Fifteen minutes later, after the sun had set and darkness was beginning to fall, we pulled up in front of the house that was next door to the ex-boyfriend's house. We positioned the station wagon so that Chuy could see the front porch of the ex-boyfriend's House. Yet, the station wagon was hidden by the darkness and by the shadow of a big tree. Chuy and I agreed that he would remain in the station wagon unless the ex-boyfriend appeared in the front of his house with one or more of his friends. This was a calculated risk because the odds were high that the ex-boyfriend would have at least one friend there. I explained to Chuy that it was my plan to ask the ex-boyfriend to step out of his house and to fight with me once and for all right then and there and to settle all of our differences.

I stepped out of the station wagon, stretched my hamstrings, did a couple of squats, took 5-6 deep breaths and walked briskly toward the ex-boyfriend's house. The screen door of his house was closed but the main door itself was opened and I could see inside his living room. No one was there but I could tell that there was some activity in the kitchen area. I stood in front of the screen door, cupped my hands around my mouth and yelled out the ex-boyfriend's name. From inside, I heard an immediate response. Seconds later, the ex-boyfriend came bouncing happily over the living room floor, swung around the sofa in happy anticipation, flung open the screen door and stepped out into the porch. He had a look of glee and gaiety about him ...until his eyes focused on mine and he realized that I--rather than one of his friends--had just called on him.

He closed the screen door behind him as we stared at each other. He knew why I was there. At that moment I confirmed, without even asking, that he was alone and did not have his usual retinue of friends. I also sensed at that moment that he was scared, weak and probably felt cornered.

I waited and let him say the first words. I wanted him to fully experience the feeling of looking at his worst nightmare right in the face. Pretty soon, his eyes started to wander--an unmistakable sign of submission that I learned from having seen many Poodles on TV. His feet then started to shuffle. A female voice from his house inquired as to whether everything was OK. He looked toward the living room and muttered, "Yeah, everything's fine."

Then he turned around and looked at me again. He asked me "Qué pasó?" ("What's going on?") I told him, "You know why I'm here." He quickly said, "Maybe Lizzie is not such a big deal after all." I knew instantly that he was mine. I stepped forward right to his face and challenged him to step out on the grass with me then and there so we could resolve all of our issues like real men. He raised both of his hands chest-high exposing his palms and shaking his head and said "We don't need to do that." Clearly, he had reduced himself to putty in my hands. I told him that he had offended me, Lizzie and her parents greatly the previous night and that I would not leave until my honor had been restored. I was acting extremely aggressively simply because he was being so submissive. He backed away, apologized and started to beg for forgiveness. I lurched forward one more time threateningly with my fists cuffed ready to pound him. He turned sideways almost in tears.

I retreated slightly and then lifted my clenched right ham-hock of a fist to his face and gave him a stern warning: If he ever looked at me or Lizzie in any threatening way that I would be back. He nodded sheepishly and said he would never do that again. I relaxed, turned around and walked triumphantly back to the green station wagon.

There in the shadow of the tree, standing outside of the driver side of the station wagon was Chuy. He said he had heard everything. He congratulated me on achieving a great victory without having to put grass stains on my blue jeans. As we drove away, I told him that I would never forget what he had just done in standing by me during a crisis. I told him that in recognition of his loyalty and friendship I would like to reward him. We then went to the *Oasis* and I bought both of us an ice-cold cherry *Coke*.

Sure enough, the next few days at school I felt like a king. I did run into the ex-boyfriend a couple of times and each time he carefully avoided making eye contact with me. Even when I ran into his buddies, I could sense that my message to the ex-boyfriend had been forwarded to them. Life was beautiful for the next few months.

The second thing that stands out in my mind about the relationship that I had with Lizzie was how I was unable to terminate it even though I recognized that our affection for each other had ended. Sure, the first few months were extremely exciting as it normally is with teenagers who are discovering things about the opposite sex theretofore unknown to them. But by the beginning of the second semester of my junior year, I rationalized that I was not as attracted to Lizzie anymore. In addition, I was finding that other girls were increasingly of interest to me and that I was of interest to them as well. Yet, despite all of that, I could not bring myself to tell Lizzie that it was over. Instead, I simply endured the matter for months hoping that somehow things would end without me being the initiator of the termination process. Then to my great surprise, by the end of my junior year, Lizzie broke up with me claiming that I was seeing or paying too much attention to other girls.

Interestingly, even though we were not going steady during my senior year, when I went to Texas A&M in September of 1965, we started seeing each other once again. We corresponded during the entire year and whenever I came home, we dated. But it was not exclusive for either of us.

When I went to West Point the following spring, she continued to be my girlfriend on the same basis as during my year at A&M. We wrote letters to each other for the first semester of my plebe year. However, around October she quit writing back. When I returned home for the Christmas holidays that year, I did not even attempt to see her at all. I later found out that, in reality, she had been very sick during the time that she quit writing. She eventually got well again. I felt badly when I discovered that she had been ill but I got over it quickly and I came to accept the fact that our relationship was truly over.

Lizzie went on to rear two kids as a single mom. She is immensely proud of how she ensured that her kids got through college despite all of the challenges she had to meet. Her daughter, Courtney, earned a bachelor of arts degree in 1997 from *Vassar College* having majored in Art History and French. Her son, Brian, graduated from *New York University* in 2002 also with a bachelor of arts degree.

Chapter 9-The Jr. Toastmasters Club

Regardless of where we grow up, our lives will likely be enriched immensely by the friendships that we formed. Most of us became friends simply by happenstance but the imprint we made on each other's lives is profound and timeless. But in addition to experiences we had with our friends, some recognition must be given to institutions, organizations or simply activities that we joined or participated in—within or outside of the *El Paso Boys' Club*--and to the impact they had on our lives.

The variety of activities offered to members at the *El Paso Boys' Club* was incredibly extensive. However, if I had to pick the one activity that I believe was the most interesting, exciting and truly helpful in the development of the boys it would have to be—without a doubt--the Jr. Toastmasters.

The idea of an activity within the Boys' Club aimed at developing the public speaking skills of members first came up in the spring of 1961. The Boys' Club had discovered that there was an oratorical contest for boys sponsored by the *Optimist Clubs International,* a community civic group. It was a national competition that involved the preparation of a speech on a given topic not to exceed five minutes in length and that had to be delivered before one of the local Optimist Clubs. In El Paso, there were at least 10 local chapters of the Optimist Clubs. One of them, the Airport Optimist Club, decided to expand the participant group beyond the normal, exclusively Anglo-American source of participants. In what I believe was a truly visionary deed, they decided to invite members of the *El Paso Boys' Club*—comprised almost exclusively of Mexican-American boys--to participate. I imagine that the Airport Optimist Club sent the invitation to Mr. Hightower at Unit 1 who then passed it down to the other Units. The Director at our Boys' Club Unit 2 at the time, Mr. D, recognized the oratorical contest as a great opportunity and urged me and a few other Club members to consider participating.

It was at this point that Joan Griffin—a volunteer mentor at the Boys Club-- came into my life. She was a secretary at the *El Paso Natural Gas Company* in downtown El Paso and she apparently offered her services to mentor and coach members of the Boys' Club in 1960. That year she organized and became the Director of the *El Paso Boys' Club Glee Club*. She taught a group of some 50 boys from Units 1 and 2 how to sing and then would take them to meetings of local civic clubs to entertain and to spread the word about all the good that was happening at the Boys' Club.

She was a single, career-oriented woman in her mid to late twenties, tall and slender with fair skin and freckles on her face and sky-blue eyes. Her hairstyle was typical 1960s: short, straight and businesslike. In addition to her Glee Club duties, she was assigned to be my coach for the oratorical contest and I was elated at the prospect of working with someone like her. I recall that she always dressed in business attire whenever she met with me. She wore tight skirts and high heeled pumps and was always impeccably made up. I thought she was extremely beautiful, very sweet and I was fortunate to be able to spend as much time as I did with her. She was the first Anglo female that I ever came in relatively close contact with on an individual basis.

I remember wanting very much to properly prepare for the contest. Therefore, some three months before the scheduled event at the local club level, I began drafting my five- minute speech. The speech topic for that year would be: "Optimism; Ingredient for True Leadership." From the moment that I first put pencil to paper, Joan was present to help. She would come to the Boys' Club Unit 2 building in the Paisano Projects every Saturday. We started working in mid-January and the contest was to take place in early April. I would prepare a few paragraphs ahead of each of our Saturday sessions and she would review and otherwise advise me on how to improve the speech. After the first three or four sessions, the speech started to take its final form. Even though it was only a few hundred words long and designed to take no more than five minutes to deliver, it did seem to me to take an eternity to write and finalize.

Once the speech was written, I started to work on my delivery. I would spend a few minutes each day memorizing the speech and then on Saturday afternoons, when I met with Joan, I would deliver the speech in a small private room where she would listen and critique. The sessions would last a few hours and I remember that we were both completely committed to achieving something as close to perfection as we possibly could.

So, Joan Griffin stuck with me for those three months like a puppy sticks to a kid covered with ice-cream. I remember having many, many coaching sessions where she would drill me repeatedly but in a very kind manner. I had a crush on Joan and so I was absolutely committed to pleasing her. That enabled me to focus on this exercise like I had never focused on anything before. By doing that, I believe I was able to create a very fine piece of oratory (for a 13-year-old kid). I would look forward to our meetings because she would give me 100% of her attention during the time that we were together. Even though I--as any other adolescent would have done--

fantasized about her constantly, our coaching sessions were strictly businesslike and the benefits derived were absolutely priceless.

When contest day at the Airport Optimist Club finally arrived in early April of 1961, I was ready. I felt enormously confident and well-prepared. A few other Boys' Club members also competed but I delivered the winning speech, complete with sweeping, punctuating gestures and inflections of my voice. I drew lots of compliments from everyone and took home the first plaque I had ever won. This was the plaque that I mentioned earlier on which my name was painted by hand by Luis Peña, the Crafts Instructor at The Boys' Club. In addition to the plaque, I earned a chance to advance to the Zone F competition which included most of the other Optimist Clubs in the city.

I went on to the Zone F competition where I again gave it my best shot. However, the competition was simply too great and I failed even to place. Other Boys' Club members who had won at the Optimist Club level similarly were not able to compete effectively at the Zone level. Nevertheless, the Boys' Club, as well as the individuals who participated, received great press from the experience. We had tasted victory and had gained valuable experience and were highly motivated to compete again the following year. The other Boys' Club members who had also been coached by adult volunteer mentors and who competed and won at contests at other Optimist Clubs throughout El Paso seemed as smitten by the experience as I had been. There's no question that lifelong impressions about the value of public speaking were formed in the minds of each of us who participated in the contest that year.

And so, for many years following this experience, I felt very grateful for what all of these adult mentors had done, particularly Joan Griffin. But interestingly, when I was around 35 or 40 years old, I realized that I had forgotten Joan's last name. Year after year, I felt pretty rotten about that because she had done so much for me and one should never forget those who do so much. But my memory was blank and I felt fairly miserable about having forgotten her name. None of my buds from the old neighborhood seemed to recall her last name either.

Many years later, in 2006, my friend, fellow Boys' Club member and fellow Optimist Speech Contest competitor, Checo Reza, told me that he had an old scrapbook filled with Boys' Club information. I asked to borrow it and sure enough, among the documents in his scrapbook was the annual report on the *El Paso Boys' Club* for 1961. One of the photographs in the report was of the *El Paso Boys' Club Glee Club* and much to my delightful surprise, I saw that the Glee Club director was my old speech mentor. The photograph identified her by name: Joan Griffin, and I was overwhelmed with joy as a burden that I had been carrying for twenty years was suddenly lifted. I now knew once again Joan Griffin's last name.

Joan, like the many other adults that I met in my adolescence, made a huge impact on my life. I firmly believe that had I been brought up in a different environment, I would probably have never met Joan and the others and, without doubt, my life would have been different. The only thing I regret is that I did not dedicate myself earlier to finding these folks to again thank them for all they did for me.

As a result of the successes the boys had enjoyed in the Optimist Oratorical contest in the spring of 1961, Homer Taylor, a member of the *Paso Del Norte Toastmasters Club* approached Mr. Hightower in May, 1961, and suggested organizing a Junior Toastmasters Club for members of the Boys' Club. The concept was to be identical to that of the adult Toastmasters Clubs. It was a noble and imaginative act by Mr. Hightower, Mr. Taylor and the Boys' Club Board to set in motion the formation of the *Linguistic Jr. Toastmasters Club*.

As many people know, there is a civic organization throughout the country called the *Toastmasters*. Once a month, the Toastmasters meet for the sole purpose of improving their public speaking abilities. They meet in restaurants in the morning, at noon or in the evening and while enjoying a meal, various members of the organization actually stand before the group and deliver a speech. Other members of the organization evaluate the speech and provide constructive criticism. The end result, theoretically, is that the speaker becomes better over time.

Mr. Taylor became the adult sponsor of the Jr. Toastmasters and was accorded the title of Director. He had the enthusiastic support of a member of the Board of Directors of the Boys' Club, Mr. George Stauning, who like Mr. Taylor, was also a member of the *Paso Del Norte Toastmasters Club*. Both of these gentlemen were well-educated and very successful businessmen employed by one of the most prominent companies in El Paso at the time, the *El Paso Natural Gas Company*.

As all that was happening at Unit 1 of the Boys' Club, Mr. D, the Director of Unit 2, continued to establish himself as a singular community organizer, a very capable leader of boys and a wonderful role model. I believe strongly that the vast majority of the Club members at Unit 2 were influenced significantly by Mr. D. There were a few who were influenced immensely. I was one of those. Mr. D always communicated to me with words and deeds that I had some potential to excel. Therefore, he was constantly pushing me to do new and different things and to get into as many different Club activities as possible. One day, Mr. Hightower apparently sent word from the main unit to Mr. D that a new public speaking activity for members was being started and that he wanted Mr. D to bring a carload of Club members from our unit to join. Mr. D had also helped me when I first competed in the Optimist Oratorical Contest and so he immediately contacted me and a couple of other boys who had also competed to help form the core of this new club. I remember very fondly that trip from Unit 2 to Unit 1--in the Club's sky-blue *Chevrolet* panel truck along with three or four other kids--to attend that first meeting. We were all somewhat excited about it but we could not have possibly known then how huge an impact this new activity would have on our lives for the next three or four years and for the rest of our lives as well.

During that first meeting in June, 1961, Messrs. Taylor and Stauning proposed organizing this new club to a gathering of 8 or 9 boys including myself. They told us that by participating in this new club, we would learn how to effectively speak publicly. They also promised that each of us would benefit further by enhancing our confidence and our ability to think on our feet. I recognized even then at the age of 14 that an ability to speak effectively before the public was very desirable and constituted one of the most powerful skills that anyone could take with them into just about any profession. I also could see that such an organization would help us enormously in future Optimist Oratorical Contests. They invited us to think about this new club and if we were still interested, to reconvene the following week so we could actually form it.

The following week, just about every one of the original attendees showed up again. From his experience at the *Paso Del Norte Toastmasters Club*, Mr. Taylor had drafted the Bylaws and the Constitution to get the organization started. He had also decided what the name of the new organization would be: The *Linguistic Junior Toastmasters Club*. The members reviewed and approved the new documents and then elected the officers that would move the organization forward. I was lucky and privileged to be elected President. The rest of the original officer slate was: Salvador E. "Chichi" Garcia, Educational Vice President; Sergio "Checo" Reza, Administrative Vice President; Armando Lopez, Secretary-Treasurer; and Ezequiel Chacon, Sergeant-at-Arms. Some of the other original members included: Antonio Alfaro, Eugene Paredes, Arnulfo Hernandez, Jose Amor, Miguel Colorado, Antonio Alba, Daniel Miranda, Robert Lopez, Salvador Valdez and my older brother Nacho.

So, from the core of 8 or 9 members, the club grew. Eventually the *Linguistic Jr. Toastmasters Club* had as many as 15 or 20 or even more, including Ray Velarde, Manny Ontiveros, Homer Reza, Bernie Del Hierro, Joe Renteria, Manny and Javier Alvarez, Juan Uranga, Arturo Estrada, Ben Garcia, Julio Pellicano and Antonio Stephens. The Jr. Toastmaster experience was essentially the following: at the end of any given meeting, the assignments for the following week would be handed out. Three members would be designated to be the main speakers. They would have a week to prepare a 5-minute speech for delivery the following week. If a kid was there for the very first time, he would be designated as one of the three main speakers for the following week and be required to give his "Icebreaker" speech. This was a 5-minute summary of his life. It would quickly give him a taste of Toastmastering and at the same time introduce him more fully to the rest of the members. Another member would be designated to be the chief evaluator for the next meeting. His job was to listen carefully to all the speeches, to take notes and to honestly—although perhaps a better word might be "brutally"—tell each speaker in great detail what he did wrong (or right). Another person would be designated to be the timer. He would be armed with a stop watch and a lamp system. The lamp system was a box with three lights on it. One light--the green one--would be illuminated from the beginning of any speech. Another light—the yellow one—would be turned on when the speaker was 30 seconds from his time limit. The third light—a red one—would be turned on when the speaker reached his time limit. The most coveted job each week was that of the "Bean Can Man." His tools were an empty tin can and a bag of beans. His job was to listen to every speech intently and to fire a bean into the can each and every time that a speaker would utter an "uh" or an "ah" or any other sound that was not a proper word. The sound of the bean clanging into the can would inform the speaker that he had just committed a public-speaking blunder. Later, as each speaker received his critique, the Bean-Can Man would announce the total number of beans he had dropped into the can for that speaker. The idea was to learn how to avoid making those blunders in the future.

All the other members who did not have a specific job during a meeting would nevertheless get a chance to get on their feet and speak during the "Table Topics" session of the meeting. The adult sponsor would simply pick a topic at random and assign it to a member who would immediately have to stand up and speak about it for 2 seemingly endless minutes. Examples of topics included: "My favorite TV program," "America's Race in Space," and even "Our Stand on Laos and Cuba." No one ever was excused from having to participate in this part of the program.

These jobs were rotated each week so as to give each kid an opportunity to either speak before the rest of the members or to evaluate a speech given by another. Generally, because boys will be boys, no one really prepared very hard for the next week's assignments. Yet, we all seemed genuinely interested in becoming better speakers and even if we were not well-prepared, we would refine our public speaking skills and have great fun each week doing that.

Mr. Taylor prepared a "Training Program" for the club based on the program followed by the adult Toastmasters. It consisted of 12 basic training speeches. The first was always the aforementioned "Icebreaker." The next eleven speeches were intended to emphasize the different vital elements of public speaking. For example, one such speech was to focus on the speaker's use of hand gestures to make his delivery more effective. Another speech was to focus on the speaker's eye contact with his audience. Another speech would focus on the organization of the subject matter of the speech. When a member completed his 12 basic training speeches, the Club would award him a Certificate of Merit in an appropriate ceremony usually attended by a senior member of the Boys' Club staff, usually the Executive Director, Mr. Hightower. As one might imagine, this event was a huge confidence builder for each of us.

One of my most precious Jr. Toastmaster memories relates to a special lectern that I built during my tenure as President. The training model of the Jr. Toastmasters Club discouraged speakers from ever resting their hands on the podium or lectern. Theoretically, a good speaker should use his hands only to make gestures to enhance the effectiveness of the speech. Otherwise, the hands should hang comfortably at his side. No matter what, the hands should never come to rest on the podium or lectern. I distinctly remember how this rule about hands was emphasized over and over during our meetings. One day, I came up with an idea to build a lectern that would sit on the table in front of the speaker and serve as an inclined platform where the speaker can place his notes. But I designed and built this particular lectern to discourage any speaker using it from mindlessly resting his hands on it. I did that by spring-loading the two side edges on the top of the lectern where speakers would normally rest their hands. I then rigged a battery-operated buzzer to them so that whenever the speaker would place his hands on the edges, a circuit would close and a buzzer would sound. A more effective bad-habit-breaker has never been invented. Unfortunately, audiences listening to speeches being delivered from that lectern usually paid less attention to the speech and more to the buzzer and to the hapless speaker who had to deal with it.

Here's another story that will stick in my mind for a long time. The Jr. Toastmasters Club met every Wednesday evening at 7:30PM at Unit 1 which was about 3 or 4 miles away from Unit 2. At around 6:15PM on Mondays, the Unit 2 1953 sky-blue *Chevrolet* panel truck would load all the Jr. Toastmasters from Unit 2 and take us to Unit 1 for the meeting. After the meeting, Mr. Hightower would take the Unit 2 boys back to Unit 2. His home was on the east side of town and so he could simply continue on home after dropping the boys off. On one such occasion, only two boys from Unit 2—Checo Reza and I--needed a ride. Mr. Hightower put us in the backseat of his white '56 *Chevy* and drove us back to Unit 2. Checo and I felt privileged that the Executive Director of the *El Paso Boys' Club* was driving us home. After all, Mr. Hightower was the most distinguished man either of us had ever met. On the way there we engaged in a bit of small talk but mostly the trip was a quiet one as Checo and I were trying hard to be respectful and courteous. Then, after a few moments of quiet and out of nowhere, Mr. Hightower started warbling. Warbling is a very distinctive form of whistling that is done by sucking air in through the mouth and passing the air stream over a small puddle of saliva gathered on the tongue. That produces a warbling sort of whistling melody. Mr. Hightower was completely absorbed in his warbling. It actually sounded pretty good. But Checo glanced over at me and I back at him and we could not believe the strange sound that we were hearing. Then—as often happens to kids--both of us started to giggle very quietly at the warbling, hoping that he would stop. Well, Mr. Hightower did not stop. We continued to listen and could hardly control our giggling as Mr. Hightower drove east on Paisano Drive. Despite all of our efforts to stifle the giggling, it was becoming impossible to hide it. Soon, Checo and I found ourselves trying to muffle our giggling with one hand and with the other hand, desperately trying to suppress a growing risk of peeing in our pants. After what seemed an eternity, Mr. Hightower became aware that we were indeed laughing at his warbling. He gave us a broad smile and encouraged us to laugh freely and so we did. He was a really pleasant sort of person.

I honestly and strongly believe that the weekly meetings that we held and the tutoring that we received from adult professional, mentor volunteers, prepared a whole bunch of us boys to deal with the future and with society much more effectively. In my mind, the Junior Toastmasters was one of the most valuable and enriching experiences that I ever went through. It was a truly wonderful coincidence that during that period of time at the Boys' Club, a few adult mentors conceived of the idea that meeting weekly to train young teenagers in the art of public speaking was a project worth undertaking. However, the idea by itself would be meaningless unless those young teenagers could somehow be persuaded to spend one or two hours per week meeting with those mentors and with their peers to pursue this goal. I very much doubt that the teenagers such as me, who ended up joining the Junior Toastmasters, would have done so except for the sometimes not-so-gentle persuasion of club staff members. Simply announcing that the Junior Toastmasters were going to meet, never had the desired effect of getting the boys to attend the meetings. In the early days of the organization, Mr. D or Huevo or some other staff member would literally snare one or two or three boys from the game room at the Club and usher them into the library for a meeting of the Junior Toastmasters. Many times, those boys did not come back to future meetings. However, many did return and discovered how cool it was to learn how to give speeches.

As I look back today, I have to say that it was extremely unlikely that an activity aimed at the development of public speaking skills of young boys in any of the neighborhoods where the Boys' Clubs existed would ever be successful. We were only young kids participating in an activity that a few adults told us was worthwhile. I suppose we had some sense that public speaking skills were useful but we really could not appreciate the profound impact that such training would have as we pursued college educations and careers later on. It must be remembered that then, and now, it was not and is not normal for residents of predominantly Mexican-American communities to speak English without a heavy Spanish or Mexican accent. When kids in these communities finally finish high school many of them carry with them a very noticeable speech accent that traditionally has been frowned upon outside of the Barrio. There is no question that when I was in high school such an accent was and would always be a significant impediment to one's future success. Yet, speaking with such an accent the accent was practically unavoidable since in most cases, the first language at home was Spanish and since that same accent prevailed in every social context including schools. To be sure, the Junior Toastmasters club did not really focus on doing something about that accent. The focus was mostly on overcoming fear when speaking before groups and on the techniques that enable speakers to communicate well. Former Junior Toastmasters today smile when recalling how some of the boys back then were dynamic speakers but were nevertheless hobbled in their communication skills by the thick Mexican accents in their speeches.

It was in the Jr. Toastmasters that I first heard the term "constructive criticism." When an organization is formed so that its members can improve themselves in any way, there has to be a way to identify shortcomings and other deficiencies so that they can be addressed and hopefully fixed. In the Jr. Toastmasters, we accomplished that through constructive criticism. When a 12-year-old kid gives a 2-minute speech to an audience of Jr. Toastmaster peers and mentors, it will almost certainly result in an avalanche of constructive criticism. That's the way it was at the weekly Jr. Toastmasters Club meeting. One of us would give a speech and get tons of constructive criticism from the rest. At the next meeting, the "target" of all that criticism would become a giver of criticism. Sometimes it was tough to hear that the speech just delivered was deficient in so many ways. Other times, it was funny. But we were learning to become better speakers and this was a pretty effective way of doing that. More importantly, I think we were discovering that each of us was far from perfect and that receiving constructive criticism in *any* context is a useful thing.

It was a wonderful coincidence that during those years, the *Optimist Clubs of America* was sponsoring an oratorical contest. That contest allowed the members of the Junior Toastmasters Club to set their sights on tangible and meaningful targets as well as rewards and recognition, all in the context of public speaking. The competition engendered by these oratorical contests was every bit as intense as the competition that existed in the basketball, baseball and touch football leagues of the Boys' Club. The rewards, however, were much more immediate and significant. Whenever we spoke, not only did we receive compliments and pats on the back from supportive and apparently successful adults, but we could win trophies and even scholarships from public speaking. We also had the distinct pleasure of going on trips as a group to compete. And, every time that a Junior Toastmaster won an oratorical contest, there would be recognition in the local as well as in the high school newspapers.

This competition proved pivotal in sharpening the speaking skills of the individual members and in grooming really outstanding Boys' Club members to compete in the national *Boys' Clubs of America* Boy of the Year competition. Suddenly, as Jr. Toastmasters started winning speech contests, more and more boys started to show up at the Boys' Club from all over El Paso wanting to join not only the Jr. Toastmasters Club but also the Boys' Club itself. In my mind, the crowning moment in that regard occurred when Mr. Stauning--who was one of the members of the Boys' Club Board of Directors and also an adult sponsor and mentor of the Jr. Toastmasters--brought his own son Rick so that he too could jump on this magic carpet ride. Rick was graciously accepted into the Jr. Toastmasters and became well-liked even though his blond hair and blue eyes quite graphically set him apart from the rest of.

In early 1962, I, along with ten or twelve other members of the Jr. Toastmasters Club, embarked on a mission to compete in and win as many local Optimist Club competitions as possible. The topic for that year's competition was "The Creative Force of Optimism." By then, I had a year of experience in Optimist Club speech contests, I was the President of the *Linguistics Jr. Toastmasters Club*, I had become a true believer in the force of optimism and I was eager to lead the other Jr. Toastmasters to victory.

The Jr. Toastmasters Club had gotten a lot of good press during the oratorical contests of the previous year and, as a result, it was attracting more and more boys from other El Paso neighborhoods. Joe Renteria joined the Jr. Toastmasters that year. He had grown up in the Second Ward area near *Bowie High School* in south El Paso and had been a Boys' Club member since his elementary school days. However, his family had moved out of the neighborhood and into the more affluent area around *Austin High School*. When he joined the Jr. Toastmasters in 1962, Joe was a freshman at Austin High. After seeing what the Jr. Toastmasters Club was doing, he brought a few of his buddies from Austin High, including Manny and Javier Alvarez and Bernie Del Hierro, to also get involved.

Johnny Uranga was another kid who grew up in Second Ward but whose family managed to move up and away, in his case, to the west side of El Paso where he attended *Coronado High School*. He also heard of the Jr. Toastmasters and ended up joining. This continuing influx of kids from the more affluent neighborhoods was a testimonial to the success and effectiveness of the Jr. Toastmasters.

In February, 1962, I started writing my *Creative Force of Optimism* speech. Mr. D was my coach that year and he suggested to me that a quotation from the *Bible* would be a very effective way to start my speech. He introduced me to *Genesis* and the opening lines in my speech became the following:

In the beginning, God created the heaven and the earth. And the earth was without form and void; and darkness was upon the face of the deep. And the spirit of God moved upon the face of the waters. And God said, "Let there be light;" and there was light.

I always thought that Mr. D and I had hit the jack pot with that introduction but I did not realize how impressive it must have been until decades later when peers as well as mentors would recall my speech by saying to me: "Let there be light!"

Anyway, in early March of 1962, after about a month of writing, rehearsing and polishing my speech with lots of help from Mr. D, I was prepared to start delivering the speech in front of the Jr. Toastmasters Club itself. In fact, every member of the Jr. Toastmasters Club had been similarly working on their speeches and we were all going to deliver our speeches before each other and accept the constructive criticism that was to be offered by our peers and mentors.

And so, I delivered my speech before my fellow Jr. Toastmasters and, as was customary, I received a barrage of constructive criticism about it from my buddies. In addition, the one or two mentors present, including Joan Griffin, provided additional constructive comments. Each of us boys went through the same exercise not just once but repeatedly for a few weeks until we actually had to compete. The whole process had the effect of generating some extremely good speeches that surprised everyone with the success that they had in the contests. Apparently, the kids that competed against us had absolutely nothing comparable in terms of assistance, time-spent and intensity regarding preparation. As with any other endeavor, proper preparation, including extremely good coaching, will very likely produce spectacular results.

During March and April, 1962, the Jr. Toastmasters, under the thoughtful guidance of mentors such as Edward S. Marquez, Homer Taylor and Joan Griffin, won 3 of the 7 Optimist Club speech contests held in El Paso. Winning at the local Optimist Club level enabled us to compete at the next-higher zone or district level which included a nice little trip to some town not too far away such as Carlsbad, NM. Then, whoever won at the zone/district level would compete at the regional level which involved a longer trip to a place like Albuquerque, NM. Winning at the regional level would enable one to compete at the national level and would involve a long-distance trip to a place such as Los Angeles, CA.

This is probably a good time to focus on the tremendous impact that Mr. Edward S. Marquez had on the Jr. Toastmasters. Mr. Marquez was a young and energetic lawyer back in the sixties when I was in high school and in the Jr. Toastmasters. During that time, he was an Assistant US Attorney. He went on from there to a successful private legal career. In 1974, he was appointed District Judge of the 65th District Court by Governor Dolph Briscoe. In January, 1997, he was appointed Senior Judge (Visiting Judge) and remained in that capacity until his death in 2006.

Judge Marquez was born on January 8, 1931, in El Paso. He graduated from *El Paso High School*, got a BA and a law degree from the *University of Texas* at Austin. He served his country honorably in the US Air Force Air Rescue service during the Korean War.

Judge Marquez was one of those individuals who had a profound impact on the lives of many of the Jr. Toastmasters. He was a volunteer mentor at the

El Paso Boys' Club and acted as counselor and adviser to the Junior Toastmasters Club. I was extremely active in both of those organizations when I was in high school.

In the sixties, Mr. Marquez--although always busy with his legal work--was able to engage in all of these activities simply because he was a bachelor. He never had to run home in the evenings to be with his wife or children. But unlike most bachelors who would rather party and otherwise have a good time with chicks, he chose to spend his free time helping the community by mentoring young men and, in effect, discouraging them from getting into trouble.

Even though he was in his thirties at the time, Mr. Mzrquez was a teenager at heart. The main differences between Mr. Marquez and the boys he mentored were that he had money and that he enjoyed a fine reputation for being an upstanding member of the community and of the local legal bar. For those reasons, he could have fun and answer to no one. The fun I refer to is, of course, harmless teenager fun.

For example, Mr. Marquez loved to go to the professional wrestling matches. But instead of inviting girlfriends or other adult friends, he would prefer to take a pack of Boys' Clubbers with him. By doing so, he would still have the fun that he wanted to have, yet he would, at the same time, be contributing to the good development of youngsters. On any given Sunday afternoon, Mr. Marquez would take a group of us to Juárez, Mexico, where we would watch professional wrestlers act out incredibly fake matches. We enjoyed these matches immensely primarily because they were so utterly unbelievable. After the matches, he would treat us to lunch there in Juárez. Checo, Fernando and I were almost always in the group that he would invite. He had met our parents and everyone trusted him. He was actually much wilder and fun-loving than anyone ever imagined.

Because Mr. Marquez was a gainfully employed attorney, he had money. But he apparently really didn't have very much of it. He drove an ancient 1949 or 1950 *Chevy* that probably had never been washed. The interior was as filthy as any I've ever seen. His glove box was a good indication of how slovenly he was. Occasionally, he would need to get something from the glove box and, when he opened it, invariably, a ton of trash would spill out causing us all to have a good laugh. But he didn't care about that and we did not care either. The group of us would pile into his car and he would take us to events such as wrestling matches or baseball games and all of us had the times of our lives.

In 1965, when I was a senior in high school, I got my first speeding ticket. Shortly afterward, I took that ticket to Mr. Marquez hoping that he might be able to help me "take care" of it. When I showed it to him, he snatched it from my hand as if it were nothing, told me not to worry about it and then stuffed it into the glove box of his *Chevy*. I relied on him completely and never gave the speeding ticket another thought. Months later, during one of these wrestling trips to Juárez, I was riding shotgun on the front seat with three or four other kids elsewhere in the car. Mr. Marquez needed something from the glove compartment and so he asked me to look in there and find it. I pushed the glove box button to pop it open and, sure enough, a mountain of trash spilled out. I noticed that among the trash there were probably fifteen or twenty old police citation forms and traffic tickets that Mr. Marquez had stuffed in there. After I handed him what he needed from the glove box, I proceeded to re-stuff all that garbage back into it. In doing so, I spotted one particular traffic ticket with my name on it. My heart stopped. It was the citation I had given to him months earlier and that he was going to handle for me. I remember feeling at that moment that soon I was going to be arrested for failure to appear in court and would be convicted, thereby seriously jeopardizing any chance I ever had to go to Texas A&M or West Point. I showed it to him without saying anything. He immediately acknowledged that he had forgotten all about it, laughed boisterously and again assured me to not worry about it. He did, however, ask me not to put it back in the glove box so that he could take care of it the next day. I recall that I worried about it for a few more days but eventually nothing did happen. I have to assume that this time he really took care of it.

During the Christmas vacation that I took while in my plebe year at West Point, I spent most of it in El Paso. One afternoon shortly before Christmas I decided to stop by the El Paso District Attorney's office to say hello to Mr. Marquez. It just so happened that they were going to have the Christmas office party that afternoon. Mr. Marquez invited me to stay for the party. The party was lots of fun. I even met a young lady (a really cute secretary) there and we both hit it off quite nicely. Of course, I had no car at the time. As the party was ending at about 8:00 PM, Mr. Marquez noticed that the young lady and I were having a good time and he knew that I did not have a car. So, he called me aside where the young lady could not hear and handed me his car keys telling me to use his car and not bring it back to him until the next day. Now that I had a car, I was able to go out for the rest of the evening with this young lady. I shall never forget Mr. Marquez' generosity and insight on that particular day.

More recently, after I had finished law school and started working for IBM, I went to El Paso for some reason and decided to stop by and visit Judge

Marquez in his courtroom. He was a State District Judge at the time. My plan had been to enter the courtroom and take a seat among all the people that were present during the trial that he happened to be presiding over. I wanted to observe him in his capacity as judge and then say hello during the first recess. I entered his courtroom very quietly trying hard not to be intrusive. Judge Marquez happened to glance up as I entered. Instantly, as he recognized me, a huge grin covered his face. He stood up and ignoring proper courtroom decorum, he hollered out, "Willie!" The proceedings came to a complete halt. Everyone in the court room turned to look at me. I was totally shocked and embarrassed. Judge Marquez then asked me to step up to the bench where he introduced me to everyone. He acknowledged to all present that I was an attorney working for IBM and then he proceeded to list every good thing that I had ever done in my life. I remember that by that time my shock and embarrassment had worn off and I started to feel really proud of whom I had become. In my entire life, no one had ever before made me feel better than he did in those moments. After forcing everyone to listen to his speech for about ten minutes, he asked me to say a few words. I simply told everyone that if I had indeed become a good member of society, it was in large measure due to guidance that I had received from Judge Marquez while I was in the Boys' Club. He then recessed the proceedings and we went to lunch.

Judge Marquez had a huge impact on my life. There are probably three main things that he drew my attention to while we were acquainted. The first one was the importance and value of being able to address large groups of people. He was quite good at it and he taught me and all the other members of the Junior Toastmasters Club how to do that very effectively. Another thing that he influenced me about greatly was a career as a lawyer. He--more than anyone else--created an image in my mind of lawyers that I found quite attractive. The last item that I learned from him was to lighten up. I believe that I have never met anyone who could mix life--including all of the nasty moments that it creates--with laughter and good times. Judge Marquez had a sense of humor and an appreciation for levity that should be emulated by everyone. I know I always tried to use his sense of humor as my own benchmark for having a good time.

While I have never regretted leaving for good the city where I grew up, I occasionally do have a sense of remorse about not staying in touch with the many men and women who helped me get a good start in life. If I had remained in El Paso, I am quite certain that I would have remained in close contact with Judge Marquez. Since I went away instead, I did not stay in touch and I regret that immensely.

Armed with an awesome stable of mentors and teachers such as Mr. Marquez, the Jr. Toastmasters flourished. As far as speech contest success went, 1962 was my year. For the second year in a row, I competed in the Optimist Oratorical Contest at the Airport Optimist Club. I had truly become a believer in optimism as a powerful booster in any and all aspects of life and I honestly felt an inexorable force working in me that year to conquer the world. In late April, 1962, I again won the Airport Optimist Club oratorical contest and earned yet another beautiful plaque and the right to compete at the District 19 competition that followed. I recall very fondly how the President of the Airport Optimist Club, Mr. Bill Rutledge, and other members including Mr. Dick Catt and Mr. H. B. "Laff" Lafferty embraced me and encouraged me with boundless enthusiasm to go forth and continue in my quest for fame and glory.

In May, 1962, the Boys' Club organized a trip for the Jr. Toastmasters to go to Carlsbad, NM, to compete in the District 19 Optimist Oratorical Contest. The three Jr. Toastmasters who had won at the local Optimist Club level were Joe Renteria, Johnny Uranga and I. We would now compete with each other and with 4 other boys to see who would win the District contest. Mr. Hightower had obtained a brand-new *Buick* station wagon on loan from the local dealer--along with some privately-owned cars of Boys' Club staff members--to drive the entire Jr. Toastmasters Club to Carlsbad. We stayed at the Carlsbad Boys' Club at the invitation of its Executive Director, Mr. De Shazo, whose son, Randy, was a staff member of the *El Paso Boys' Club*. During the trip, the Jr. Toastmasters managed to play softball against the Carlsbad boys and beat them although Carlsbad gained revenge when the two teams later played basketball.

On Friday, May 18, 1962, the District 19 Optimist Oratorical contest was held. I won first place; Dick Azar also from El Paso won second place (he had been the District 19 winner the previous year); and Brian Gratton of Roswell, New Mexico, won third place. I received a beautiful trophy for my efforts and earned a slot to compete at the Regional contest two weeks later. The trophy was about 12 inches tall and consisted of a polished mahogany base with a gold-plated figure of a man on top. The figurine-man was standing straight and tall, wearing a suit with both arms bent at the elbow with hands open as if making a point during a speech.

In June, Mr. Hightower again organized a big trip for the Jr. Toastmasters to accompany me to the Regional competition in Albuquerque, NM. This was a momentous event for the Jr. Toastmasters as well as the *El Paso Boys' Club* and our hopes soared as we contemplated a non-stop ride to fame and fortune. Unfortunately, I did not even place in the competition although I did receive a nice *Elgin* gold watch to commemorate the event. I was not even 15 years old at this time, yet I had gone through some experiences in these competitions that would forever stay with me and affect me more positively than anything else I had ever experienced. The Jr. Toastmasters had become so successful that we could barely accommodate the number of speaking engagements that were being offered to us. Given all that I had just learned, I looked to the following year with great anticipation. I, in particular, was giving speeches at local civic clubs about once a week. Things were going absolutely perfectly. I was riding fast and high on a magic carpet and no matter where I looked, the view was clear and infinite.

The Board of Directors of the *El Paso Boys' Club* was also enjoying unprecedented prominence due to the successes of the Boys' Club. After all, the Club had produced the National *Boy of the Year* in 1961, as well as a few Regional and Sectional *Boy of the Year* winners. In addition, a succession of victories in speech contests all over the Southwest had gotten the Club incredibly good press. It was a great time to be a part of the *El Paso Boys' Club*. It was also a great time to be a member of its Board of Directors. These fine people were all community activists and when things went well for the Club, they could certainly take credit.

I have a particularly bittersweet memory of one thing that happened to me during that wonderful period. One day after a few months of establishing myself as an effective speaker for the Boys' Club cause, I received an invitation to speak at a meeting of the Boys' Club Board of Directors. The meeting was held at the ballroom of the *Del Camino Hotel* and over 100 people attended. I was asked to give my five-minute speech that had taken me to the Optimist Oratorical Contest Regional finals earlier that summer. This represented an amazing opportunity for me personally and, because the press would cover the event, I also knew that the Boys' Club would also benefit tremendously.

On the evening of the event, I wore the same dark plaid suit that I always wore. It had no lapels. That was fashionable because of the *Beatles* who were invading America. I was cocky as heck since I had given the speech many times before. Also, I knew the audience would be friendly. I felt in those days that absolutely everybody liked me. Sure enough, my speech was a home run. Everything went perfectly. The applause that I received seemed to run forever. The evening was completely successful.

When the meeting was adjourned, the secretary of the Board of Directors, a distinguished lady named Mrs. Chris Aranda, came over to where I was standing by the dais. She was truly an elegant lady who was one of the most powerful figures in El Paso. She happened to work as the executive assistant to the El Paso County District Attorney, but she was very popular and influential in her own right and she could make things happen in El Paso, particularly as those things might benefit the Boys' Club.

Mrs. Aranda was a sweet lady who seemed to really like me. At that point, I had known her for about a year and I felt that she was one of my biggest fans. She could have been my grandmother the way she hugged me and fretted about me. She also was a very fashion-conscious dresser. Her outfits were strikingly attractive and presumably very expensive. She always wore a wide brim hat at these functions. I liked her also and I was always delighted to chat with her whenever the opportunity came up.

And so, she and I stood by the dais and chatted pleasantly as the busboys and waiters began clearing away the dishes. I cannot recall the topic of our conversation--probably nothing but small talk--but we were having a swell time just talking and visiting.

As we were conversing, I noticed a small collection of creamers that were sitting in a tray on the table next to us. These were the little glass bottles about 2 in. high and maybe three-quarters of an inch in diameter, filled with cream and capped with a little cardboard disk about the size of a dime. The creamers were the customary method in those days of delivering cream for coffee drinkers at restaurants.

I absentmindedly picked up one of the creamers and started to fiddle with it as I tried to charm Mrs. Aranda with conversation. She listened intently to everything I would say and whenever I delivered a lame, funny remark, she would laugh gleefully. We continued chatting for maybe a minute or two and I continued fiddling with that creamer I had picked up. Then, as we chatted a bit more, I placed the creamer on the table and put my index finger on the cardboard disk on top. As I listened to Mrs. Aranda speak, I gently pushed down on the disk. Why? I don't know. Maybe I was hoping to cause the disk to harmlessly collapse into the cream.

The disk did not budge and so I pushed a little harder with my index finger. I was still listening to everything Mrs. Aranda was saying but I was more focused on getting the cardboard disk to gently fall into the cream.

Just as Mrs. Aranda was delivering what must have been a significant conversational point, the cardboard disk gave way. But instead of its slow and meaningless descent into the cream, the cardboard disk--along with the force of my index finger--caused the cream to *explode* upward from its little container and to create a 3 ft. geyser of milk and bubbles that promptly cascaded all over Mrs. Aranda's sweet face, lovely hat and magnificent dark outfit that quickly turned polka-dotted in white.

I was completely stunned at what I had just done and could not believe that I could have done something so stupid. But then I compounded the disaster by grabbing a cloth napkin and trying to pat her all over to remove the cream from her dress. It was an act of chivalry until I realized that I was patting her on her breasts. She backed away quickly, of course. My embarrassment became total humiliation.

That had to be the worst moment of my life. Not only did I commit a gross act of stupidity, but it affected one of the grandest ladies I had ever known. To make matters worse, all this occurred at the moment in my life when everything was almost completely under control and during which I honestly felt like I could do no wrong.

If I recall correctly, on more than one occasion during those days people would refer to me as the *"crème de la crème"* of El Paso youth. How ironic it was that cream had so much to do with this humiliating but memorable event.

1963 quite possibly was the finest year ever for a Boy's Club anywhere. In April of that year, my brother, Ignacio (aka "Nacho" and "Lefty") Chavez, a member of the *El Paso Boys' Club* and the Jr. Toastmasters, was named the *Boys' Clubs of America's* National Boy of the Year. What made that so special was that only two years earlier, another El Paso youth had won that same honor. In 1963, it was as if nothing could go wrong. I personally felt an irresistible force pushing me forward and without limits and I believe that many other Club members felt the same way.

That year, 1963, was a banner year for the Jr. Toastmasters as well. It also turned out to be my friend, Joe Renteria's, year. I first met him when he showed up at a Jr. Toastmasters meeting at the Boys' Club in 1962. He was a freshman at *Austin High School*. I did not understand then how or why a kid from *Austin High School* ended up coming to the south side of El Paso into a rough neighborhood to attend the Junior Toastmasters Club meeting. Kids and families in South El Paso always looked to schools such as Austin—which was predominantly Anglo—as a much more desirable place to get educated. It became even more baffling to me later when Joe left Austin High and enrolled at Bowie, a South El Paso school. Well, I learned many years later that his older brothers and sister had all graduated from Bowie

High and so at the beginning of his sophomore year, he decided to go to Bowie also.

Nevertheless, in 1963, Joe--who had joined the Jr. Toastmasters a year earlier--began to really impress everyone greatly with his innate public-speaking skills and his natural ability to speak perfect English. That may sound strange, but, as I've pointed out previously, most of us in the Club struggled with English since most of us had not been born in the US and/or only spoke English as a second language.

Not long after he joined the Jr. Toastmasters Club, he started his own rise toward the presidency of the Club. I--like everyone else--saw that potential in him. As a seasoned veteran who had arrived at the scene a year earlier, I treated Joe as my protégé as he developed his public speaking skills to the level that I had achieved over the past year. Within a short time, he became so good that he became more my rival than my protégé. It was inevitable that he would soon run against me for office and that he would beat me. The Boys' Club also recognized Joe's potential and started to groom him as a Boy of the Year candidate as well. I saw clearly then that we were destined to compete against each other in the foreseeable future.

Sure enough, Joe, who had been a member of the Jr. Toastmasters for over a year, developed into an extremely good public speaker. In June of 1963, he was elected President of the Jr. Toastmasters. I sensed early on that my hope of repeating and even exceeding the success I achieved the previous year would be significantly complicated now that I would have to contend with someone with the skills of Joe.

As had become the pattern, boys from the *El Paso Boys' Club* again started winning the majority of the Optimist Oratorical contests held at the local club level throughout El Paso. Some 18 Jr. Toastmasters actually competed that year and at least 8 managed to win at the local Optimist Club level. For the third year in a row, I won the contest at the Airport Optimist Club; Joe Renteria won the Cielo Vista Optimist Club; and Ben Garcia won at the West Side Optimist Club. The three of us went on to win in three different Zone contests. This set the stage for the three of us to compete against each other at the District level where I had won the previous year.

On Saturday, May 7, 1963, the District 19 Optimist Oratorical Contest was held in Albuquerque, NM. Once again, a trip was organized by the Boys' Club staff so that all 18 of the Jr. Toastmasters who competed in the local contests could attend and support their club-mate competitors. I was a junior in high school and felt as confident as ever knowing that I had prepared fully with the best coach available, yet I knew that Joe had become a formidable threat to deny me the victory. Joe was a sophomore in high school and he showed up at the District contest with unbounded determination and also reeking with optimism. We all drew lots regarding the speaking order and of the three Jr. Toastmasters competing, Ben Garcia went first followed by me and then Joe. I had always believed that it was best to be the last speaker in these situations. That way you would know what your competition had done and you could take your delivery one notch higher to hedge your chances of winning. I felt a bit distressed that Joe and not I had drawn the last slot.

After Ben and the other five contestants and I had delivered our speeches, I felt that I was still the boy to beat. Joe would have to hit not only a Home Run but a Grand Slam to take the prize. Joe proceeded to deliver a truly memorable speech. I say memorable because as he was reaching the final part of his speech, his microphone neck-strap broke. I will never forget how he took this potentially disrupting and possibly even devastating misfortune, and transformed it into an act of mature and calm recovery. When the strap broke, without interrupting the flawless delivery of his speech, and without taking his eyes away from his mesmerized audience, he somehow gracefully and, almost unnoticeably, placed his hand over his heart and caught the falling microphone. He kept his hand there until he finished his speech. Then as the audience erupted in much more applause than any of us had received previously, he finished removing the microphone and returned to his seat next to me. I knew then that Joe had hit his Grand Slam. His performance indeed earned him the first-place trophy; I came in second.

The next step for Joe was to compete at the Regional finals of the Optimist Oratorical contest which was held in San Francisco in early June, 1963. The region—one of four regions--covered the entire US west of the Mississippi River and parts of Canada. Again, the Boys' Club treated the entire Jr. Toastmasters Club to an all-expenses paid trip to support Joe. If Joe won there, he would then be eligible to compete in the Optimist Oratorical International finals in Ontario, Canada.

That trip to San Francisco in the summer of 1963 is one of the best memories of my life. Even though Joe had beaten me at the District contest, I was rooting enthusiastically for Joe to keep on winning. After his District win, Joe had received a check for $200 to cover the expenses he would incur at the Regional contest. At one of our meetings of the Jr. Toastmasters, Joe announced that all twenty of us in the Jr. Toastmasters Club should go with him to San Francisco and that he would commit that $200 check to funding the trip.

The Boys' Club agreed to organize that trip. They managed to get the *Lydia Patterson Institute*, a local school for girls, to lend us their school bus to get us there and back. In exchange, the Boys' Club agreed that it would have boys' clubbers re-upholster the seat cushions on the bus. Mr. George Stauning, the President of the Board of Directors of the Boys' Club—and a Jr. Toastmaster mentor--volunteered to act as leader and chaperone during the trip. Ernesto Madrid, a staff member at Unit 2 would do the driving. My brother, Nacho, a former Jr. Toastmaster who, two months earlier, had been selected as the *Boys' Clubs of America* National Boy of the Year, would also make the trip with us. Joe's parents would also accompany the group but they would drive their own car and stay at hotels while Joe hung out with the rest of us. Overnight stays were planned at Boys' Clubs along the way in order to save on lodging costs, and meals would be taken at fast-food places. They estimated that we would need an additional $300 to cover the rest of the expenses, and so, for the next 3 or 4 weeks, all of us became fund-raisers. On weekends, we would have car-washes and on weekdays after school we would sell chocolate candy bars door-to-door. Eventually, we managed to put together the $300 we needed.

The trip started on the morning of Wednesday, June 5, 1963. We drove from El Paso to Phoenix and upon arrival, played a friendly game of softball against Phoenix Boys' clubbers. We slept on folding cots that had been set up in the gym. The following morning, we drove to Los Angeles and spent the night at the Los Angeles Boys' Club. On Friday morning we drove to San Francisco. Bernie Del Hierro, one of the Jr. Toastmasters who made the trip, reminded me recently how the bus had gotten pelted with stones as we drove through the rough Boys' Club neighborhood in San Francisco as we neared the Club. Nevertheless, we arrived safely and, in the evening, we again competed with local Clubbers, this time in basketball, before again bedding down in the gym.

On Saturday, June 8th, Joe competed unsuccessfully at the Regional competition. He gave it a good shot but some other kid won. We felt devastated yet proud of what Joe and the rest of us had accomplished during the month leading up to that moment. We would all give it another shot next year.

The following day, we drove back to Los Angeles arriving early enough for us to be treated to a late afternoon at *Disneyland*. On Monday, as we were heading to Phoenix, we ran into some trouble. Several miles west of Indio, California, the bus motor threw a rod and the repair job would cost $324. The bus was towed into Indio. That night and the following night, all of us slept in a public park while we waited for the motor to be replaced. Fortunately, the weather was warm and, for the most part, none of us had any problems. I, however, managed to develop a bad case of Tonsillitis. I don't know how he did it, but my brother, Nacho, somehow managed to put me on a *Greyhound* bus that took me from Indio to El Paso. The Unit 2 director, Mr. D was waiting for me there and took me home to my anxious parents.

Even though Joe did not win in San Francisco, his accomplishments for that year had been amazing. Simply stated, he had completely overshadowed me. As I look back on those days when Joe and I competed against each other, I know that he made me strive to be better like no other person, thing or event had ever done before. I recently spoke with Joe and asked him whether any Boys' Club peer had significantly influenced him. He flattered me immensely when he replied: *"You* made me better," acknowledging the similar feelings that I had about him.

In 1964, the Jr. Toastmasters continued to move forward, but something had happened on January 30th that changed everything. On that day, after a long battle with Leukemia, Mr. Hightower passed away. Nothing at the *El Paso Boys' Club* would ever be the same. Even the Jr. Toastmasters began to fade away. The passing of Mr. Hightower occurred just a few months after the assassination of President Kennedy and I know that I--as well as most of my peers and a lot of adults as well--was having great difficulty dealing with such monumental losses. The weekly meetings continued and new but still awesome mentors such as Edward S. Marquez appeared to keep the speech program as viable as ever. Yet, there seemed to be a palpable sense that the best was over. A new crop of youngsters always seemed to be available to emulate the kids that had been Jr. Toastmasters before them, but the contest victories of the successors never came even close to what the Toastmasters of 1962 and 1963 managed to achieve. Even the original Jr. Toastmasters seemed to be growing up and moving to new distractions.

I recently had occasion to speak with Lane Smith, the Director in 1964 of the *El Paso Boys' Club* Unit 2. I asked him what was most memorable about his years at the Boys' Club. He replied: "The process of transformation of the Jr. Toastmasters." He recalled how Mr. Hightower, Sal Ramirez and Mr. D. had no real plan about how such a program might work but suddenly it started exceeding everyone's expectations. He felt that the entire Jr. Toastmaster experience was for him "very thought-provoking." He saw the Jr. Toastmasters as the best example of how the Boys' Club used its most valuable asset—the boys themselves—and capitalized on their successes. Lane thought it was amazing how community volunteers became involved in that activity and actually spent time mentoring and training the boys. The Jr. Toastmasters Club literally put the Mexican-American kids of South El Paso in the middle of the rest of the city's Anglo community. He was impressed at how the local civic organizations changed their views about and their attitudes toward the Boys' Club neighborhoods when they heard the Jr. Toastmasters. He remembered how competitive speaking dramatically and without introducing prejudices broadened the perspective of each boy. It was simply "super-powerful" to him. He believed then and even now that nothing else about the Boys' Club did more to enhance the dignity of each boy than the Jr. Toastmasters. He told me how he specifically remembered that I, as a Jr. Toastmaster, had been a good influence on my peers but he did not think any of us really had any idea how much good we were doing to ourselves, to the Boys' Club and to the community.

I think about the experiences I had as a Jr. Toastmaster and I have to agree with Lane Smith that we probably did not understand how much good we were doing. I did have a sense then as I do now, that the benefits that we gained as Jr. Toastmasters were extreme and priceless. However, it remains somewhat of a mystery when I try to figure out why the Jr. Toastmaster experience happened when and where it did. Our parents, the Boys' Club staff members and leadership, our mentors, our coaches, our teachers, the economic and political realities, our peers, our heroes, television and God-knows-what-else all converged during that special period of time and afforded us with learning and tools that no one in South El Paso has since seen or heard of. I am certain that my recalling those days with such pleasure is in large part due to a strong need on my part to express the gratitude that I feel toward those remarkable people that made them happen.

Other Spinoff Activities

It is my considered opinion that the single most significant attribute that Jr. Toastmasters imparted and honed on each of us was an unusually strong sense of confidence. Armed with that confidence, many of us were eager to do other things within the Boys' Club program that opened new avenues of excitement and learning. Mr. Hightower understood very well the value of allowing members of the Boys' Club to promote the organization at local civic clubs. The Jr. Toastmasters frequently were called upon to be guest speakers at the regular meetings of these clubs. But he also realized that the boys could effectively give the same speech only so many times before it raised the risk of being boring. So, the mentors and sponsors of the Jr. Toastmasters introduced us to drama.

Casey at the Bat is a wonderful poem about baseball and personal expectations. It was written in 1888 by Ernest Thayer. Miss Joan Griffin, my former Optimist speech contest coach, invited four of us from the Jr.

Toastmasters to make a small traveling production of that poem and to use it to show yet another dimension of the good work that was being done at the Boys' Club. Checo Reza got the lead role of Casey; Sal Garcia was the pitcher; Daniel Miranda was the catcher; and I got the part of the Muse/Narrator. We all wore appropriate costumes (our baseball uniforms) and, as I recited the poem, the three other players acted out their roles in the poetic drama.

The poem is about a baseball team from the town of Mudville and its star batter, Casey. In it, five thousand fans at a Mudville game are hoping that their team can salvage a victory even though they are behind by 2 runs at the bottom of the last inning. The fans believe that Casey can win the game but he is the fifth batter up. Their hopes are dimmed when the first two batters fail to get on base. But then the emotions of the fans sky-rocket when the next two batters get on base thus giving Casey a chance to win it all. Casey, makes it even more exciting by pompously ignoring the first two pitches which the umpire calls "Strikes!" The conclusion of the poem is a lesson for all as the pitcher and Casey battle it out:

...

The sneer is gone from Casey's lip, his teeth are clenched in hate;

He pounds with cruel violence his bat upon the plate.

And now the pitcher holds the ball, and now he lets it go,

And now the air is shattered by the force of Casey's blow.

Oh, somewhere in this favored land the sun is shining bright;

The band is playing somewhere, and somewhere hearts are light,

And somewhere men are laughing, and somewhere children shout;

But there is no joy in Mudville—mighty Casey has struck out.

Our little group of 4 made this presentation frequently before local civic clubs and invariably it was received well. Each of us felt the thrill of accomplishment and approval every time we did it and undoubtedly, with each presentation before yet another community organization, the reputation of the Boys' Club was further enhanced as an institution that made boys better.

A similar result came to pass at the local military installation, Fort Bliss. The Recreation Center at Fort Bliss was dedicated to providing recreational activities and entertainment for the soldiers and families stationed there. The

El Paso Boys' Club was invited regularly to compete in its talent shows and - once again, many of its members—again pumped up with Jr Toastmaster confidence and enthusiasm—made appearances and walked away as winners.

In anticipation of one Fort Bliss talent show competition, Mr. D approached the arguably most talented member of Unit 2, Checo Reza, and asked him to put together an act that could represent the Boys' Club. Checo considered the usual variety of acts such as singing and dancing but instead recruited Sal Garcia and me to come up with a fresh, innovative idea through which we could set ourselves apart. We came up with silent movie rendition of *The Mummy*. It would be a 3-minute act involving 3 characters: The Mummy, a beautiful girl and her boyfriend. The girl and her boyfriend, while enjoying a moment of peaceful romance were suddenly attacked by the Mummy. A sequence of fighting and chasing each other around a table then followed until the Mummy was defeated. I took the role as the Mummy, Checo got the role of the hero-boyfriend and we recruited a sister of one of our friends to be the girlfriend.

What made this act unique was how we achieved the appearance of a silent movie. We had discovered earlier that if, in a darkened room, two or three continuously oscillating flashlights are shined on a character who keeps himself in constant jerky motion, the result is remarkably similar to a silent movie, particularly when a fast piano score plays in the background.

The talent show took place and the usual array of acts came and went and the audience, composed mainly of military personnel, politely acknowledged each with subdued applause. When *The Mummy* was performed, the audience responded with an unprecedented level of applause, cheering and whistling and that prompted the judges to award the First-Place trophy to the act from the Boys' Club Unit 2.

The confidence-building effect of the Jr. Toastmasters was not limited to activities of the mind. The sense of self-assurance that we picked up learning how to speak in public also seemed to empower us in other more physical arenas even if we did not always emerge as victorious.

One day in 1961, Mr. D arrived at Unit 2 with a half-dozen pairs of genuine, professional quality boxing gloves. Everyone knew what they were but I daresay no one had ever actually worn a pair of real boxing gloves, much less, engaged in a real boxing match.

But we were normal kids who always were attracted by the challenge of a sporting opportunity and so, not surprisingly, it wasn't long before the Boys

Club created a boxing league. I happened to be a junior staff member of the Club at the time and so I participated more as a referee and organizer in the league rather than as an actual boxer.

Every afternoon or evening in the main hall of the Club we would roll out a thick gray 9'X12' vinyl pad on the floor and arrange to have boxing matches for members of all ages. The youngest members called "Midgets," would have incredibly entertaining boxing matches where there was an enormous amount of movement and flailing of arms but very little contact and thus virtually no damage to human tissue. Those were simply funny things to watch. The participants who were older were a little bit more aggressive and more skillful and thus produced boxing matches that were somewhat realistic. Sometimes one of the kids would get a bloody nose. The older members of the Club called the "Intermediates" or the "Seniors" would get involved in boxing matches that were really good. They were not much different from what you actually see on television or in the Golden Gloves competition. One particular boxer stands out in my mind. He was Ramon Gonzalez. We called him "Mon" and he was an exceptionally good boxer. Everyone feared him.

And so, for about a month or so during that particular year, I was quite content to participate in the boxing program merely by organizing the bouts and refereeing some matches, but I never had to--nor did I really want to-- actually fight. The success of the program was such that eventually we started to compete with boxers from the other Boys' Club unit and were making fairly good showings at those matches. One day, we heard about the most famous youth boxing program in the City. It was operated at Fort Bliss. We heard that the annual championships were about to take place there and, perhaps naively, we decided that we probably had the right stuff to go compete there.

In preparation for this tournament, I was tasked to be the assistant trainer of the boxing team of the *El Paso Boys' Club*, Unit 2. After engaging in a few more local matches and doing some real training, we decided that we were ready to go fight at Fort Bliss. Until that moment, however, all of our boxing had been limited to Boys' Club level matches.

One fine day, we gathered up the team and our measly equipment and got ready to go fight at Fort Bliss. A few minutes before actually departing (in the sky-blue panel truck) Mr. D told me that one of the members of the team was not going to be able to make it. After pointing out that that the missing boxer and I were in the same weight class, Mr. D asked whether I could take his place. I was bursting with self-confidence from the many successes I had been enjoying in other Boys' Club contexts and was familiar enough with boxing at that point that, even though I had not yet fought even one match, I agreed to fight that night.

When we arrived at Fort Bliss the setting was awesome. They actually had a gymnasium that had been converted into a boxing auditorium. There was a full-scale boxing ring complete with lights and a bell and little stools for the boxers at each corner. We all were very impressed.

Then we saw the team that we would be fighting. These guys were physically very similar to us but they were all wearing uniforms and boxing shoes. And they all seemed have rubber mouthpieces. We were dressed in odd lots of shorts and t-shirts and dirty sneakers. Even though we were somewhat unnerved with the cosmetics of the situation, in our hearts we knew that we were destined to win that night.

There would be a total of eight fights. The first fight would be the real small guys; the last fight would be the heavyweights. I remember that I was roughly in the middle of the bracket weighing in at a semi-solid 105 lbs.

And so, the first fight took place. The kid from the Boys' Club was defeated badly. Yet, I did not think that his opponent had been a significantly superior fighter. In any event, the same thing happened in the second and third matches. At that point, the Boys' Club was down 3 to 0 and my match was coming up.

I remember so well seeing my opponent for the first time. He was a short, stocky 105 pounder named Paul DeMarco. He seemed to be at least a foot shorter than I was and he just did not look like a fighter of any kind. As soon as I sized him up, I just knew that the momentum in the series was about to turn in our favor. I had never been more confident in my life about being able to defeat an opponent. This guy simply looked like he did not even belong in a boxing ring. I felt like a shark in a bloody pool and I wanted very badly to avenge our first three losses.

Before the first bell, Mr. D meekly told me that Paul DeMarco was an experienced fighter but that I should not be afraid. He told me to go out there and fight for the honor and glory of the *El Paso Boys' Club*.

It is a good thing that even then in the early '60s, youth boxing matches required participants to wear protective headgear. As soon as the bell rang, I charged to the middle of the ring possessed with a rare and deep sense of vengeance and aggressiveness. As soon as Paul DeMarco came within range of my lethal, yet never-tested, right hook, Paul landed a jab in my nose that sent me back reeling. I felt as if I had been hit by a fast-moving truck.

I instantly decided to revise my strategy. Rather than attack and destroy him immediately, I decided to dance around the ring until I could figure out what to do. Unfortunately, Paul DeMarco would have no part of that strategy. He started to pursue me and whenever he was within 3 ft. of my face, he would fire off another jab that seemed never to miss. I then started to think about the clock. I only had to fight three rounds and each round was going to last 1 minute. I decided that, even if I did nothing more than back-pedal and try to evade Paul DeMarco, I could certainly last three rounds.

Within seconds, Paul had pummeled me so much that the referee declared the bout a technical knockout. I was stunned in a variety of ways. First, I was stunned because he hit me so powerfully. Second, I was stunned by the speed that he possessed that enabled him to catch up with me seemingly without even trying. Third, I was stunned at how little stamina I possessed. All of these elements reduced my fight to one of the most embarrassing and humiliating moments of my life

So, my fight left the score at 4-0 and by the end of the day Fort Bliss had won 7 and the Boys' Club only 1: Mon almost killed his opponent. The one good thing that I remember about that event is that despite the pummeling that Paul DeMarco gave me, my bout with him was really not the most devastating loss of the day. Three of the four fights after mine involved slightly bigger guys than me but were even worse losses for the Club than mine. The Boys' Club representatives in those three fights were hurt worse than I and their fights were terminated even sooner than mine. Mr. D told me after the fight that Paul DeMarco had been the previous year's Golden Gloves champion at the 105 lb level. I felt a whole lot better knowing that I had lost to a champion. Paul DeMarco went on to win that division again that year.

Chapter 10-Crossroads of the Americas

But life in the Projects in the early 1960s was not all Jr. Toastmasters or Boys' Club. Many of us were also somewhat consumed by other things we did at school, after school and even during the summers. One such amazing summer activity was known as *Crossroads of the Americas*.

This was a program that was started in El Paso back in the early 1960's. The founder was Dr. Cleofas Calleros. He immigrated to the US from Mexico without any formal education but managed to become a pretty renowned authority on Southwestern US and Northern Mexico history by reading a whole heck of a lot. He eventually got an honorary degree and henceforth became known as Dr. Calleros.

Dr. Calleros was a very tall man (around 6 feet 3 inches), very skinny, dark complexioned, practically bald but had just a few long strands of white hair growing in the top and sides of his head, always wore gold-rimmed granny glasses, always wore a dark suit, tie and white shirt, and always wore high-top highly-polished black shoes reminiscent of the first half of the twentieth century.

Dr. Calleros had to be one of the most arrogant, abrasive, offensive, know-it-all, in-your-face, persons that I've ever known. At least, he would impress you that way until he got to know you better and became your friend. When that happened, despite his status as a fairly influential member of the community, you would discover that he was warm, quite charming, down-to-earth and very likeable. Nevertheless, he was a genuine authority on the subject of southwestern US history and one of the power-brokers in El Paso. He was a life-long member of the *Knights of Columbus* and ultimately honored through his investiture as a *Knight Commander of St. Gregory the Great*. He was also designated a *Knight of the Order of Isabella* by the Spanish Government for his work on Spanish history in the Southwest. In addition, Dr. Calleros was awarded an honorary Master of Fine Arts degree by *New Mexico State University* and an honorary Doctor's degree in history by the *University of New Mexico*.

Here's how I came to know Dr. Calleros. During his junior year in high school, my brother Nacho achieved some prominence because of his baseball skills and because he had been selected as the Regional Boy of the Year by the *Boys' Clubs of America*. All this made Nacho one of the most distinguished members of his class at Jefferson High. During the summer of 1962, Nacho was selected--along with a dozen other seniors from the rest of the high schools in El Paso--to participate in the *Crossroads of the Americas* program. I describe that program more fully later on. In any case, Nacho participated in this program that year and the program was declared a smashing international success by the local and national media. Dr. Calleros' stature grew immensely as a result of all this. My parents and I became acquainted with Dr. Calleros for the first time as we accompanied Nacho to functions and events related to *Crossroads of the Americas* 1962.

The following year, while I was a sophomore, Dr. Calleros was invited to speak at our high school. I attended his presentation and the only thing I remember is that he impressed me as being extremely arrogant and somewhat of a bull-shitter. I thought he was a bull-shitter because he would tell stories about his past that to me, sounded incredible--or at least wildly exaggerated--and I simply did not think many of them were true. I knew then that he was an interesting man but I really did not like him.

During the summer of 1963, I had achieved a certain measure of local prominence in my own right and was therefore selected to participate in that year's *Crossroads of the Americas* program. It took place in the city of Parral, Mexico. Then, in the summer of 1964, I was asked to again participate in the *Crossroads* program, but this time in the capacity of one of two Assistants to the adult project leader. That year, the project was undertaken in the city of Chihuahua, Mexico.

Then, during my senior year, my high school band, the *Jefferson High School* band, was selected to participate in musical exchange programs in three cities in Mexico: Juárez, Chihuahua and Parral. All this was also in conjunction with the *Crossroads of the Americas* program. One might have asked why it was that of 13 high schools in El Paso, only *Jefferson High School* got to do this? Well, I believe the choice was truly based on merit since at that time, the *Jefferson High School* band was absolutely the best in the city.

All of the above *Crossroads of the Americas* activities caused me to change my mind about Dr. Calleros and, eventually, we formed a very strong bond. I believe that he viewed me as a person who could contribute greatly to his programs. I just participated in these things because I enjoyed them. Yet, there was simply a great amount of mutual respect between us. He even extended an open invitation for me drop by at his home to visit with him and his wife whenever I could spare the time. Even though he and his wife were in their mid-sixties, I truly enjoyed going to their home and listening to the incredible tales that he would tell. At that point, I had no doubt about their authenticity. The entire time that I would be there, he would be chain-smoking *Record* cigarettes, which were a brand from Mexico that, in those days, only cost 10¢ a pack. (American cigarettes cost 30¢ a pack). I never was able to conclude whether he smoked *Records* because he was cheap or because he was fiercely proud of his roots and therefore would only smoke Mexican cigarettes.

The bond that existed between Dr. Calleros and me extended itself not only to his sweet wife, Benita, but also to his daughter, Margarita and her husband, Raul Blanco Sr., and their three children, Cecilia, Raul, Jr. and Martha. I actually ended up dating Martha.

I probably visited Dr. Calleros at his home about a dozen times. One of those visits occurred in December, 1965, when I was home for the holidays from Texas A&M. We were just chatting when he inquired what my plans were for the future. I revealed to him for the first time, that I had started the application process to try to get into West Point. He was extremely pleased with that and he thought that it was a very appropriate choice that I had made. He then asked me whether I was certain that that's what I wanted. I enthusiastically assured him that I was extremely certain. He then made a statement that I shall never forget. He said that since I felt so strongly, he would make sure that I got an "appointment" from our local congressman to enter the academy. My instantaneous reaction was that he had once again--as he frequently did--overstated his importance by making that remark. I really did not believe that he had that kind of power. I was nevertheless happy to hear him say that. It was certainly an encouraging remark.

In the course of the next few months, it came to pass that I did receive an appointment to West Point. I really never thought that the appointment had been anything other than the result of my application, my qualifications and the merit that I represented. As time passed, I have come to suspect that maybe a little bit more than simply my qualifications enabled me to get that appointment. I do not know this for a fact; however, I do know how aggressive and outspoken Dr. Calleros had always been and it would not surprise me at all if, at the time of my application, he, in fact, did contact the Honorable Richard C. White, Congressman, and applied just the right amount of pressure to cause the application to be approved and my appointment to be granted. I visited Dr. Calleros a few more times after I graduated from West Point and on one of those occasions, I tried to express my gratitude for all that he had done for me by presenting him with a gift. It was a West Point sword and scabbard just like the one I had worn at my graduation. He was very touched by the gift. I then asked him to tell me exactly what he did when I was seeking that appointment. I remember that he looked at me and smiled as the *Records* cigarette smoke swirled around his head, but he simply said absolutely nothing. Hence, I shall never know whether Dr. Calleros affected the course of my life in more ways than I knew... but I have a very strong suspicion that he did. Dr. Calleros died in 1973.

In any event, back in 1962, after taking office, President Kennedy got lots of acclaim for starting a goodwill program between the US and Africa. The program was called *Crossroads Africa*. Dr. Calleros saw a similar opportunity for the US and Mexico and, capitalizing on the Africa precedent, he started *Crossroads of the Americas*.

The first *Crossroads of the Americas* program was undertaken in the summer of 1962. A little town in northern Mexico named Rio Florido (also called Villa Coronado) was selected. I was only a freshman in high school at the time and my brother Nacho, was a junior. He--along with a second boy from *Jefferson High School*, Louie Olivas--was nominated to participate in that first *Crossroads* project.

At the conclusion of that first program, a strong connection between the *Crossroads of the Americas* program, the *El Paso Boys' Club* and my school, Jefferson High, began to evolve. My brother, Nacho, who had been one of the two representatives from Jefferson High in that first *Crossroads* program, got selected as the *Boys' Clubs of America* National Boy of the Year in April, 1963. All three institutions--*Crossroads of the Americas*, the *El Paso Boys' Club* and *Jefferson High School*--for good reasons I am sure, started to exploit their connections with Nacho. But instead of competing with each other for attention, they formed an informal alliance for their mutual benefit. The offshoot of all this was that in future activities of the 3 institutions, a common denominator would be that all three institutions would be well represented by participants in those activities.

The second *Crossroads of the Americas* project took place in the summer of 1963. I was a sophomore and was selected to participate as one of the representatives from my high school. Three other classmates from my high school along with 13 others from 5 other high schools were also selected to participate. Raul Blanco, the grandson of Dr. Calleros, also got to participate as the so called "mascot" of the program. In 2007, a fellow participant and *Jefferson High School* classmate—and a fellow member of the Boys' Club--Salvador E. "Chichi" Garcia, gave me a copy of the original roster of participants. The roster is reproduced in the table below.

Name	Address	Phone	School	Religion	Birth Date	Birthplace
Abbott, Alan Ray	1316 Mathias	PR2-4892	Burgess	Methodist	4-16-47	San Diego, CA
Blanco, Raul C.	6204 Ute	PR2-5071	St. Joseph	Catholic	3-19-52	El Paso, TX
Cantu, Rene Jerome	2304 N. Kansas	KE2-9183	El Paso Hi	Catholic	10-4-45	Los Angeles, CA
Chavez, Guillermo D.	3922 Paisano Dr. Apt. 3	KE3-5376	Jefferson	Catholic	6-15-47	El Paso, TX
Caro, Humberto	3022 Grant Ave.	LO6-1953	Bowie	Catholic	1-10-46	El Paso, TX
Diaz, Federico	1509 E. 12th		Bowie	Catholic	3-2-43	Cd. Juárez, Mex
Gutierrez, Ernesto A.	4404 Wallington	KE7-8749	El Paso Hi	Catholic	6-17-46	El Paso, TX
Garcia, Benjamin	462 S. Glenwood	PR8-2448	Jefferson	Catholic	4-14-47	El Paso, TX
Garcia, Salvador E.	Webber Way		Jefferson	Catholic	10-21-45	Gomez Palacio, Mex.
House, Samuel P.	5217 Jerry	SK1-0205	Andress	Catholic	12-4-47	El Paso, TX
Hair, Jerold F.	3815 Monroe	LO6-3538	Austin	Jewish	10-12-48	El Paso, TX
Martinez, Arturo	605 S. Ochoa	KE2-8690	Bowie	Catholic	12-30-45	El Paso, TX
Pimentel, David V.	6231 Taos Dr.	PR2-5754	Burgess	Protestant	7-25-47	Mexico City, Mex.
Pellicano, Julio	Collingsworth		Jefferson	Catholic	8-8-46	El Paso, TX
Sellers, James K.	520 Prospect	KE2-2189	Emporia	Protestant	5-31-47	Emporia, KS
Stephens, Antonio M.	413 S. Florence	KE3-3528	Bowie	Catholic	10-31-45	El Paso, TX
Karr, Michael E.	520 Prospect	KE2-2189	El Paso Hi	Episcopalian	3-26-47	Linz, Austria

I am sure it was no coincidence that of the 15 participants, 5 were Boys' Club members as well as students from Jefferson High or Bowie High, the two schools that served the Boys' Club neighborhoods.

The Mexican town selected to be the host for the 1964 project was Parral, Chihuahua, located about 300 miles south of the border. One of the local elementary schools, Escuela 282, was closed for the summer and so it became our residence for a month. The man selected to be the Executive Director for the program that summer was Mr. Sal Ramirez. He happened to be the Unit 1 director of the *El Paso Boys' Club*. He was a good acquaintance and mentor of mine and undoubtedly had much to do with my selection and with the selection of the other five project participants who happened to be Boys' Club members. The group of 15 plus the Executive Director arrived in Parral on July 24, 1963.

The overall objective of the *Crossroads* projects was to foment better relations between the youth of Mexico and the youth of the United States by sending a group of boys to a town in Mexico for 3 or 4 weeks where they would engage in an effort to restore or rehabilitate some local structure and also where they would offer conversational English classes to the local folks.

What exactly did we do in Parral? First, we taught English to a large group of children as well as adults. Second, we painted the entire interior of the elementary school where we stayed. The daily schedule was simple. We would wake up at about 6:30 in the morning and have breakfast in the dining room that had been set up in the school. Two local ladies had been hired to cook for us right there in the school kitchen. After breakfast, we would conduct the English classes for the local students. The classes would normally run from 9 in the morning until around noon. We would teach in teams of two ensuring that at least one of the two teachers spoke Spanish. Every single class was oversubscribed. By the end of the project some 250 students were attending the classes each day. The mutual benefit of these classes was enormous. At the end of the project, many of the students told us that they clearly had learned more English during that period than most had learned in their entire lives. The teaching experience and the sense of contribution that we, as teachers, felt were also enormous.

After the classes each day, we would have lunch in the dining room. In the afternoon we would spend approximately the first three hours painting the interior of the entire school. We actually used oil-based paint and we would work in teams of two or three. The teams would go from one room to the next until an entire wing was finished. We even organized ourselves into a subgroup that we called the "Brush Association." To add formality to that association, we took an extra, white bath-sized towel and one of the participants from *Bowie High School*, Humberto Caro, drew upon it an image of crossed brushes on a background of paint buckets. We started each afternoon's painting sessions with an elaborate parade and march-in whereby the two- or three-man teams would line up in a single formation and then disperse to their assigned rooms to march music blaring in from the dorm room.

I will never forget how the artist/comedian of our group, Humberto Caro, handled his painting assignments. The existing paint on the classroom walls was off-white and the color we were applying was dark green. At the beginning of each painting session, Humberto would select the largest wall of the room he would be painting and he would proceed to paint on it an enormous penis and balls complete with pubic hair. The image was huge, covering most of that wall. Then all of the guys would come into the room to check it out and to get a raucous laugh out of the experience as only young, unsupervised boys can do. Then, before any of the adults could show up, Humberto would proceed to paint the entire wall in dark green, forever obliterating his work of art. The school had many such rooms and I remember how Humberto did his penile rendition at every single room he painted. What should have been tedious and dirty work became pure fun and entertainment, all thanks to the talents of Humberto.

In the late afternoon we would normally engage in either sports or other recreation. Sports included basketball and soccer amongst ourselves or against groups of local boys. We also had access to a huge swimming pool directly across the street from the elementary school where we could have fun and cool off. The most athletic kid in the group was Alan Abbott from *Burgess High School*. He was a football player who seemed to do well in all sports. I was a mediocre swimmer at best at that time, but Alan showed me how to do the "sailor's dive," which I have, in turn, used to impress many a young kid including my two sons. The sailor's dive is the one which involves keeping your hands by your side as you enter the water head first.

The other recreational activities could be a tour of some local point of interest or a visit to a sporting event. Then we would have dinner in the dining room. In the evenings we would normally attend some social event, a lecture presented by a local dignitary or a party celebrating someone's birthday. Finally, it was bedtime between 10 and 11PM. All this went on for the 18 days that the project lasted.

During this visit in Parral, I was asked by Dr. Calleros to be the project reporter to the local newspaper, *El Heraldo de Parral*. It just so happened that the newspaper offices were located directly across the street from the school where we were billeted. Every evening when we were getting ready to go to sleep, I would prepare a 300-word article in Spanish that I would submit to the editor first thing the following morning. The article would then appear in the afternoon or evening edition of the newspaper.

As I alluded earlier, the social content of this trip was fairly intense. In addition to any number of weekday parties thrown for us at private homes, we also had at least one huge dance every weekend at the local country club called *El Casino de Parral*. Every young, single girl of means in this small town was invited and we literally would dance with them nonstop during these events. The most spectacular ball occurred on August 10, 1963, when a local girl was crowned as the Queen of the Casino. Dr. Calleros got our entire group invited and even brought his two granddaughters, Cecilia and Martha Blanco, to attend from El Paso, Texas. Cecilia was accorded the honor of being *Ambassador of the Crossroads of the Americas*. The number of beautiful girls that showed up for the event was astounding. I have always been amazed at how a town as small as Parral could produce so many stunningly attractive girls.

These *Crossroads* trips to Mexico each year received incredibly good press in the cities and countries that were involved. In El Paso, there was almost daily newspaper coverage of what was going on in the programs and thus the participants became small local celebrities during the summers. The same type of press coverage and recognition also took place in the towns where the programs were playing out. For that reason, we, the participants, felt that we were really making a difference. We felt that we were, in fact, improving relations between the two countries. Whether that was true or not, one thing I know for sure is that all of us had a really great time.

In early 1964, when I was a junior in high school, I found that because of my involvement in the summer *Crossroads* project, I had become a close friend and protégé of Dr. Calleros. As a result of our friendship, he became aware of my involvement with the *Thomas Jefferson High School* Band and of its accomplishments. In late 1963, the band won the coveted "Sweepstakes" trophy at the annual El Paso high school marching bands competition, and I had the honor and privilege of being that band's Drum Major. I knew that Dr. Calleros was very proud of the fact that I was an alumnus of the *Crossroads* program, but he was also extremely proud of the fact that the *Jefferson High School* Band was comprised almost exclusively of Hispanic boys and girls who came from disadvantaged neighborhoods of El Paso. I suppose that all this inspired him to come up with his next idea for a *Crossroads* project: To take the Jefferson High Band to a few towns in Mexico for goodwill concerts and marching demonstrations. And so, Dr. Calleros invited me, the seasoned veteran of the Parral, Mexico, *Crossroads* program, to accompany him on a weekend planning trip in January, 1964, to the cities of Chihuahua and Parral, Mexico, to help arrange this musical endeavor.

Certain parts of that planning trip remain etched in my mind. Dr. Calleros had recently purchased a new *Plymouth* Fury equipped with *General Dual 90* tires, which were characterized by 3 red rings instead of white walls. We drove to Chihuahua together in that car and I was duly impressed with the comfort and pleasure of riding in it even though Dr. Calleros smoked incessantly during the entire 5-hour trip. Once there, we stayed at the *Hotel Fermont*, the newest and most luxurious hotel in the city. For dinner that evening, I remember having the biggest and most tender beef steak I had ever tasted. During dinner we met with the Mayor of Chihuahua and a few other dignitaries to make arrangements for the upcoming concerts and parades. The next day we visited with an old friend of his, the last wife of Pancho Villa. She personally entertained us in the parlor of Pancho Villa's hacienda--which had been partially converted to a museum--and told us some riveting stories about the great Mexican general. The experience continued the next day when we drove to Parral. There we stayed at the *Hotel Burciaga* and at dinner met with the Mayor of Parral and with other dignitaries including the Editor of the local newspaper, Mr. Ruben Rocha, with whom I had worked the previous summer as I submitted my daily columns reporting the activities of the *Crossroads* group. In short order, all the necessary arrangements were made. My high school band would be making a modest but international tour within 3 months. There I was, a kid of 17 experiencing all those things for the very first time ever. My sense of confidence and chutzpah got a shot of a lifetime.

Now that this musical odyssey had been planned, all that was left to be done was to get the necessary funds. Dr. Calleros and all the other amazing mentors that I ran into in the 60's were people of stupendous vision and energy but not a one of them had great wealth. They would create great opportunities for me and the other kids that they worked with, but the opportunities rarely, if ever, came with the money needed to exploit them. It was no different in this case. Dr. Calleros showed up at a *Jefferson High School* band rehearsal in early February, 1964, and announced that the band had been selected to make a goodwill concert and marching trip to Mexico later on in the spring. He also directed us to come up with ideas for raising the required funds. I suppose that participating in such projects builds character. Raising the money to fund such projects must build even more character.

After undertaking numerous car washes, cake sales and door-to-door candy sales, the Jefferson High Band collected the money needed for the trip. At 7AM on April 24, 1964, the band boarded two buses and departed for the city of Chihuahua. Upon arrival at noon, we were greeted by a huge crowd of well-wishers and benefactors. Each band member would be an overnight guest at the home of a local family. I had the good fortune of staying at the home of the Mayor. Later that afternoon, the band assembled in the center of town and did a parade routine for the gathered crowd. In the evening, the band presented a concert in a filled-to-capacity gymnasium at one of the local schools. Later in the evening, the son of the Mayor who was about my age, invited me to accompany him on a bar-hopping tour of night life in Chihuahua. That day in Chihuahua was an extremely interesting and unforgettable experience for me and, as I found out later, for just about all of us.

Early the following day, the band boarded the buses again and this time headed for the magical town of Parral. The schedule was identical to that of Chihuahua and everything went without a hitch until the parade started. Apparently, the local folks—particularly the young men—had never seen a marching unit that included Majorettes wearing skimpy outfits. The usual formation of the band had the five Majorettes at the very front followed by the Drum Major followed by the 10 or 12 ranks of marching musicians. The band started marching in formation through the designated route playing an assortment of military marches. We had not even completed the third number when I noticed from my vantage point that the people—mostly the young men—were not staying on the sidewalks but were instead getting closer and closer to the Majorettes. In a matter of seconds, the groups of men had the Majorettes surrounded and some of the men were actually pawing and fondling them. I saw in the faces of the Majorettes a look of panic as they retreated toward me and so I moved toward them waving and swinging my 4-foot chrome baton. The men immediately backed away and I directed the Majorettes to get inside the ranks of the marching musicians. It was apparent to the rest of the band that the Majorettes were being accosted and they closed ranks to protect them. Despite the commotion, the music and the marching did not stop. The band continued with the parade—with the Majorettes secured within the band ranks--until it reached its destination. No further incidents of that sort occurred.

The concert performed by the band that evening went according to plan and again, there was standing room only from beginning to end. The band spent the night at different hosts' homes and the following day returned home to El Paso.

In the course of the next few years, these international marching and concert tours continued to be organized by Dr. Calleros under the sponsorship of *Crossroads of the Americas*. I accompanied the *Jefferson High School* band to three Mexican towns the following year and other El Paso high school bands followed in later years. Bands and orchestras from towns in Mexico also performed for US audiences in El Paso under the sponsorship of *Crossroads of the Americas*. Once again, this time with music and marching, Dr. Calleros had introduced yet another means through which young people from El Paso and from Mexico could better understand each other's cultures and at the same time build up their senses of confidence and invincibility.

How fortunate we all were to be beneficiaries of the thoughts and acts of people like Dr. Calleros.

The summer that followed that first marching and concert tour—the summer of 1964—had to be the best summer of my life. I had completed a very successful junior year in high school and was about to start my final year. The union comprised of the *Crossroads of the Americas* program, the *El Paso Boys' Club* and *Jefferson High School* continued to flourish. Dr. Calleros again organized a *Crossroads* summer project for 1964 and I was invited to return, this time as an assistant director. Another high school classmate of mine, Ben Garcia, who had also participated in the 1963 program, was also invited to participate as an assistant director. The man selected to be the Executive Director for this project was Mr. Joe Mares, an Assistant Principal at *Jefferson High school*. And, at least six of the 21 participants in the 1964 program came from Jefferson High. They included Fernando Casas, Sergio Reza, Ben Garcia, Julio Pellicano, Robert Porras and me. The remaining 14 participants came from eight other high schools in El Paso. They were: Bernie Del Hierro and Manuel Alvarez from Austin High School; Xavier Bañales and Heinz Geisel from Bowie High School; and William Aylor, Steve Ward, Jamey Murray, Herman Ahumada, Jerry Barrett, Rudy Chavez, Daniel Campos, Steve Tipton, Ernie Morales and Steve McNeil. Then there was Raul Blanco, grandson of Dr. Calleros, who for the second year in a row was the mascot of the project (since he was only 10 years old). The total number of participants included six Boys' Club members.

The site of the 1964 *Crossroads* program was the town of Chihuahua, Chihuahua, Mexico. We were housed in a fairly large but empty (during the summer) two- or three-story school building named *Colegio Morelos* located right next to a big river in Chihuahua. There were three or four large dorm rooms where bunk beds had been installed for us. The building was like a large hacienda on a street that dead-ended on the river. It had a main entrance that opened to a fairly large courtyard where a basketball court had been set up. I recall playing basketball there almost on a daily basis and I particularly remember playing against program-mate Fernando Casas who despite his smaller size would use his body aggressively to push me and the others all over the court.

The *Crossroads* program was to last a month. As in the previous years, the program had two main objectives. The first was to engage in some physical labor activity that would benefit the community. The second was to conduct informal English classes for anyone wishing to attend.

The physical labor activity portion turned out to be the digging of a foundation for a church in the neighborhood. This entailed grabbing a pick and shovel and digging a trench about 2-3 ft. wide and 3 ft. deep that ran the entire perimeter of a church that was under construction. I would estimate that perimeter to have been 300-400 ft. in total length. And so, every day, right after breakfast we would board a bus and go to the site and dig for a few hours. The earth was hard caliche and progress came slowly. By the end of the project I believe we might have completed half of the foundation trench.

The English classes which we taught for two hours every afternoon were a lot more productive and enjoyable. Once again, as in previous programs, a bilingual member of the project would be paired with one who only spoke English and together they would teach conversational English to classes that normally numbered well over 30 pupils. I truly believe that the community really enjoyed the classes and that all of us really enjoyed teaching them. Fernando Casas, because of his superior knowledge of English and Spanish managed to get the most basic classes of all since he could most effectively communicate with the students. At the conclusion of the project, he received a gift from his class. It was a book entitled *Las Estrellas Miran Hacia Abajo*, by A. J. Cronin. He still has it today along with 4 little cards signed by some of his female students.

At the end of each day, immediately following the dinner meal, a group of us would go to the grocery store next door to the school building and each would purchase a liter-size bottle of milk. Since the milk was not homogenized, the cream was always sitting on top. We would shake the bottle vigorously for five minutes and then guzzle it down. I remember quite well how good it tasted. We felt that we needed that milk because the meals that we were getting, which were based on the local economy, were somewhat lacking in the nutrition that we required.

Among the interesting characters that we met during the program was a really amazing Catholic priest named Gaspar who had been appointed to be available for us during the entire project. He was an incredibly friendly young man who was universally liked and who played a mean game of basketball. For a few days, this priest lived under the impression that the real name of one of the project participants, Sergio Reza, was "Foxes." This was because Sergio had been wearing an athletic T-shirt that had the imprint "FOXES" on it. He had gotten it from playing football at Jefferson High where the mascot was the Silver Fox. Father Gaspar called him "Foxes" from the outset and even after Sergio revealed to him his real name, Father Gaspar continued to call him "Foxes" until the program ended.

Another interesting set of characters were the photographer and reporter from the local newspaper who had been assigned to the program. One (the photographer) was a fat, jolly guy who was somewhat slow but quite likeable. The other guy (the reporter) was small and skinny and really looked like a weasel. Together, they shadowed us wherever we went and reported our activities to a local newspaper. Fernando Casas was the group's interface with these two representatives of the local newspaper. Fernando would actually write the periodic articles and they would then be published in the newspaper the following day. We became close to that pair, particularly after they started to supply us with beer and liquor.

One of the most memorable events of that summer's program was a talent show that we presented to the community. We had a number of skits that we rehearsed and then performed for an audience that probably numbered 200-300. The school where we were housed had a large auditorium and a stage and so we invited the community on a Saturday to attend the show for free. I can only recall 4 of the skits that we presented. The first was an impersonation of the *Beatles* who were really big even in Mexico at that time. We got wigs and suits and guitars and a drum set and with a great amplifier, we put on a pretty impressive impersonation of that famous British rock group. The crowd sang along, applauded lustily and really loved it.

The second skit that I recall was Fernando Casas lip-synching *Venus*, the popular Frankie Avalon song. The girls in the audience almost assaulted him at the end of his song.

Then there was a short flute recital put on by Xavier Bañales who was a standout musician at *Bowie High School*.

Finally, and by far the most memorable--and controversial--skit was the one during which I stood on stage and sang *Granada*. *Granada* is one of the most famous and beautiful Spanish songs ever written. The composer, Agustín Lara, is arguably the greatest musical composer in Mexican history. *Granada* is probably his greatest accomplishment. Mexicans revere that song.

As far as the audience knew, I was going to do a serious rendition of that song. Julio Pellicano, a fellow participant from Jefferson High and an accomplished pianist, was going to accompany me on the piano. He would do a lengthy and dramatic introduction on the keyboard and then I would start singing the song. The first time we did this, a fellow participant, Bernie Del Hierro, appeared on the stage behind me dressed as a confused waiter carrying a large tray full of pots and pans high above his head and looking for the kitchen. While I dramatically sang the first lyric of *Granada*, he quietly acted disoriented and pretended he had accidentally lost his way and somehow ended up on the stage. The audience could see him but I could not and so I continued to sing. I had not gotten past the first verse when Bernie stumbled on the stage and dropped all the pots and pans creating an incredible ruckus. We originally thought that the audience would erupt in laughter but instead, it seemed stunned and remained silent.

We stopped the song and allowed Bernie to gather the pots and pans and to depart. Then after Julio and I regained our composure, Julio once again did his slow, dramatic piano introduction and, once again, I started to sing. This time, another fellow participant, Sergio Reza, suddenly appeared behind me on stage doing an imitation of *Tarzan*. He was hanging on to the end of a long rope that was suspended from the ceiling over the center of the stage and he swung from one side of the stage to the other and as he did, he let out a loud but very real Tarzan scream. I stopped singing again and pretended to be totally distraught by this second interruption. I could sense that the audience--which was expecting a serious rendition of *Granada*—did not think this stunt was any funnier than the first and was starting to get really annoyed with the interrupters.

After getting rid of Sergio and after composing myself one more time, I asked Julio (maestro) to please start again. As we started our third attempt at the song, yet another fellow participant, Robert Porras, who had earlier situated himself right in the middle of the audience next to a pretty girl (who was also part of the conspiracy) put his lips to his palm and created a loud kissing sound and pretended to be kissing that girl. The sound was so real and so disruptive that I once again had to stop the song. At that point, my part of the skit had ended. I ran off the stage pulling at my hair in total frustration hoping that the audience would be roaring with laughter. The audience, however, did not find any of the interruptions--particularly the last one--to be funny. Some of the women sitting next to "Robert the kisser" proceeded to angrily swat at him with their fans and handbags and to otherwise beat him about the head and shoulders. The audience was going to make poor Robert pay for ALL of the interruptions. I had to return to the microphone and quiet the mob down. It was only then that the audience understood that the skit was supposed to be funny and that I really never intended to sing *Granada*. The audience nevertheless wanted me to do the song. I had to explain that I did not know all the words nor did have a suitable voice to do so. The audience finally understood and applauded politely as Julio and I bowed and exited.

Another memorable event of the summer occurred on the last night of the month that we had been there. With the assistance of the aforementioned journalists and by using a 40 ft. rope with a huge straw basket tied at the end, we—led by Bernie Del Hierro--hoisted four or five bottles of tequila, whiskey and gin to the top floor of the school to one of the windows that faced the river. The hoisting of the liquor needed to occur right by the window of the Executive Director, Mr. Mares, *while* he was in his office. Therefore, we dispatched Fernando, to distract Mr. Mares, as the liquor was elevated right behind his unsuspecting back. Fernando made sure that Mr. Mares did not notice the basket of booze as it was raised just a few feet behind him. Later on, Mr. Mares left to attend some social function and put Ben Garcia and me in charge while he was gone.

As soon as the door to the school building closed behind Mr. Mares, all of us proceeded to get drunk for the next few hours. We played loud music and horsed around as we consumed the liquor. This went on for a few hours. Late in the evening, Bernie Del Hierro, who had drunk too much, vomited all over the dining room floor. Moments after he puked and before any of us even thought about how to clean up the mess, Mr. Mares returned, threw the doors open, made a slow and elegant entrance into the dining room and while standing deep in Bernie's puke, asked in overly perfect Spanish: "Qué chingados está pasando aquí?" ("What the hell is happening here?") The only answer that he got was derisive laughter from the entire group, all of whom were slightly or completely drunk. What happened next has conveniently been forgotten apparently by all of us.

As young men are prone to do, the group became polarized in the course of the month. I became the *de facto* leader of one group and we called ourselves *The Playboy Club*. Ben Garcia was the leader of the other group and they called themselves *The Jockey Club*. There was a lot of friendly competition between the two groups both at the foundation digging area as well as on the sports fields. I remember getting great satisfaction and a feeling of final victory over *The Jockey Club* when one time during a tour of the local newspaper press, they offered to print placards for the two groups bearing the club names. The placard for *The Playboy Club* was done without incident and we were justly pleased and proud. *The Jockey Club* placard, however, did not get done as anticipated. The typesetter confused the English word "Jockey" with the Spanish word "Yaqui"--which is the name of an Indian tribe--and created a placard for *The "Yaqui" Club*. For lack of time, the press man could not correct the error despite shameless begging and crying by the members of *The Jockey Club*. *The Playboy Club* has laughed for decades at their misfortune.

At the conclusion of that year's program, Dr. Calleros gave each participant a blank *Crossroads of the Americas* certificate which was then passed around for each to sign. The certificate also bore the signatures of Dr. Calleros and then Mayor of El Paso, the Honorable Ralph Seitsinger. It was a wonderful memento of the program and I certainly treasured it until it went up in smoke in that fire I mentioned earlier.

When it was all said and done, *Crossroads of the Americas 1964* was a huge success. As with previous projects, I am sure that all of the participants walked away with a tremendous sense of accomplishment. We saw with our own eyes the results of our work in digging the foundation for the church and we heard with our own ears the results of the classes that we taught. We knew simply that if we could do all that, we could do anything. We got yet another taste of what confidence is and what it can do and we gained an appreciation of another culture from close and personal encounters that we all lived through during that incredible month. Once again, my peers and I found ourselves as fortunate beneficiaries of an unprecedented and unlikely convergence of persons and institutions that enabled us to become better in so many ways.

I believe that it is very important to also consider the national context when one recalls the happenings of the *Crossroads of the Americas* programs. The country was undergoing changes in its social fabric that had not been seen since the *Civil War*. The *Civil Rights Act of 1964* was being enacted in those days and all of the cultural minorities of America were feeling a new sense of liberation. I personally remember feeling a new sense of cultural identity. I was no longer reticent about my Mexican roots. I felt proud and fortunate to know how to speak, read and write in Spanish and, coupled with my learned ability to do the same in English, I started to feel advantaged over my Anglo peers who could only communicate in English. I no longer felt compelled to be in the lower rungs of American society as I believed my parents had always felt. And, I felt an irresistible urge to be an active and productive *American*. I believed then and now that the Mexican-American community of El Paso was also experiencing these same feelings at that time. My participation in the *Crossroads* programs reassured me in spades that those cultural feelings were absolutely correct and that they represented the future for me and for the entire Mexican-American community.

As I participated first in the Parral project, then the Chihuahua City project and finally in the band tours, I could see that the Boy of the Year development process of the Boys' Club had a very strong connection with the *Crossroads of the Americas* program. I could be cynical and say that the Boys' Club somehow maneuvered Dr. Calleros to stack his programs with Club members so as to enhance their chances for the Boy of the Year honors but I really do not think that was the case. I prefer to believe that when Dr.

Calleros would invite the different high schools to nominate candidates for programs, the counselors or administrators at those high schools would contact those boys that they believed were most outstanding in their respective schools and at Jefferson High and Bowie High, those boys just happened to also be members of the Boys' Club. I know that when I was asked to participate in those programs, in the back of my mind I certainly did think of how participation would in all probability make me a better candidate for Boy of the Year. However, I also knew from my own brother's experience and from the press coverage that I had seen about those programs, that these were rare and highly coveted honors as well as exciting and potentially extremely gratifying experiences that were being offered to me. There was no way that I would ever consider passing them up.

And so, the impact that Dr. Calleros had on my life was profound. He probably enriched my life in more ways than anyone else ever did and I am certain that there are quite a few other 1960's high school kids from El Paso who feel the same way. I was recently thrilled to no end when I heard that a fellow participant in one of the *Crossroads of the Americas* projects in the 1960's anonymously endowed the "Cleofas Calleros Scholarship" at UTEP. From wherever he may be, Dr. Calleros must be beaming at this wonderful tribute to him and his deeds more than 50 years after he caused them to happen.

Chapter 11-The Jefferson High School Band

I did not know it at the time but the four years that I spent as a member of the *Jefferson High School* Band probably constituted my first real experience with an organization that truly achieved excellence. In 1960, after mi Papá caused the family to move into the house in the back of a restaurant where he would attempt one more time to open a business, I enrolled at *Jefferson Intermediate School*. I would be entering the 8th grade that year. My brother, Nacho, would be a sophomore in the same campus at *Jefferson High School*. For two years, I had been listening to the wonderful stories that he would tell me about Jefferson High, particularly stories about the Band. That year, 1960, I joined the Intermediate band and each day was thrilled to learn more and more about playing the trombone. I eagerly anticipated the day when I could join my brother in the Senior Band.

In the fall of 1960, the Band Director, Mr. Berne Glover, put together an awesome and, to me, a very memorable half-time show. In essence, for that particular half-time show, he split up the band into two units and pitted one against the other in friendly competition. In the course of the 7 minutes allotted to the Jefferson Band during the half-time break, the two units entertained the crowd by marching and playing and trying energetically to outdo each other. Eventually, the two units discovered that they were infinitely better if they quit competing with each other and instead merged into one (married each other) and so they did. Then to symbolize the successful consummation of the union, a smaller unit comprised of 6 members of the intermediate band wearing diapers and bonnets marched onto the field. In conclusion, the combined band and their "offspring" marched into the sunset to live happily ever after. Mr. Glover had selected me to be the drum major of the "baby band" and had given me a toilet plunger to use as my baton. I had never felt so honored in my life. From that moment forward, I all but worshipped Mr. Glover. I finished up the 8th grade and was excited at the prospect of finally becoming a freshman at Jefferson High. But more importantly, I was extremely thrilled to know that I would be joining that amazing band.

The Jefferson High School Band was the perennial winner in the band competitions held each year in El Paso. Without a doubt, the biggest reason for that success was the director, Mr. Glover. I don't know if he ever liked me very much. I don't think he did. I don't think he ever gave any indication that he liked anybody. I know for a fact that he really did NOT like my good friend and band-mate, Checo Reza. Anyway, he always treated me very formally although he did use me for his educational and organizational purposes as much as possible. I became, after all, the Senior Band drum major for two years and so he knew that I could and did help control the band. Since I did not turn out to be a very good musician, I frequently ended up being the butt of some of Mr. Glover's jokes or as an example of how to play a trombone badly. In the first two years before I became drum major, I recall that he swatted my butt in front of the entire band on at least one occasion when I arrived in the band room late one morning. It only happened to me one time although butt-swatting was a daily occurrence as someone invariably arrived late every day. I'll never forget how painful and humiliating the experience was. I came very close to crying in front of the entire band. But I didn't.

As I look back today, I appreciate more fully how good a teacher Mr. Glover was. He was a talented musician who could play most instruments but specialized in the reed instruments. He was also an extremely creative and gifted choreographer who was way ahead of his peers in coming up with amazing half-time shows that truly dazzled Friday night football audiences. He was always being copied by the other band directors in the school district except that their shows always appeared a year later that ours. He was also relentless in making the band work hard and for long hours until we perfected those shows. But most importantly, he was a wise teacher and leader who inspired a generation of kids and who gave many of us our first taste of what it's like to be the best. The end result was a highly regarded marching band comprised of extremely proud and enthusiastic students. Once again, I tasted excellence under Mr. Glover's supervision and I honestly believe that it carried me into the future always searching for that same taste.

My freshman and sophomore years at Jefferson High were good years for me as far as grades and extracurricular activities went. I also tried out for athletic teams but always seemed to get cut. The competition for making those squads was not particularly tough yet the other kids trying out seemed to make it while I did not. I finally concluded that I was simply not a jock and thus focused instead on doing well in the band. Well, to my dismay, I soon discovered that I was not a promising musician either. By the end of my sophomore year, I had been playing the trombone for 5 years and I seemed locked in the 3d chair of the section. The better players were in the 1st and 2d chairs. Furthermore, and probably for good reason, I had failed to impress Mr. Glover in any way. I suspect that during those two years he might not have known at all who I was.

It was customary for the Drum Major for the following school year to be selected just as the spring semester ended. Around April, 1963, I had never forgotten the trust and confidence that Mr. Glover had placed in me two years earlier when he selected me to be the toilet-plunger-bearing drum major of the baby band and since then I had always envisioned myself as a future Drum Major of the Senior Band, I decided to give it a shot. I had trained hard for the position and knew that my chances were good simply because I was one of the few members of the band who was at least 6 feet tall. By lucky coincidence, my brother, Nacho, who was about to graduate and had been a member of the band until his junior year, was selected as the *Boys' Clubs of America* National Boy of the Year at around the same time that the band was selecting its new Drum Major and, being his brother, much of his good press spilled onto me. In any event, I became the new Drum Major.

During my junior year and as Drum Major, I got to know Mr. Glover very well. I saw firsthand how he would create those spectacular half time shows. The music and the themes that he came up with along with the intricate formations that he arranged were very different from those done by the rest of the schools. And his ability to extract superior effort from his students was becoming legendary. My job was to lead the band whenever we were on the field practicing or performing and I felt that the band truly followed and respected me. But it was Mr. Glover who raised everybody up to perform at the highest level. By the end of that year, the Jefferson band had established itself as one of the best.

In April, 1964, I was about to begin my senior year and my second year as Drum Major. During my first year as Drum Major, I had been the sole drum major. As I mentioned earlier, for 1964-65, Mr. Glover decided that we would have two drum majors. When I first heard of this dual arrangement, I felt that something had been taken away from me. Instead of being able to pursue the glory in front of this magnificent band all by myself as I had done the previous year, I now had to share it with someone else. Mr. Glover explained to me that he needed two drum majors because he was planning halftime shows for that year that required the band to be split into two units much of the time and each unit would need to have its own leader on the field. I felt better after the explanation although I still felt to some degree that something precious had been taken from me. The idea of having two Drum Majors leading a marching band was unheard of until then. Nowadays, most bands have *at least* 2 drum majors and maybe even more. But way back then, this was radical, creative thinking and that is what made Mr. Glover special.

The other drum major turned out to be my good friend Armando "Mando" Gallego about whom I wrote in an earlier chapter. He was a skilled member of the percussion section and was very well-liked and respected by everyone. He had been one of my best friends throughout high-school and after he became the co-drum major with me, we became even better friends. I had a good feeling that the two-unit idea each with its own Drum Major was going to be a good one.

Sure enough, the band halftime shows that we put on in the fall of 1964 did indeed reflect the idea of splitting the band into two groups. The Jefferson High band was pretty large for those days. We probably had between 100 and 120 members marching at any given time. Most bands in El Paso only marched a little over 70. The Jefferson High football games in those days tended not to be very exciting. The team was not very good. The band, however, was regularly the best in the city. It was well understood in those days that the majority of the people who went to the Jefferson High football games in those years really went there to watch the band.

At the end of each football season, around December, the annual interscholastic marching band competition would take place. The Jefferson High band seemed to always be one of the favorites to win. In conjunction with the band competition, they also awarded a trophy to the "Outstanding Drum Major," and Mando and I wanted very much to win it that year. And so, we developed the flying-batons routine that I described in an earlier chapter and practiced hard. On the day of the competition we had two objectives: First, we wanted our band to win the "Sweepstakes" trophy; Second, Mando and I wanted to take home the "Outstanding Drum Major" trophy.

As I related earlier, Mando and I were fortunate and ended up winning the "Outstanding Drum Major" trophy. The band also did win the "Sweepstakes" award. I was happy that I was graduating because I knew that the competition would get really stiff the following year. I later found out that the year following my graduation at least four or five other schools adopted the co-drum major approach at football games and band competitions and that drum major batons started flying all over the place.

Successes like those that we experienced in the Band will make anyone feel supremely assured and invincible. And I did feel invincible. I and the other members of the band had gotten a taste of what being the best feels like and I know I really liked it. Once again, for many reasons, our own expectations as students and the expectations of the community were not only surpassed; they were blown away. My band-mates and I were fortunate that we had a teacher like Mr. Glover who taught us what it took to be winners. The experience that he afforded us propelled many of us to continue the quest. I know it served me amazingly well when the following year, I enrolled at *Texas A&M University* and joined *The Fightin' Texas Aggie Band*, indubitably the finest military marching band in the world. That organization, under the direction of Lieutenant Colonel E. V. Adams, continued to inspire and challenge me to keep working hard in pursuit of excellence. I found it interesting too that the Aggie Band at that time--like my high school band--also consisted of two units: The White Band and the Maroon band. I was honored at the end of that year to be named "Best Drilled Fish (Freshman)" of the White Band.

Chapter 12-Other Enriching Experiences and People

Boy Scouts

My Scouting experience--which started before my Boys' Club days--was a rich and interesting one even though I never got any higher than the rank of Star Scout. It all began in 1955 when we were living at our grocery store/home on Alameda Avenue in El Paso. There was a neighbor family there which was very close to my family. They were the Rojas family and they lived at 125 Locust St. The father was Luis Rojas; the mother was "Acho" Rojas and they had four kids: Leo who was one year younger than me; Thelma who was 1 year younger than Leo; Bonnie three years younger than Leo, and Jimmy who was a toddler. Leo and I were "pals" and absolutely the closest of buddies.

Leo's family was one of the few in our neighborhood who were Protestant. They worshipped at the *United Methodist Church* located a few miles away from our neighborhood on Tays Street in the part of the city known as Second Ward. Their church was affiliated with the *Houchen Community Center* which happened to sponsor Boy Scout Troop 39. Leo had joined as a cub scout and after a few months he invited me to also join. Our Scoutmaster, Mr. Al Burciaga, made a tremendous impression on me and without doubt on all the other scouts. He was the type of person that helped give scouting the great reputation that it enjoyed during those years.

Everything about the scouting experience seemed ideal. Leo's father would put us in his '55 red and white *Plymouth* and drive us to the scout meetings every Wednesday evening. He would also drive us to any scouting activities such as camps and picnics. Since my family did not have a car, this arrangement was perfect for me and my family.

Because he had gotten an early start, Leo always was one rank ahead of me. When I was a Bobcat, he was a Wolf. We then progressed up the ranks steadily although he always remained at least one step above me. This relationship did not change for a few years and I never felt a need to try to catch up with him. Eventually, he became a Star Scout while I was only a First Class. One day in early 1957, Leo and I had a quarrel. I do not recall what the quarrel was about. But when I showed up at his house the following Wednesday evening to attend a scout meeting, he would not let me get into the *Plymouth*. I knew we had quarreled but I believed that our relationship transcended what the argument had been about and so I appealed to his father to let me go with them. His father preferred to not get involved and certainly would not intercede on my behalf. I suppose being his dad, he had to support Leo's side. Anyway, I'll never forget how I stood at the curb in front of Leo's house with tears in my eyes as I watched the *Plymouth* pull away. I was so hurt by that event that I terminated my pursuit of scouting with the Rojas family and never spoke to Leo again for the rest of our lives.

I did not return to Scouting until July, 1958, after my family moved to the Paisano Projects. I had just turned 11 years of age. I had not yet become a member of the Boys' Club and had enough free time and interest to continue with Scouting. Troop 39 was still operating as it had previously but my old friend Leo was no longer involved. I re-kindled my love for camping and scouting and enjoyed frequent camping trips to places like nearby *Zach White Scout Camp* and to more exotic places like *Piedmont Ranch* in New Mexico. Eventually I attained the rank of Star scout and had the opportunity to attend the *Boy Scout National Jamboree* in Colorado Springs, Colorado. A handful of other Scouts from my Troop and I were there between July 22nd and July 28th, 1960.

I am really thankful that my youth was filled with interesting times and events even though my family did not have too many material advantages. I know that we did not have much money. But as usual, through a variety of fund-raising events, my troop raised enough money to cover the expenses of a few of us. The entire contingent of Scouts from El Paso traveled to Colorado Springs in one *Greyhound* bus. The bus ride turned out to be a great opportunity to interact with Boy Scouts from other El Paso Troops.

The Jamboree was held at a place called the *J Diamond Ranch* which lay in the shadows of 14,100 ft. *Pike's Peak* near Colorado Springs, Colorado. Over 53,000 scouts descended into this ranch from all over the world and set up a small city of tents. The population of the entire town of Colorado Springs at that time was only 25,000.

I remember rooming (or should I say "tenting"?) with another kid from El Paso named Felipe Gonzalez. He proudly insisted that he be called "Felipe" (pronounced "feh-LEE-peh") rather than the easier to pronounce "Phillip" or "Phil." He was a very nice guy but he looked a lot like "Goofy" because of his protruding ears and widely-spaced, over-biting teeth. As a result of his looks, a lot of the other scouts made fun of him. Most memorable to me was how they took his name and deliberately distorted it so that he became known far and wide as "Full-of-pee" Gonzalez.

The most popular activity during the entire jamboree was to gather at various points of the gigantic camp site to buy, sell or exchange trinkets. There was a huge variety of scout patches, neckerchiefs, pins, neckerchief slides and other memorabilia available. Among the items I brought home were: a green cotton jacket with a huge circular jamboree patch stitched onto the back, a commemorative chest patch and a neat gold-colored neckerchief also commemorating the Jamboree.

The Jamboree was a huge national event. President Dwight Eisenhower attended although I do not remember seeing him. A few times during the week, the entire body of scouts would assemble at a huge natural amphitheater where we would sit on the grass that gently sloped downward toward the bottom of the amphitheater where they had set up the stage. I do remember a comedian whose name I believe was Dick Shawn who entertained us. The one line of Dick Shawn that I remember from his monologue was when he told us about his "sunburned goose bumps." It was a funny but accurate characterization of life at the Jamboree since in the evenings it was so cold that you had goose bumps, yet the days were so hot that your goose bumps would get sunburned.

I remember also that one of the guest stars at the Jamboree was James Arness who played Matt Dillon in the television show *Gunsmoke*. Again, I don't remember actually seeing him. The reason why I don't remember seeing some of these stars has to do with size of the amphitheater. We always ended up sitting so far away from the stage that it was difficult to pick up every detail of the entertainment going on there.

At the opening ceremonies, I do remember seeing the US Air Force *Blue Angels* do a fly-by that was absolutely spectacular. Also, on the final evening, the 50,000 attendees gathered at the amphitheater and, after the entertainment concluded, we were directed to take the candle that we had been given earlier and to light it. All the artificial lights were turned off and a beautiful sea of flickering flames surrounded me in the darkness as far as I could see.

The Jamboree lasted a whole week and it was the most interesting and exciting week that I had spent in my entire life up to that point. I collected a huge number of souvenirs and photographs of the Jamboree and I cherished them and the experience for years. Unfortunately, they were all in the foot locker that was lost in the fire that I mentioned earlier. I suppose that if I still had some of those souvenirs and pictures, I would remember many more of the facts relating to the Jamboree. But the fact is that I remember very little other than it was a wonderful experience.

Scouting for me was immensely important. The values taught by scouting have never left me. It was one of those institutions that molded and enriched me and which gave me memories that I will treasure forever. For some reason--probably the fact that I had become extremely busy at the *El Paso Boys' Club*-- I quit scouting for good in 1961.

My old friend Leo and I attended *Jefferson High School* together although he was one year behind me. I really never did speak to him for the entire time that we were in high school together. He was the quarterback of the varsity football team and a very popular student. I heard that upon graduation from high school he apparently got into drugs and died of a drug overdose after dropping out of college. I felt terrible when I heard that. Twenty or so years later, his mother, Acho, gave me Leo's high school yearbook (*El Capitan 1966*) because she had found out that mine had been lost (in that fire). It is somewhat ironic that my high school senior-year yearbook today is the one that once belonged to Leo.

Jr. ROTC and ROTC

My affinity for order, regimentation and ceremony probably started in the Boy Scouts. ROTC in high school attracted me for those same reasons and other reasons too. From my youngest days, I felt comfortable and probably somewhat more important than my peers whenever I was part of a military-style organization, particularly one whose members wore distinguishing uniforms. I also know that I felt a deep sense of patriotism whenever I could honor American soldiers of previous generations by enthusiastically following their footsteps. I cannot recall exactly when I determined that one day I would serve in the armed forces of our country. But that feeling finally morphed into reality when I joined the Jr. Reserve Officer Training Corps or ROTC program at my high school in September, 1961.

ROTC was an elective course but I felt drawn to it and so I joined. I was already a member of the high school band yet I wanted more regimentation in my life. My first three years in the corps of cadets were fairly typical: We wore uniforms once a week, drilled with real rifles, learned how to keep them clean, studied diverse subjects such as military tactics and first aid and practiced marksmanship at the indoor range right there in the school. I took the ROTC thing very seriously particularly with respect to my uniform. Lorenzo Candelaria, the Boys' Club staff member who I mentioned earlier and who was active in the Sr. ROTC program at *Texas Western College* had taught me how to spit shine shoes and I honestly believe that in my school program no one ever had shinier military shoes than mine. Mi Mamá had taught me how to starch and press my clothes many years earlier and so I made it a point whenever we wore our khaki uniforms to have the sharpest uniform in the battalion. As a result of all this, I accumulated a decent ROTC performance record and could tell that the instructors saw some potential in me.

At the beginning of my senior year, the school decided to organize a separate military marching band to support the school's ROTC battalion during parades. That same year I was selected to again be one of the two Drum Majors of the Senior Band and so, because of my prior connection with the ROTC program, I was given the position of ROTC Band Commander with the rank of Cadet Major.

Soon thereafter, the Jr. ROTC program for the entire city school system (The Jr. ROTC Brigade) did what was customary each year: It selected the three cadets who would act as the Brigade staff. The Brigade staff consisted of the Brigade Commander, the Deputy Brigade Commander and the Brigade Adjutant. Each high school in the city would nominate a cadet to undergo the Brigade Staff interview and selection process. The usual nominee would be that school's senior cadet, the Cadet Colonel who held the position of Battalion Commander. At my high school that year the Battalion Commander was Gilbert Sanchez and he should have been the school's nominee. However, the school's ROTC instructor cadre, Sergeants Victor Barrera and Kenneth Andrade and my band director, Mr. Glover decided to nominate me instead.

At the conclusion of the Brigade Staff interview and selection process, I was honored to have been selected as Brigade Deputy Commander along with Gustavo Lucas from *Bowie High School* (Brigade Commander) and Alan Gold from *Austin High School* (Brigade Adjutant). This event catapulted me to the position of Cadet Colonel and made me the senior cadet at my high school. From that point forward until 1975, when I finally resigned my regular army commission as an Air Defense Artillery Captain, I felt a compelling bond with the military. For a good portion of those years I also felt an irresistible urge to become a career officer.

My year as the Deputy Brigade Commander enhanced my self-esteem immeasurably and took my self-confidence off the chart. As a result of my Boys' Club accomplishments, particularly with respect to the Optimist Oratorical contests, I had managed to establish a good reputation as a teen in El Paso. This ROTC honor, which was solidly scholastic and military, was yet another significant boost in my quest to be an exemplary youth. Suddenly, I was rubbing elbows with the best and the brightest students from the other schools and, more importantly, was acting as one of their leaders. I became good friends with the other Brigade Staff members and that was significant because, generally, students from my high school--which was predominately Mexican-American—did not associate with students from schools which had predominately Anglo populations. I even found myself getting phone calls from female students at these Anglo schools and ended up dating some of them. If I did not believe prior to this that I was a student leader, I certainly remember feeling that way after my ascension to Brigade Staff.

This experience at the Jr. ROTC level proved invaluable the following fall when I enrolled at *Texas A&M University* in College Station, Texas, some 700 miles east of El Paso. As mentioned earlier, I joined the Corps of Cadets there as a member of the *Fightin' Texas Aggie Band*. I had an amazingly interesting and educational freshman year there and again experienced a reality far removed from what I had known in El Paso. The student body was almost exclusively male and Anglo and the number of brown or black faces there truly was quite small. In the *Fightin' Texas Aggie Band* that year there were around 120 freshmen ("fish") none of whom were black and of whom maybe 5 of us were Mexican-American. And, the almost century-old tradition of physical hazing within the Corps remained as strong as ever. Regarding Mexican-Americans, the prevailing attitude in those years and in that part of Texas was pretty much the same as it had been since Texas gained its independence from Mexico in 1836. In a twisted sort of way, I was very fortunate to have spent that year there. Whenever an upperclassman decided to spend time hazing me—and for me and the other band fish, that would happen almost every day—I never would attempt to figure out whether the hazer had an ulterior racist motive or whether he was just trying to build character in me. I did not enjoy the hazing but I also never let it bother me. Interestingly, one of the upperclassmen who hazed me the most—all of it in the absolute purest traditional sense—was my squad leader, Henry G. Cisneros, a proud Mexican-American himself who went on to become Mayor of San Antonio and US Secretary of Housing and Urban Development under President Bill Clinton. In addition, during that one year I spent at A&M, I formed some of the strongest friendships of my life. Most prominent among those friends were Morris Vogel and Jonathan Magnus Beall, my two "fish" roommates. Regrettably, Morris passed away in 2014 but I remain in close touch with Jon Beall and some 20 other Texas A&M classmates particularly when we reunite annually at Aggie Musters.

At any rate, I realized soon after getting there that my high school band and Jr. ROTC experiences had prepared me well for A&M. I felt privileged to be there and as the year progressed, I sensed that I would complete the ordeal without any problems. All of this plus a strong desire to pursue a career in the US Army enabled me at the end of that year to obtain an appointment to the *United States Military Academy* from which I graduated in 1970.

I remember thinking in 1966 when I arrived at West Point how fortunate I was. The war in Vietnam was escalating and it had not yet become unpopular and there I was, about to get the best training on earth that would allow me to achieve my life-long ambition of serving my country in a war just as the Greatest Generation had done a few decades earlier. My only regret—and it was a big one--was that I had to cut short my career at Texas A&M. In the one year that I spent there I underwent experiences that most certainly strengthened me physically and spiritually forever.

Civil Air Patrol

In the fall of 1964, as I was beginning my senior year in high school, I came upon an opportunity that I simply could not pass up. I was very much into the military way of life, having been selected the Deputy Brigade Commander for the entire school district R.O.T.C. organization. I was also planning to compete for the last time in the *Boys' Clubs of America* National "Boy of the Year" competition. In light of that competition, I needed to continue to pad my resume with more and more activities, particularly community service activities, to make myself more competitive.

At the beginning of that academic year, a new teacher had reported to work at *Jefferson High School*. He was Mr. Phillip Ortego, a retired US Air Force pilot and a Major in the Civil Air Patrol. He was excited to be at Jefferson and highly motivated to work with his students to make them more active in the community. Thus, he decided to organize a junior unit of the Civil Air Patrol and act as sponsor. The Civil Air Patrol, to the best of my knowledge, was nothing more than a bunch of civilians who formed units all over the country, wore really neat Air Force blue uniforms, and when invited, participated in search and rescue operations. The junior Civil Air Patrol was really nothing more than a bunch of teenage jet-pilot wannabe's who provided eyes in airplanes when search and rescue missions were undertaken by their senior counterparts.

Mr. Ortego started looking for candidates for his new organization from among the students at Jefferson High. Soon, he put the recruiting moves on me and a classmate named Robert Porras. Robert had become an extremely popular student among the faculty because of his participation in *Crossroads of the Americas* that summer. Robert and I were pretty good chums primarily from our experience in that *Crossroads* project. We had become real buddies as the school term started.

Mr. Ortego, without knowing anything about me--except what he had heard or read--offered me the post of Squadron Commander of the junior Civil Air Patrol unit that he was forming. Similarly, he offered my buddy, Robert, the post of Deputy Squadron Commander. We both eagerly accepted. For me, it was excellent fodder for my resume but, much more importantly, he promised that we would get to fly in an airplane every once in a while. Plus, we would be issued those neat Air Force blue uniforms that looked so cool.

Two events relating to the junior Civil Air Patrol stand out in my mind. The first of these was the organizational meeting that was held a week after Mr. Ortego made me the Squadron Commander. The meeting place was the *Delta Recreation Center*, which was a brand-new facility that happened to be only a 10-minute walk from my house in the Paisano Projects. He decided that the meetings would be held weekly on Saturdays at 10:00AM. I thought that was a bad move because like all kids, we liked to sleep in on Saturday mornings. However, most of us were busy every afternoon at school and evenings were generally taken up by homework making time-slot options very limited.

The organizational meeting was rather impressive. Somehow, Mr. Ortego got six or seven new recruits to show up for that meeting. He presided over the first meeting resplendent in his CAP uniform which consisted of navy-blue pants, a light blue shirt with shiny Major and CAP insignia, his Air Force decorations and ribbons and a very cool navy-blue garrison cap, the type that are all fabric and flat and can be tucked under your belt. I remember being very impressed with everything. He proceeded to announce the new command structure and I recall looking at the puzzled faces of the other recruits when he identified me as the squadron commander. After all, I was just another dumb recruit attending the first meeting of this new organization. Then we took a tour of the facility, which had nothing to do with the US Air Force or the Civil Air Patrol. It was, after all, just a big gymnasium. Everyone was very excited when Mr. Ortego announced the plan for next meeting: We were to gather at the *El Paso International Airport* at 9:00 AM the following Saturday and Mr. Ortego was going to take all of us on a plane ride.

The second event that vividly stands out in my mind was the plane ride the following week and some other things that happened that day. Mr. Ortego knew that Robert and I had no cars at home and since we both lived near each other in or near the Paisano Projects, he offered to pick us up. That Saturday morning, Mr. Ortego showed up in a 1963 *Mercedes-Benz* 300SE automobile that he kept perfectly clean and detailed. When we got into the car, Robert and I were overwhelmed by the smell of newness and leather.

When we arrived at the airport, only two of the other recruits had shown up and so Mr. Ortego took us all up at once in a small *Piper Cub* single-engine plane that could carry six. I sat next to my friend, Robert. We flew all over the El Paso desert areas. It was a bright sunny day in October, a bit cool but nevertheless perfect for flying and for converting reluctant recruits into Air Force zealots.

During the flight, Mr. Ortego showed off a bit by doing some minor flight acrobatics although nothing extreme such as flying upside down. About a half-hour into the flight, my buddy Robert started to look pale. He quickly took one of the vomit bags and held it under his chin for the remainder of the flight. My biggest fear was that he would throw up and that I would get splattered with his vomit. I kept as far away from him as I possibly could.

After the hour-long flight, we touched down and to everyone's relief no one had gotten sick. Robert still felt a bit queasy and he still looked pale as we walked from the parked airplane back to Mr. Ortego's *Mercedes* for our ride back home.

We started the drive back home and it seemed that only Mr. Ortego and I were talking. Robert was uncharacteristically quiet. Suddenly, after maybe two minutes of driving, Robert, who was in the back seat alone, (I was riding shotgun) let out a loud belch and then violently threw up all over the back of the front seat and on the floor in the back. It was a lot of vomit and smelled really bad.

Mr. Ortego quickly pulled over to the side of the road. Robert climbed out of the car and continued to try to finish throwing up outside but he was empty. Robert then awkwardly and pathetically tried to clean the backseat and floor with some Kleenex tissues but the mess was too much. We drove the rest of the way back in silence. Despite the cool weather, all the windows of the *Mercedes* were left open as we drove. I was certain that I would throw up next so as to ensure that any remaining clean part of the interior would get fouled as well. Thankfully, I did not.

The next week in school, Mr. Ortego hardly spoke to Robert or me. A certain chill pervaded the air whenever we saw him. I suppose Robert was embarrassed and would simply never get over what he did to the *Mercedes*. So, prior to the next meeting, Robert resigned. While the flight had been fun, the vomit aftermath seemed to dominate every thought that I recalled about it. Also, I was too much into the military and decided that I really didn't care to become an Air Force "zoomy" after all. So, I turned in my resignation too.

And so, that was it...my month-long stint in the junior division of the Civil Air Patrol. I concluded that kids from our neighborhood were simply not ready for airplanes and flying. Most of our fathers or even older brothers who had served in the armed forces had served in the Army or Marines and, therefore, could not impart exciting flight experiences to us. I could relate to flight only because of movies I had watched or books and comics that I had read and, finally, when I took my first flight, the many pleasant thoughts that came of it got devastated by Robert's vomit. I imagine that he felt the same way. Nevertheless, I must give credit to Mr. Ortego. He saw potential in the kids from my neighborhood and he was a generous visionary who tried to introduce us to the exciting world of flying. He stands tall among the many adults who mentored us even though the results of his work probably never reached his expectations.

Jefferson High School

As I was attending High School, I always felt as if I was having the best time of my life. Of course, there were many moments of extreme stress and frustration as any high school student will endure, but overall, I have always looked back at those 4 years as years of great personal pleasure, accomplishment and gratification. When I reflect and try to figure out why I had such a meaningful time there, I end up fondly remembering the many different experiences that I went through while there. Those experiences involved many close friends, some very well-run organizations and a few very talented and dedicated teachers. I have already written about some of them but there were more.

Mrs. Sallie Leonard

Somewhere, somehow, as I grew up, I acquired a great interest and a strong affinity for the subject of English. I believe I can trace that to my 11th grade English teacher, Mrs. Sally Leonard. My brother, Nacho, had been a student of Mrs. Leonard and he would constantly tell me about the pleasure that he felt when he attended her classes. He recently recalled how, as a junior, in order to gain more from her classes, he would sit in the front row even though that would preclude him from keeping an eye on a real cute girl, Olga Olivas, who preferred to sit in the back row. It turns out that on Parents Night, the two English papers that Mrs. Leonard posted on the bulletin board for viewing by parents were those of Nacho and Olga. Incidentally, Nacho and Olga eventually got married. At any rate, I also started to believe that Mrs. Leonard was really special and I couldn't wait to experience what Nacho kept telling me about. When I finally got into her class, I was not disappointed.

Mrs. Leonard was not only a good teacher, who was widely liked and respected, but she also had the classic good looks of the quintessential female teacher. She was tall, thin, and very pretty. She always wore extremely attractive business suits or dresses along with high heels and she never seemed to get excited about anything. Her style of teaching was soft, calm, deliberate and very entertaining. She basically taught me how to write and, therefore, gave me a skill that helped very much to get me through college and law school and, even today, helps me whenever I write anything.

Mrs. Alice Bosworth

In all fairness, I should give credit to another teacher who contributed significantly in getting me to like English. That was Mrs. Alice Bosworth. She was my ninth grade English I teacher who probably first whetted my appetite for writing and for literature. Unfortunately, despite her effectiveness as a teacher, I only seem to remember her very attractive long legs. I, along with a few of my classmate-buddies from the Projects, would daydream about going to her classes and hope with all our hearts that she would sit on the tall stool at the front of the class facing us and cross her legs and drive us crazy for 45 minutes. We still talk about her today.

Mrs. Mary Diaz

My love for history--which is greater today than ever before--probably can be traced to my ninth grade American History teacher named Miss Mary Baquera. During the course of that year she got married and became Mrs. Diaz. I don't believe that she was an exceptionally gifted teacher and she had no unique style or method of teaching. Yet I always looked forward to her classes. This may well be a good example of how a student can be motivated to learn a subject simply because the teacher happens to be very attractive.

Mrs. Diaz was extremely attractive; perhaps the only teacher for whom I had a genuine crush. I suppose that I subconsciously wanted very much to communicate to her my admiration and affection for her. I probably believed that I could only do so by excelling in history. Regardless of what motivated me, I remember developing a great interest in that subject and ending up getting straight A's. I wonder if the outcome would have been different if she had been homely. I have a strong suspicion that it would have been different indeed.

Mr. C. E. Neal

In 1963, when I was Junior, I had the privilege of having Mr. Neal as my speech teacher. I will always remember him for two reasons: First, he taught me how to be a better public speaker. He was my coach at the speech interscholastic competition where I took second place in the El Paso School District. I think he also recognized some special skill in me and he took the time to help me to develop it. The second reason why I will always remember him is because it was in his class that I first heard the news that President John F. Kennedy had been shot. Even though I will always be grateful for what Mr. Neal did for me in developing my public speaking skills, I felt that he was too formal and rigid and not very friendly in our daily communications. I honestly can say that I never really cared for him or for his style of teaching, yet, he gave me tons of confidence that helped me immensely once I got out of school.

And so, now that the 50th anniversary of my high-school graduation has passed, I look back and find that I have one huge regret: I regret that I did not stay in touch with these teachers. I wish today very much that I had told them in the past, and that I could again tell them now, that they really made a big difference in at least one life: mine. Unfortunately, the years have passed so quickly that even if they were still alive some may not fully appreciate what I would be saying.

Living near the City Dump

South El Paso has always been the tough part of the City. In the 60's the only thing between the residential neighborhoods of South El Paso and the *Rio Grande* was the City Dump (these Dumps are now called "landfills"). It was situated right along the *Rio Grande*. The only thing that separated the river from the Dump was a gigantic levee whose cross-section measured some 40 to 50ft. in height and maybe 100ft. at the base. The Dump was probably like any other Dump. All sorts of garbage could be found there and all sorts of people as well. I did not frequent the Dump having been warned by my parents about the hazards that existed there, but it seemed to me that many of the kids of our neighborhood did go there frequently in search of usable discarded stuff or just high adventure.

This story is about my only visit ever to the Dump. The year was 1960. It was the fall or winter of that year--light jacket weather in El Paso--and the past-time that had become extremely popular among the boys that I played with was hunting with BB guns. This fad began when one of the neighborhood kids got his own BB gun. He made an appearance with his rifle at the large playground located in our neighborhood. The playground included a baseball park and so it provided lots of open space. Nature then provided suitable targets in the forms of sparrows and pigeons. Soon thereafter, it seemed like every other kid in the neighborhood had somehow acquired a BB gun and was hunting these fearsome creatures.

At our home, we certainly could not afford one BB gun for each of the two boys. Therefore, the older of us, Nacho, got the BB gun. As was almost always the case, Nacho was reasonably generous in sharing the BB gun with me. I remember on many occasions sitting in the backdoor concrete slab at my good buddy Checo's house--which faced directly toward the playground-- and with Checo and other buds shooting sparrows and pigeons with our guns as they perched on telephone poles or power lines or playground light poles. One thing that particularly stands out in my mind is this: Whenever we were playing baseball or football on the playground field, we would always be amazed by the number of birds that were perching nearby. We could have shot them like fish in a barrel. However, it was amazing how as soon as we went to our homes and returned with our BB guns, all of the birds suddenly disappeared and simply were nowhere to be found. Nevertheless, we learned that with patience, the birds would inevitably return and allow us to consummate that timeless passion of boys to hunt.

Within the housing projects, the only type of rifle that could be found for these hunting activities was indeed the BB gun. Immediately south of the Paisano Projects and closer to the City Dump, there was a residential area comprised of individual homes. Unlike the Projects, these homes were owned by the people living in them. Generally, the standard of living in that neighborhood was slightly higher than in the Projects but still considerably lower than the rest of the city. Anyway, in that residential neighborhood, because of that higher socio-economic reality, one could find an occasional upgrade to a BB gun: The pellet gun. The pellet gun was distinguishable from the BB gun by two characteristics. First, it fired little pellets shaped like small bombs (round but with a set of rear stabilizing fins). And second, it was equipped with a pump mechanism that enabled the operator to increase significantly the amount of air pressure with which an individual pellet could be fired. For a standard shot comparable to a BB gun, the mechanism needed to be pumped two or three times. If, however, the operator wanted to fire the pellet farther or with greater velocity, it could be pumped 10 to 15 and even as many as 50 times.

I remember one individual in particular who owned a pellet gun. His name was Eddie Lerma. Eddie lived in one of those privately-owned homes closer to the Dump. He was exactly my age and he and I participated in just about all of the same activities in school and in the Boys' Club. He was a good buddy but not as close as Checo.

One day, Eddie Lerma and another good buddy named Robert Cervantes (known as "Pelón") were in my neighborhood. Eddie had brought his pellet gun and Pelón had his BB gun. I had Nacho's BB gun. We started shooting birds from the bleachers at the baseball field. A few minutes later, a group of kids to showed up. Each of them was carrying a case of 24 cans of *Coors* beer. They were going from house to house trying to sell it. When we inquired, the kids told us that they had found all this beer in the Dump. Apparently, the *Coors* brewery would regularly get rid of "spoiled" beer by leaving truckloads of it at the Dump. *Coors* beer was different from most beers. Since the brewery did not pasteurize the beer, it had a tendency to spoil if it was not kept refrigerated. Any cases that lost their refrigeration would end up in the Dump.

Eddie suggested that we take our hunting party to the Dump and see if we could find some of that beer. And so, in the late morning, the three of us started to walk the two miles to the Dump. We arrived at around noon. We saw lots of pigeons and sparrows and other birds that we could have shot. But we also saw lots of people there and so we put off the hunting a bit more. We spotted the river levee farther to the south so we walked toward it. We climbed the north side of the levee, reached the very top and then started to walk east along the top of the levee. From there, we could see the *Rio Grande* down below on the right and Mexico just on the other side of it. There were lots of bushes and shrubs growing in isolated places by the riverbank. We did not see anybody or anything else down there. We just kept walking along the top of the levee. We had not seen anything to shoot at so Eddie kept pumping the pump mechanism of his pellet gun over and over and over waiting for the first target to present itself.

We decided to go look for birds or small animals closer to the river. So, we started walking down the south side of the levee until we reached the level of the river bank. We had not taken more than a few steps along the river bank when, suddenly, two men stepped out from bushes where they had been hiding. They were approximately 20ft. away from us looking at us in a somewhat menacing way. They asked us for our rifles. Eddie said, "No way," and told them to go to hell. They started walking toward us in a more threatening manner. We started backing away. Then one of the men picked up a couple of stones and started to throw them at us. We deftly dodged the stones and then turned around and started running back up the levee. As we ran up the levee, I felt those sizable stones flying by my head but fortunately, none of them struck us. As we ran, I remember feeling fear as I have rarely, if ever, felt it in my life. I just knew that these men would certainly rob us and probably hurt us if they caught us.

We scrambled to the top of the levee. From the top we looked back down at the two men who were now halfway up the levee and still coming after us. The three of us were standing in a line at the top of the levee. We saw one of the men throw more stones at us and then bend down to pick up a few more. At that moment, the three of us quietly--without looking at or speaking with each other--aimed our BB and pellet guns at the two men below. Before the bent-over man could stand up again, we fired. I have no idea where the BBs landed that Pelón and I fired. For all I know, we missed them completely. Eddie's pellet, however, hit the bent-over man squarely on the right shoulder. I concluded that it must have been Eddie's pellet because I noticed a fairly large cloud of dust rise from the man's jacket at the point of impact. Also, the man instantly reached for his shoulder as if in great pain. He then looked up and made an ugly face--either of pain or anger--and let out a howl. For what seemed like long minutes, the three of us froze and stared alternatively at each other and at the two men below. The silence was broken when Eddie started pumping his rifle again. The men below saw what he was doing, looked at each other, looked back at us then turned around and started running back down the levee toward the river.

Eddie, Pelón and I stood for a few moments longer at the top of the levee contemplating whether the pellet had actually penetrated the jacket that the man had been wearing. We knew that the pellet had been fired with just about as much force as the gun could possibly generate. We did not know whether the man had fled because he was injured or because he was just scared. Nevertheless, they both had run and we had beaten them. We conveniently assumed that the man had not been injured but had been taught a good lesson. We continued our walk back toward the Dump.

We passed the Dump and continued walking toward Eddie's house. We did not say very much to each other. I think that we all felt a sense of guilt at having possibly hurt that man, so we spent lots of time trying to rationalize what we had done. I don't believe Eddie, Pelón and I ever discussed that episode again although the story did circulate among the neighborhood boys that Eddie had shot a "mojado" or "wetback" who had attacked us. I seem to recall that the fad involving BB (and pellet) guns did not last much longer. It's hard to say whether that levee incident had anything to do with the passing of the fad but I know that for me personally, it left me fearful of the damage that even small rifles can do and prompted me never to shoot my BB gun again.

Commuting to School

One of the most enjoyable opportunities in my life to communicate, rejoice, commiserate or acquire useful knowledge used to occur daily as I walked back and forth from school with my buddies. From 1961 until 1965, while I attended high school, we lived in the Paisano Projects. The exact address was 3922 East Paisano Drive, Apartment 3. *Thomas Jefferson High School* was approximately 1 mi. east of our apartment on Paisano Drive. My routine, therefore, was to walk to school every morning, come home for lunch, return to school after lunch and then come home at the end of the day every day.

For some strange reason, the twice-a-day round-trip commute became incredibly systematic. Without actually making any special arrangements, at precisely 8:00AM, a group of my neighborhood buddies would gather at the intersection of Paisano Drive and Boone St. The group generally consisted of Eloiso De Avila, Rogelio Felix, Sal Garcia, Jesús Reza and me although sometimes there were more of us and sometimes there were fewer. No one actually waited for anyone else. It just so happened that everyone in our group of four or five would arrive at that corner within seconds of each other. And so, without even slowing down, the group would merge and proceed to school.

We would walk on the south side of Paisano Drive heading east for about ¾ of a mile. Then we would cross Paisano Drive and finish the walk on the north side of Paisano Drive. The reason we stayed on the south side for most of the walk was simple: it had a sidewalk. They had actually built a pedestrian overpass right at the high school to cross Paisano Drive (a busy six-lane highway), however, because in order to use it you had to climb and descend a total of 50 steps, no one ever used it. We avoided the north side because it was dusty and no one wanted to get their shoes too dirty before getting to school. Once we arrived at the campus, we would scatter in all directions to go to our morning classes.

Then, at precisely 11:40AM, a school-bell would ring releasing all of us for lunch. Once again, without any one of us having to wait, the group of four or five would merge at the school gate that led to Paisano Drive and we would start our walk home. We used to walk quite rapidly covering the approximate 1-mile distance in about 13 minutes. At the intersection of Boone St. and Paisano Drive the group would scatter and each of us would head for our respective homes for lunch. For me, that intersection was exactly 140 paces from the rear door to our apartment. So, at approximately 11:54AM every day, I would enter the back door of our apartment where mi

Mamá was waiting with a hot lunch. I would eat in about 10 minutes, go the bathroom for a maximum of five minutes, brush my teeth, kiss mi Mamá and I would be heading out for the commute back at exactly 12:12 PM. The merging process would repeat itself again, the group would head back to school and we would arrive on campus at 12:28 PM to start classes at 12:30. The exact same merging and marching process would occur when the afternoon bell would ring at approximately 3:15PM.

We did not follow this exact procedure for every single day but I know that the majority of the time we did just that. Here are some of the things that I remember most vividly about these commutes.

In March of every single year, the winds from Mexico would sweep over El Paso. These winds were not only strong but they carried huge quantities of fine Mexican dust. Normally, they would start picking up in intensity right after noon. So, our lunchtime commute generally was unaffected by them. However, later in the afternoons, the stronger winds would be waiting for us. The skies would be colored a soft, khaki-brown color and visibility would be just a few feet. Sometimes, those winds were so strong that we would literally be walking at 45-degree angles into the westerly wind in order to not be blown back. The dust was so thick that we never tried to open our eyes nor to look up from our feet. We would just point our bodies westward, lean forward and start walking. I really despised those March winds.

The March dust storms managed to aggravate our lives in at least one other way. During those days in high school, I used to use hairdressing to keep my hair slicked down. The brand that I preferred was *Royal Crown* hairdressing. It was really nothing more than sweet smelling petroleum jelly and I remember that a little inch-and-a-half tall container of it would cost about 15¢. I would apply the hairdressing on my hair every day in the morning so that I would look cool and attractive all day. On those days when the March dust storms were happening, I would arrive home with hair that was a dull shade of khaki-brown and twice as voluminous as normal. The Mexican dust would find resting places all over my hair and would sit there firmly secured by the adhering qualities of *Royal Crown* hairdressing. I hated this because it caused me to have to again take a shower that evening. Normally, I only showered in the mornings before going to school. It was really amusing when the three or four of us would walk home during a dust storm after each of us had applied a generous helping of hairdressing. We would all arrive at the intersection of Boone St. and Paisano Drive with what appeared to be khaki-colored hats on our heads.

The last thing I remember about these commutes was that we took full advantage of all opportunities to walk behind girls. Coincidentally, as my group of four or five would gather for the commute, a similar gathering of girl school-mates would occur at roughly the same intersection and at roughly the same time every day. We would maneuver our group so that it would be walking at a discreet distance behind that group of girls. We would never walk ahead of the girls. We would do this primarily so that we could enjoy looking at and talking about the group of girls in front of us. Of course, we never actually spoke to these girls and we never cared to date them. However, it was of utmost importance that we position ourselves behind them whenever we engaged in the commute.

For many of us, these commutes provided a great and frequent opportunity for us to communicate with each other about subjects that we did not have time to discuss on athletic fields or other venues. Eloiso De Avila recently reminded me of the conversation we had on our noon commute of November 22, 1963. He recalled that as we walked home in a somewhat stunned state after hearing the news of Kennedy's assassination just moments earlier, we each related to the others precisely what we were doing as the announcement was made to the entire school over the public address system. He reminded me of what I told the group: At that particular moment, I was scrunched in my desk trying desperately to hide a raging erection that I had been experiencing during most of the class period and which had been caused by a really pretty girl who sat near me and regularly excited me to no end when she would cross her legs.

On another commute as we returned to school from lunch, one of the older boys brought with him a small collection of post-card-sized, black and white pornographic photographs. I had never seen anything like that before and by the time we reached the school grounds I had become so nauseated by them that I was ready to puke mi Mamá's lunch all over the sidewalk.

During these commutes, we also frequently talked about the future and about older boys who had graduated before us and were attending college. We seemed to reassure each other that we were also destined to do the same.

Driving

Despite the lower socio-economic state of our neighborhood and thus the paucity of family cars, it was, nevertheless, every teenager's dream to learn how to drive and to acquire a car as quickly as possible. Learning to drive for me was not so much an event as it was a process or evolution. I seem to recall that it all started in 1960 when I was 13 years old. Prior to that, since we had no car at home, I had gotten no offers from anyone at home to be taught how to drive. But life goes on and interesting things inevitably happen.

One day that year, while we were living in the Paisano Projects, a friend of mi Mamá's was visiting with us. She had arrived there in her car and was there just for the afternoon. As she chatted with mi Mamá she offered to sell us her car. It was a huge, light-green 1950 *Dodge*. For an 11-year-old car, it was in pretty good shape. She wanted $250 for it.

The lady seemed to have amazing sales skills. Mi Mamá gave her lots of reasons why we couldn't possibly consider buying it. After all, mi Papá was blind, mi Mamá was ill, we had no money and the only possible driver, my big brother Nacho, was not even there to test it. Next thing you know, I got designated as the driver by the shark lady and, as she handed me the keys, she told me to take the family on a test drive. While we did the test drive, she went off to visit someone else in the neighborhood.

I don't believe I had ever driven a car prior to that day. However, with all the adults saying it's OK, the bizarre event became legitimate. Mi Mamá and my little 7-year old sister Hilda Luz got into the backseat. They really seemed thrilled and excited to be going on a ride. With great cockiness and impunity, I started it up and off we went.

We departed the Projects and somehow, I managed to cross Paisano Drive-- one of the busiest highways in the city--to go to our old neighborhood where *Albro's Grocery* used to be. A round trip to that point would complete our test drive. The total distance from our house to the old neighborhood was a little over a mile. It's interesting that mi Mamá asked that I take all of us to the "old neighborhood" for the test drive.

I recall driving east on Alameda Ave. feeling extremely confident and managing the situation quite well. Finally, we got to Locust Street. (*Albro's* was on the southeast corner of Locust Street and Alameda Ave.) I turned right on Locust. I was deliriously happy driving down Locust Street slowly hoping to see old buddies that I could impress. Unfortunately, no one was around.

Suddenly, I saw a car backing out from a driveway on my left in front of me. I was only going less than 10 miles per hour yet I decided not to stop. I felt that if I accelerated instead, I would get past that car before it reached the street. I pressed the accelerator but the 106 HP engine didn't exactly make the car jump. Then I prayed that the car pulling out of the driveway would see us and stop or that it would just miss our rear end as we passed.

My prayers were answered with a soft crunching sound as the right-rear fender of the other car hit our rear driver side fender. We all heard and felt the crunch but I just kept on driving slowly. None of us knew what we were supposed to do in situations like this. I looked in the rearview mirror and saw the other car continue to back up and then to drive away from us on Locust Street.

We drove in silence all the way back home. We all felt a heavy burden as we considered the dilemma we were facing. If we didn't disclose the accident to the seller, we knew that God would eventually send us to the eternal flames of hell. If we did disclose, we would have to buy the car or else the seller would turn me in and I would have to rot in prison for the rest of my life. When I parked the car in the street next to our home and looked at the damage, mi Mamá decided that it was minor and hardly noticeable and, therefore, we would not say anything to the seller. Mi Mamá saw the seller-lady, smiled at her, gave her the car keys and said "Gracias, pero nó." ("Thanks, but no.") That, thank God, was the last we ever heard about that car.

My next learning-to-drive experience occurred not long after that. It is interesting that once again, I was "compelled" by a presumably responsible adult (mi Papá) to drive even though I had no driver's license. As far as I was concerned, parental compulsion meant that I could not get in trouble if anything happened.

This experience took place in 1961. I was 14 years old but my parents kept telling me that I was wise way beyond my years. My total driving experience thus far was limited only to that test drive and minor accident in the 1950 *Dodge*. This time, the sequence of events started when mi Papá decided to buy a car now that Nacho had a license. One Saturday, he and I got on a bus (I have no idea where Nacho was that day) and we went to a used car lot on Montana Avenue. Someone had recommended the lot to mi Papá. It was owned by a guy named Joe Quijano. Somehow, upon meeting us, Joe decided that we really had to have this 1957 white *Ford* sedan that he had sitting in his lot. He was so convinced about how the car matched our needs that he handed the keys to mi Papá and told him to take the car home for the weekend. Mi Papá held up his white cane with a red tip and told him that he'd love to do that except that he was blind. We all laughed. Mr. Quijano then pushed the keys into my hand and said "You can drive it." Next thing I knew, I was driving down on Chelsea toward our home on Paisano Drive. Mi Papá was with me and we both knew that I did not have a driver's license and yet we pushed on. I was thrilled and had no fear. After all, mi Papá was right there and knew everything about what I was doing. I essentially felt that I had "full immunity" from possible prosecution.

That night, since I had a car, I called my two best buddies, Fernando and Checo, and I invited them to join me on a trip to some bars in Juárez, Mexico, in my "new" *Ford*. I found out later that as soon as I had left to pick up Fernando and Checo, Mr. Quijano had called mi Papá to get my driver's license number. Mi Papá told him that I did not have a license and that I had gone out in the car and wouldn't return until after midnight.

All of that was unbeknownst to me until the following day. Mr. Quijano arrived at our front door on Sunday morning, very early. He was agitated and he wanted the car keys. He started yelling at me for not telling him that I didn't have a license. Mi Papá intervened on my behalf and we told Mr. Quijano that the car was overpriced at $550 and to get lost.

All I know is that the driving experiences I had that Saturday night were invaluable in ultimately getting me to become a licensed driver. The bar-hopping that we did must have resulted in my drinking a beer or two. So, I must have been somewhat impaired. Driving in the downtown area of Juárez had to involve some of the most complex and risky maneuvering that anyone could possibly ever face. Nevertheless, I managed it all just fine. Checo and Fernando both had access to cars owned by their parents and were considerably more experienced drivers than I was; yet they properly never offered to drive and I never asked them to do so that night. I know also that the car was so neat and clean that a few heads actually turned on one particular occasion that night as I parallel-parked it in front of a bar. I never felt fear or even apprehension that night. I only felt cool and invincible in that *Ford* in the company of my very best buddies.

Then I turned 15. Both of my parents were eager to sign the parental consent form that would allow me to get a driver's license at that age. I asked my good friend and classmate, Julio Pellicano--who had a license--to help me prepare for my driving test. Julio was one of my very best friends whose family happened to be relatively well-to-do compared to the rest of the people that comprised my high-school society. His parents had various automobiles including a 1960 *Pontiac Tempest* that had a push button shifter on the dash.

On three or four afternoons in a row in the summer of 1962, I walked a mile to Julio's house where he showed me the basics in order to get licensed. Then one day late in June, Julio drove me to the Department of Motor Vehicles and he stayed with me until I passed my tests and got my license. From that day on, I felt as empowered as any other peer in my neighborhood. My dream was now half complete. I eagerly anticipated making enough money very soon thereafter to buy my own car. Little did I know or even suspect that the second half of my dream would not become reality until 8 long years later when I graduated from West Point and purchased my very first car: A brand-spanking-new1970 *Buick Grand Sport*.

An Interim Car

Even though I would not actually own a car until many years later, I managed to get wheels anyway for my last year of high school as a result of an amazing set of fortuitous events. These events occurred during the winter of 1964 and the spring of 1965. I lived with my parents and sister at 3922 East Paisano Drive Apartment 3 in El Paso, Texas. My brother Nacho was in college at the *New Mexico Military Institute*.

During those times, mi Mamá had the habit of opening our home to Mexican aliens of questionable legal status who needed a place to stay. Somehow, mi Mamá would become acquainted with these persons who worked in El Paso as maids but who had entered the US--in most cases--illegally, from Mexico. These ladies worked Monday through Friday at their employer's home and they would actually sleep there on those days. They were not needed on weekends and these maids normally would go back to their own homes from Friday night until Monday morning. But they couldn't really go back to Mexico because they might not be able to come back into the US. So, through some strange network, they would end up spending weekends with some facilitating family in El Paso. Mi Mamá somehow was in that network and she regularly would hear about one of these maids needing a place to sleep over the weekend. They would be put in contact with each other and mi Mamá would invite the maid to stay in our home and sleep on the sofa in exchange for some small fee or some minor domestic work.

One of these maids was a lady named Aurora. We called her Rory. She was an illegal alien around 40 years old, about 5ft. 8in. tall and somewhat overweight. She was a very gregarious woman, however, and seemed to always be laughing loudly particularly at mi Papá's jokes. She was extremely energetic and always managed to clean our house thoroughly before the weekend ended. I recall that all of us in my home enjoyed the company of Rory because she was such an upbeat and pleasant person.

Usually, these guest-maids would sleep at our home during weekend nights but they loved to party heavily during the weekend days and evenings. On one particular occasion Rory met a man while she was partying in downtown El Paso. That man was Charlie Coleman.

Charlie was a man of approximately 50 years of age and he was a chain smoker. His brand of choice was *Camel* cigarettes but any other unfiltered cigarette would also do just fine. Consequently, he was afflicted by a horrible hacking cough. Like Rory, he also loved to laugh boisterously but because of his hacking cough, his laughter frequently ended up in a near-seizure that required him to sit down in order to get over it. He had a pot belly, was short of stature (approximately 5ft. 5in.) but had a personality very similar to Rory's in that they constantly seemed to be laughing loudly. To me, he was a likable but not an admirable man.

Charlie lived and worked in Hatch, New Mexico, which was approximately two hours from El Paso. After their initial meeting, Charlie decided to come to El Paso every weekend to spend it with Rory. They arranged for Charlie to simply come to our home on Friday afternoons after work where he would meet Rory. Rory would complete her work at her employer's home in the early afternoon of Friday and come to our house. Charlie would arrive from Hatch a little bit later.

Charlie used to drive a 1955 four-door slate-blue *Chevy* sedan. It must have been the absolute cheapest model available when new because it had no optional equipment at all. And, it appeared to me that Charlie never washed that car.

One day after arriving at our home, Charlie declared that the car was actually a bit of a problem since he thought he would be drinking and partying all night with Rory and probably should not be driving. Mi Mamá suggested that they instead use taxis to get around and that he simply leave the car in the adjoining parking lot where we could keep an eye on it. Charlie looked at me and seeing that I was an eighteen-year-old high school senior without a car, told me to feel free to use it while it was parked there. I had never had such access to a car before. I immediately offered to protect that car with my life and to wash and wax it while it was under my control. Charlie was quick to accept. Thereafter, he always expressed great admiration and gratitude for the amazing transformation that occurred after I worked on his car.

During that period of my life, I was fortunate in that I was extremely busy socially almost every weekend. Since I was the number 2 ranking high school ROTC cadet in the entire city, I got invited--along with my date--to attend the military ball of every high school in El Paso. This meant that there would be a dance that I could go to just about every Saturday night beginning in late November and running through the end of February. I was lucky also to have found a girl, Maria Luisa "Tita" Velarde, who would attend every one of these functions with me even though we weren't going steady. Yes, this was that same girl that I wrote about earlier who had the audacity to pick a fight with me when we were younger. Of course, I was incredibly even more fortunate to have had placed before me some wheels by this saint, Charlie Coleman.

During that same period of my senior year, after dancing the night away on Saturdays at the military balls, I would spend Fridays and other Saturday nights with my buddies Fernando and Checo. Even though they had access to cars, they were somewhat restricted since they had to share that access with other family members. When I told them about this *Chevy* and its availability for what turned out to be three or four months, we could not believe our luck. I felt as if I had become one of the most fortunate young men on earth. Every Friday, I would get Charlie Coleman's '55 *Chevy*, I would wash and wax it, and I would enjoy it for the entire weekend. And, believe it or not, Charlie always made it a point to leave me the car with a full tank of gas.

I remember distinctly a particularly unpleasant part of the process of washing and waxing Charlie Coleman's car. Because he was a chain smoker, and because he smoked unfiltered cigarettes, I would always find a large number of little shreds of tobacco all over the steering wheel, the steering column, the dashboard, and inside the windshield. Apparently, as Charlie drove his car, and while he smoked cigarettes, every time that a shred of tobacco got into his mouth, he would merely spit it out. In so doing, little shreds of tobacco would end up sticking all over the inside of his car. I was a little bit grossed out when I first saw this, but the benefit that I was gaining more than justified the hassle of cleaning the shreds. Anyway, I would wash the exterior of the car, vacuum the interior, and wax it every Friday afternoon. If Charlie arrived a little bit late, I would only wash it that evening and not wax it until the following day.

This routine went on month after month during my senior year. In order to appreciate how good that stroke of luck actually was, one needs to understand that very few of my peers around El Paso actually had cars. Those of my peers who lived in the Projects had an even lower likelihood of owning a car or of even having regular access to one. All of a sudden, I became much better than my peers in that respect because almost without exception, on any given Friday or Saturday, Willie Chavez had a cool '55 *Chevy* in which to have fun.

Just when I thought that life could simply not get any better, Charlie Coleman one-upped himself. One day in the spring of 1965, while I was waiting for his arrival and looking for the *Chevy*, Charlie showed up in a stunning 1962 *Corvair Monza Club Coupé*. It was banana-yellow with a matching interior and it was almost in brand-new condition. Charlie had not planned on getting this car but basically bought it on a whim. He was trying to impress Rory and Rory was, in fact, very impressed. But even on the very first day that he brought it, he elected to go into town with Rory and have a good time on a taxi rather than in his new car.

I will never forget the excitement that I felt when I surprised Fernando and Checo by driving up to their homes in this almost new *Corvair* and honking for them to come out. I was "the man" and we were having the time of our lives.

One of those weekends when Fernando, Checo and I were cruising in the *Corvair,* I got my first traffic ticket. As we were cruising, we reached an intersection and discovered that parked right next to us was some nondescript automobile with three gorgeous girls in it. As we waited for the light to change, they actually revved their engine. As I slowly turned to face the girls and confirm the challenge, Checo and Fernando immediately pointed out that I was not a man unless I drag-raced and whipped these girls with the *Corvair*. I needed no persuasion. As soon as the light turned green, I popped the clutch and floored the accelerator. The *Corvair*, with its 6-cylinder 80 horsepower engine jumped nicely. However, the girls must have had a V-8 automatic that simply was much faster. Despite my best efforts, they were at least one full car-length ahead of me during the first half of the next block. Eventually, I overtook them. As I passed them, I noticed three things. First, I was doing 50 miles per hour in a 35 miles per hour zone. Second, I saw in my rear-view mirror the flashing red light of a police car right behind me. And third, the girls in the other car never went faster than 35. I got pulled over and got my first speeding ticket; the girls who incited the whole thing got off scot-free.

I don't remember exactly what became of the relationship between Rory and Charlie. I believe that it continued even after I graduated, took a job for the summer and eventually went to Texas A&M. It never ceases to amaze me how even a young kid like me can stumble upon a huge dose of good luck. There's no question in my mind that the availability of Charlie's *Chevy* and *Corvair* during my senior year was one of the factors that made that the most exciting year of my entire life. In my mind, I knew that I had been very, very lucky but, nevertheless, these events continued to develop in me an irrepressible sense of confidence and self-assurance that caused me to believe without any doubt whatsoever that there was absolutely nothing that I could not do.

The *Royal Duchesses*

Even though today the institution is known as the *Boys and Girls Clubs of El Paso*, in those days back in the 1960's it was just the *El Paso Boys' Club*. And, even though there were just as many young girls as there were young boys living in the neighborhoods where the Boys' Clubs were established, society simply declined to pay attention to their needs in any way resembling what was done for the boys. But the presence of the girls could not be ignored. At both Unit 1 on South Florence Street and at Unit 2 in the Paisano Projects, the neighborhood girls were allowed to form social organizations that functioned under the auspices of the Boys' Club and served to keep them entertained. Compared to the boys, however, their activities were severely limited. One could even argue that they were permitted to exist solely so that the boys could have dancing partners at the Friday night dances.

In my neighborhood, the Paisano Projects, the girls' club within the Boys' Club was known as the *Royal Duchesses*. During my years there, the *Royal Duchesses* added a stimulating dimension to everything else that was happening within the Club. After all, they were teenage girls and we were teenage boys and for the first time ever, many of us were feeling the attraction that comes so naturally between the sexes. The *Royal Duchesses* were allowed to organize into a group of maybe 10 or 12, to elect officers, to have weekly meetings there at the Boys' Club, to plan and conduct social activities and to support the Boys' Club in whatever other way they could. The *Royal Duchesses* were invited to attend all of the dances and hops sponsored by the Boys' Club and to participate in events such as talent shows, holiday parties and drama presentations.

These are some of the names of *Royal Duchesses* that I remember: Isabel Bencomo, Celia Valenzuela, Gloria Frias, Teresa Saucedo, Linda Ortiz and Cecilia Lozano.

Hot Dogs

The year was 1962. I had been working as a popcorn and peanut vendor at the *El Paso Coliseum* for least a year. I had become pretty good at it. The money I made there was modest and yet a windfall not only to me personally but also to my family since we forever seemed to be struggling to make ends meet.

The concession operation manager at the *Coliseum*, Mr. Ralph Licona, also ran the concession operation at *Kidd Field*, the football stadium at *Texas Western College* (TWC). Because the stadium was located on the extreme West end of El Paso, it was simply too far away for young kids like my brother Nacho and me to travel there to earn a few bucks. However, Mr. Reza, the father of Checo and Chuy--and a dear friend of my parents--had become a cold beer vendor extraordinaire at the *Coliseum*. For that reason, Mr. Licona offered Mr. Reza a position behind the concession stand counter at *Kidd Field* for the entire football season that year. That amounted to four or five home games where Mr. Reza could be guaranteed to at least earn the minimum wage, $1.25 per hour. That was actually a really good deal.

On those Saturday nights, Mr. Reza would take his green and white 1958 *Ford* station wagon and head for *Kidd Field*. He would bring along Checo and Chuy to get jobs selling popcorn or *Cokes*. Since we were all good friends, they would invite my brother Nacho and me to join them to see if we could also get jobs.

The games normally would start at 8:00PM. The concession vending operations would normally start at 7:00PM. We would arrive there at around 6:30 PM. and invariably, we would all manage to get one job or another.

Despite all of the different varieties of assaults that your senses would experience at a football game--including the game excitement, the crowd noise, and the cold weather just to mention a few--the most potent and most memorable of all in my mind was the smell and taste of the *Kidd Field* hot dogs. These were nothing more than steamed frankfurters stuffed into a soft bun, bathed with mustard and smothered with chili beans in a meat sauce. But they packed a powerful wallop whenever one smelled them.

These amazing hot dogs could be purchased at the concession stand for 25¢ or from vendors in the stands for 30¢. Vendors were given insulated aluminum carrying cases for the hot dogs. The vendors would earn 5¢ on each hot dog they sold. It was not uncommon on a very good night for a vendor to sell as many as 100 hot dogs thereby earning $5. In those days, and in those circumstances, that was a huge wage. Mr. Reza would earn at least that much behind the concession stand counter but it was a much more pleasant work experience and it was not as backbreaking as lugging the hot dogs or beer up and down the stadium steps.

During the first home game of the season, the concession operations overestimated demand for hot dogs. Lots of them were left over. After the game, the concession stand reduced the price for each to 10¢. I had earned about $1.50 that night so I splurged and bought one. It was absolutely heavenly. I can taste and smell it to this day! I remember sliding the dime across the concession stand counter to Mr. Reza. He, in turn, slid a hot dog to me. It was wrapped in white waxed-paper, was warm and soft and was extremely aromatic. The combination of the diverse smells of the steamed frank, the chili beans and the pungent mustard coupled with the unrelenting late-night hunger pangs that I was feeling, made the experience almost religious. I was thrilled to no end as I slowly ate it.

For the week or two that preceded the next home game, I was fixated on those hot dogs. I prayed that another hot dog bargain would be available again. I could never pay full price for a hot dog because it was too expensive and simply not part of our extremely frugal lifestyle. Fortunately, the same thing happened during the next game. I was once again able to purchase a 10¢ hot dog and indulge myself one more time.

But it was at the final home game of the season that the real miracle occurred. The big crowd that was expected did not show up due to extreme cold and because the home team had not had a good season. As a result, an extraordinarily large number of hot dogs were left over. After the game, with the same eagerness and anticipation that a young boy feels when picking up a girl for a date, I went to the concession counter and offered Mr. Reza my dime. He quickly pushed it back and in a low, secretive voice, told me to wait a few minutes. Apparently, there were so many hot dogs left over that eventually, they were simply going to have to give them away *free*. If that indeed happened, his two sons, my brother Nacho and I were--by a mysterious stroke of luck--first in line to get them.

Sure enough, when the crowd had departed and only vendors were left loitering around the area, the manager of concessions announced the hot dog giveaway. We were immediately surrounded by the rest of the vendors trying to get some for themselves. Since we were first in line, Mr. Reza gave each of us six hot dogs. I could not have been more thrilled if Mr. Reza had given me six bars of gold bullion. I stuffed those puppies inside my jacket and, with my brother, snuck into a dark corner under the cavernous spaces below the stadium seats to contemplate our booty. We felt great not only because we were about to feast but also because we would be able to take some home for our parents and my sister. Even if we each ate two of them right then and there, we would still be able to bring eight dogs home and that would certainly make everyone happy.

The drive home was almost joyous. All of us seemed elated. Even though we had not earned very much in commissions from sales, the hot dog windfall more than made up for that.

I will never forget the excitement that Nacho and I created when we arrived home and opened our jackets to reveal the still warm hot dogs. It's not as if my family was starving, but stadium hot dogs were a delicacy that we rarely experienced and the eight hot dogs really made everyone very happy.

I felt so grown-up and so capable as I watched my parents and my sister enjoy those dogs. I actually felt like a father who had just delivered big-time on his obligation to feed his family. Yet, I was only 15 years old. I really felt proud of what I had just done and felt as if I had done something really special for my entire family. We even enjoyed a few of those hot dogs the next day.

Dancing

As much as I wish to have been born or to have developed into a good dancer, I know quite well that I am and have always been a fairly bad dancer. I have no recollection of even trying to dance prior to 1959 when I was 12 years old. In that year, the Boys' Club was established in our neighborhood and I started watching with renewed interest the dancing of my peers. It was around that time that I made my first attempt to dance. I have no specific memory of when that occurred or with whom I danced, but I believe that I did not do well. I do know, however, that in 1961, after I met my friend for life Fernando Casas, I certainly went through a period of really trying to become quite the dancer.

It seems that Fernando was pretty good at dancing and would go to Juárez regularly to participate in Sunday afternoon dances called "Tardeadas" (pronounced "tar-deh-AH-dus" and derived from the Spanish word "tarde" which means "afternoon"). When Checo and I started hanging with Fernando we would go to these tardeadas together. The music was strictly Mexican and the dancing, for the most part, consisted of a step called the "danzón" (pronounced "don-SOHN"). It was a relatively slow step in a very traditional style and did not require very much coordination. Therefore, we all could do it very comfortably and we never lacked for partners with whom to enjoy this pleasure. The basic steps in a danzón were: 1-2-3-lean left, 1-2-3-lean right, and the pattern did not vary. As you took these steps, you, together with your partner, would twirl around the dance floor. You could even hold a partner very close and dance cheek to cheek in a danzón. I think we did this for a few years and even though I was not a natural dancer, I honestly enjoyed doing it very much.

Back on the American side, things were still not going quite as well for those of us who lacked coordination or imagination. There, the prevailing dance step was pure rock-and-roll. For us in the Projects, there were essentially two dance steps associated with rock-and-roll. One was very fast where partners are moving quickly with the guy holding the hand of the girl and then raising it over her head for her to twirl under. Then the partners come close but while still moving fast start rocking and rolling until once again the boy partner throws the girl away but holds her hand again and then raises it over her head for her to twirl under again. A typical song to which this fast step was danced to for example was *Palisades Park*. I did not really care for the fast rock and roll dance step because I could never seem to be able to do it.

The other prevailing dance step in rock-and-roll was the slow dance. This step I *did* like and because of its simplicity, I could do it without any effort or fear. It could be danced to songs like *Earth Angel* and essentially consisted of gluing together the boy's body to the girl's body from face to thigh and rocking gently from left to right moving the left foot two steps then rocking slowly to the left and then moving the right foot two steps and rocking slowly to the right and repeating this over and over as the couple slowly twirls around the dance floor. This was absolutely the most sensual dance of that era.

I was no good at all at doing the fast step but I became an expert at the slow dance. During the early to mid-1960's, the Boys' Club sponsored those Friday-night dances that I mentioned earlier. I was a Jr. staff member at Unit 2 at that time and one of my responsibilities was to spin the records at the Friday night dances. When I was not acting as the disc jockey, I would be on the dance floor trying to dance with one particular neighborhood girl that I had the hots for. Her name was Celia Valenzuela who was exactly my age, very short with long curly black hair and with the most curvaceous body and well-defined legs of the neighborhood. She would always wear a tight skirt that went below the knees and flat shoes and so the top of her head barely reached my chin. She also always smelled really good. Slow dances with her were all I lived for. Unfortunately, she had a boyfriend... but fortunately, he lived in another neighborhood and, therefore, was not always present at these dances.

Checo was his usual gregarious self and he was an excellent fast dancer. He never had any problems finding a dance partner and it seemed apparent that he was always having a good time. The absolute best dancer of the neighborhood was Chichi. He was a very smooth fast dancer that never had an awkward moment and always appeared absolutely confident in everything he did including dancing. Girls always wanted to dance with him. I envied him greatly for that.

I apparently was so bad at dancing that Checo even created a little mimicking act of how I danced and he could entertain lots of people by occasionally performing it. According to his mimicry, I danced like *Frankenstein*. I was absolutely rigid, and I rocked from left to right just like a robot. I must admit that whenever he imitated my dancing, I was among those who laughed the hardest.

During that same era, beginning around 1963, two things happened that led to some high-intensity and very memorable dancing for me. The first of those things was that I met my high school flame, Lizzie Varela. That meant that I didn't have the problem of ever finding a partner at a dance so long as we were going steady. The second thing that occurred were the *Fox Hops*. A *Fox Hop* was a dance held the at the *Jefferson High School* cafeteria immediately following every Friday night football game. (We were the Silver Foxes from Jefferson High.) The admission charge was 35¢ and the dance would last from 10PM to midnight with one of the top bands in the city always available to perform.

I was in the high-school band at the time and so I would return from the football game in the band bus to the band hall where I would remove my wet T-shirt which got that way from all the perspiration under the heavy wool uniform. I would put on a clean T-shirt and a clean shirt all over my black band uniform pants which happened to have a 2 in. wide white and red stripe down each side. Then in that outfit and while wearing my white band shoes, I would walk over to the cafeteria where Lizzie would be waiting for me. For the next two hours, we would then slow dance every single song--whether it was fast or slow. It generally would become so hot in the cafeteria that everyone would be sweating profusely. Dancing cheek to cheek with Lizzie would always result in the hair on the side of my head getting plastered over my right eye without my even knowing it. My buddies would make fun of me by causing their hair to come over their eyes and mimicking me. I didn't mind the mimicking because I knew that I was in heaven while I was dancing with Lizzie at these hops.

I was always very nervous and perhaps even afraid to try to dance fast. Therefore, at any dance, I only danced the slow dances. Then something wonderful happened. The era was the mid-1960's and the British invasion began and with it came a whole bunch of new steps that didn't really require any kind of skill or coordination. These included the *Twist*, the *Mashed Potatoes*, the *Watusi*, the *Locomotion*, the *Swim* and other steps that didn't require you to hold a partner at all. All you had to do was to stand in front of each other and jump up and down at the beat of the music, flap your arms around occasionally, jerk your head up and down once in a while and, by the then current definition, you were dancing. I did that extremely well. Unfortunately, this music became so popular that the slow dancing sometimes did not occur at all in some hops.

The *Golden Key Club*

One of the fondest memories that I have relating to my teenage years involves the *Golden Key Club* also called the *Key Club*. The timeframe of this memory is between 1960 and 1963. It was then that the *Key Club* emerged and thrived in El Paso. It was a dance hall specifically for teenagers that evolved out of nothing and, for the owners, turned into a fairly large financial boondoggle.

There was--and still is--a strip mall at the southwest corner of the intersection of Chelsea and Montana streets in El Paso. It was called *Chelmont*. Hidden among the storefronts in that strip mall, was a large building that had a relatively small front but was huge toward the back. Its size suggests that at some time, it must have been a warehouse. There was very little parking available in that strip mall and, therefore, as the popularity of the *Key Club* grew, the traffic problems that would develop when it was open were horrendous for the relatively small town that El Paso was. At any rate, some enterprising folks decided to open this place up as a liquor-free establishment intended for the entertainment of teenagers in El Paso. The original idea, I believe, was for teenagers to go there on evenings and weekends to play arcade games such as pinball or to listen to music from a jukebox. The target audience at the start was the predominantly Anglo teenage population that attended Austin High, El Paso High, Irvin High and other high schools in the north and central parts of the city. Right from the start, the *Key Club* was a smashing success.

Initially, the only kind of music offered at the *Key Club* was from a jukebox. Later on, they started to offer record music managed by a disc jockey. Given that this was non-live entertainment, it was truly amazing how many kids would pack into the *Key Club* on any given Friday or Saturday night. The music played at the *Key Club* generally followed the *Billboard* Top 40 songs by artists such as Bobby Lewis, Patsy Cline, Roy Orbison, Del Shannon, Dee Clark, Bobby Vee and The Shirelles.

Later in its first year, the *Key Club* started to invite the popular local bands to perform on weekends. That only made the club even more popular and successful. There were at least two bands that dominated the *Key Club* entertainment scene. They were the *Night Dreamers* and the *Drifters* (a local group different from the *Drifters* who sang *On Broadway*). There was something extremely ironic about the popularity and success of these two bands. Even though the El Paso fans of these bands came very solidly from the teenage Anglo community, the bands themselves were composed of teenagers that were mostly Mexican-American or African-American. It seems that the Anglo teenage community in El Paso simply could not produce any wildly successful bands.

I remember going to the *Key Club* to hear the *Drifters* or the *Night Dreamers* and there was simply no space to move among the crowd. Here's what I remember about one of those bands, the *Night Dreamers*. The lead singer was an African-American rock and roller who had a gift for being able to mimic the original "Godfather of Soul," James Brown. His name was Sonny Powell but was known simply as "Sonny" and in my view he was every bit as good a singer and entertainer as James Brown himself. Then there was the lead guitar (an older guy from Bowie High, I think) as well as a base guitar. The bass guitarist was a guy named Alfonso Tinajero who I knew from elementary school. He was known as "Goofy." As the bass guitarist for the *Night Dreamers*, he was the envy of lots of teenage boys and a heartthrob to lots of teenage girls. Then there was the tenor saxophonist, Juan Valles (nicknamed "Uvas" which means "grapes"), saxophonist Fernie Aceves, trombonists Roberto Moreno and Mando Perez, and the lead trumpet player, Armando Lucero. Then there was the drummer, Manny Tinajero, brother of Goofy. All of them, except for Sonny and the lead guitarist, attended Jefferson High. And all of those were in the Jefferson High band and were either classmates of mine or classmates of my brother, Nacho. In that era, they achieved what all teenagers desperately sought but few ever tasted: Success in a teenage rock and roll band.

In its heyday, the *Key Club* would get mobbed every Friday and Saturday night and every Sunday afternoon. There is no doubt that the number of kids that were permitted to enter the dance hall had to be in violation of local fire ordinances. Yet, every weekend, if you weren't in the *Key Club* or clawing your way in, you were simply "nowhere and square." The admission to enter the *Key Club* was, I believe, 50¢ if the music was recorded and $1.00 if there was a live band. The lines to get in would form very early in the evening and would wrap around the entire strip mall. As you entered and paid your admission, you would get an ink stamp on the back of your hand that would indicate that you had paid. The stamp was invisible to the naked eye but was visible when placed under a black light. And so, if you left the building and wanted to come back in you would place the back of your hand under the black light so that they could see that you had paid. Wearing the residue of the stamp (the visible dirt that over the weekend got stuck to the invisible ink) on your hand on the following Monday morning at school was always a significant sign of coolness among the teenagers of El Paso.

In 1961, when the *Key Club* was enjoying its most popular days, El Paso happened to be the home of Richard Lopez, the first of two National Boys of the Year for the *Boys' Clubs of America,* who hailed from El Paso. In early April of that year, Richard Lopez went to Washington and New York to be recognized and honored by some of the national leaders of those days including President Kennedy, Vice President Johnson and FBI Director, J. Edgar Hoover. When Richard returned to El Paso from that trip, he was invited to be a special guest at the *Key Club.* Since I was a member of the Boys' Club, I made it a special point to be at the *Key Club* that night to welcome Richard. Up until then, I had not been to the *Key Club* on a regular basis because my buddies and I considered it to be a hangout for the Anglo teenagers of the central and north parts of the city and we were from the south side.

But on the evening when Richard Lopez was honored at the *Key Club*, there was total gridlock for two or three blocks around the club. Eventually, I managed to get in along with a bunch of classmates from Jefferson High and buddies from the *El Paso Boys' Club.* When Richard entered the *Key Club,* it was as if some rock and roll superstar had just entered. Everyone--Anglos, Mexican-Americans and African-Americans--cheered and reacted as if Richard was a genuine All-American kid. I will never forget what happened that evening and the deep admiration that I felt that moment for this kid who had done well despite the disadvantages that surrounded him as he grew up. Richard, like my brother Nacho, inspired me to seek tougher challenges and thus bigger rewards in later years as I worked my way through life.

Following Richard Lopez's appearance at the *Key Club* and because it had attracted so many teenagers from the Mexican-American community, the *Key Club* started its conversion from the Anglicized music to the Mexicanized music. Even though, the music was never purely Mexican, it did become decidedly Mexican-American in that "oldies but goodies" became the most popular music played there rather than the currently popular music. For the next year or so, as I entered the first few years of high school, the *Key Club* remained a Mecca for the Mexican-American teenagers.

By the time I was a junior in high school in 1964, the *Key Club* had decayed back to what it started as: a place where kids would go to play arcade games or to listen to jukebox music. The live music and dance aspects disappeared and it reverted back to nothing more than a small hangout for Anglo teenagers. I'm not sure when the *Key Club* finally closed down but it had to have been around the time when I was a senior in high school in 1965. Those years were a great time for teenagers in El Paso back then and the *Key Club* added immensely to that experience.

Steve Crosno

I suppose that I will never tire of reminiscing about life in the Projects in El Paso in the early 1960's. There were many extraordinary people who entered our lives in that era and who re-defined it into what we truly believe was so wonderful as to make us believe we were indeed very lucky to have been able to live through it. One such person was Steve Crosno.

Steve was born in Las Cruces, New Mexico, a town just 35 miles north of El Paso. He was a disc jockey at KELP, a radio station that played the weekly top 40 tunes. He started working there in 1959, the same year that the Boys' Club opened Unit 2 in the Paisano Projects. He was extremely successful because his unique style of programming somehow happened to appeal strongly to an audience that was pretty evenly split between the Anglo and the Hispanic communities of the area. In 1961, San Diego lured him with an offer no one could have possibly refused and so he was suddenly gone from the El Paso airwaves. Within a few months, the Crosno program was deemed ineffective in San Diego and he quickly returned to El Paso. Upon his return that same year, his radio program ratings started sky-rocketing and soon, in addition to his radio program, he was given his own television program, *The Crosno Hop*, closely mirroring Dick Clark's wildly successful *American Bandstand*. His radio program on KELP and *The Crosno Hop* as I remember them remained on the air until 1968 although he, of course, continued in radio and TV for many more years.

Television was pretty much still in its infancy during the early 60's. Some families in our neighborhood still did not own a TV. Radio, however, was ubiquitous. Every household had at least one radio. Every car had one too. Battery powered transistor radios were also becoming popular. I was 12 years old in 1959 and suddenly, I—along with just about every one of my friends--discovered rock and roll. I am sure we made this discovery because of the Steve Crosno radio program.

In those years, Steve Crosno played only the US Top 40 tunes. His programs, commercials and even commentary were witty, timely, innovative and frequently hilarious. The local Anglo community—particularly the teenagers—became fanatical listeners. He did not, however, routinely play any Mexican or Mexican-American music. Even though Steve would occasionally broadcast a word or two in Spanish, his programs were almost exclusively in English. Nevertheless, the Mexican-American community in El Paso—at least that portion of it that was young and could speak English--similarly embraced him.

I liked Steve Crosno and his radio program because he played the music that my friends and I liked. My friends and I were Mexican-Americans well aware of the benefits of assimilation and for the most part deeply in love with the culture of America. We were reasonably knowledgeable about and quite proud of our Mexican heritage, but we knew keenly that our futures were as Americans and our language was English. Thus, the top 40 tunes were our music and no one delivered them to us better than Steve Crosno.

I believe that Steve Crosno and his program needed the support of the Anglo community audience in order to survive financially. Like so many other local disc jockeys and radio stations, Crosno and KELP could easily and predictably have ignored the Mexican-American community and left it to those in the industry that customarily catered to it. But it seems to me that Crosno was probably the first to note that the Mexican-American community in El Paso was evolving and adapting and that the then-current generation of teenagers was decidedly more Americanized than even those teenagers themselves knew. And so, he reached out to those teenagers. As far as I could tell, he spoke Spanish sufficiently well to make many believe that there was some Spanish blood somewhere in his genealogy. And, he injected just enough Mexican culture into his programs for us to identify with them. I recall, for example, how he played records by *Sunny and the Sun Liners*. This was a rock group from San Antonio that produced a number of songs in English that really appealed to Hispanic teens like me. The group was so good, however, that eventually their appeal went national. Crosno also created content that was genuinely funny and fresh regardless of your ethnicity. But most importantly, he played the music that El Paso teenagers liked. And therefore, we listened to him religiously.

Whenever Unit 2 of the Boys' Club was open, the hi-fi radio in the main game room was tuned to KELP. Hours of operation at Unit 2 included the daily 4PM to 6PM shift which provided a place for the kids from the neighborhood to gather right after school. The Crosno show was broadcast daily from 3PM to 6PM. So, anyone at Unit 2 during that shift and within earshot of that hi-fi radio got to listen to Steve Crosno and his music. And everyone truly seemed to enjoy his programs. On Friday nights, when Unit 2 turned the game room into a teenage dance hall, the records that were played and danced to were the same ones that Crosno played on his programs.

When the televised *Crosno Hop* first aired in 1961, it was broadcast from the KELP studios on Delta Drive in El Paso. Curiously, the studios were located next to that landfill that I described earlier. Unit 2 of the Boys' Club—and my neighborhood--just happened to be located a half mile away from the studios. I remember watching the first few *Crosno Hops* and thinking how cool it was to have something so similar to *American Bandstand* right there in El Paso. I also noted that just about every kid that showed up at the studio for the first few shows just happened to be Anglos from the nice parts of town. As the popularity of the *Crosno Hop* grew, so grew the courage of kids from my neighborhood to start going to those shows. Pretty soon, the majority of the teenagers appearing on the shows were from the Hispanic community. I was immensely proud when I made my own appearance on one of those shows even though I feared deeply that I would end up publicly embarrassing myself since I was such a bad dancer.

Today, I see Steve Crosno and his radio and television programs as just another of the many benefits meted out to me and every other kid that grew up in El Paso in the 1960's. I did get to meet Steve at the KELP studio once but he did not become a mentor or coach to me and he certainly did not inspire me to even consider a career in entertainment. But what he did do for me and for many other kids from El Paso's Hispanic community was to plant and cultivate in our minds the idea that we were valued members of society. I believe that, because of the access he gave kids from the Hispanic neighborhoods to the *Crosno Hop*, he validated emphatically--and in brilliant black and white—the fact that kids like me were indeed assimilating into the American mainstream.

National Leaders and Laws

When I look back and ponder why the experience of growing up in South El Paso in the 60's was so rich and meaningful, inevitably I think about the men that were leading our country in those days and about the impact they had in shaping our minds. I believe that two such leaders were Presidents John F. Kennedy and Lyndon B. Johnson. It is not as if we, the kids of the Boys' Club, were interested in politics or if we even really knew or understood what these men were up to in Washington. What we did know—through the wonder of television—was that these men were causing great excitement and change in American society and their words and deeds seemed to touch all of our lives constantly and in very distinct ways.

John F. Kennedy became President as my Boys' Club friends and I were entering high school. Kennedy aroused our Mexican-American community as no other person—politician or otherwise—had ever done. Sure, the vast majority of our community had always embraced the ideas of the Democratic Party but that was mostly through default rather than thoughtful consideration. Perhaps his appeal was because he was Catholic. In any event, when the images and the voice of Kennedy entered our homes through the airwaves, it seemed that everyone fell in love with him. It did not matter that a substantial portion of our parents could not even understand the language with which he spoke. What did matter was that he inspired hope and optimism and that apparently a majority of the country felt the same way.

In school, the speeches of Kennedy suddenly became the subjects of classes the same way Lincoln's *Gettysburg Address* had been for the past century. In one class in particular--the one called Speech X taught by Mr. James Burton—the speech was used for two purposes. First, it was used to convey to our particular "new generation of Americans," Kennedy's enlightened view of the future. The message was clearly one of boundless opportunity and prosperity for America's future and my classmates and I were mature enough to know that we were destined to be the principal beneficiaries of his vision. Second, and notwithstanding the President's Boston accent, the speech was used by Mr. Burton as a benchmark for all Americans—particularly those for whom English was not the primary language—as to how English should be used and how it should be spoken.

What we learned in the Speech X classes did not stay at school. Many of us memorized passages from Kennedy's Inaugural Address and found ourselves quoting him whenever the situation required a generous dose of enthusiasm. Many of my classmates and I found it a rich source of relevant and easily understandable quotations that we regularly used in our speeches when we competed in the Optimist Oratorical Contests. Two passages from the inaugural address stand out in my memory even now: "And so my fellow Americans, ask not what your country can do for you; ask what you can do for your country." And, "With a good conscience our only sure reward, with history the final judge of our deeds, let us go forth to lead the land we love, asking His blessing and His help, but knowing that here on earth God's work must truly be our own." In those heady days of the 60's, we used these words often because they enabled us to believe that we did not have to be bound by the constraints that our parents and grandparents grew up with. More importantly, the more we referred to Kennedy's words, the more we believed in them. That remarkable speech by Kennedy convinced me more than anything else that America was my country, that English was my language and that my future was secure.

President Kennedy did something else in 1961 that would later have a profound impact on me and many of my Boys' Club buddies. He introduced America to the concept of "affirmative action" as a new way to combat certain types of discrimination that existed in the hiring process. Affirmative action was first created through Executive Order 10925 which was signed by President Kennedy on March 6, 1961. It required that Federal Government employers "not discriminate against any employee or applicant for employment because of race, creed, color, or national origin" and "take affirmative action to ensure that applicants are employed, and that employees are treated during employment, without regard to their race, creed, color, or national origin."

On September 24, 1965, President Lyndon B. Johnson signed Executive Order 11246, thereby replacing Executive Order 10925 and affirming the Federal Government's commitment "to promote the full realization of equal employment opportunity through a positive, continuing program in each executive department and agency".

These two Executive Orders worked their way through the policies and practices of the Federal government and eventually became models for hiring by corporations and public and private educational institutions as well. As a result, when my buddies and I finished high school and began looking for admissions to and financial assistance from colleges, we discovered that the doors to opportunity had been opened considerably wider. Those of us who continued on to graduate programs and eventually even to employment, found that there too the doors had opened wider. Once again, we found ourselves at the right place at the right time.

Kennedy could have remained a powerful but still distant force in my life and in the lives of other members of the Boys' Club but, once again, fate somehow intervened to bring the Kennedy mystique even closer to us. As I alluded to earlier, in 1961, a fellow Club member, Richard Lopez, was selected as the *Boys' Clubs of America* National Boy of the Year. The recognition that Richard received included a visit to the White House where he met President Kennedy. Richard even got the remarkable honor and privilege of going to the Major League Baseball season opener that day with President Kennedy and got to see him throw out the first pitch up close and personal. Two years later, the unimaginable happened: My own brother, Ignacio (Nacho), became the second boy from El Paso to receive that same honor from the *Boys' Clubs of America* and he too was personally greeted and recognized by President Kennedy for his achievement. There is simply no way to put in words how these events transformed my mind and, I'm sure, the minds of the other members of the Boys' Club. All of us knew these two boys. I even shared a bedroom with one of them. They were in many ways much better than we were but, in more ways, they were just like us. And they had achieved the amazing distinction of meeting and chatting with the most powerful and inspiring man on the planet. The rest of us simply started to believe that a similar fate might also be waiting for us in the not too distant future.

It just so happened that during their Boy of the Year visits to Washington, DC, Richard Lopez in 1961 and Nacho Chavez in 1963, also got to meet Vice President Lyndon Baines Johnson. Richard and Nacho told me that neither of them was as impressed by the Vice President as they had been by the President. And their Boys' Club friends in El Paso paid almost no attention at all to the fact that Richard and Nacho had also met the Vice President. Yet, in my view, it turned out that, substantively, Johnson eventually did much more for our community than Kennedy.

To be sure, the assassination of John Kennedy in 1963 stunned the country as few things had ever done before. The small community of South El Paso, generally indifferent to national politics, was shaken even more deeply because Kennedy had infinitely endeared himself to us not only by his world-wide popularity but also by his connection with Richard Lopez and Nacho Chavez. It just seemed as if the promise of a better world that Kennedy had made to us had suddenly been dashed. From one day to the next, Kennedy--and everything that we believed he represented--was replaced by Johnson. Maybe the insiders in Washington never doubted that Johnson would pick up and carry the torch that Kennedy had lit, but my community almost certainly did not think so.

History, however, shows that as far as real federal legislation goes, no President has ever done more to improve the state of the Mexican-American community than Johnson. He, more than anyone else, was responsible for designing the "Great Society" legislation which included laws that upheld civil rights, Medicare, Medicaid, aid to education, and his "War on Poverty." The War on Poverty helped millions of Americans—including many of us who lived in South El Paso--rise above the poverty line during Johnson's presidency. Civil rights bills signed by Johnson banned racial discrimination in public facilities, interstate commerce, the workplace, and housing, and a powerful voting rights act guaranteed full voting rights for citizens of all races. With the passage of the sweeping Immigration and Nationality Act of

1965, the country's immigration system was reformed and all national origin quotas were removed. For young people growing up as minorities in that era, Johnson opened up huge opportunities that their ancestors never had. So as far as our national leaders were concerned, while Kennedy provided the inspiration, it was Johnson who truly enabled me and the other kids of the Boys' Club to rise above the fate that otherwise surely waited for us in El Paso.

Another piece of federal legislation that turned out to be of enormous value to my community was the *Servicemen's Readjustment Act of 1944*, popularly known as the *GI Bill of Rights*. It was intended primarily to benefit the veterans of World War II, that is, those veterans in the generation of my parents. Interestingly, however, I do not remember too many of the dads in the Paisano Projects as having served in World War II. That may be because they had not yet immigrated. But I know that mi Papá—who immigrated as a kid--once told me that he did not serve in that war because he was too old. He was 42 years old when Pearl Harbor was attacked by the Japanese. In any case, when my peers from the Boys' Club and I were called to serve during the Vietnam era, there is no question that following our service, a very large percentage of us were greatly enabled in the pursuit of a college degree by the *GI Bill*.

Civic Organizations

During the time that I was a member, the question of how the *El Paso Boys' Club* got its money to continue operating, rarely became visible to me. All I knew was that the doors of Unit 2 always opened on time, the air conditioner always seemed to be on, the staff was always present and the sky-blue panel truck that was used to transport boys to activities always seemed to have a full tank of gas. Even the modest $15/month salary check that I received while I worked as a Jr. Staff member always got delivered to me on time by Mr. D or my immediate supervisor, Checo Reza.

I do recall, however, that the Boys' Club relied heavily on the *United Fund* for paying its operating expenses. I also recall that when unanticipated costs came up—such as taking the entire Jr. Toastmasters Club to San Francisco in the summer of 1963—the boys themselves would become fundraisers by selling chocolate candy door-to-door or by having car washes. I also recall that a number of local civic organizations always seemed to step up when the Boys' Club needed additional financial assistance.

My own personal experiences at that time told me that one civic organization seemed to do much more than the others. That was the *Pan-American Pilot*

Club, a civic club that was comprised entirely of ladies. Four ladies of the *Pan-American Pilot Club* in particular still linger in my mind as ever-present and deeply committed to the Boys' Club. They were Mrs. Chris Aranda, Mrs. William R. Blackburn, Mrs. Norma Fierro and Miss Teresa Peña. In the years 1962-1964, because of my involvement in the Jr. Toastmasters Club and at the request of Mr. Hightower, I found myself making lots of appearances before the *Pan-American Pilot Club*. Most of the time, these appearances were in connection with an event intended to raise funds for the Boys' Club. In just about every instance, I was asked to deliver the speech that I had prepared to compete in the Optimist Oratorical Contest. I'm sure that Mr. Hightower was using me to reassure the members of the Pan-American Pilot Club that their support was having a very positive effect within the community.

Another civic club that I remember was the *Young Matron's Auxiliary* of the *El Paso Women's Club*. In 1959, they undertook the funding of the remodeling of the kitchen at Unit 1. There were any number of other civic clubs that helped the Boys' Club in similar ways and it is apparent to me now that without their support, the effectiveness of the Boys' Club would most likely have been significantly diminished.

Other civic organizations had a tremendous impact on the Boys' Club even without actually raising or providing funds to it. In my view, the civic organization that did the most for the boys in the early 1960's was *Optimist International*. Then—as now—they were and are committed to bringing out the best in kids. As I detailed earlier, *Optimist International* sponsored an oratorical contest for boys that turned out to be the absolutely most significant learning experience that I and scores of other Boys' Club members went through in the early and mid-1960's.

Finally, there was the *El Paso Kiwanis Club*. I have no doubt that the Kiwanis Club did a whole lot not only for the *El Paso Boys' Club* but for the entire El Paso community. The one thing in particular that I recall and for which I will always be grateful is how the Kiwanis Club made a personal loan to me in 1966 so I could purchase my airline ticket to get to West Point. The loan was interest-free and payable 15 years later. Indeed, I paid it back in 1981 when I was employed by IBM as one of their corporate counsel.

The Vietnam War

Growing up in the 1960s caused all of us to spend an inordinate amount of time thinking about the Vietnam War. It is difficult for me today to reconstruct in my mind all of the thoughts and other forces regarding that war that were at work on me and on all of my peers during that incredible period, but there is no question that it consumed all of us.

I cannot recall any specific event that signaled the start of my thinking about the Vietnam War. Obviously, sometime after 1962, discussions of the war began creeping into conversations with our parents or teachers and certainly with our friends. By the time I was thinking of college, the United States was completely engaged in that war. And so, it was impossible to think about college without also thinking about the need to fulfill one's military service obligations.

Even though the war in Vietnam was very enigmatic in terms of military and political objectives, it nevertheless was still a war where American men were fighting--and dying. That being the case, I became driven by the thought that I also had to eventually be one of those men. I had always viewed the American soldier as one of the great pillars of this wonderful country. Whether it was because of soldier games that I played as a boy or war stories that I read in school or war movies that I saw in the theaters or on television, to be an American soldier was a proud tradition and an obligation that I was more than happy to take on. The images that had been cultivated in my mind regarding the American soldier were all extremely positive, romantic and full of all of the ideals that an American boy would want to pursue. Even though mi Papá had not been in the military and I really had no family connections with the military, I believed very strongly that it was my destiny and my duty to serve my country in its military units if the need ever arose. By the mid 1960's, the need to serve had become clear and inevitable.

Along with the compelling military service consideration raised by the war, there was an equally significant need to continue pursuing my educational goals which absolutely included finishing high school and going on to college. I knew from my earliest days in high school that I would go to college. I also knew that I would not simply go to the local college/university. Somehow early on, for reasons that I cannot explain, I felt an urge to get out of town. I also seemed driven by the naïve notion that I should go to some exotic location to attend college and that it would be an institution that no one in my socio-economic status could possibly hope to attend. Maybe that was starry-eyed thinking on my part, but I knew that scholarships existed and that I had positioned myself pretty well to benefit from them. I felt great confidence that when that intricate education bridge finally stood before me, I would cross over it one way or another.

Many of my peers looked upon this convergence of forces-- namely military duty and college education--as a tough situation. Many of them wanted to go to college but couldn't afford it and therefore got drafted. Other young men of the sixties went to college simply to avoid the draft. Some went to college, enrolled in ROTC and prepared themselves not only to obtain a degree but also to provide military service once they graduated. I generally fell in the last category. But I took it one step further. I decided to seek an appointment to West Point where I would get a superior education at no cost. At the same time, I would get the best possible military training and end up with a commission to serve in the US Army. I did not kid myself at the time. I knew that upon graduation from West Point, I would probably end up serving in the military in Vietnam. But I also knew that I would have gotten the very best training available anywhere in the universe for such an undertaking.

During my senior year, I discussed this plan with a couple of my high school teachers and counselors. As I mentioned earlier, I was told that the plan was a bit too ambitious. I was told quite frankly that the high school education I had received at *Jefferson High School* probably was not good enough for me to succeed at West Point. The principal purveyor of this depressing bit of information was the Senior Class Counselor, Miss Rosalie Hamrah. That meeting with Miss Hamrah and the other teachers was incredibly significant. I was enormously confident and ambitious as I was concluding my high school years and very eager to get on with my drive to success. Yet, there I was being told that I probably was not ready to take the next step. In hindsight, the advice given to me by Miss Hamrah and the others probably saved me from becoming a likely failure at West Point, assuming I could have gotten in. For that reason, Miss Hamrah will remain prominent in my mind forever and will symbolize to me the best in the teaching and counseling profession.

Nevertheless, none of those teachers and counselors suggested to me that I should give up on my West Point dream. They suggested instead that I spend a year getting additional preparation at some college or university and then apply for the West Point appointment. I did not fully understand what I was hearing because I never for a second thought that I had been getting an inferior high school education. But soon my idealistic outlook gave way to the reality of what they were telling me and I decided to consider their suggestion. But, even after agreeing that a year of preparation was the best way to proceed, I was still in a quandary because I had no idea how to go about finding the right college to attend for that purpose.

This is a good place for me to acknowledge and to express my deep gratitude for the role Mrs. Ruth Thompson and her family played in shaping my life. Mrs. Thompson was a teacher at Thomas Jefferson High school for the entire time I was there. I never had her as a teacher and I only interacted with her a tiny bit otherwise. But, as it turns out, she was the prime factor in one of the most momentous events that I lived through. Mrs. Thompson turned out to be the main reason I ended up attending *Texas A&M University* right after high school.

Shortly after the meeting that I had with those teachers and counselors, Mrs. Thompson explained how Texas A&M had one the largest corps of cadets in the country and would most certainly be a great place to prepare for West Point. She then told me about how her husband had graduated from Texas A&M and how one of her sons would be starting his junior year there and how another son would be starting his freshman year there in the fall. Most importantly, she gave me a clear and warm signal that she would do everything she could to make sure I got into A&M. Before long, she invited me to her home for dinner with her family and after listening to the enthusiasm with which all of them spoke about this institution, I decided to go for it.

During the summer following my graduation from Jefferson High, I became friends with Mrs. Thompson's younger son, Matt. Even though he had never been a student there, he knew everything there was to know about Texas A&M and its Corps of Cadets and he shared all of that knowledge with me. Matt's older brother, Tommy, was home for the summer and he too reassured me about the value to be found there. I was also invited by Mrs. Thompson to attend a few of the *El Paso A&M Hometown Club* meetings during that summer where in no time I started to feel some of the emotion and spirit felt by most Aggies. Mrs. Thompson and the *El Paso A&M Hometown Club* were also instrumental in finding for me a work-study job once I arrived at A&M. The job turned out to be a huge godsend. Since I was going to join the Texas A&M Band (*The Fightin' Texas Aggie Band*), I was offered the job of Band Librarian which would pay $1/hour. I would work 20 hours per week *as my schedule would permit*, and my workplace would be the Band Library which was a small room directly across from my room at the Band Dormitory. To top everything off, the Band Library—my work area--was the only room in the entire Band Dormitory that had its own room air-conditioner!

In late-August, 1965, when the fall semester was about to start, the Thompson brothers invited me to bring my footlocker and ride with them to College Station, Texas, in Tommy's car so Matt and I could finally get a taste of what it was really like to be a Texas Aggie. For the entire year that I spent at Texas A&M, the Thompson family was always near and available and made the "fish year" experience in the *Fightin' Texas Aggie Band* and at the University not only bearable but incredibly valuable and memorable as well.

In the spring of my freshman (fish) year at A&M, I applied for an appointment to West Point from Texas Congressman Richard C. White. During that year I tried to maintain good grades and completed all of the exams and other requirements for the appointment. That year at A&M was a great year for me. I achieved all of my academic goals and even got selected as "Best Drilled Fish" of the Texas A&M White Band. In April, 1966, I received the appointment and on July 1st of that same year, I reported to West Point to start my Plebe (freshman) year. Coincidentally, 1966 was one of the worst years for the United States as it fought the war in Vietnam. So, the thought of serving in Vietnam was absolutely paramount in my mind on the day I reported to West Point.

The next four years saw a pretty amazing transformation of my thinking. As a freshman at West Point, the war in Vietnam--as unconventional as it was-- still generally was viewed as eminently winnable. I was as gung-ho as anyone as I undertook the academic and the physical training that would take four years to convert me into a Second Lieutenant in the U.S. Army. I took on all of the West Point courses with great enthusiasm and optimism believing strongly that this was the correct thing to do. All the military training that I received at West Point was clearly aimed at providing us with skill and experience on how to fight a jungle war against the North Vietnamese regular army and the Communist Vietcong. I never doubted that the world and I would be better after I graduated and served my country.

Sometime during the second and third years at West Point (1967 and 1968), it became apparent that the war in Vietnam was becoming a huge disaster. The number of American casualties was rising dramatically and the antiwar voices were getting louder and more insistent. As a third-year cadet at West Point (1969), I remember being very concerned about where the American military was heading. It did not seem to be heading where history told us that it was supposed to go. I remained committed to the four-year program at West Point followed by the five-year service obligation, but the enthusiasm and pride that I had felt as a Plebe and before that, as a fish at Texas A&M, were decidedly gone at that point.

As a senior at West Point (1970), I started to hear the stories about young lieutenants who had been at West Point as upperclassmen when I was a freshman and who had lost their lives in Vietnam. The loss of life in a war situation was not what was troubling me. I knew that is part of what will happen in any war. What was troubling was the fact that the United States appeared to be losing too many young men while our government leaders seemed lost in a maze of political problems. They seemed to have no idea as to what they were trying to do in Vietnam, how they were going to do it and when they would get it done. Even though we, as cadets, were isolated and protected by the granite walls of the Military Academy, we were well aware of the fact that the Vietnam War was a mess and that American society was being ripped asunder as those who opposed it clashed with those who supported it. It got to the point that West Point cadets were ordered not to wear their uniforms off campus for fear that they might be assaulted by antiwar demonstrators. This was America? I could not believe it.

I continued to cling to my naïve belief that America was right and that the war was appropriate. But I could sense that I was wavering. By the time I graduated and received my commission in June, 1970, I had a great, great sense of doubt that the war could ever be won. As it turned out, the majority of American society was generally feeling the same way. I also no longer felt that the military was a place for me to spend the rest of my life. The efforts to escalate the war had come to a screeching halt. The number of American soldiers being sent to Vietnam had been on the decline for some time. As I was considering my first military assignment following graduation, I discovered that no one in my graduating class was being involuntarily sent to Vietnam. Only volunteers were being considered. By the time I reported to my first assignment (1971), I had formed a very strong relationship with my girlfriend and, together, we decided that going to Vietnam to serve only made sense if one had already decided to pursue a military career. By then, I had already decided that I would not make the military my career. I wanted to serve my five years and then leave. Therefore, serving in Vietnam simply would not be part of my plan.

By then, many of my high school friends had military experience and some had served in Vietnam. A few had been killed or wounded. I felt really badly that they had made those sacrifices and that I was not going to follow them to do my duty. However, I also knew by then that Vietnam was not the place for anyone to do their duty. Even though many Americans continued to serve there honorably until the bitter end, too much of the American involvement in the last years of the Vietnam War got reduced to focusing on an embarrassing, small collection of out-of-control soldiers more involved in drug abuse, insubordination and racial violence then in pursuing American military objectives. In light of all that, I was able to easily rationalize my decision to forgo serving in Vietnam. However, for a while afterward, I did entertain some doubts because lingering thoughts of serving in the military as generations ahead of me had done still told me that I should have gone to war for my country no matter what.

Soon thereafter, it became clear that the American involvement in Vietnam was coming to a halt. By 1973, all of the American troops had been withdrawn. As everyone knows, the withdrawal of troops and the termination of involvement by Americans in Vietnam was one of the worst humiliations in American military history. By that time, I was married and halfway through with my 5-year service obligation and more convinced than ever that I wanted no part of the military as it existed then. I was actually stationed in Korea in 1973 as the Vietnam operation was being dismantled. My wife was there too but not as an authorized dependent of mine. From that point on, our objective was to terminate the military service, get as much additional education as possible and, as soon as my military obligation was completed, for me to enroll in law school. And that's the way it happened.

Chapter 13-The National Boy of the Year Contest

Up to this point, everything that I have written has been for the purpose of providing the reader with a context about what life was like for a teenage boy growing up in the 1960's in South El Paso. The dynamics and the circumstances that I personally experienced were probably not atypical of what most teenage boys were experiencing in those days in that neighborhood: The Boys' Club, with all of its activities and personnel; the Projects and the families that lived there; *Jefferson High School* and the teachers who taught us; the friendships that we formed; the adventures we had; the parents, mentors and other adults who showed us the way. All of these factors in different ways guided, propelled and enabled us to get through those years. But, as I stated at the outset, I believe that kids like me in that context were moved upward and forward dramatically by yet another undeniable force: The annual *Boys' Clubs' of America* "Boy of the Year" contest.

The national *Boys' Clubs of America* organization had its beginnings in 1860 and eventually took form as the *Federated Boys' Club* in Boston in 1906. In 1931, the name was changed back to *Boys' Clubs of America*. By then, it had become an organization of 258 Clubs nationwide with some 250,000 members. In 1947, the *Reader's Digest Foundation* began its sponsorship of the "Boy of the Year" contest within the *Boys' Clubs of America*. After 1990, when the organization formally adopted its new name, *Boys and Girls Clubs of America*, the "Boy of the Year" contest became the "Youth of the Year" contest.

When the title of "Boy of the Year" first became known in El Paso during the late 1950's or early 1960's, the contest was relatively new. Under the leadership of Mr. Hightower, the *El Paso Boys' Club* apparently decided to participate very enthusiastically in all activities sponsored by the national organization. The "Boy of the Year" contest was one of those activities.

The contest was open to any member of the *Boys' Clubs of America*. During the 1950's, the number of local Clubs throughout the US had grown to over 600. Each local Club could nominate one of its members to compete for the title. The process for identifying the local nominee probably varied substantially from Club to Club. However, the idea was for each local Club to identify the one member who had done the most in terms of service to Club, family and community and to submit his name along with corroborating documentation for consideration by the national office.

In those days, the national organization of the *Boys' Clubs of America* was divided into 4 geographic Regions: The Northwest, Northeast, Southwest and Southeast Regions. Each Region was further divided into Sections with each Section containing anywhere from 10 to 20 local Clubs.

The national office would presumably review all of the nominations and select a Boy of the Year from each Section. These Sectional Boys of the Year comprised the set of finalists who would then go on to the next step of the contest—the selection of the 4 Regional Boys of the Year. It was from those four Regional Boys of the Year that the National winner was selected. The timing of the selections was such as to permit the winner to be identified and presented to the nation during National *Boys' Clubs of America* Week which occurred each year during the first week of April. In order to meet that schedule, the local Club nominations had to be submitted by January 1 of each year. The selection process would take place during the following three months to allow for the announcement of the winner on or about April 1st.

And so, in early April, 1961, the announcement was made that Richard Lopez, a Mexican-American boy from El Paso, Texas, had been selected as Boys' Clubs of America's *National Boy of the Year*. During the days following the announcement, the local newspapers and television stations saturated their media with related information. The city of El Paso, which was predominantly Mexican-American, erupted in pride and celebration as the notion sank in: A local youth from a relatively disadvantaged social status had risen to recognition at the national level for being a shining example of what a model American boy should be.

Richard Lopez-National Boy of the Year 1961

My story and the story of the other South El Paso kids who somehow managed to defy the odds and who went on to surprising levels of educational achievement are stories of incredible complexity. The factors that materialized and that affected all of us during that period were not atypical. They included the usual people/players: Parents, siblings, teachers, clergy, social workers, employers, Boys' Club professionals, mentors, friends and politicians. They also included the usual institutions: Schools, churches, civic and social clubs, Cub Scouts and Boy Scouts and government units. Then there were the activities that we all got involved in: After school jobs, school athletic teams, bands, ROTC, drama clubs, youth gangs, public speaking clubs and religious education. All of these factors were essential to what was happening to each of us and each of us was affected in different ways. However, if there had not been any "boys" on which these factors could work then the factors all may have simply passed over the neighborhood without any impact whatsoever.

But, fortunately, a crop of boys did exist who could and did benefit from the effect of these factors. The first of these boys was Richard Lopez.

Richard was born on September 3, 1943. He was the third oldest of 4 boys and a girl who were brought up by their mother, Maria Luisa Franco Lopez. His real name was Jose Ricardo Lopez but he became known from his earliest days as "Richard" to be distinguished from his father, Ricardo. Later on, when he started playing Little League Baseball, he also became known as "Lefty."

Richard's father graduated from high school and became a butcher. He managed to acquire a small grocery store on South El Paso's Stanton street and did extremely well although eventually, according to Richard, he squandered the money he made. Richard recalls that his father gambled and was a womanizer who made life very difficult for Richard's mother. When Richard was seven or eight years old his parents divorced. Richard never saw his father again until he went to his funeral in the early 1980's. He had apparently died of cancer although Richard suspects cirrhosis. Richard claims that he never had any feelings for his dad.

Richard's mother became known by her Americanized name, Mary Louise Lopez. She also graduated from high school and, according to Richard, became quite a businesswoman. She always was a strong proponent of education and constantly encouraged her kids to do well in school. While that may sound normal in most environments, such zeal for schooling was—and may still be--rare in that neighborhood. Richard remembers that when he was still very young, she would walk to work 5 miles each way in order to save the 25¢ bus fare so she could put it into the education fund of her children.

She was previously married to the love of her life, Adan, who fathered Richard's two older siblings, Adan Jr. and Martha. In addition to Richard, his parents produced two younger twin brothers, Robert and Armando.

Richard grew up in a house located at 504 South Florence Street in the heart of a tough South El Paso neighborhood known as Second Ward (El Segundo Barrio). Unit 1 of the *El Paso Boys' Club* was located nearby at 801 South Florence Street and so Richard naturally and conveniently found a place there in which to hang out. His elementary school, *Roosevelt Elementary*, was right across the street from the Boys Club. He remembers how he would sit in his classroom and look out the window with great curiosity about what the Boys' Club building across the street was all about. He thought it was a factory. At age seven, Richard's curiosity got the best of him and so he crossed the street one day to inquire about joining. One of the staff members there, Sal Ramirez, welcomed him but told him that he was too young to join and to come back when he was eight. At age eight, sometime around 1951-1952, Richard became a member of the *El Paso Boys' Club* by paying the 25¢ yearly dues.

From a very young age, Richard showed signs that he was unique. During his days at *Roosevelt Elementary School* he showed remarkable leadership and athletic potential. He was selected as Captain of his Patrol Boy organization. The Patrol Boys (and Girls)—as I described in an earlier chapter--were the street crossing guards of those days. On the sports side, by the time he finished elementary school, he had won recognition as an All-Star Little League selection, played in the El Paso *Little League World Series* and, despite his young age, won the *West Texas Sportsman of the Year* Award.

When he entered high school at Bowie High, he became an active participant in a variety of school teams or activities and received numerous honors. He was in the Student Council, served as President of his sophomore and senior classes, made the El Paso city baseball team that played in the *Babe Ruth Baseball World Series* in Vancouver, British Columbia, was Captain of the varsity tennis squad, Captain of the varsity basketball team, Captain of the varsity baseball team, played in the varsity football squad, was selected as a member of the 4-AAAA All-District and All-State Baseball Teams and received a special invitation to attend the San Francisco Giants baseball training camp in 1960.

In addition, Richard managed to maintain good enough grades for selection into the *National Honor Society*. He also was the sports editor and photographer for the Bowie High newspaper, *The Growler*, managed to hold down a part-time job while a senior as part of the school's *Distributive Education* Program, found time to act in the *Masque and Gavel Society* and even got selected to participate in the national *Scholastic Sports Association* sponsored by the *Los Angeles Examiner*.

Perhaps most significant, Richard was a major contributor to ensuring that everything went well at home. Since his mother was the sole wage-earner, Richard learned how to be a homemaker and did much of the housework required in his home. He did the family wash, ironed his and his brothers' clothes and cooked one meal each weekday for his younger brothers. Richard also ensured that his younger brothers did their homework and otherwise stayed abreast of their school requirements.

Richard recently recalled: "I came from an environment—not my parental environment but a community environment—that says: If the thing gets tough, quit. We have a good excuse to quit. But something in my demeanor...I don't know if it was inbred, I think it had to do with competitiveness and competing and getting your ass whipped and on occasion just winning...but I attribute that to mi Mamá...I mean mi Mamá was hell-bent...if you don't put forth a concerted effort, a determined effort, you can't tell me that you failed. And that's the philosophy I took with me."

In January, 1961, the *El Paso Boys' Club* for the first time in its history decided to nominate one of its members to compete for the title of *Boys' Clubs of America* National Boy of the Year. Richard Lopez was the candidate. The nomination process was simple. With the assistance of the Boys' Club staff, Richard prepared a scrapbook which contained any and all references that somehow attested to his exemplary qualifications. The scrapbook was then submitted to the national office of the *Boys' Clubs of America* for consideration along with the submissions of the rest of the candidates from all over America.

The news of Richard's selection as National Boy of the Year came in two spurts of publicity. On April 9, 1961, an article in the *El Paso Times* reported that Richard had been selected as one of the winners of the "Regional Boy of the Year" title. The Region included 6 states: Texas, New Mexico, Louisiana, Arkansas, Colorado and Oklahoma. Before the community could digest the significance of Richard's Regional honor, a second article appeared on Wednesday, April 11, 1961, in the *El Paso Times,* describing how Richard, having been selected as *National* Boy of the Year, had spent the previous few days being honored and recognized by national dignitaries. The article highlighted how then President John F. Kennedy had presented Richard with a plaque commemorating his selection as National Boy of the Year and how the President, noting their mutual love of baseball, had invited Richard to attend that year's *Major League Baseball* season opener with him and other dignitaries, including Vice President Lyndon B. Johnson.

It was that second article that really opened the eyes of the El Paso community as to what had happened. This kid from South El Paso was being recognized by some of the most powerful figures in the *world*. Even though I had not met Richard at that point in time, I knew that El Paso, the local Mexican-American community and particularly the *El Paso Boys' Club* had a real hero in their midst. Everywhere I went and anything I did during those few days were consumed by thoughts and words relating to Richard Lopez.

Even at my high school—which happened to be the arch rival of Richard's high school—there was genuine admiration for what he had accomplished.

On Friday, April 13, 1961, Richard returned to El Paso and was greeted by the largest and most tumultuous crowd ever to greet anyone at the local airport. Every important local dignitary was there including then Mayor, Raymond Telles. The size and excitement level of the crowd that showed up to greet Richard was a surprise to everyone since there had been no coordination to make a big scene. It was spontaneous yet huge probably because all segments of the community saw something really neat about Richard. I was among the contingent there from the *El Paso Boys' Club* and I can only remember how little success I had in getting close to him on account of the size of the crowd.

Shortly after Richard was selected National Boy of the Year, I ran into him at the Boys' Club. I introduced myself to him and congratulated him. He struck me as incredibly modest in light of everything that had happened to him. He then proceeded to explain how he had been coping with his new-found fame. He acknowledged that he had been very lucky and that he was very grateful for all that had recently happened but that he would always remember what Sal "Huevo" Ramirez, the Boys' Club Unit 1 Director, told him just before he went to New York to receive his award. Huevo told him to "always pray for humility." Richard confessed to me that he kept Huevo's guidance in mind constantly and he advised me to do the same. Humility, in the personal as well as material sense, was indeed a huge deal for Huevo. He was happy to spend his life helping the Mexican-American community even if it meant having to give up material advantages that he might have obtained in other pursuits. Both Richard and I found great inspiration for the rest of our lives in those words from Huevo.

So now El Paso had a Boy of the Year. Is it possible to measure or understand what that fact meant particularly with respect to other boys--and girls--of El Paso? I for one believe that the selection of Richard Lopez as *National Boy of the Year* deeply inspired an extraordinarily large number of kids who witnessed this event and who privately wondered, "Why can't I do the same?" I know that that is precisely what happened to me. I was in awe of Richard and, at the same time, I didn't think he was much different from me or many of my peers. It may have been a naïve determination on my part but there was no doubt that a fire had been lit in my belly and that it would propel me to levels of achievement that I ordinarily would probably not even have dreamed of reaching. I believe that a remarkable number of my Boys' Club buddies were equally impressed by what Richard had accomplished and that they also believed that they could be like Richard. I was a 14-year-old freshman in high school when all this was happening and I felt a great sense of certainty that by the time I was a senior, I also would be a national Boy of the Year.

Boy of the Year Competition -1962

In 1962, the *El Paso Boys' Club* nominated two boys to compete for National Boy of the Year honors. They were Jesús Murillo from Unit 1 and my brother, Ignacio (aka "Nacho" and "Lefty") Chavez from Unit 2. The sentiment at the Boys' Club was that there was no reason why El Paso could not win the national award in consecutive years. After all, the achievements of the 1962 candidates compared very favorably with those of Richard Lopez. However, there was the risk of making the contest appear too localized if winners kept coming from the same town. So, for the 1962 Boy of the Year contest, the expectations of the Boys' Club and, for that matter, of the entire community, were somewhat reserved.

For the 1962 contest, El Paso's nominees were selected from a total membership of approximately 1200 boys. They would compete with candidates from 600 Boys' Clubs serving more than 600,000 boys throughout the US. The winner was to receive a $500 scholarship from the *Readers' Digest Foundation*. In addition, there would be a trip to New York and Washington, DC to be recognized by government leaders, including the President of the United States.

Jesús Murillo

Jesús Murillo was an 18-year old senior student at *Bowie High School* when he received the nomination. His life to that point had been one of significant achievements given the forces that he had faced. At that time, Jesús lived alone and supported himself since his entire family--which included six brothers and three sisters--had moved to California two years earlier. He had been a factor in the raising of his nine siblings since he was in the sixth grade when he would contribute his earnings from a newspaper route to help with his family's financial needs.

He started to show signs of exceptional potential as early as 1952, at the age of 8, when he was named Best Arithmetic Student at *Aoy Elementary School*. During the course of his elementary schooling he got double-promoted and was selected Class President. While at Aoy, he also received reading and hand-writing awards and was selected Captain of Patrol Boys.

While at *Bowie High School*, he continued to excel in just about all phases of his education. He became Captain of the Varsity Tennis squad and was once a runner-up in the *El Paso City Tennis Doubles Tournament*. He was also a letterman in the varsity basketball team and in the football B-Team (Jr. Varsity). He was continuously an honors student and named "Draftsman of the Year" in 1960. He was active in many other high school activities including the Drama Club and the Writing Club in which he received poem and essay awards.

In the South El Paso community, he was active by being an altar boy, chairing a "Get out the Vote" campaign and a canned-goods drive, and participating in *United Fund* solicitation programs and parades.

Finally, at the Boys' Club he was a table tennis champion and a homework tutor to younger kids. He coached baseball and basketball teams of younger boys and was generally looked upon by many other members as a role model and unpaid staff member. Jesús was simply an incredibly good kid who was mature way beyond his tender years.

Ignacio "Lefty" Chavez

The second nominee from the *El Paso Boys' Club* in 1962 was "Lefty" Chavez who was a 17-year-old junior student at *Jefferson High School*. Lefty was my older brother and probably no one knew him better than I did when he entered this competition.

Lefty's real name was Ignacio Enrique Chavez. He was named after mi Papá but unlike mi Papá, whose name was spelled "Ygnacio," Lefty's name was spelled "Ignacio." From an early age, he acquired the nickname "Nachito" again to differentiate him from mi Papá who was called "Nacho." By the time we lived in the projects, he had become known as "Lefty" or the Spanish version of Lefty: "Surdo." At home, we continued to call him "Nachito."

Lefty's days in the Boys' Club started when Unit 2 was opened in the Paisano Projects in the summer of 1959. We had lived in that neighborhood for about a year by then and had formed friendships with many of the other kids and their families who also lived there.

Since mi Papá had struggled financially during our entire lives, Lefty started helping with family finances from an early age. He was a shoe-shine boy while still very young and later on supplemented the family income by working as a soda vendor at the *El Paso Coliseum* and at other local sports venues. I remember quite well how he would arrive late at night from these gigs and hand most--if not all--of his earnings to mi Mamá so she could buy groceries. Lefty was a rock of stability and wisdom and nicely complemented mi Papá who was 63 years old, blind and who relied on welfare to support our family.

Lefty was also a very successful student. From his elementary school days, he too showed signs of significant potential. He received Citizenship Medals, perfect attendance, writing and band awards and made the honor roll regularly. In high school he excelled in the varsity baseball team and participated in the band and in the Student Council.

Lefty was an altar boy for a few years and was active at the local Catholic Church. He also captained or coached a variety of athletic squads at the Boys' Club. He was a charter member of the *Linguistic Jr. Toastmasters Club* and participated in various speech contests sponsored by the Optimist Clubs. He considers even today that the Jr. Toastmasters constituted the most significant and valuable development experience that he ever undertook at the Boys' Club.

When Lefty moved to the Paisano Projects in 1958, he met another neighborhood kid who seemed to love baseball even more than he did. That kid was Jesús "Chuy" Reza who was the eldest son of Jesús Reza, Sr. affectionately known then in the professional baseball leagues of Mexico as "La Borrachita." Lefty acknowledges to this day that Chuy and his father profoundly influenced the development of his own passion for baseball. Lefty believes that it was fortuitous that at around that same time in the Paisano Projects, the Boys Club opened a branch that enabled baseball to flourish and to provide a precious distraction from the traditional and sometimes troubling activities that boys might otherwise have pursued. Mr. Reza became the coach of many different baseball teams populated by Boys' Clubbers. Lefty—like many other boys—learned how to play and developed his skills significantly under the watchful eyes of Mr. Reza.

On April 9, 1962, word reached the *El Paso Boys' Club* that Lefty had been selected as one of four *Regional Boys of the Year* for 1962. He was awarded a $200 scholarship. Jesús Murillo, the candidate submitted by Unit 1, was selected as one of the *Sectional Boys of the Year* and was awarded a $100 scholarship. Jesús, who was a high school senior that year, indicated at that time that upon graduation from high school he would re-join his family in California and use that scholarship to attend *Sacramento State College*.

In the Chavez family, there was tremendous elation at Lefty's accomplishment. But there was also a bit of disappointment since he did not get the national award. I recall thinking how close Lefty had actually come to winning (given that he won a Regional title) and after this near miss how unlikely it was that he could ever again win the big one. More importantly, I saw an opportunity open up for me as well as for others who were following in the footsteps of guys like Richard, Jesús and Lefty. I saw clearly that there was a huge educational benefit in store for those who emulated these pathfinders and I became determined then to do all I could to earn it. I also noted that most of my peers had been similarly affected. At athletic contests, social gatherings and club meetings, all of us were abuzz about how a Boy of the Year title might also be won by any of us. I remember seeing among my buddies a type of resolve to also try to do what these Boys of the Year had done. There was a palpable renewed interest in doing better in school, in doing good things for the community and in being better sons at home so that we too, in the next year or so, might consider entering this contest.

Boy of the Year Competition -1963

When the Boy of the Year competition opened in 1963, the attitude at the *El Paso Boys' Club* was aggressive and wildly optimistic. Boys interested in the competition now had two years of knowledge and experience which they could apply as they prepared their scrapbooks for consideration by the national office. The staff of the club also had learned much about grooming kids for the contest and about how to prepare the materials that each boy submitted. But much more importantly, it was widely believed that the huge obstacle of the previous year—the unlikely possibility of the same city winning the national prize for two years in a row—was no longer a factor. At least, it seemed that way to all who competed in that year's contest. The candidates were: Joe Renteria, Johnny Uranga and Ezequiel Chacón from Unit 1 and again, Lefty Chavez from Unit 2.

Lefty Chavez

All bets this year were being placed on last year's Regional winner, Lefty Chavez. Now in his senior year at Jefferson High, Lefty had evolved into precisely the type of youth that the *Boys' Clubs of America* was looking for in the Boy of the Year competition. His leadership qualities and oratorical skills earned him the position of Assembly Manager at his high school, a coveted position that required him to be the master of ceremonies during all student assemblies. Also, his athletic skills had been honed during the previous year and made him one of the key contributors in the varsity baseball team's quest for a district title.

During the summer prior to his senior year (1962), Lefty was selected to participate in the *Crossroads of the Americas* program. *Crossroads*—discussed in more detail in an earlier chapter--was a youth program whereby a group of the best and brightest high school students in El Paso were selected to spend a month during summer vacation in some location in Mexico promoting good will between the two countries. Lefty, along with 16 other high school standouts from El Paso, journeyed to Rio Florido, Chihuahua, a small town in northern Mexico, and endeavored to realize the program objectives. It turned out to be an enormous success bringing accolades and honors from both the US and Mexico to the participants.

At home, Lefty's contributions also grew dramatically. Our parents' dependence on Lefty as a source of income, particularly during the summer, was substantial. Furthermore, as mi Papá's age advanced and his eye-sight continued to deteriorate and, as mi Mamá's health worsened (those violent seizures of an undetermined source) all of us looked to Lefty to assume the role of head of the household. He never dodged the responsibility.

So, all of the proverbial eggs of *The El Paso Boys' Club* were placed in the one basket called Lefty Chavez. There was confidence bordering on recklessness that everyone felt regarding his chances of winning that year. However, Mr. Hightower and his staff were appropriately sensitive to the future and, therefore, came up with three younger boys whose names would also be submitted to compete with Lefty for the honor of Boy of the Year.

Joe Renteria

Joe Renteria, born on September 6, 1948, was Christened José Renteria and was affectionately called "Pepe" by his family. He lived in South El Paso on South Mesa Street just south of Paisano drive when he became affiliated with the *El Paso Boys' Club* unit on Florence Street. He was a Boys' Club member from 1956 until well after his high school graduation in 1966. While at *Bowie High School* and afterward, while he attended the *University of Texas at El Paso*, Joe worked as a disk jockey at local radio stations. Also, during those years, he was a volunteer supervisor at the Boys' Club working with boys to teach them about life as a disk jockey.

Joe grew up in a very loving family environment. He was the youngest of four kids. Brothers Louie (10 years older) and Richard (8 years older) and sister Dolores (6 years older) all were role models who preceded him at *Bowie High School*. He also had another brother Raymond (1 year older) who died while still very young.

His father, Luis, was somewhat atypical from other parents in the barrio in that he finished high school with a technical diploma. His mother, Josefina, did not get a high school education probably because she married Luis at age 16 or 17. Joe credits his parents with many things, but in particular, instilling in him a strong sense of the value of a good education.

Joe first went to the Boys' Club because it constituted a sanctuary from all of the violence that was happening in his neighborhood. He remembers that gang wars and knife fights were all too common and, one day, as he was heading home from school, he ended up being chased by a pack of young thugs. He ran straight for the Boys' Club facility on Florence Street and remained there until the thugs left him alone. That's when he first met Sal "Huevo" Ramirez. Joe considers Sal to be the staff member who most influenced him during these formative years.

Although Joe was born in the underprivileged barrio of South El Paso, he was reared in a home that was probably one socio-economic level higher than the homes of the rest of the members of the Boys' Club. His parents simply were more successful than other South El Paso parents in breaking the bonds that kept them there and managed to move to a more affluent section of town as Joe entered high school. In that regard, Joe was very fortunate. Joe started high school at Austin High, which, unlike Bowie High and Jefferson High, was mostly populated by Anglo students from relatively affluent families. The boys who were members of the *El Paso Boys' Club* Unit 1 located in South El Paso almost exclusively went to Bowie High. The members of Unit 2 located in the Paisano Projects almost exclusively went to Jefferson High. Students at Bowie and Jefferson were almost exclusively Mexican-American.

I met Joe in 1962 when he attended a meeting of the Junior Toastmasters Club. I was the club president at the time and the club was enjoying city-wide fame due to its amazing series of speech contest victories. I had achieved the highest level of success that year among all club members by winning the Zone level of competition (West Texas and Eastern New Mexico) of the *Optimist Oratorical Contest*.

Then Joe showed up. He was a very cool and popular boy who was much better looking than me, blessed with extremely good social skills and with a radio broadcaster's voice. He also seemed to have at his disposal many of the material things that young boys wanted, including a car and some money. Most importantly, he seemed to know lots of pretty girls. On many occasions, my buddies and I ended up looking to Joe to supply us with dates.

I recall that he did just that two or three times when we participated in the local version of *American Bandstand* called *Crosno's Hop*. Anyone who met Joe could not help but be swept away by his engaging personality and charm.

That year an intense rivalry between Joe and me began. We were always good friends and we generally liked each other but we were constantly competing against each other in Jr. Toastmasters Club elections and in speech contests. Even though I was a year older and one year ahead of him in school, he definitely kept me on my toes. At around the same time, both of us became involved in a *YMCA Youth Council* which had been established for student leaders from El Paso schools to try to address the growing problem of juvenile delinquency. We both ran for office in that organization but Joe handily beat me and became president. And his appeal was not simply local. In 1962, when Joe was only 14 years of age, the then *Attorney General of the State of Texas*, Waggoner Carr, was so impressed with him that he invited Joe to be the Keynote speaker at a statewide youth conference at *Rice University* in Houston.

By 1963, Joe—a freshman at Austin High--was "the" rising star of the Boys' Club and had compiled an impressive record of academic, community, home, church and Boys' Club accomplishments. When Joe was nominated for Boy of the Year in 1963, his nomination scrapbook was pretty impressive. It showed that he was an honor student that year and, before that, had been president of his class, president of the choir, *Spelling Bee* champion while in grammar school and had earned a perfect attendance certificate. His other activities and honors included Student Council Secretary, Captain of Patrol Boys and *Rookie of the Year* in the *Coldwell School Little League* team.

He also was an active member of his church. He and his family were parishioners at *Our Lady of Guadalupe Catholic Church* and Joe always found time to help out there whenever he could. At Christmas time he was regularly involved in helping set up decorations, and after bazaars, he could be counted on to help with the clean-up. During masses, Joe was one of the regular attendants and would help in conducting the collections.

He contributed heavily to making sure everything got done around his home. For example, he was handy and was credited with helping remodel his home by helping to build a garage, a bathroom, a garden patio and a bathroom. He was helpful also by occasionally cooking a family meal, by doing the dinner dishes three times a week, by ironing all of his clothes and by frequently even doing the family laundry.

His older siblings had all graduated from Bowie High. One day, while Joe was a freshman at Austin High, he was washing the family car in his driveway. The Principal of Bowie High, Mr. Frank C. Pollitt, happened to drive by and started to chat with him. Joe was an aspiring track athlete at Austin High and Mr. Pollitt had heard that Joe had indicated that he would prefer to attend Bowie but couldn't because he lived in an Austin High neighborhood. Mr. Pollitt offered to arrange a transfer. That enabled Joe to move to Bowie High in 1963 for his last three years of high school.

As a sophomore in high school in 1963, I too was enjoying enormous success. I was doing well academically and also excelling in extracurricular activities in school. I was also participating in community activities such as *Crossroads of the Americas*. And I was up to my ears in Boys' Club activities since I—along with maybe another dozen of my peers--was being groomed to be the next National Boy of the Year. I felt that I would have been a better candidate for Boy of the Year than Joe, but Unit 2 already had a nominee—my brother, Lefty, and so I accepted that I would stay on the sidelines for the 1963 competition.

Joe recently told me that the experiences that he had in the Jr. Toastmasters were life-changing. He believes that the events that he participated in as a Jr. Toastmaster converted him from a shy and very guarded kid who had great difficulty expressing himself, to an articulate and expressive communicator. He sees those years today as a powerful educational experience that more than anything else propelled him to the successful career in entertainment that he eventually realized. He remains eternally grateful to Sal Ramirez for taking him by the arm back in 1962 and leading him for the very first time into the meeting room of the Jr. Toastmasters Club.

However, in 1963, when he first competed in the National Boy of the Year contest, he was not likely to win the honor, particularly when matched with Lefty Chavez. But Mr. Hightower, the Executive Director of the Boys' Club, probably was simply grooming Joe to compete in future years.

Johnny Uranga

Everyone at the Boys' Club called him Johnny but his real name was Juán just like his father. He was another true product of the tough neighborhood known as Second Ward in South El Paso. He lived at 911 South Virginia Street and first joined the Club when he was in the third grade. He remained an active member until he graduated high school in 1966.

Johnny was the son of Juán Uranga, Sr. and Catalina Amparán Uranga, neither of whom completed high school. As he was growing up in South El Paso, Johnny had two younger brothers, Ricardo and Carlos. He was very fortunate in that his father was able to move away from that neighborhood in South El Paso just as Johnny was entering high school. The family moved to the west side of El Paso where Johnny could attend the predominantly Anglo *Coronado High School*, a school which was reputed to be considerably superior academically to Bowie High, the school in South El Paso which he otherwise would have attended.

Despite moving away, Johnny saw the value of the Boys' Club in his old neighborhood and he remained a member. He was another one of the kids that was inspired by the Unit 1 Director/Assistant Executive Director, Sal "Huevo" Ramirez. Johnny recalls to this day that Sal was the very first "successful" Latino—as defined by the dominant Anglo culture--that he had ever met. Johnny remembers that even at that early age, he saw in Sal a man of integrity and authenticity. Johnny had also been impressed by Sal because Sal was also a product of South El Paso and because Sal had not only gotten a degree from *Texas Western College* but had also played football while there.

In the spring of 1962, Sal Ramirez suggested to Johnny that he also join the Jr. Toastmasters. The Jr. Toastmasters had been in operation for a year and had established a pretty good record of speech contest victories and as a result started attracting more and more boys who either realized by themselves how valuable this activity was, or who trusted someone who told them so. Johnny arrived at the Jr. Toastmasters and quickly established himself as a force to be reckoned with as he competed and quickly won at one of the local Optimist Clubs. His coach for that contest was Sal Ramirez.

By 1963, Sal Ramirez and O. D Hightower could see that Johnny was yet another example of an outstanding youth coming out of the Boys' Club and so even though the leading Boy of the Year candidate had to be Lefty Chavez, they saw fit to also nominate Johnny to give him the experience of competing.

When Johnny was nominated to compete for the National Boy of the Year title in 1963, he was a freshman at Coronado High. Nevertheless, Johnny's nomination scrapbook showed that even at that young age, he had become a model of juvenile decency who deserved recognition.

In school, beginning in the third grade and continuing through junior high school, Johnny had consistently made the honor roll. He managed to get elected as class president one year in grade school and had always been very active in football, baseball and football and was elected captain of several of his teams.

At home, Johnny frequently assumed the role of a junior parent. Since both of his parents worked, Johnny regularly prepared the meals for his two younger brothers, one of whom was a victim of Polio. Johnny also routinely did the dishes after meals, maintained the front and back-yard lawns and helped his mother operate a neighborhood grocery store.

Despite all of these demands on his time, Johnny still found time to do things for his community. He regularly solicited contributions for the *United Way*, the *March of Dimes*, the *Muscular Dystrophy Campaign*, the *Heart Fund*, the *Cancer Drive* and, of course, the Boys' Club. In recognition of his accomplishments, the *Kiwanis International* organization awarded him a Citizenship Award.

The training and experience that Johnny gained in the Jr. Toastmasters Club and in the *Optimist Oratorical Contest* turned him into yet another public relations asset of the Boys' Club. As a result, that year he was a frequent guest speaker at local civic clubs and one time even before the *El Paso City Council*.

Later on, at *Coronado High School*, Johnny succeeded in becoming an outstanding all-around athlete. He played varsity baseball, basketball and football and became the Captain of the football team as a senior. He recently recalled for me a somewhat tough experience that he had when he had to choose between playing baseball and participating in the Student Council. His baseball coach at the time, the legendary William C. "Nemo" Herrera, who took the *Bowie High School* baseball team to the state championship in 1949, had come out of retirement to coach at Coronado High in the mid 1960's. Johnny was a solid member of Coach Nemo's team but wanted to also attend a state-wide Student Council convention which conflicted with the baseball schedule. Coach Nemo told Johnny to make a choice: baseball or Student Council. Johnny elected to attend the Student Council Convention. Upon Johnny's return, Coach Nemo kicked him off the baseball team.

In the summer before his senior year at Coronado High, Johnny was invited to participate in *Camp Rising Sun*, an invitation-only, international, full-scholarship leadership summer program in upstate New York for students aged 14-16. He recalls that his Jr. Toastmasters experience helped him immensely at that Camp so much so that one of the representatives attending from *Columbia University*, in essence told him that if he could get admitted to Columbia the following year, there would be a scholarship waiting for him. When Johnny completed his senior year, he applied for admission at Columbia and got in and, sure enough, obtained that scholarship that had been offered.

Despite having kicked Johnny off the team, Coach Nemo had a lot of respect for his baseball skills. When Johnny was about to graduate, Coach Nemo managed to find for him a baseball scholarship at *Texas State Teacher's College*. When Coach Nemo told Johnny about the scholarship, Johnny found himself in yet another quandary. Unbeknownst to Coach Nemo, Johnny had also been offered that scholarship to *Columbia University,* and Johnny, once again, had to make a choice. According to Johnny, Coach Nemo simply could not understand why Johnny would choose Columbia over baseball at *Texas State Teacher's College*.

Ezequiel Chacón

Of all of the kids that I knew from the Boys' Club Unit 1, Ezequiel "Zekie" Chacón was probably the one with the deepest roots in that South El Paso neighborhood. He lived in a small house on Charles Street in a neighborhood known as "Chihuahuita." His family had lived there for a number of generations after his ancestors had fled from Mexico in the early 1900's to avoid getting caught in the revolutionary turmoil.

Zekie was nominated by Boys' Club Unit 1 to compete in the Boy of the Year contest in 1963 when he was only a 14-year-old freshman at *El Paso High School*. His father, Ignacio, had died two years earlier and that made Zekie the man of the house for his mother, Julieta, and his younger sister, Dolores. They had to make ends meet on a monthly *Social Security* check plus a small pension left by Ignacio.

There was never any doubt in Zekie's family as to the value of an education. When Zekie entered high school, his mother decided to enroll at *Texas Western College* there in El Paso and pursue a degree in elementary education so she could become a teacher. Even though he himself had his work cut out for him in high school, Zekie decided then that he would help his mother as much as he could to ensure that she realized her ambition.

I remember when I first met Zekie. He was invited to attend one of our Jr. Toastmasters Club meetings in early 1962 when he was in the 8th grade. He was one of the youngest boys in the Jr. Toastmasters, yet he embraced the training program with rare zeal and quickly learned all of the basics of public speaking. He was different from most of the other boys in that he always seemed to be in a happy and bubbly mood. Whether we were practicing speeches or playing basketball, he was extraordinarily energetic and positive in his disposition. He was not a big guy but one always sensed his presence and that enthusiastic aura that always seemed to surround him.

He became quite a successful public speaker that year winning the *Optimist Oratorical Contest* at the *Bel Air Optimist Club*. The topic that year was "The Creative Force of Optimism." Like the rest of us, he also was considered a public relations asset for the *El Paso Boys' Club*. In one year, he was invited to deliver his speech on behalf of the Boys' Club some 27 times before local civic organizations.

As a freshman at *El Paso High School*, he impressed his Military Science instructors sufficiently to earn a promotion to Cadet Sergeant, a rank more commonly given to sophomores and juniors. He also joined the senior band and eventually, as a senior, became the Drum Major. Given Zekie's age at the time he was nominated for the Boy of the Year title, it seems apparent that Mr. Hightower and the rest of the Boys' Club staff were again merely grooming a promising younger boy for later competitions.

Lefty Wins

And so, in the fall of 1962, I remember Mr. D telling my brother, Lefty, to update his scrapbook so that he could be nominated for the 1963 National Boy of the Year title. Lefty then gathered all the information that he had saved during the past year and added it into his pretty amazing scrapbook. It was again filled with photographs, certificates, report cards, letters of recommendation, medals, ribbons, newspaper articles, and every other conceivable record that substantiated the many good qualities that he possessed. It was this scrapbook alone that was reviewed and judged throughout the country in order to determine the winner.

The scrapbook went into the selection process early in 1963. Then, around mid-March, Mr. D, who was the Unit 2 Director, and Mr. Hightower, who was the Executive Director of the *El Paso Boys' Club*, dropped in to visit my family at home. Mr. D did most of the talking while my entire family sat on a sofa; my parents on the end seats with my sister in the middle while my brother Lefty and I sat on the armrests at each end. Mr. D started by telling us that he had some good news. He announced that Lefty had been selected-- for the second year in a row--as the *Southwestern Regional Boy of the Year*. At this, all of us jumped up from the sofa and started to holler in happiness. After we settled down a bit he told us that, as in the previous year, this was a huge honor. And he confirmed that Lefty was now one of the four finalists being considered for National Boy of the Year. We initially had feared that by winning the regional award again, he would not be able to go any further. But the news that he was still in the hunt for the national prize made my entire family hysterically happy. Mr. D proceeded to explain that we should understand carefully the implications of what was happening. He asked all of us whether we were truly prepared for the possibility that Lefty could indeed become the National Boy of the Year. It would mean lots of travel for him and having to take lots of time off from school and from the athletic teams that he was a part of. It would also be extremely stressful for the entire family as we experienced what it was like to have somewhat of a famous person living among us. He pointed out how with that honor came pretty enormous responsibilities, duties and obligations to the Boys' Club, to the community and even to the *City of El Paso* not only for Lefty but also for our entire family. Mr. D basically warned us that the experience could be as traumatic and disruptive as it could be joyful. We all looked at each other and smiled and enthusiastically communicated to Mr. D that we, as a family, were certainly prepared for all of that in the event that Lefty was to win the national title. Mr. D acknowledged our response and smiled broadly and with great calmness proceeded to tell us that they expected that the final results would not be announced until sometime in the next few weeks. We then felt as if the meeting had come to an end and that Mr. D and Mr. Hightower would leave us to privately celebrate Lefty's regional victory and to contemplate the possibility that he might yet win the national award. However, Mr. Hightower then took over the conversation and told us that it was official: Lefty had, in fact, been selected as the 1963 *National Boy of the Year!* We all again started jumping up and down and then all of us— including Mr. D and Mr. Hightower--seemed to be crying with joy. In my entire life, I have never felt as happy as I did that day.

And so, a few days later the preparations began. We were all sworn to secrecy. Lefty was taken to local clothing store by Mr. Hightower and discreetly given two brand new suits that Lefty would wear during the upcoming trip to Washington, DC and New York City. Arrangements were made at school and elsewhere for him to disappear for about a week during the week of April 12th. And we could hardly contain our excitement as each day passed prior to the public announcement.

Then one day in mid-April, 1963, a news release was published that announced that he had been selected as National Boy of the Year. By that time, he had already flown to New York City with Mr. Hightower and was being prepared to receive the award at the *Boys' Clubs of America* National Headquarters on the day that it was announced. On that same day, after receiving the award, Lefty was given a tour of New York City where he met many local dignitaries. Lefty recently recalled how he and Mr. Hightower had had dinner by themselves on the first night in New York so that Mr. Hightower could coach him on how to behave, what to say, what to do, how to eat, etc. during the next few days. On one of the evenings of that week Lefty appeared on *The Tonight Show* with Johnny Carson where Mr. Carson walked up into the studio audience and introduced him on national TV and did a brief interview with him.

After a few days in New York City, Lefty and Mr. Hightower then went to Washington, DC. While there, Lefty met just about every important person who lived there at the time. He met President Kennedy, Vice-President Lyndon Johnson, former President Herbert Hoover, FBI Director J. Edgar Hoover and a whole bunch of others. During their visit, President Kennedy at one point looked down at his tie, straightened it out and then removed the gold PT-109 tie clasp that he was wearing and gave it to Lefty.

Eventually, Lefty flew back to El Paso. When he arrived, he was given one of the biggest hero's welcome that the city had ever seen. Classes at Jefferson High were canceled for that day so that everyone could be at the airport and at the homecoming parade that followed. The newspaper carried a huge number of different articles that all related to him. And all of the television stations carried the news reports about him for quite a few days that week. He was absolutely at the top of the world for a while.

One of my most vivid memories revolves around the pop band that was formed to welcome him to the neighborhood following that homecoming parade. Six or seven members of the *Jefferson High School* band also happened to live in the Paisano Projects. We dressed as beatniks and played music as he got off his plane at the airport, as he walked through the terminal and, finally, as he arrived at our home. I honestly do not remember feeling any jealousy or resentment about all the attention that Lefty was receiving. I actually felt extremely proud and fortunate that he was my brother. I've always felt that he was special. I never really knew for sure that he was National-Boy-of-the-Year material but at the same time, it did not come as a huge surprise when he actually won the title.

As a result of this honor, Lefty accumulated a ton of mementos. Regrettably, the majority of these mementos were lost in that warehouse fire I mentioned earlier where our household goods were stored. A few photographs did survive including some of Lefty with President Kennedy. I also ended up with the suit that Lefty wore when he met President Kennedy. Lefty gave it to me a few years after he used it on that memorable occasion since he had put on some weight and I had grown enough so that by then, it fit me perfectly. I used it a few times and, eventually, I also outgrew it, but I held on to it. In 2014, I returned it to Lefty in perfect condition so he could pass it on to his grandsons who might appreciate such an heirloom.

So, the main objective of the *El Paso Boys' Club* in 1963 was achieved: The Club produced another *National Boy of the Year*. But they also got a bonus. The nominee that represented their best hope for the future, Joe Renteria, was awarded the title of *Sectional Boy of the Year*. The machine that Mr. Hightower built seemingly had become an unstoppable producer of exceptionally fine examples of juvenile decency.

Boy of the Year Competition -1964

Finally, the year arrived when I became an official nominee for *National Boy of the Year*. Here's what the situation looked like at that point. Richard Lopez, an *El Paso Boys' Club* member, won the National award in 1961. In 1962, El Paso did not claim a National winner but had a Regional winner (Ignacio "Lefty" Chavez) *and* a Sectional winner (Jesús Murillo). In 1963, another *El Paso Boys' Club* member, Lefty Chavez, again snared the National award and Joe Renteria got a Sectional award. As I contemplated the contest for 1964, I knew that the odds were overwhelmingly against having another El Paso boy win the National contest. However, the prospects of a Regional or even a Sectional award were enticing not only because of the scholarships but also because of the prestige and recognition that came with them.

I had always been an unrelenting optimist and three years of competing in the *Optimist Oratorical Contest* had honed that particular personal outlook to a razor sharpness. Yet, I understood very well then that the Boy of the Year contest would no longer ever be a shot at a final destination (the National award) but rather a stepping stone to my future. My objective changed from *becoming* the *National Boy of the Year* to instead using the experience of running to help get me ready for college and whatever else came after. It was then that I realized that while winning the National award was, without doubt, a monumental experience, it was the annual ritual of the competition that really produced the returns for the *Boys Clubs of America* and the benefits for all of the contestants and their communities.

The nomination process at the *El Paso Boys' Club* for the 1964 Boy of the Year competition culminated in January of that year when an announcement was made in the *El Paso Times*. That announcement just happened to occur at around the same time that our beloved Mr. Hightower finally succumbed to leukemia on January 30th of that same year. I truly believe that with the passing of Mr. Hightower, so ended the amazing era at the *El Paso Boys' Club* which is the subject of this book. The *El Paso Boys' Club* announcement of the 1964 contest nominees was as exciting and hopeful as any previous similar newspaper article. However, even a kid like me could sense that things at the Boys' Club were about to change and not for the better. One reason as to why I felt that way was the fact that I was growing older and would not be enjoying the benefits of that organization for much longer. As I alluded to earlier, I was thinking more and more about the future after the Boys' Club and less about what was actually happening at the Boys' Club. More importantly, however, I had a gut feeling that all of the good that had come from the Boys' Club in the past 5 or 6 years--including the benefits that accrued to the community as well as to individual boys such as myself— were directly and almost totally attributable to Mr. Hightower. And now, he was gone. My irrepressible optimism was to be taxed to the max.

The six nominees from the *El Paso Boys' Club* in 1964 were Joe Renteria, Ricardo Monzón, and Manny Alvarez (representing Unit 1) and Salvador E. Garcia, Sergio Reza and myself (representing Unit 2). Joe Renteria was the only nominee who had competed previously; the other five of us were first-timers. In keeping with the "grooming" process that had been in effect for the past few years, the crop of contenders was impressive, if I may say so myself.

Joe Renteria

This year, Joe Renteria was the most promising candidate. He was now a sophomore at Bowie High. In addition to all that he had accomplished up to the previous year (all set forth in an earlier part of this book) he continued to be an honor student, a class officer and very active in high school sports.

Joe was such an effective public speaker that he was regularly on the radio and making appearances on local TV. He was also frequently speaking on behalf of the Boys' Club before local service and civic clubs. The image that he conveyed during these appearances represented solid evidence to all who watched or listened that the Hightower model for running a Boys' Club and combatting juvenile delinquency was working well.

Joe's reputation as a youth leader was by then firmly established not only in El Paso but even throughout the State of Texas. In 1964, Even President Lyndon Johnson saw in Joe a story that could be used in the President's War on Poverty so he invited Joe to speak before the US Congress on how to prevent juvenile delinquency.

Anyone who followed the Boy of the Year competition could not have helped believing that despite the two recent winners, Joe really had a good shot at winning the national title that year.

Ricardo Monzón

But the slate of nominees for 1964 was deep and another boy from Bowie High, Ricardo Monzón, an exceptional athlete, was going to give every candidate a run for his money. The *El Paso Times* article that announced the Boy of the Year nominees for 1964 said the following about Ricardo:

> Monzón, a real product of the Boys' Club, whose list of accomplishments are included in eight type-written pages, has been outstanding in school, home, church and Boys' Club activities for several years.
>
> Currently the high scorer on the Bowie High basketball team, Monzón was also the first-string quarterback for the Bears while weighing only 122. He has been selected All-Boy Favorite in competition with over 2000 students and has served as captain of the football, basketball and baseball teams. ...
>
> A champion chess player, he has also excelled in boxing, track, Ping-Pong, checkers, swimming, softball, arts and crafts, billiards, marble tournaments, and in Little League, Pony, Babe Ruth and Connie Mack baseball programs.

I knew Ricardo personally primarily from the Boys' Club competitions in baseball, touch football and basketball between Unit 1 and Unit 2. A few times a year, each Unit would form an All-Star team in each sport to play against the All-Star team from the other Unit. I was privileged to have made the All-Star teams from Unit 2 on a number of occasions and I thought that each of those teams were pretty darn good. However, whenever we ended up facing a team that included Ricardo, we almost always got beat and it was almost always Ricardo who was the dominant player.

Manny Alvarez

The third nominee from Unit 1 in 1964 was Dionicio Manuel "Manny" Alvarez. He was a sophomore at Austin High and had been an honor student since grammar school. At a very tender age, he started helping his father operate a produce business by making deliveries, supervising workers and helping maintain the business books. In the Boys' Club, he was a member of the Jr. Toastmasters Club and had won the *Optimist Oratorical Contest* that year at the *Northgate Optimist Club*.

Probably the most impressive item on his nominee resume at the time was his junior volunteer work at *Providence Memorial Hospital* there in El Paso. While in high school, he regularly volunteered 16 hours per week to train new volunteers and to perform other hospital duties including taking of patients' temperatures, blood pressures and heart rates. His medical supervisors appreciated his work so much that they even allowed him to participate and assist in tracheotomy operations and spinal taps. It came as no surprise later that Manny completed medical school in 1981 and became a successful Nephrologist practicing in El Paso.

I have known and remained in touch with Manny since our Jr. Toastmasters days in the early 1960's. On Mothers' Day, 1963, just 6 months before he received this 1964 Boy of the Year nomination, he was right there with me and those other Jr. Toastmasters when our colleague, Sergio "Checo" Reza got knifed while we were attempting to raise money to attend a speech contest in San Francisco by serenading neighborhood mothers on Mother's Day. I covered this event in great detail at an earlier part of this book. I have always thought that it is interesting that of the six Boy of the Year nominees for 1964, four of us, including the victim himself, had been involved in that incident.

Salvador E. Garcia

Salvador E. Garcia, the first of three nominees from Unit 2, is the "Chichi" that I wrote about earlier. In my opinion, he was by far the brightest kid that I grew up with. He was a junior in high school when he got nominated for Boy of the Year and his resume was impressive. He had always been at the top of his class, was an incredibly good athlete and had done lots of good around the community. I knew exactly how strong a nominee he was because I had known him since the fourth grade and I forever seemed to be playing catch-up with him. In high school we always competed with each other in school elections and in extracurricular activities. In the Boys' Club, we were competitors in sports, in speech contests and in Jr. Toastmasters. In 1963, we had both been honored when we were selected to represent our high school in the *Crossroads of the Americas* program, that international goodwill venture involving high school students from El Paso who spent a month in Mexico.

Finally, in the spring of 1964, Chichi and I would compete with each other and a few other local boys for the biggest honor that we had ever heard of: *National Boy of the Year*. It was an incredibly exciting time for all of us.

Sergio Reza

The second nominee from Unit 2 was my best friend, Sergio "Checo" Reza, about whom I have also written extensively in an earlier part of this book. I have always maintained that if any kid from the South side of El Paso in the 1960's personified the "Boy of the Year," it had to be Checo. He did not have the best grades in school and he was not the best speaker in the Jr. Toastmasters or the best athlete in the many teams he joined. However, he had to be the best-liked and most-respected boy in the whole area served by the *El Paso Boys' Club*. Everybody liked Checo. His peers, *including the kid who knifed him*, the younger and older siblings of his peers, their parents, his teachers, his mentors, his employers, his employees, his teammates, his coaches and practically anyone else who ever met him, simply had to like him. If anyone had lost the title of Boy of the Year to Checo, I'm sure they would have understood why.

Willie Chavez

I was the third nominee from Unit 2. I knew that the Boys' Club had been preparing a number of boys to compete in this contest for a few years and that this grooming process would continue forever with other boys. Well, my time had finally arrived. The credentials that I brought with me were, I suppose, pretty good. They have been liberally scattered throughout this book and each reader can come to his or her own conclusions. But I also felt that the brother of last year's winner of the *national* title was at a substantial disadvantage, particularly with competitors such as the 5 other local boys, not to mention similarly outstanding boys from the other 625 Boys' Clubs throughout America. Nevertheless, I was thrilled and honored to no end to be included in this year's competition and I was determined to grow from the experience and to continue enjoying what I have always believed to have been the best year of my life.

The results of that year's Boy of the Year competition were fairly impressive as far as the *El Paso Boys' Club* was concerned. Of the six local nominees, three were selected as among the top 50 finalists in the nation. They were Ricardo Monzon, Joe Renteria and myself. Joe Renteria then went on to receive an award as *Regional Boy of the Year*. So, for anyone keeping track, the El Paso Boys' Club, under the leadership of Mr. O. D. Hightower, had thus managed to produce 2 Regional and 2 National winners between 1961 and 1964.

Boy of the Year Competition -1965

Mr. O. D. Hightower, the Executive Director of the Boys' Club had passed away in January, 1964. I recall that his replacement was not identified for a while. Meanwhile, I became a senior in high school and turned 18 years of age. I was no longer a child and could not understand why the Board of Directors did not immediately appoint the Assistant Director, Mr. Salvador Ramirez, to succeed Mr. Hightower. After all, in my eyes—and in the eyes of just about every other Boys' Club kid—he certainly seemed eminently qualified. In any event, after some months, the new Executive Director was named. He was Mr. Bob Lothridge. I have no official information about where Mr. Lothridge came from and what Boys' Club experience he brought with him. All I know is that a gentleman appeared one day at the Club and was introduced as the new Executive Director. He certainly looked the part. He was Anglo, in his mid- to late-thirties and he always wore a suit. I naively assumed that the transition from the Hightower era to the Lothridge era would be seamless and that the successes of the past would simply continue into the indefinite future.

1965 would be my last year as a member of the *El Paso Boys' Club*. I had become extremely active in representing the Boys Club in a variety of activities, including appearances at luncheons and dinners of local civic clubs always proudly communicating by live example all of the good that was being accomplished in the constant war against juvenile delinquency in South El Paso. I recall vividly how different it was that year to be introduced at these events by the Boys' Club Executive Director, Mr. Bob Lothridge instead of Mr. Hightower who had always done that prior to his passing a year earlier. There were two things in particular that bothered me about Mr. Lothridge. First, he always seemed to mispronounce my surname. He pronounced it: "sha-VEZ" instead of "CHA-vez." I let it go for a while but eventually politely told him how it was pronounced. He tried hard to do it correctly but simply could not get it right consistently. I was troubled by that inability of his to properly pronounce my name. The second thing that bothered me was Mr. Lothridge's dismal ability to speak in public. In sharp contrast to Mr. Hightower, Mr. Lothridge was nervous and awkward and frequently would stumble as he read from his notes. But more significantly, he seemed to misuse or mispronounce too many English words as he spoke before these civic groups. Sure, I was probably hypersensitive to these matters due to my training in the Jr. Toastmasters, but I could see that many in his audiences were snickering when he would make these mistakes. The one blunder that I'll never forget was when Mr. Lothridge stated that "juvenile delinquency had turned South El Paso into a *'grotesque'* neighborhood." Even if I could forgive his use of "grotesque" in that context,

I was not able to avoid doing a double-take when he pronounced it "gro-tes-CUE."

For these and other reasons, it did not take long for me to begin thinking that Mr. Lothridge would not be a good successor to Mr. Hightower. But it was not for me to ponder those issues. I diligently continued to represent the Boys' Club whenever he asked and I found myself too distracted by the new and pressing forces that I was feeling as a senior in high school to worry about him and the impact he was having on the Boys' Club. But I was acutely aware that the Boys' Club staff, the members themselves and probably anyone who came in contact with Mr. Lothridge could see that the Boys' Club had failed miserably in filling the shoes of Mr. Hightower.

And so, it was in this context that the *El Paso Boys' Club* quest for success in the 1965 Boy of the Year competition was launched. The candidate list included two boys who were veterans at competing and two who were newcomers.

Mario Lewis

Mario Manuel Lewis became a member of Unit 1 of the Boys' Club in 1964. That was somewhat of a curiosity because at that time, unlike most of the other kids at Unit 1 who attended *Bowie High School*, he was a sophomore at arch-rival *Jefferson High School*. Furthermore, he did not live in the neighborhood around Unit 1. He lived at 2011 Olive St. Apt. 27 in the Tays Projects which were located roughly between Unit 1 (in South El Paso) and Unit 2 (in the Paisano Projects). The *El Paso Boys' Club* had actually opened yet another branch called Unit 3 in the middle of the Tays Projects but Mario ended up at Unit 1 because his neighborhood chums attended Bowie High and they all gravitated toward Unit 1.

Mario remembers that one day he was trying to unsuccessfully join a sports club at Unit 1 while the club was practicing basketball. These clubs were equivalent to teams and, as such, competed with each other in Boys' Club sports leagues. And Mario was not impressing them with his basketball skills. Sal (Huevo) Ramirez, Director of Unit 1, saw Mario and knowing that he was not a particularly good athlete, pulled him aside and suggested that Mario identify what he otherwise could offer the other members that would make him a good candidate for the sports club. Mario knew that they all shared a strong wish to have their own club jackets so he proposed that the sports club not take any action on his request for membership until they raised the money to buy 30 club jackets. He then offered to take the lead in raising the funds. They accepted his proposal and eventually they got their jackets and not only accepted him as a member but shortly thereafter elected him as their President.

Mario recalls that after that club jacket experience, Huevo became a cheerleader for the group and for him especially. Huevo made a point of asking how things were for Mario and how he was doing in school and kept asking if he had a financial plan for getting into college. He never even asked if Mario thought he was capable of getting through college. In Huevo's mind it was a given.

To Mario, his Boys' Club experience with that sports club was pivotal. He will certainly never forget how Huevo brought out the best in him. And he will never forget how his friends who were already in the sports club--and were all students at Bowie High--nevertheless motivated him to be their leader. One of them, Salvador Alvarado, initially was completely against letting Mario join the sports club. At every turn in the process of getting those jackets, Salvador was the naysayer, convinced that the jackets would never become a reality. In the end, however, Salvador was the one who nominated Mario for club president. Another of his friends, Butch Campa, was the true leader to whom everybody in the sports club gravitated. Butch weighed carefully the jacket ploy and decided to support it from the beginning. This was an enormous endorsement for Mario. A third friend, Pablo (Honker) Saenz was like a sponsor to Mario. Mario remembers Honker often saying "Este chavo tiene cabeza" ("This kid's got brains") when referring to Mario. Mario remembers these interactions with his peers and how they gave him enormous self-confidence not only then but in years to come. As for his experience at the Boys' Club, Mario will tell you today that "it instilled confidence in me by reinforcing the value of and my ability in analysis, persuasion and leadership."

The story of the club jackets could not avoid an ironic ending. Shortly after the sports club members got their jackets, Mario proudly wore his to school at Jefferson High one day. The principal, Mr. Howard Aycock, saw him and told him to report to his office. There he told Mario that he did not approve of "gang" jackets and to take it off and never to bring it back to school. When Mario protested that it was from the *El Paso Boys' Club,* Mr. Aycock simply told him that he did not care.

Mario went on to become successful at *Jefferson High School*, in the Boys' Club and in his community and, thus in 1965, while a junior in high school, was nominated by Huevo as the Unit 1 candidate for National Boy of the Year.

Xavier Bañales

Xavier was another boy who was born and raised in the South El Paso neighborhood around Unit 1 of the Boys' Club. His father never got beyond the 8th grade although his mother finished high school in Mexico before immigrating to the US. Even though he lived in the area, he did not become active in the Club until he got into High School.

I became acquainted with Xavier first when he joined the Jr. Toastmasters Club and later when we both participated in the *Crossroads of the Americas* Program in 1964 in Chihuahua, Mexico.

By the time Xavier was a senior at *Bowie High School,* he was President of the Student Council, played first chair flute in the High School band, selected to the All-City Band and was an outstanding baseball player.

Joe Renteria

In 1965, Unit 1 again nominated Joe Renteria. This would be Joe's third nomination in as many years. Having won the Regional award the previous year, he was probably the strongest candidate from El Paso, particularly since he had accomplished so much more during 1964.

Willie Chavez

For the second year in a row, I was nominated by Unit 2 to participate in the competition. I was a senior in high school and this would be my last year of eligibility. I was having a very successful year at Jefferson High remaining in the top ten percent academically, getting named as the All-Jefferson Boy, being selected—along with my Co-Drum Major, Armando Gallego--as the Outstanding Drum Major in El Paso, getting elected as Senior Class President and becoming the Deputy Commander of the entire El Paso Jr. ROTC Brigade. I was also continuing to frequently represent the Boys' Club in speaking engagements all over the city. And, I continued to remain involved in the *El Paso Youth Council* advocating juvenile decency and in *Crossroads of the Americas* promoting goodwill between the US and Mexico. I was very happy that I had been nominated but my outlook remained guarded and sober. I had always considered my chances for a national award to be slim since El Paso had produced two such winners in the last four years, including one of whom was my older brother. To make matters worse, I was now in competition with Joe Renteria, last year's Regional Boy of the Year. There were few, if any, more optimistic humans on earth than me in those days, yet, I could not see myself coming out of this as the winner.

Some would say that it would make the perfect ending for this book if despite everything that I believed was stacked against me, I somehow managed to win the *National Boy of the Year* title in 1965. Well, I regret to say that I did not win it. This is not--and has never been--what my story is about. My story is about the contest itself and the benefits that each boy derived from the competition rather than the rewards that came from winning. I was extremely surprised and pleased that year when I learned that I had won another *Regional Boy of the Year* title for the *El Paso Boys' Club* that year. I felt deeply honored particularly because of whom I had competed against. I knew all of the nominees extremely well and I knew that they were all as worthy as I was. As far as I was concerned, my quest had finally ended and I was very happy with the results.

Boy of the Year Competition -1966

When I was doing some research recently to make sure I got this information right, I noticed an interesting development in the coverage that the local newspapers were providing for this competition. Between 1961 and 1963, when the *El Paso Boys' Club* produced 2 National Boys of the Year, the local newspaper articles that announced the candidates and their accomplishments were huge. Sometimes they ran stories for 2 or 3 days in succession and, including pictures, some took up full pages and sometimes even more. The articles provided lots of details about what each local boy had accomplished and they gave the readers a fairly intimate view of who each of them was. In 1964 and 1965, newspaper coverage of the competition was still pretty robust but somewhat diminished despite the fact that El Paso claimed a Regional Boy of the Year in each of those 2 years. I was surprised when I read the article in the *El Paso Herald Post* of March 19, 1966, which announced the nominees for Boy of the Year at how extremely short and superficial it was.

When the *El Paso Boys' Club* announced its Boy of the Year nominees in the spring of 1966, I had graduated high school and was a freshman at *Texas A&M University*. The tumultuous year of 1965 ended with the departure of Mr. Bob Lothridge as Executive Director and the ascension of Mr. Salvador "Huevo" Ramirez as his replacement. The "pipeline" of Boy of the Year candidates that Mr. Hightower and Mr. Ramirez had installed in 1961 was still functioning but my personal acquaintance with the nominees was fading. By then, the *El Paso Boys' Club* had opened a third unit (Unit 3) in the Tays Projects and each Unit was able to nominate a candidate. They were: Manuel

Ontiveros from Unit 1, Homer Reza from Unit 2 and Leonard Anthony Bolds from Unit 3.

Manuel Ontiveros

Manuel Ontiveros has gone by the name "Manny" all of his life. He grew up in South El Paso in the vicinity of the Boys' Club Unit 1. His parents, Crescencio and Isabel, never made it past the 8th grade. Both of them had lost their spouses and were struggling to bring up their own sets of kids when they met and got married. The union resulted in a family that included a total of 13 children some of whom were already adults. It was then that Manny was born and by the time he was 14, he was the only one left living with his parents.

Manny was a member of the Boys' Club Unit 1 from 1955 until 1966. During those years he—like so many other kids in the Club--became acquainted with and came under the influence of Sal (Huevo) Ramirez, the Unit 1 Director. Manny remembers how Sal taught him how to play the games the Club offered in the Game Room such as Ping-Pong and Billiards. But more importantly, he recalls how Sal made him and other boys take the time to read books and to do their homework. Manny remembers Sal as stern but fair when meting out discipline and also as very compassionate with the boys while constantly instilling in them the need to do the best they could in everything they did.

Another staff member that influenced Manny was the Unit 2 Arts and Crafts Instructor, Luis Peña. Manny remembers how Luis taught him how using his imagination helped to make him creative but not only in arts and crafts but in everyday life as well.

Finally, he fondly remembers Mr. Hightower, the Executive Director, who he believes served as the consummate role model for being respectful to others. Manny specifically recalled two things about Mr. Hightower: First, how Mr. Hightower's primary concern was to have the boys do well in school. Second, the remarkable sensitivity Mr. Hightower demonstrated to him personally by stopping by his home to pay his respects on the day Manny's father passed away in 1963. Somehow, Mr. Hightower found out about his dad's passing and he went to their apartment with a box full of groceries for Manny and his mom.

Like so many of the rest of us, Manny was also highly influenced and motivated by Richard Lopez and Lefty Chavez who became National Boys of the Year. Manny recalls that:

At the time it happened, it seemed to send a signal to all of us that reflected what our mentors had been saying all along. That if we kept our heads straight, we could do great things, and many of us did and continue to do so.

When I recently asked Manny to pinpoint how the Boys' Club shaped his future, he replied:

> Through its variety of activities, such as sports, arts and crafts, table games, or field trips, I learned the meaning of following rules, sharing with others, and striving to do the best in everything we did. Each activity or event was structured and geared toward fairness and learning that to win, you sometimes had to lose, and that hard work and honesty would cause you to be a better person. The Boys' Club exposed us to many things outside the barrio environment, and taught us that there was more to life than living in our neighborhood. That is, that a whole world could be ours to explore and improve. And, in many respects, I believe that many of us have done just that over the course of our lives.

He specifically noted how the experience he had in Jr. Toastmasters Club, particularly the guidance offered by one of the mentors, Judge (then Assistant District Attorney) Edward Marquez, taught him skills that served him immensely in his career in private practice and federal public service.

Manny was a senior at *Bowie High School* in 1966 and had established a fine record of academic achievement there. He had also been an outstanding member of the Boys' Club at Unit 1 and therefore he probably represented the best shot that the El Paso Boys' Club would have that year at producing another *National Boy of the Year*.

Homer Reza

Homer joined Boys' Club Unit 2 in 1959 at the age of 9 along with his older brothers, Jesús (Chuy) and Sergio (Checo) and me. But he was a few years younger and so he spent most of his time engaged in Club activities involving the "midget" age group (ages 8-10). For that reason, I did not associate with him as much as I did with his older brothers. Yet, I knew him well enough to see that he was a really good kid.

In 1962 and 1963, when the Jr. Toastmasters started attracting attention by winning oratorical contests all over the city, he was still too young to join. However, as soon as he came of age, he was invited to sign up because the rest of us could see that he had lots of potential to contribute to it and to benefit from it. As I finished high school in 1965, I remember thinking about the kids who would be taking our places as we moved on. The one kid who seemed to me to be the most promising was Homer. By 1965, when he was a sophomore at Jefferson High—and the kids in my age group had graduated--he was one of the stars of the Jr. Toastmasters. The torch had been passed and he eagerly took it going on to win a number of *Optimist Oratorical Contests* himself. He recently told me that participating in the Jr. Toastmasters did to him what all the rest of us had also experienced: He got a huge dose of additional self-confidence, particularly when it came to interacting with other neighborhood kids including the "bad" guys.

Even though his older brother, Checo, was also eligible to compete in the Boy of the Year competition in 1966—and, in fact had competed in 1964—it was Homer who instead got the Unit 2 nomination. Homer had become an honor student at Jefferson High that year and, armed with the remarkable public speaking skills that he acquired in the Jr. Toastmasters, he made an excellent first-year nominee.

Leonard Anthony Bolds

For the first time in history, all three Units of the *El Paso Boys Club* felt that they had a qualified candidate who they could nominate. Unit 3, located in the Tays Projects, nominated Leonard Anthony Bolds. Even though I had been away from the Boys' Club and from El Paso for a year, I personally knew the Unit 1 and Unit 2 nominees from our mutual participation in a variety of Club activities, particularly in the Jr. Toastmasters. However, I did not know Leonard Anthony Bolds. All I can say about him is what the newspaper article said about the three candidates: "All have excellent records of participation in home, school, church, club and community activities."

When the Boys' Clubs of America announced the results of the 1966 Boy of the Year competition, El Paso once again got recognized. It turned out that Homer Reza was selected as one of the *Regional Boys of the Year*. Even though I was far away from home at that moment, I remember thinking at the time that the *El Paso Boys' Club* seemed to have continued with its success in generating boys worthy of such recognition even though the Executive Directorship had passed from Mr. Hightower to Mr. Lothridge and finally to Mr. Ramirez.

Boy of the Year Competition -1967

As the Boy of the Year contest got underway in 1967, I had all but severed my ties with the *El Paso Boys' Club*. It was not that I did not care about the Boys' Club but rather that I had become consumed by my West Point training. I was in my second semester there and between academics and summer training, we were only getting 30 days of leave during the summers. When I came home on leave, I simply had too many things to do and that left little or no time to even drop by at the Boys' Club. Furthermore, on those times that I did drop by, I hardly recognized the boys there and even the staff members were new.

But the Boy of the Year contest went on. Once again, even though I had been gone from the scene for 2 years, I knew all three of the nominees fairly well since we had been involved in Jr. Toastmasters together. But I had known them when they were much younger and before they had become outstanding. But even when they were younger, I could see that they were Boy-of-the-Year material.

Antonio Stephens

The nominee from Unit 1 for the 1967 competition was Antonio Stephens. In 1958, when he was 9 years old, Antonio Stephens' family moved into a home at 413 South Florence Street, a block away from Unit 1 of the *El Paso Boys' Club*. He lived with his father, Antonio, who dropped out of high school in the 10th grade, his mother, Refugio, also a high school drop-out, and his younger brother David.

As was typical, he started working to help with family expenses at the age of 10. He recently reminisced about his first jobs.

> My job at this age was selling newspapers in downtown El Paso. The newspaper boy that I worked for held the right to sell at a certain corner in downtown, and I invested 2-3 hours daily (Monday through Friday) selling newspapers and earning 50 cents a day. On Saturday nights, we would load up our bikes with the Sunday Edition of the *El Paso Times* and deliver these to all the hotels, drug stores and newsstands in downtown El Paso. I think we made maybe 75 cents on Saturday nights. Other jobs through high school and college included mowing lawns, "cleaning" cotton fields (i.e., cutting weeds), ticket taker at teen dances and events at the *Coliseum*, high school tutor, stock boy, warehouse flunky, mail boy and technician's assistant at *White Sands Missile Range*.

I occasionally helped my father, a carpenter, on small contract jobs. I was not paid to help my father.

He joined the Boys' Club in 1960 and remained active in it until 1967, a year after he finished high school. He went by the barrio nickname of "Sonny" but when I met him in the Jr. Toastmasters Club in 1962, we started calling him just "Tony."

As he grew up in South El Paso and attended elementary school, he proved to be smarter than his peers and got double-promoted twice. When he recently recalled his Boys' Club experience, he said it basically consisted of two major activities: Sports (league play, tournaments, etc.), and the Jr. Toastmasters Club. His engagement in Club sports occurred mainly when he was in grade school. He believed that the sports activities were the major tools available to the Club as alternatives to boredom and the gang life. Although he experienced success in school, he considered himself as an "at-risk" youth because he was growing up in the midst of "Pachucos" (the barrio term for hoodlums) and many of his friends were, in fact, gang members. He credits Boys' Club sports and later, varsity wrestling at *Bowie High School* as main contributors to helping him avoid gang life.

To Tony, however, the Jr. Toastmasters Club was much more than just another activity for "at-risk" youth. Sure, it kept kids occupied and off the streets but he could not help notice that most members of the Jr. Toastmasters were doing well in school and otherwise and simply did not appear to be "at-risk." As he looks back today, Tony believes that the Jr. Toastmasters Club was an innovative experiment meant to bolster the skills of a group of kids that would likely go to college. He will always be grateful to Mr. Hightower and Sal Ramirez and the many mentors, particularly Eddie Marquez, who envisioned this opportunity and who helped the Jr. Toastmasters develop their public-speaking skills.

It was a seminal moment in Tony's life when Sal Ramirez asked him to join the Jr. Toastmasters. He characterizes the Jr. Toastmaster experience as "phenomenal" because he learned so much about public-speaking, competing, team building and about friendships. He went on to further refine his public-speaking abilities by competing successfully in city-wide high school impromptu and extemporaneous speech contests. And even in his professional life, which required him to regularly make presentations, he felt that his Jr. Toastmaster training came in very handy, especially in controlling stage fright.

Tony's nomination was interesting in that when he was nominated in the spring of 1967, he had actually already finished high school. I believe he was the only boy ever nominated from the *El Paso Boys' Club* who was a college student (freshman engineering student at the *University of Texas at El Paso*) rather than in high school. He achieved this distinction because he had been an exceptionally bright student in grade school and got those two double-promotions. That enabled him to graduate from Bowie High School at age 16.

Homer Reza

Unit 2 nominated Homer Reza. This would be Homer's second year of competing for Boy of the Year and, having won the Regional title the previous year, everyone felt confident that he had a pretty good shot at winning the National title this year.

Raymundo Velarde

The 1967 Boy of the Year competition nominee from the Boys' Club Unit 3 was Raymundo "Ray" Velarde. I know for a fact that Ray lived in the neighborhood around Unit 1 so I was surprised to see that he had been Unit 3's nominee. I suppose that's because Unit 3 could not come up with its own nominee and Unit 1 probably had at least two worthy candidates. Anyway, he was a junior at *Bowie High School* that year and had been a Boys' Club member for 11 years. He had earned the nomination because he had distinguished himself as a leader in high school, in Jr. ROTC, in sports, at the Boys' Club and in his community.

My personal recollection of Ray was from our days as Jr. Toastmasters. He was three years younger than me when he joined and I was getting ready to graduate from high school and move on to other activities. But I got a chance to see him compete at a number of *Optimist Oratorical Contests* and it was obvious to me that Ray would become the best orator in the club in the foreseeable future. I have to assume that he did.

The results of the Boy of the Year competition in 1967 were remarkable though probably disappointing. Even though Homer Reza had been selected as Regional Boy of the Year the previous year, it was newcomer Ray Velarde who got the highest recognition in 1967 by being selected as *Sectional Boy of the Year*. El Paso would not have a Regional winner that year.

Here is a summary of how the boys from the *El Paso Boys' Club* did in the Boy of the Year competition from 1961 through 1967:

1961- Richard Lopez won the National title
1962- Lefty Chavez won a Regional title and Jesús Murillo won a Sectional title.
1963- Lefty Chavez won the National title and Joe Renteria won a Sectional title.
1964- Joe Renteria won a Regional title.
1965- I won a Regional title.
1966- Homer Reza won a Regional title.
1967- Ray Velarde won a Sectional title.
That's 2 National titles, 5 Regional titles and 3 Sectional titles in 7 years.

By 1968, my connection with the *El Paso Boys' Club* became extremely attenuated. I had been away from El Paso for three years and was at that time in my second year at West Point. I know that in the Boy of the Year contest for 1968, Ray Velarde was again nominated and was able to get a notch higher by winning the title of Regional Boy of the Year. Then in 1969, David Stephens, younger brother of Antonio Stephens, captured yet another Regional Boy of the Year award. That would change the totals to 2 National titles, 7 Regional titles and 3 Sectional titles in 9 years.

So, the *El Paso Boys' Club* continued to produce young men whose records of service to their homes, communities, schools and to the Boys' Club earned for them the recognition of the *Boys' Clubs of America* as well as a scholarship that each would soon put to good use. More importantly, I believe that each such instance of success in this contest delivered a priceless dose of encouragement to the participants, regardless of whether or not they won anything, which would in turn continue to motivate and propel them as they moved on from South El Paso. But I had completely lost my association with all of the boys at the Club by that time and I really could no longer sense whether the Boy of the Year contest affected them as it had affected me. That is why I decided not to include in this book the Boy of the Year contests after 1967.

Chapter 14-Why This Surge of Juvenile Decency?

Now that I am in my 70's, I frequently find myself wondering how it came to be that the mean streets of South El Paso managed to pour forth into American society so many properly motivated kids during the 1960's. I have come up with some possible reasons. Certainly, there were many institutions that had a hand in it. *Jefferson* and *Bowie High Schools* and the teachers and counselors there without doubt were prime cultivators of our young minds. The *El Paso Boys' Club* and the Board of Directors and staff that watched over us were invaluable in giving our hearts inspiration and confidence to compete and to move forward. The local corporations and civic clubs such as the *El Paso Natural Gas Company, Mutual Federal Savings and Loan Association,* the *Optimist Club,* the *Pan-American Pilot Club,* the *Catholic Youth Organization,* the *Boy Scouts of America,* just to mention a few, gave us mentors to coach us and a stage on which to hone our developing skills and talents. And *Crossroads of the Americas* carried our energy and enthusiasm across international boundaries.

There were also many individuals whom I would have to credit heavily for the success that we achieved. First and foremost, among those would be our parents. Then there were the teachers and counselors that we got to know personally and who tailored their instruction and advice to each of us as individuals. Then there was the Boys' Club cadre who became fathers and big brothers to us. Then there were mentors and coaches whose time was surely valuable yet who found enough of it to spend some with us not only teaching us how to be better but also inspiring us as to what we could become.

I also strongly believe that our peers provided a unique framework in which I, for one, could develop into something uncommon. My peers certainly became models for me to emulate at home, at school and at the Boys' Club, and I know that I competed harder at everything because of them. The older boys that I knew at the Boys' Club such as Richard Lopez and my brother, Lefty Chavez, had clearly demonstrated that recognition at the national level was indeed reachable. The boys I hung out with such as Checo Reza, Fernando Casas, Sal Garcia, Joe Renteria and Armando Gallego simply made me work harder in order to gain their respect and their friendship and in many cases to out-perform them in friendly competition. There is no doubt in my mind that this peer pressure was absolutely reciprocal and that every one of us became so much better because of it.

The Boy of the Year contest sponsored annually by the *Boys' Clubs of America* was also of tremendous import in prompting me and other Boys' Club members in those days to try to achieve more. Every Boys' Club in the

US could nominate as many of its members as it wanted to compete for Boy of the Year recognition. Being a local Club nominee was not insignificant. Your picture would be prominently displayed at the Club, there would always be local press coverage and even your school would likely announce the honor. That nomination, at a minimum, would be a loud statement to your Club peers that you were a stand-out. The *El Paso Boys' Club* in 1961 and again in 1963 had the distinction of nominating boys that went on to become National Boys of the Year. I believe that every kid that joined the Boys' Club in those days could not help but believe that they too could achieve that honor. And many of us competed for and some of us won the Sectional as well as the Regional titles. This went on seemingly without end and created high expectations and excitement for most of the 1960's. I am convinced that this atmosphere helped significantly in producing a solid crop of exemplary candidates and winners every year. The Boy of the Year contests each year had the effect of re-affirming in our minds the notion that we were truly capable of competing successfully against other high-achieving kids from all over the US.

But perhaps the most significant factor that helped us to imagine and to pursue and achieve ambitious outcomes and which gave us real opportunities to elevate ourselves was that intangible and difficult-to-measure phenomenon called *timing*. I truly believe that of all of the factors that ultimately enabled this lot of kids to excel, the key was the calendar. The late 1950's and early 1960's comprised a period that was laden with optimism and opportunity, and we, as kids, had the great fortune of finding ourselves right there in that time slot ready and eager to exploit it.

Kids like me were basking in the knowledge that our country was without any doubt the greatest that ever existed. We knew that America was the main reason why the Allies had won World War II. We knew that our country was militarily the most powerful in history and even though we drilled often on how to survive a nuclear attack, in the backs of our minds we knew not only that we would we certainly survive it, but that we would then go on to destroy the evil aggressor.

In addition to all that, there was yet another fortuitous and incredibly impressive event that permeated our young lives in those days: The race for space. Beginning in 1957, we started to hear about the Russian "*Sputnik*." In the next few years we heard about how America responded with *Explorer, Pioneer and Vanguard*. A few years later, the world was introduced to the *Mercury Seven* Astronauts, who absolutely represented the "right stuff" to all kids, even to those from South El Paso. Then we came to hear about Russian Cosmonaut, Yuri Gagarin, the first man to go to space. Less than a month later, we heard about American Astronaut, Alan B. Shepherd, the first American in space. Like most other Americans, we too were stirred when we heard John Kennedy in 1961 tell us that we would land a man on the moon by the end of the decade. And so, for the remainder of our teen years, we would be challenged by--and at the same time treated to--an incomparable variety of achievements and discoveries in that arena that indeed culminated with Neil Armstrong and Edwin "Buzz" Aldrin becoming the first men to walk on the Moon in 1969.

I knew in my heart—and I believe most of my friends also knew—that we would never experience the despair and hardships that our parents had lived through. Yes, our parents had become stronger by surviving the *Great Depression*, by struggling desperately as they tried to assimilate into the culture of the United States of America and by enduring the worst war ever fought by humanity. And having done that, they also managed to provide— even if only minimally--for their children. But if we simply dared to look beyond our families and our communities, we would see that this country was indeed special. We had a President that was telling us in terms we could embrace, that the future was bright and ours for the taking. We had a Congress that was making laws that would enable and ensure that we could scale the ladders of educational and economic opportunities. We had industry that seemed to be offering boundless employment options. There simply was no question in our minds that this, *our* generation of Americans, even before they became adults, was indeed going to land on the moon.

Not only did we feel fully engaged with the changing political and economic processes, but we were also in lock-step with the emerging world of entertainment. Television continued to evolve and we witnessed the introduction of color to that medium, which was becoming so important in the lives of everyone. Through it, we also saw "up close and personal" those events that were not so nice such as the assassination of President Kennedy, the racial turmoil in the South and the worsening war in Vietnam. But regardless of the content, kids like me got to see through television so much more of the world that was out there. This unquestionably enabled us, more than any earlier generation, to prepare ourselves to enter it and to take it on.

The entertainment world also brought us Rock and Roll which comprised that one genre of music that transcended all socio-economic, racial and cultural boundaries. In that not-so-narrow sliver of life, Rock and Roll made all of us more homogeneous and allowed us to communicate--and thus associate better--with each other. Another incredibly timely corollary of Rock and Roll that we witnessed in those magical years was the British Invasion. If Rock and Roll drew the different segments of American society closer, then the British Invasion had the same effect except on an international scale.

Timing was also of vital importance to me and the kids I grew up with in that we lived in a world where people still trusted one another. Parents could send their kids to school, to the Boys' Club, on *Boy Scout* camping trips, to cross-country speech contests and to cross-border goodwill excursions knowing all along that the adults in charge were trustworthy. Behavior patterns among adult supervisors in that era did not dictate that parents be as wary as they have become in the years that followed. What this meant was that we as kids had the benefit of a multitude of adults that could teach, motivate, guide, inspire and care for us just as our own parents did. And in many, many cases those adults did all that even better than our parents ever could.

In summary, the boys who grew up around the *El Paso Boys' Club* in the late fifties and early sixties were blessed with an almost miraculous coincidence involving people and events that truly represented a large-scale change in how we would live our lives in the future. Simply stated, we had been at the right place at the right time.

Epilogue: Where the Boys Are Today

Richard Lopez

Immediately after graduation from high school in May, 1961, and while still basking in the glory of having been selected *National Boy of the Year*, Richard enrolled at *Macalester College* in St. Paul, Minnesota. DeWitt Wallace, owner of *Reader's Digest* magazine and A.L. Cole, Managing Editor of *Reader's Digest* and Chairman of the Board of the *Boys' Clubs of America*--both alumni of *Macalester*--had arranged for Richard to receive a $40,000 four-year scholarship.

Richard recently told me, "I always thought that college was a little beyond my capability. In my senior year when the Boy of the Year thing happened, I was influenced by the fact that people like [El Paso] Mayor Telles, and Mayor Williams were well educated and maybe I could go to *Texas Western College*." He painfully recalled how one teacher told him, "Richard, you are simply not college material." Fortunately, many other teachers told him "You've got what it takes." Richard remembers that when he met President Kennedy, the President told him that he too could go to *Harvard*. Richard confesses that he then did not think he really could. "I was blessed with boldness and chutzpah," Richard told me, "and so I went to *Macalester* but I regretted it as soon as I got there because it was a long way from home."

Richard only stayed at *Macalester* for one year and then went to *Georgetown University* where he made the dean's list and, in 1965, earned a Bachelor's degree in Political Science. He remembers that he needed a 3.7 to make the Dean's list and, by making the Dean's list, he could avoid taking finals. So, even though he did not consider himself brilliant, he worked hard to get that 3.7 and he succeeded.

While at *Georgetown*, Richard started working for US Senator Ralph Yarborough from Texas. At around the same time, he ran into some serious health issues and ended up having three operations for a brain tumor. He left northern Virginia and moved to Perth Amboy, New Jersey, with first wife Patricia to be close to Patricia's parents. At that time, they had one son (Richard Michael Henry born in Arlington, Virginia) and another son on the way (Scott). Their third son, Nicholas and daughter Kimberly were born while the family lived in New Jersey.

Richard started working as a nurse recruiter in a hospital in Elizabeth, NJ. Three years later, a nurse administrator at that hospital sent Richard to graduate school at *Columbia University* where he received a Master's Degree in Health Care Administration in 1967.

Richard commuted to *Columbia University* in New York City three days a week after work from his home in Perth Amboy (45 minutes on the train). It was while Richard was studying at and commuting to *Columbia* that I, then a cadet at West Point, ran into Richard. I was on a weekend pass getting on a bus at *Port Authority* terminal when we ran into each other. Johnny Uranga, Boys' Club member from 1964-66 whom I mentioned earlier, also went to *Columbia University* between 1966 and 1970. I think it is remarkable that the three of us—all Boys' Club alumni of the 1960's--were in that part of the country at about the same time all engaged in educational pursuits.

Richard was then recruited to work for a hospital company in Birmingham, Alabama. He became Director of Placement for a company that had 9 hospitals with 2000-3000 beds. They needed to find health care administrators, nurses, doctors, surgeons, cardiologists and technologists that would come to Alabama and Richard was hired to help find them. He got a recruitment budget of $1M and he went all over the country trying to find these employees. Eventually, the 9 hospitals became 14. At that point in the early 1990's, Richard retired from that company and started his own consulting firm.

His consulting business managed to engage a major client, the *Hospital Corporation of America (HCA)*. Richard specialized in setting up placement programs at hospitals all over the country. The *HCA* had 237 hospitals and he consulted practically with all of them.

Then he noticed that companies in Alabama that were in the shirt manufacturing business were losing jobs to Mexico and so he expanded into the business of economic development. He authored a study of Alabama as a retirement locale and was hired by various municipalities to assist in their economic development.

At that time while he was doing economic development for these municipalities, he ran into a couple of struggling, undocumented immigrant laborers and decided to enter the business of assisting them.

As of 2011, Richard was running three companies: A marketing company that specializes in marketing to the undocumented Spanish-speaking immigrant community in Spanish with clients that include *Burger King* and *Compass Bank*; A development company that builds homes for the undocumented Spanish-speaking immigrant community; and *Richco*

Enterprises, a consulting company that specializes in immigration issues doing advocacy as well as reform work.

Lefty Chavez

Lefty has always acknowledged that he was positively influenced by many, many people as he was growing up and experiencing his successes. In addition to Mr. Hightower and Mr. D, he also recalls how at least two of Mr. D's assistants, Douglas Cooper and Ernesto Madrid, sharpened and reinforced his interest and skills in baseball.

Doug Cooper was a fine baseball player and coach who once took a team from Unit 2 to play at a competition at Fort Bliss, the local military establishment. During the pre-game warm-up, Doug was hitting hard grounders to get the infield ready. Hard grounders were considered the best way to train infielders. Lefty recently remembered one grounder that Doug hit to him. It took a bad bounce and ended up breaking his thumb. Lefty never considered the injury as anything more than as the normal cost of becoming better.

Ernesto "Neto" Madrid was a product of the Paisano Projects who, in the minds of many, was the finest baseball player ever to come out of *Jefferson High School*. That was one of the reasons why Mr. D hired him in 1959 as one of his assistants when Unit 2 was first opened. Neto was one of Lefty's baseball coaches and Lefty has always attributed much of his baseball prowess to Neto. Lefty also remembers Neto as a good friend since Neto used to lend him his car every so often so Lefty could take a girl out on a date.

As Lefty completed his senior year at Jefferson High in 1963, there was no doubt in anyone's mind that he would be going on to college. He reminded me recently that from our youngest years, mi Papá had been insisting to everyone that Lefty was destined to become a lawyer and that I was destined to become a doctor. Lefty believes that mi Papá said that so often and to so many people that it essentially channeled Lefty to always believe that he had no choice but to become a lawyer. Lefty knew that one cannot become a lawyer unless one goes to college and thus the idea of college took root in his mind very early on. In addition, Lefty recalled that he had been deeply impressed when Richard Lopez became Boy of the Year and received a large college scholarship. The chance of also getting a scholarship was paramount in Lefty's mind as he competed for the Boy of the Year title in 1962 and 1963. Despite all that, Lefty believes that probably the strongest force that convinced him to go to college was the realization that his teachers and counselors were all college graduates. Four teachers/counselors in particular made huge impressions on him. They were Mrs. Tomasa Dominguez, a math teacher; Mr. James Burton, a Speech and Government teacher and class counselor; Mrs. Sallie Leonard, an English teacher; and Mrs. Rosalie Hamrah, also a class counselor.

In April, 1963, when Lefty spent that week in New York and Washington, DC, being recognized as National Boy of the Year, the idea entered his mind that rather than become a lawyer, he might want to go to the *United States Naval Academy* and pursue a career in the Navy. Upon returning to El Paso he discussed this with a trusted high school teacher and counselor, Mr. Ronald Miller, who happened to be a retired *Marine Corps* General. Mr. Miller told Lefty—as my counselors told me two years later—that the education he received at Jefferson High was inadequate to succeed at a Service Academy. Mr. Miller suggested instead that Lefty enroll at *New Mexico Military Institute (NMMI)* in nearby Roswell, New Mexico, to get further prepared for the rigors of the Naval Academy.

Following graduation from high school he enrolled at *NMMI* in September, 1963. While there, he sought and obtained an appointment to the Naval Academy and reported there in July, 1964. In the spring of his plebe year at the Academy, he sustained a knee injury while participating in intramural wrestling. He ended up having a knee operation with an extended stay at the Academy hospital and, as a result, fell behind sufficiently in his studies to not be able to complete the academic requirements by the end of the term. Even though he was offered the opportunity to repeat the year, he declined to do so and left the Academy for good.

During the summer of 1965, he moved to California where he took on a series of jobs while he continued to pursue his studies at a Jr. College. In the meantime, the war in Vietnam continued to escalate and, in February, 1967, Lefty got drafted into the US Army. He attended Officer Candidate School at Ft. Sill, Oklahoma and was commissioned as a 2d Lieutenant in Field Artillery. In the spring of 1968, while Lefty was at Ft. Sill, his mom (mi Mamá) died suddenly back in El Paso. Even though he had orders to be deployed to Germany with a Sergeant Missile unit, he was instead given a compassionate re-assignment to report to Ft. Bliss in El Paso, where he could help provide for our aging father and our sister, Hilda Luz, who was 14 and about to start high school.

At Ft. Bliss, Lefty worked in the office of the General Staff for Intelligence (G2) for 18 months until the fall of 1969. He then decided to volunteer for a tour in Vietnam. Lefty arranged for our father (mi Papá) to live alone and for our sister, Hilda Luz, to move to Maryland to live with our cousin, Alma. He then got deployed to Vietnam in September, 1969.

Lefty served in Vietnam for a year and returned in September, 1970. His assignments in Vietnam included 3 months as a forward observer for an artillery battalion with the 1st Infantry Division, 3 months in the artillery battalion staff, then 6 months as the Headquarters Battery Commander for the 52d Artillery Group. In November, 1970, while still in the Army, Lefty married his high school sweetheart, Olga Olivas, who had earlier moved back to El Paso from the Los Angeles, CA area where she had been working as a registered nurse at a *Veteran's Administration* hospital.

In March, 1971, Lefty left the Army as a Captain. By September, Lefty was again in pursuit of a degree. In May, 1973, Lefty completed the requirements for a Bachelor's Degree in accounting from *Cal State University-Long Beach*. Upon graduation, he went to work for the City of Los Angeles as an auditor.

In the summer of 1974, Lefty, Olga and their newborn baby, Amy, moved back to El Paso to be closer to family. Lefty got a job there as an accountant for a jean manufacturing company and Olga went to work again as a nurse. After a year, they decided to move back to Los Angeles where he again got an auditor job with the county.

He went back to school full-time in pursuit of a Master's Degree in business at *The University of Southern California*. In January, 1979, as he was nearing the completion of that program, he was offered a marketing job with *IBM* in Ft. Worth, Texas. He could not resist the opportunity presented and so he took it. He left for Texas one course short of completing the requirements for his MBA.

Lefty was employed by IBM as a Marketing Representative and as a Marketing Instructor until 1992 when he took a bridge to early retirement. His beloved wife, Olga, succumbed to breast cancer in 1990. He continued in the data processing industry and in procurement until he suffered a mild stroke in May of 2004 which left him disabled.

Lefty lives with his wife, Athena, in Ft. Worth, Texas. He continues to be extremely active as a member of the *Boys and Girls Clubs of El Paso Alumni Association*. Lefty's daughter, Amy Chavez Foreman, received a BS in Business from the University of Texas.

Joe Renteria

At the tender age of 14, while a member of the Boys' Club, Joe became a professional disk jockey in El Paso. He started as a talk-show host at radio station KIZZ, then moved to KINT and finally KROD where he hosted easy-listening programs featuring singers such as Frank Sinatra and Tony Bennett. As he played their songs, he would shut off the mike and sing along until he developed into quite a singer himself.

Joe only completed 2 years at UTEP. He had been in the music industry since high school and he left UTEP in 1968 to travel all over the country with a band in pursuit of a singing career. Joe did not serve in the military during the Vietnam era because he got a medical deferment due to a perforated eardrum. However, Joe remembers being politically aroused even in those days and was not sympathetic with the war effort.

One day in 1968, while Joe was still working at KROD, he went to the *King's X Inn*, a popular night club in El Paso, to listen to the *Jimmy Olivas Band*. During the course of the evening, Joe asked Jimmy if he could get on the stage and do the vocals on some of the songs. The audience was impressed enough to prompt Jimmy to invite Joe to become their lead singer. From then on for the next few years, Joe became part of a pretty successful musical group that hit it off in other local El Paso night spots such as the *Desert Inn* and the *Rodeway Inn*. Later, Joe and the group were invited to perform at the biggest showplaces across the border in Juárez, Mexico. They included *El Camino Real, El Madrigal* and *Adrian's*. Then they got gigs in major American cities including Nashville, St. Louis, Louisville, Denver and Kansas City. I was a cadet at West Point during those years and on at least one occasion when I came home on leave, I went to one of Joe's concerts and it was apparent to me that Joe was clearly destined for the big time. Joe himself characterized these years as a period when everything started "snowballing" for him. His brother, an electrical engineer, would joke with Joe telling him that despite all the years of engineering training and education he had gone through, Joe was making more money in a weekend than he would make in a week. Joe has pursued his singing interest up until present day. He even performed a benefit concert for the *Boys and Girls Clubs of El Paso* in May, 2011.

At about the same time that Joe's musical career started taking off, he also became interested in acting. In 1968, during a break in performances with the *Jimmy Olivas Band*, he took a 2-week vacation from KROD, threw all of his sheet music into his car and headed for Los Angeles. He showed up at the *Etcetera* nightclub where aspiring singers could get auditions. After he finally got his shot--well after midnight--a theatrical agent named Diane Davis summoned him, signed him up and offered him an acting audition the next day. Before long, he had landed acting spots on television programs such as *The Interns* and *The Bold Ones*. In the next 40 years, Joe's acting career landed him in over 200 TV shows, feature films and commercials with performers such as Rock Hudson, Steven Seagal, Broderick Crawford, Patty Duke, Linda Evans and Robert Blake, to name a few. I'll never forget the sinister character that he played opposite Steven Seagal in the motion picture *Marked for Death*. He was "Raoul" (also called "Screwface") who was one nasty guy. In addition to his acting work he also took on producing and directing films and writing of screenplays. At around that time, we all were certain that he was going to bring great recognition to El Paso and to the Boys' Club. Eventually, he achieved a measure of success that matched the potential that he had always shown as a member of the *El Paso Boys' Club*.

But then he crashed and burned. Unfortunately, during his steady rise as an actor in Hollywood and as a singer doing extended gigs in Vegas where he befriended Frank Sinatra, he got involved in a drug conspiracy and served time for reasons which, and with individuals whom, he is not at liberty to discuss to this day. But immediately upon his release, Joe went right back to work in the industry he loves and continues to thrive in today. "It's all I know," he says. "It's all I ever wanted." In 1992, Joe married Paula Baird from Santa Fe, New Mexico. They live in Los Angeles and have 3 children: Carlee, Camille and Raymond.

Joe has remained connected with El Paso even though his career in entertainment has kept him in California. Through benefit concerts that he has performed in El Paso on behalf of alumni associations of *Bowie High School* and of the *Boys and Girls Clubs of El Paso*, he has enabled scholarship programs to be established for the benefit of young people from South El Paso.

Johnny Uranga

Johnny joined the Boys' Club in 1957 and remained active until he graduated from *Coronado High School* in 1966. Right after high school, he attended *Columbia University* in New York City where he graduated in 1970 with a BA degree in Government. In 1971, he enrolled at *Georgetown University Law School* and graduated in 1974 with a JD degree.

He started his law career with *California Rural Legal Assistance (CLRA)*, a non-profit legal services program in Salinas, CA whose mission was to strive for economic justice and to fight for human rights on behalf of California's rural poor. In 1980, he became the first state-wide Director of *CLRA's* Migrant Family Project. He remained with the *CLRA* until 1988.

From 1993 until 1996, Johnny served as a Congressional Aide to US Representative Sam Farr. Then in 1997, Johnny became the Executive Director of the *Center for Community Advocacy (CCA)* a non-profit California corporation which operates in Monterey and Santa Cruz Counties and whose purpose is to find, recruit, develop and sustain farmworker leadership.

For most of his career, Johnny has devoted his public life to improving the quality of life for farmworkers and other low-income working families and to helping decision-makers and other stakeholders join the effort. In his work, Johnny has helped to forge strategic alliances between growers and organized labor and between social justice advocates and private residential developers. These strategic alliances have supported investment opportunities in housing and economic development in the area.

He is licensed to practice law in all courts of the State of California and has argued cases in the United States District Court for the Northern District of California and the United States Court of Appeals for the Ninth Circuit.

Johnny lives with his wife, Anna Caballero, in Salinas, CA.

Ezequiel Chacon

Ezequiel (Zekie) Chacon graduated from *El Paso High School* in 1966. In December, 1971, he was awarded a Bachelor of Arts degree from the *University of Texas El Paso*. He had been active in the ROTC programs in high school and at the University and was commissioned as a Second Lieutenant that same year. For the next 22 years he proudly served in the US Army until he retired in 1994 having attained the rank of Lieutenant Colonel. In 1978, while still serving in the Army, he also managed to complete the requirements for a Master of Arts degree from the *University of Northern Colorado*.

Following his retirement from the US Army, he became a teacher at various schools in the San Antonio, TX area until he retired once again in 2005. He passed away in 2013 at age 64.

Zekie and his wife Margie ensured that the value of an education was passed on to their children. Their son, Albert, received a Bachelor of Arts degree from *Southwest Texas State University*; daughter Isabel, a Bachelor of Arts degree from *St. Mary's University* and a Master's degree from *Texas A&M University*; and son, Ezequiel, an Associate degree.

I recently had the pleasure of visiting with Zekie's mother, Mrs. Julieta Chacon, and his sister, Dolores. Mrs. Chacon was still living in the same house where Zekie grew up on Charles Street in South El Paso. We recalled many of the rich experiences that Zekie and I went through while in the Boys' Club back in the 60's. She agreed that the skills learned in the Jr. Toastmasters Club had to be some of the most significant that any kid anywhere could possibly acquire. She remembered one particular event that occurred in 1962 while she was a student at *Texas Western College*. She was in her 30's at the time and despite the late start, she was determined to graduate and to become a teacher. Anyway, she was taking a speech class and one day her professor had invited some special guests to show the students some examples of effective public speakers. She was pleasantly surprised to see that the special guests were three boys from the Jr. Toastmasters Club of the *El Paso Boys' Club*. She remembered two of them specifically as Joe Renteria and Johnny Uranga but she could not recall who the third kid was. The three boys went on to deliver to the class the speeches that each was using in that year's *Optimist Oratorical Contest*. Mrs. Chacon told me that she had been very impressed by the speech that Joe Renteria delivered. I was not surprised to hear that since I knew how good a speaker Joe was in those days. In fact, she was so impressed by Joe that she actually could remember there and then (some 52 years later) some of the specific words that Joe had used. Mrs. Chacon noted that Joe had started his speech that day in 1962 with a quote from the Bible. The quote was from *Genesis* and she remembered vividly how Joe had ended his stirring introduction with the words, "And God said, 'Let there be light!'"

When Mrs. Chacon said that, I practically fell off the couch on which I was sitting. In reality, Joe's speech did not have that quote in it at all. However, the speech that I had written for that competition and which I also had been practicing at every opportunity, did contain that introduction and those specific words. We concluded that I had been that third special guest at her speech class and that even though the speaker that she best remembered was indeed Joe Renteria, the content of the speech that impressed her had been mine. I was very sorry to hear recently that Mrs. Chacon passed in 2015.

Interestingly, a few months earlier while I was interviewing another Jr. Toastmaster, Manny Ontiveros, also for this book, I asked him about the speeches we competed with in the *Optimist Oratorical Contest* back in the 1960's. I asked whether he had saved or whether he remembered any of the speeches or the topics of the speeches we had used in the competition. He replied that he recalled almost nothing at all but that a small part of one of Joe Renteria's speeches did seem to permanently etch itself into his memory. He then proceeded to recite those same words that Mrs. Chacon remembered ("And God said, 'Let there be light!'"). So here again, I discovered that yet another person was attributing my speech to Joe Renteria. As I acknowledged earlier, Joe was indeed a better public speaker than me and he proved that when he beat me head-to-head at the *Optimist Oratorical Contest* District finals in 1963. I am nevertheless delighted to know that the words from my speech managed to remain embedded in the minds of at least two people even though they remember Joe delivering them rather than me.

Willie Chavez

I left the Boys' Club when I graduated from Jefferson High in May, 1965. Shored up by the $200 "Regional Boy of the Year" scholarship that I received from the *Boys' Clubs of America*, I enrolled that fall as a freshman or "fish" at *Texas A&M University*. I was following the advice that my high school counselors had given me that spring. That is, to go to college somewhere for at least one year and then to seek the appointment that I wanted in order to attend West Point. At that point in my life, I had decided to become a career officer in the US Army. In those years, Texas A&M was mainly a military college and the idea was for me to enhance my readiness for the academic demands of West Point while at the same time feeling the full effects of round-the-clock regimentation.

By the following May (1966), I truly felt that my objectives at Texas A&M had been accomplished, perhaps, much more so that I really wanted. I had managed to receive the appointment to West Point earlier in the spring and as I wound up my year at A&M, I was genuinely torn between the prospect of going off to West Point or staying at A&M. I had become a true Aggie during that year and I really did not want to leave. Not long thereafter, however, I was again swept up by the idea of going to the *United States Military Academy* and so I headed east in July, 1966, to start my second "fish" year or "plebe" year as it is called at West Point.

My reporting date at West Point was July 1, 1966. Upon completion of my A&M fish year in May, 1966, I was broke. I had managed to pay for all of my college expenses up to that point through my "Boy of the Year" scholarship and the job as A&M Band librarian and so I had no debts. I also knew that it would cost me nothing to attend West Point. However, I somehow needed to get from El Paso to West Point, New York, and I knew I had no money and that I could not look to my parents for any support along those lines. So once again I turned to my *El Paso Boys' Club* connections.

In the summer of 1966, Mr. D, (Manuel De La Rosa) who had been the Boys' Club Unit 2 Director from 1959 until 1964, was the Director of the *General Assistance Office* of El Paso County. As I had done so many times in the past, I went to see him and shared with him my financial predicament. Even though I could only work during the month of June, he found a full-time job for me with Project BRAVO. Project BRAVO had been established in 1965 as a private IRS 501(c) (3) non-profit tax-exempt Corporation and was the designated *Community Action Agency (CAA)* for all of El Paso County. I remember making $1/hour working as a youth counselor and was grateful that I would have some money to make that trip to West Point.

At around the same time, I visited with Sal "Huevo" Ramirez, the newly appointed Executive Director of The *El Paso Boys' Club*, to share with him my experiences at Texas A&M. When he learned about my challenge of making enough money to get to West Point on July 1st, he contacted the local *Kiwanis Club* and arranged for them to loan me $300. The loan would be for 15 years at zero interest. So, as my West Point reporting date approached, I finally felt that there would be no financial issue in my getting there.

My four years at West Point were interesting and extremely enriching but very conflicted. The Vietnam War became something other than the war that that I earlier had felt duty-bound to fight. A year before graduating, I had tasted first-hand in New York City the contempt that the public seemed to feel for the members of the US armed forces. Even as a cadet at West Point, I was feeling serious doubts about whether the Vietnam War was worth fighting. By the time I graduated and got my commission in June, 1970, I had become very ambivalent about a military career. Nevertheless, I had an obligation to serve 5 years and I knew I would have plenty of time to decide during that period.

I was commissioned a second lieutenant in the Air Defense Artillery. I attended Airborne (parachutist) training and Ranger School and served tours in Florida, South Korea and Texas during my 5 years of service. Earlier, in 1971, I married a girl from New York City, Licia Eda Mastrangelo. While serving in Texas in 1974-5, I managed to complete the requirements for an MBA while Licia obtained a Master's degree in Education from *Sul Ross State University*. In the course of my 5 service years, I decided that I would leave the military and so, in August, 1975, I resigned my commission and enrolled at *Columbia Law School* in New York.

In August, 1975, I started the 3-year JD program at Columbia. In my third year, I was named Editor-in-Chief of the *Columbia Journal of Environmental*

Law. In 1978, I received my Juris Doctor degree and started working as a corporate counsel for the IBM Corporation. Our first son, Alexander, was born in 1978 and our second son, Christopher was born in 1980. My assignments with IBM took me and my family all over the country including, Armonk, NY, Chicago, IL, Dallas, TX, Endicott, NY, Houston, TX and Tucson, AZ. In 1997, I left IBM and joined *Compaq Computers* in Houston. In 2002, *Hewlett-Packard (HP)* acquired *Compaq* and I worked for HP until I retired in 2005.

Both of my sons received bachelor degrees from the *University of Arizona* and are pursuing real estate careers; Alexander in Tucson, AZ and Christopher in Houston. Licia and I presently commute between Houston and Tucson so that we can remain close to them and their families including grandsons Dashiell in Tucson and Vince in Houston.

Sergio "Checo" Reza

Checo ended his affiliation with the Boys' Club when he graduated from Jefferson High in 1966. The war in Vietnam continued to escalate and within a few months after graduating, he received his draft notice. He told me recently that because he was not a US citizen at that time, he was actually given the choice of either serving his country or going back to Mexico. He certainly was not going back to Mexico so he enlisted in the US Air Force. By February, 1968, he was in Camranh Bay trained as a *C7A Caribou* aircraft mechanic. During the year that he served there, his unit's primary mission was re-supplying field units and evacuating casualties. On June 10, 1968, he volunteered to be part of a mission to deliver some pallets of ammunition to a Marine unit that was under siege in a place called Dak Pek. As his *Caribou* was attempting to land, the two tires in the front landing gear were shot flat leaving the aircraft disabled at the end of the runway. In a hail of enemy mortar and small weapons fire, the crew evacuated the plane. Checo saw a foxhole not too far away occupied by a marine and a green beret Special Forces troop. Checo ran for it and jumped into it only to have "his butt kicked out of the foxhole" and to be told by its occupants to go dig his own foxhole. Luckily for Checo, they threw a shovel at him as well.

As mortar rounds fell nearby, Checo quickly dug a foxhole and jumped in. Eventually, the hostile fire stopped for a while and a US helicopter appeared. It dropped off two fresh tires and a jack in the middle of the runway near the disabled *Caribou* and flew off. Checo's commander then ordered him to recover the jack and tires, then to go back to the disabled aircraft, jack up the front, replace the flat tires, and open the cargo door (so that the pallets of ammunition could be dropped off as they took off again). Checo, all by himself during the most frenetic 45 minutes of his life, performed all of these duties even as more mortar rounds and small weapons fire tried to stop him. Miraculously, not a single round found him. When Checo told me this story, he was overcome with emotion as he recalled how scared he felt and how amazing it was that despite the deafening sounds of exploding shells and bullets whizzing by and ricocheting ever so close to him, he was somehow completely spared. The aircraft was repaired, they took off successfully, the pallets of ammunition were jettisoned and the crew managed to return back to base camp safe and sound. For their efforts, the pilot and co-pilot were each awarded the *Distinguished Flying Cross* and Airman First Class Sergio Reza-Martinez (his legal name) was awarded the *Bronze Star Medal* with "V" Device.

Upon his return from Vietnam in 1968, he married his girlfriend, Anna Rubio, and remained in the Air Force until he was honorably discharged as a Staff Sergeant in 1974. During that period, he pursued the final few courses at *Texas Christian University* that would lead him to a degree in Business Administration. However, in 1975, just ½ of a semester away from his degree, while living in the Dallas-Ft. Worth area, he got hired by the *IBM Corporation* in an administrative capacity. Even though he planned to return to school to finish that degree, IBM quickly offered him a job in sales and after he took it, he never looked back.

Checo remained with IBM for 27 years as a salesman, first with the *Office Products Division* and later in the *National Accounts Division*. He retired from IBM in 2002 as the Development Manager for the Hispanic Market. He lives with his wife, Anna, in Richardson, Texas. Their daughter, Christina, received a Bachelor of Arts degree from *North Texas State University*; their son, Sergio, a Communications degree from the *University of Texas*; and their other son, Paul, is still pursuing his degree.

Manny Alvarez

I first met Dionicio Manuel "Manny" Alvarez in 1963 when he and his younger brother, Javier, joined the Jr. Toastmasters. I learned then that he was a freshman at *Austin High School* and that he did not live in the impoverished areas that were close to the Boys' Club. Yet, he was a very friendly and likeable kid that fit in nicely with the rest of us. It turns out that he had actually grown up in Second Ward, the barrio that surrounded Unit 1, but that his family had managed to break out into more affluent neighborhoods eventually ending up around *Austin High School* because his father and grandfather ran a produce business that had done well for them. I remember how on many evenings after a Jr. Toastmasters Club meeting, as my buddies and I from Unit 2 waited for the humble van (a retired sky-blue Army ambulance) that would ferry us back to the Paisano Projects, a magnificent late-model Cadillac with its unmistakable soaring fins would pull up to the curb to pick up Manny and Javier.

Unlike most families who lived in Second Ward, Manny's was fortunate in having a father who not only finished high school but who excelled while there. He finished in the top 2% of his class at Bowie High in 1945 and was the commander of the school's Jr. ROTC unit. Manny's father did not go on to college but instead took over his own father's produce business. Manny, however, had other plans.

After graduating from Austin High School in 1966, Manny decided that he would not follow his father's and grandfather's footsteps into the produce business. He instead enrolled at the *University of Texas El Paso* and graduated in 1971 with a Bachelor of Science degree in Biological Science. He went on for a few years to pursue a Master's Degree but when a new Medical School was inaugurated in Juarez, Mexico, right across the border from El Paso, he enrolled there to pursue a Medical Degree instead. In 1981, Manny completed the requirements for his MD from the *Universidad Autonoma de Ciudad Juarez Escuela de Medicina*. He completed his internship at *Texas Tech University Medical School* in 1983 and a fellowship in Nephrology at the *University of Arizona* in 1986. As of 2019, he remains in practice in El Paso with his firm, Kidney Consultants of El Paso, P.A.

Manny and his wife, Alicia Vasquez Alvarez, never lost their focus on the value of a good education. Alicia went so far as to earn a Master's Degree in Theology. Their children followed in their footsteps: Older son, Dionicio Manuel Jr., earned a college degree in Law Enforcement and became a police officer; younger son, John Jacob earned an MD and is currently pursuing a fellowship in Gastroenterology.

Javier Alvarez

Javier was three years younger than me and so except for activities related to the Jr. Toastmasters, I did not hang out with him very much. Yet, I could see that he had a sense of confidence and a positive outlook about everything that were certain to make him successful. After graduating from *Austin High School* in 1968, he enrolled at the *University of Texas at El Paso* and in 1973 earned a Bachelor of Arts degree. In the next two years, he completed all of the hours to receive a Master's degree in History but did not complete his thesis and thus was never awarded the degree. In 1979 he earned a Juris Doctor degree from *Texas Tech University School of Law*.

From 1979 until 1991, Javier practiced law in Lubbock, Texas. Then, he moved to El Paso and practiced law there until 1994. In 1994, he was appointed Judge of the County Court at Law Number 1, by the El Paso County Commissioner's Court. He continued in that capacity until he was elected as Judge, County Court at Law Number 3, El Paso, Texas, in 1995. He continues to serve in that capacity to this day.

Salvador E. "Chichi" Garcia

Chichi joined the Boys' Club in 1959 and remained an active member until he graduated from high school in 1965. As I mentioned earlier, Chichi competed against me and four other local boys in the Boy of the Year competition in 1964. He recalled recently that his mother, Francis, was a very strong force in keeping him focused on finishing high school and going on to college. He also gave credit to the staff members of the Boys' Club and to Richard Lopez and Lefty Chavez, for keeping him on course to attend college. Richard and Lefty had gone off to college right after getting their National Boy of the Year honors and finishing high school and Chichi was determined to do the same. Upon graduating from high school, he earned the coveted full four-year *Stevens Scholarship* to attend *Texas Western College* there in El Paso. However, after one year he dropped out due to the break-up of a relationship that he says essentially left him foundering aimlessly. In April, 1967, he got drafted into the Army but managed to get into Officer Candidate School at Ft. Sill, OK and got himself commissioned as a 2d Lieutenant in March, 1968. He served a tour in Germany and then resigned in March, 1970.

Chichi returned to El Paso and completed the requirements for a degree in Accounting in 1973. In 1976, he became a Certified Public Accountant (CPA) and for the next 38 years worked in that capacity for a variety of firms. He has two children: Chris, who attended the *University of Texas* at Austin but did not receive a degree, and Teresa, who earned a teaching degree from the *University of Texas at El Paso*. Chichi is retired and lives in El Paso with his wife Jana.

Mario Lewis

Mario indeed was yet another example of a kid who was destined for something much better than his parents ever dreamed of. Even though his father, Oscar Alfonso Lewis only went as far as the 7th grade in Mexico, and his mother, Mercedes Schwartz Lewis only got to the 6th grade, they were proud but probably not surprised when he graduated high school in 1966.

But Mario's drive and ambition would take him even further. He attended the *University of Texas at El Paso* and in 1970 earned a Bachelor of Arts degree. Three years later he earned a Juris Doctor degree at the *University of Southern California*. His legal career began in Modesto, California, where he joined the *California Rural Legal Assistance* organization. There, he provided legal services to farmworkers and their families for a few years. Eventually, in 1977, he moved to Washington, DC, where he took a variety of legal positions in federal agencies. In 1982, Mario returned to El Paso and practiced law privately until 1998 when he was appointed General Counsel for the US Section of the *International Boundary and Water Commission*. In 2005 he returned to the Washington, DC, area and became an advisor to the *US Army Audit Agency*. Mario was a member of the Texas, California and District of Columbia Bars when he retired in 2011. He and his wife, Lupe, live in Austin, Texas.

The value of higher education was passed on to and embraced by Mario's two children, Diego Mario Lewis and Elena Angelika Lewis. Diego obtained a Bachelor of Science degree in Computer Science from *De Paul University* and Elena earned a Bachelor of Science degree in Anthropology from the *University of Texas* at Austin.

Xavier Bañales

Xavier graduated from *Bowie High School* in 1965 and then, on a music scholarship, went on to earn a Bachelor of Arts degree at the *University of Texas at El Paso* in 1969. Right after graduation, he was drafted into the US Army. Upon discharge he enrolled at UTEP once again and by 1973 had earned a Master's degree in Education.

His career has been heavily laced with youth work, first as a teacher, then with the *Girls Scouts of America* for 24 years and finally with the *El Paso County Juvenile Probation Department* for 7 years. After that, he became CEO of *Project Amistad* of the *League of United Latin American Citizens (LULAC)* in El Paso. *Project Amistad* is a non-profit agency dedicated to serving the elderly, disabled and other at-risk persons in El Paso.

Manny Ontiveros

When his days at the Boys' Club ended and he graduated from Bowie High, Manny attended the *University of Texas at El Paso* and graduated in 1970 with a Bachelors' Degree in Journalism. From 1971 until 1974, Manny served his country by enlisting in the US Army. He served tours in the US and Germany and left after attaining the rank of Specialist 5. He never ceased his pursuit of educational achievement completing an Associate Degree in Applied Science, then a General Business Degree in 1977 and finally, a Master's Degree in Public Administration from UTEP in 1985.

Manny had a variety of interesting jobs throughout his career including restaurant dishwasher, inventory clerk, department store stock clerk and sales person, college intramural sports official, Sports and News Reporter for the *El Paso Herald-Post* and Staff Assistant to US Congressman Richard C. White. He then started his career in Federal service as a Management-Employee Relations Specialist at the US Army base at Fort Bliss, Texas, and finally retired in 2009 as Supervisory Labor-Employee Relations Specialist at *U.S. Customs and Border Protection, Department of Homeland Security* after 34 years of service.

Manny has been an active member of the *Boys and Girls Clubs of El Paso Alumni Association* since its inception in 1998. He oversees the scholarship program for the Association. Manny and his wife, Lydia, live in El Paso, Texas.

Homer Reza

Homer, a Regional Boy of the Year in 1966 while only a sophomore in high school, wound up his Boys' Club days in 1968. That year was a tough one for him. The Vietnam War was still raging and his two older brothers, Checo and Chuy, were both in the US Air Force. Checo was, in fact, deployed in Vietnam that year for the second time. Their father, Jesús, Sr. was tragically killed in an auto accident that same year. Suddenly, Homer had to assume the role of father at least until Chuy was able to obtain a compassionate discharge from the service later that year.

Nevertheless, Homer stayed focused on higher education and enrolled at *UTEP* that fall. In 1972, he graduated with a Bachelor's degree in Political Science.

From 1972 until 1977 he took positions as a case worker and manager with the *El Paso Department of Welfare*. In 1977, IBM hired him as a Copier Salesman with the *Office Products Division* in Houston, Texas. He remained in that capacity until he moved to *Eastman Kodak* from 1988 until 1995 where he also was in copier sales. In 1995 he returned to *IBM*, this time with the *Services Division*, where he remained until 2001. From 2001 until the present, he has held a variety of positions in El Paso, mostly in the insurance business. His latest is as a Senior Medicare Account Representative with *Molina Healthcare*.

All four of Homer's children also went on to obtain college degrees. His oldest, Sophia Monica Reza Schwerin, received a Bachelor's degree in Communications from the *University of Texas* in Austin. Isabel Margarita Reza earned a Bachelor's degree in Technical Writing from *Texas Tech University*. Homero Reza Jr. graduated from *Arizona State University* with a Bachelor's degree in Business Administration. And Gabriel Alejandro Reza received a Bachelor's degree in Engineering from *Arizona State University* as well as a Master's degree in Biochemical Engineering from *Texas A&M University*.

Homer and his wife, Margie, still live in El Paso where he remains very active with the *Boys and Girls Clubs of El Paso Alumni Association*.

Antonio "Tony" Stephens

Following graduation from Bowie High in 1966, Tony enrolled at the *University of Texas at El Paso* and in 1971 graduated with a Bachelor of Science degree in Electrical Engineering. He was immediately hired by IBM to work in its Boulder, Colorado location. Subsequently, he worked at IBM locations in San Jose, CA and Austin, TX. While working in San Jose, he earned a Master of Business Administration degree from the *University of California-Santa Clara*. He worked for IBM for 38 years. During his career with IBM he worked a myriad of engineering jobs including logic designer, test engineer, software engineer (programmer), new product planner, project manager, and staff to senior engineering managers. In his last engineering job, he served as project manager for the RS/6000 Model 590 which served as the base computing hardware for *Deep Blue*, the computing cluster and software that defeated Russian champion Kasparov at chess. In 1997, he changed his focus from engineering to market intelligence. In this new capacity, he performed competitive analysis, Information Technology market analysis and some primary market research until he retired in 2009.

Tony has one daughter, Raquenel, who earned a Bachelor of Science degree from *Syracuse University*.

Tony now lives with his wife, Janie De La Cerda, in San Antonio, TX where he spends most of his time caring for his elderly mother-in law.

Ray Velarde

Immediately after high school, Ray enrolled at the *University of Texas at El Paso* where he became a student activist on Mexican-American matters and in student-body politics. He got his degree and a few years later got admitted into *Harvard Law School*. By his own admission, Ray did not get along with *Harvard* and after finishing his first year, transferred to *Boston College Law School* where he completed the requirements for a law degree in 1977. Ray has been practicing law in El Paso ever since.

Other Inspired Boys

The 18 boys who actually competed in the Boy of the Year competition between 1961 and 1968 were not the only ones affected by that contest. In the years that followed, a few other boys competed and also did well. I leave it to someone else to tell their stories. But a few more boys that I grew up with but who never competed for Boy of the Year deserve mentioning because it looks to me as if they nevertheless got wrapped up in the events that they saw in and around the Boys' Club and, as a result, became inspired to also be better.

Eloiso De Avila

Eloiso was a member of the Boys' Club Unit 2 from the day it opened in the summer of 1959 until shortly after he graduated high school in 1964. He was as active a participant at Unit 2 as any other boy but particularly enjoyed playing baseball. He recently told me that he essentially cruised aimlessly through high school until he met and started dating Dolores Stevens. (They eventually got married and remain so to this day.) Until his junior year he simply got by. But during his senior year he managed to get straight A's. He credits Dolores with infusing in him a desire to do well in his high school studies and to keep pursuing educational goals for the rest of his life. He remembers four high school teachers who were particularly influential in convincing him to continue his education after high school. They were Mr. Ronald Miller, an English teacher and counselor; Mr. Stanley Wright, his Distributive Education teacher; Mr. Wilson Jennings; and Mrs. Mollie Spindle also an English teacher.

As a senior in high school he remained in touch with older Boys' Club buddies who had gone on to college. They included Ignacio "Lefty" Chavez, Lionel Nava, Gilbert Montes, Anthony Ayala and Robert Lerma. He knew them all well from playing with them in sports teams and from other Boys' Club activities and he was impressed with how they seemed to be enjoying college. All of this reinforced his decision to go on and follow them.

Although no staff member at the Boys' Club specifically talked to him about college, he was strongly influenced by the fact that they were all either college graduates or were attending college while they worked at the Club. He could not help but notice how smart and articulate they all seemed to be, particularly Mr. D, the Unit 2 Director, who had a degree from *Purdue University*.

Eloiso's parents were somewhat unique among the parents who lived in the vicinity of the Boys' Club in that they actually *owned* the house in which they lived. However, they—like so many of the other parents—also did not have much of a formal education. His mother never went to school and like so many of our mothers, she never learned how to speak English. His father, only got as far as the 5th grade. Nevertheless, Eloiso remembers how much his father wanted him to finish high school and to go on to college.

For all these reasons, Eloiso enrolled at the *University of Texas-El Paso*, right after high school and in 1968 graduated with a BA in Political Science. He promptly went to the local draft board and volunteered for the draft even though he opposed the Vietnam War. He served in the US Army until July, 1970, including a tour in Vietnam.

Following his return from the service, he worked as a middle school teacher and as a federal civil servant and, at the same time, returned to *UTEP* finally completing the requirements of a Master of Arts Degree majoring in Political Science and minoring in Public Administration.

Armed with his new degree, he worked in Labor Relations at Ft. Bliss, TX until 1998 and then became a supervisor with the *US Customs and Border Protection* organization. He retired in 2005 from that agency where he had been responsible for Labor-Employee Relations for the entire Texas and New Mexico border.

The value of higher education was not lost to Eloiso and Dolores as they raised their two sons, Armando and Mario. Armando received a Master's Degree in Fine Arts and Mario received a Bachelor's degree in Criminal Justice. Eloiso and Dolores still live in El Paso.

As the years passed and the kids from the Boys' Club grew up and grew old, Eloiso De Avila evolved as our true leader. He is the current President of the *Boys and Girls Clubs of El Paso Alumni Association*. The Association is a non-profit organization dedicated to providing scholarships to kids affiliated with the *Boys and Girls Clubs of El Paso* and to funding selected operational requirements of the Clubs that are not covered by traditional funding sources. Eloiso is the only person who has presided over the Association since it came into being in 1998 and whatever success it has had in achieving its objectives is largely attributable to his efforts and to his leadership. He is a tireless and incredibly effective crusader on behalf of the *Boys and Girls Clubs of El Paso* and a huge advocate of the value of education and of developing the public speaking skills of Club members.

Jesús M. Reza

Jesús Martinez Reza, or "Chuy" as we used to (and still) call him, joined Unit 2 of the Boys' Club along with his brothers Checo and Homer on the day it opened in June, 1959. He was an active member until he graduated from Jefferson High in 1965. Chuy was perhaps the best baseball infielder that I have ever played with. As I mentioned earlier, his father, Jesús Sr., known as "La Borrachita," had actually played baseball professionally and it was obvious to all that his son, Chuy, inherited a large dose of his father's baseball DNA. Around the Boys' Club, Chuy had a lock on the shortstop position in every team he played in. And, he was always looked upon as the leader in those teams. Unlike his younger brother, Checo, Chuy was quiet and always happy to be the observer rather than the actor.

While at *Jefferson High School*, he took a bookkeeping course with a popular teacher named Mr. Windle Andrus and decided then that he was destined to have a career filled with numbers. As Chuy remained in contact with his neighborhood Boys' Club buddies who had graduated a year or two earlier, he noticed that they were all enrolled at UTEP pursuing a college degree. He therefore decided that he too would go to UTEP and try to get a degree in accounting as soon as he finished high school. However, after one semester, he concluded that he was not ready and so decided to take a year off and simply work.

At around that same time, his best friend from our neighborhood, my brother, Nacho, had decided that he would not return to the Naval Academy and so he teamed up with Chuy and headed for California to simply find work until the cob webs cleared from their minds and they could figure out what to do about the future. Within a few months after arriving in California, Chuy got his draft notice. He opted to go into the US Air Force in the summer of 1966 and was stationed at Fort Sumter, North Carolina.

In 1968, Chuy's father died tragically in an auto accident and as a result, Chuy was given a hardship discharge from the US Air Force so he could return home. Once at home and burdened with the responsibility of being the male head of his household, he immediately took a job with *Coca Cola* delivering product to local retailers. He quickly realized that this was not a good option and so, with the *GI Bill* to help pay for expenses, he enrolled once again at UTEP in September, 1968, to try for that degree one more time. In June, 1972, Chuy completed the requirements for a Bachelor's degree in Business Administration with a major in accounting.

Right out of college, Chuy took a job as an Accountant with *Prepared Foods*, an El Paso fast-food restaurant supplier. He remained with *Prepared Foods* until 1984 when the business was sold off. For the next two years, he went into the marble-importing business. Then in 1985 he went to work for the *Phelps Dodge Corporation* as an Accountant in the copper mining industry. He remained with *Phelps Dodge* until 2007 when he retired with the title of Assistant Controller of the Morenci Mine, the second largest copper mine in the world. Chuy continued to provide consulting services for two years following his retirement.

Chuy lives in El Paso. His wife, Irma, who happened to be my cousin and was a retired elementary school teacher, lost a tough battle with cancer in 2018. They produced three children, all of whom have also continued the quest for higher education. Their oldest, LoRayne, also became a teacher with a Bachelor's degree in Elementary Education and a Master's degree in Language and Literacy from *Arizona State University*. She lives and works in Marin County California. LoRayne's daughter, Gianna, is a junior at the *Massachusetts Institute of Technology*. Chuy and Irma's other daughter, Rebecca, received a Bachelor's degree in Organizational Communications from the *University of Texas at El Paso* and lives in El Paso. Their son, Nick, received a Bachelor of Science degree in Electronics Engineering Technology from *DeVry University* and works for *Nikon Corporation* in Portland, Oregon.

Fernando Casas

As detailed in an earlier part above, Fernando "Ferna" Casas was one of my two best friends back in the 1960s. The third side of this triangle was Sergio "Checo" Reza. We remained in touch and as best friends for the next 4 decades and continue that way to this day.

Despite Checo's and my efforts to recruit him to join the Boys' Club, Fernando never did. The main reason for this was that his home was not in the Paisano Projects but some two miles away at 134 Chelsea Drive. Nevertheless, the Boys' Club did have an impact on him. He wrote about that recently:

> I was never a member of the Boy's Club but several of my closest friends were. Thus, I knew about Jr. Toastmasters and the importance of public

speaking. I even attended several meetings and practiced the principles I learned. This plus additional formal training served me well in future years. Also, the Boys' Club provided role models, Lefty Chavez in particular, to whom I could look up to. Willie Chavez also shaped my thinking about leadership and extracurricular activities in high school.

His father, Rito, and his mother, Esther, were similar to the rest of our parents in that they did not get past the 6th and 10th grades in school respectively. Fernando, like so many of the rest of us, decided early on that, unlike our parents, he would pursue a college degree. Upon graduation from Jefferson High in 1966, he was accepted at several colleges but decided to attend the *University of Texas at El Paso*. A year later, while I was in my third year at West Point, he sought and obtained an appointment to join me at West Point as a plebe (freshman). Even though he did extremely well at West Point finishing that year in the top 5% academically, he decided that the military life was not for him and so he resigned and returned to UTEP to finish his college education there. He graduated with a Bachelor of Science degree in Physics and Mathematics in 1971.

Immediately after receiving his degree, he was recruited by IBM. He started as a Systems Engineer in El Paso and in 1978, he became a Systems Engineering Manager for IBM in Dallas. In 1982 he was promoted to Branch Market Support Manager and then in 1985 to Regional Market Support Manager while still in Dallas. His 30-year career with IBM culminated with his appointment as Director of Storage Systems Division Products in Paris from 2000 to 2001. In that position he had product sales responsibility throughout Europe, the Middle East and Africa as well as countries in the Asia-Pacific region with sales teams located in Singapore, Taiwan, Korea, Australia, the United Kingdom and in Paris. He presently lives in Portland, Oregon, with his wife and high school sweetheart, Bertha.

Fernando's daughter Cynthia, received a Master's Degree in Business Administration from the *University of Michigan* and his son, Fernando, a Bachelor of Science Degree from *American University*.

Lionel Nava

I remember Lionel Nava very well as a kid primarily because he was the star pitcher in the best of the baseball teams that came out of Boys' Club Unit 2 in the early 1960's. The team started out as the "Lancers" and was made up of boys in the "Intermediate" age group. These were boys between the ages of 14 and 16 and included Gilbert (Givi) Montes, Lucio Serna, Robert

(Tomato) Lerma, Ignacio (Lefty) Chavez, Anthony (Glue) Ayala, Jesús (Chuy) Reza, Ramon (Ramonsito) Gerardo, Ramon Corral, and Carlos (Curly) Carrillo. From 1959 until 1963, this team became well known throughout the city particularly after one of the neighborhood dads became the coach. That dad was Mr. Jesús Reza, Sr., father of Boys' Clubbers Jesús Jr., Sergio and Homer. As mentioned earlier, Mr. Reza also just happened to be a former professional baseball player in the Mexican League. I was two years younger and therefore could not even try out for that team but the team became quite celebrated for its successes against many teams in El Paso as well as teams from Juárez. Lionel recently recalled for me the thrill that he felt when he pitched for the Lancers during a tournament that included the "Little Giants" from Monterrey, Mexico, who had won the Little League World Series in 1957. This tournament is described in more detail later.

The Lancers had an unusually strong influence on Lionel. He remembers how tightly bonded they were and how they allowed sports to totally consume their free time at the Boys' Club or at Jefferson High. From the Boys' Club days to this day, most of the Lancers have continued to play in softball leagues and in weekly golf outings.

Lionel joined Unit 2 of the Boys' Club when it opened in 1959. He was one of 5 boys in his family and all but the oldest, Lorenzo—who was too old to join--were very active Club members. His father passed away in 1954 when he and his brothers were still very young and so his mother reared them all as a single mom. Initially, they lived in a home on Cordova Drive that they had purchased while their father was alive. Unlike most parents in our neighborhood, their father had finished high school and had gotten a good job with the federal government which enabled them to actually buy a house. Lionel vividly remembers how neighborhood gangs permeated his neighborhood before the Boys' Club arrived. He even recalled how his mother once confronted and chastised some gang leaders who were recruiting boys in the neighborhood barber shop. She ran a tight and disciplined house and was glad when the Boys' Club opened its doors.

Lionel believes that the Boys' Club was successful in keeping boys in line for two main reasons. First, it provided a "structure" consisting of a facility and a playground as well as a program that kept the boys pre-occupied with good rather than bad things. Second, it emphasized sports as the proper outlet for energy and for developing competitiveness and sportsmanship. To him, the total Boys' Club environment seemed to have been created so as to set up the boys to be successful. In addition, the daily immersion into the Club that we all experienced built up in each of us a great sense of camaraderie that we all seem to still feel even today.

Even though most of the kids that grew up around the Boys' Club in the early 1960's seemed to have been blessed with an unnatural appreciation for the benefits of an education, no one took it more seriously than Lionel. Lionel credits the Boys' Club and particularly the Unit 2 Director, Mr. Manuel De La Rosa, as the main reason why he decided to pursue an education career. Lionel has spent his entire professional career in communities where the kids were economically disadvantaged just as they were in the community where he grew up.

He graduated from Jefferson High in 1963 and proceeded to enroll at the *University of Texas at El Paso* in pursuit of a career in education. In 1967, he received a Bachelor of Arts Degree majoring in Political Science and History. In 1967, he was drafted and served with the US Army for two years until he was discharged as an E-5 in 1969. When he returned home, he took a job with the *US Post Office* and at the same time, again enrolled at UTEP, this time in pursuit of a Master's Degree in Education and Administration. In 1972 he received his Master's Degree along with a Superintendent Certification from the State of Texas.

His teaching career actually started at *Riverside High School* in El Paso in 1971 where he taught History and Government. He continued in that capacity until 1975 when he became the School's Activity Director. From 1976 until 1992, he served as Assistant Principal at Riverside High. Then from 1993 until 1996 he was the Principal at *Del Valle High School*. He returned to Riverside High in 1997 to become Principal and remained there until 2003. From 2004 through 2005 he served as the Executive Director of Administration for the *Ysleta Independent School District*. Since retiring in 2005, he has continued to serve as Interim Principal wherever he is needed in the District.

Lionel's two children, Melissa Nava Staab and Gabriel Nava have carried on their father's appreciation for education. Melissa obtained a degree in Marketing and Education from UTEP and Gabriel received a degree in Criminal Justice, also from UTEP. Lionel and his wife, Leticia, live in El Paso.

Gilbert Montes

Gilbert "Givi" Montes was a member of Boys' Club Unit 2 from 1959 until 1964. He was a few years older than me but was a classmate and Boys' Club teammate of my brother, Nacho (Lefty), in the aforementioned Lancers team/club. I remember Givi primarily because he was one of the best athletes in the Boys' Club. He played every sport offered at the Boys' Club, including touch football, softball, basketball and baseball and he excelled in every one.

He recently recalled that the main attraction towards the Boys' Club back then was one thing: sports. He heard from a friend that, at the new Boys' Club, there were opportunities to play baseball, basketball and touch football in *organized* teams. Up to this point he was only familiar with playing "sand lot" games in or around the neighborhood. The idea of playing in actual baseball fields or basketball courts was a big lure for him.

Like so many other boys in the neighborhood, Givi believes that in many ways, just about every member/peer at the Boy's Club motivated him in some form or another. However, one particular group of peers who were fellow members of the baseball team that he joined when he signed up for the Boys' Club became a very influential part of his life. That group was the aforementioned "Lancers."

One of Givi's favorite memories of his Boys' Club days occurred on the first night he showed up to play softball for the Lancers. Being an "unknown" player at the time, he was asked to play the least significant position: right fielder. Since this was his first time at the Boys' Club softball park, he failed to notice that the right field wooden light post (at least 18 inches in diameter at the base) was precariously close to the right field foul line. On the first fly ball hit to right field he managed to catch it and to collide with that light post at the same time. He was knocked unconscious by the collision. He remembers waking up lying on a billiards table in the Boys' Club building where his teammate "Tomato" Lerma was tugging at his glove saying: "Hey, let go of the ball. You're holding it too tight. We can't get it out of your glove. It's the only ball we have and you're holding up the game."

Givi also remembers how on or about 1961, the *El Paso Boys' Club* was invited to play in a baseball tournament right across the border in Juárez, Mexico. There would be four teams in the tournament, three from cities in Mexico: Laguna, Monterrey, and Juárez; and one team from the *El Paso Boys' Club*. The competition was formidable. Laguna was the then champion of Mexican boy's baseball; Juarez consisted of an All-Star team put together to win the tournament; and Monterrey consisted mainly of players from the Little League World Series Champions of 1957. Their main star was their pitcher, Angel Macias, who had pitched a perfect game in the Little League championship game in 1957. He did not pitch in this tournament because he was in Los Angeles trying out for a spot in the *Dodger* organization. The team that was selected to represent the Boys' Club was comprised mostly of Lancers. Givi--a member of that team--recalls that the Boys' Club team was beaten in close games by both Laguna and Monterrey. On the third game they played Juárez and beat them before a rather large crowd. After the final out, as the Boys' Club team headed to the dugout, the crowd started throwing stuff at them, including newspapers that were set on fire. He will never forget the thrill of playing in that tournament with the Lancers and winning that third-place trophy.

Givi's home was not in the Projects and, therefore, he was not as physically close to the Boys' Club as many more of us were and he believes that for that reason, he was not able to participate in many of the educational activities such as the Jr. Toastmasters. He was somewhat unusual among us because both his parents actually completed high school. Givi believes that no one had as much influence on his education as his older siblings: Rosa, Ramon (Cano) and Luis (Pelón). Being eight to ten years older, they inculcated in his mind the many concrete benefits of getting an education and doing as well as possible in school. And so, Givi graduated from *Jefferson High School in 1963*. He served in the US Air Force from 1966 to 1970. In 1973, he received a Bachelor of Science degree in Chemistry from the *University of Texas at El Paso*. He worked for *Phelps Dodge Refining Corporation* from 1973 until he retired in 2003.

Of Givi's 3 children, one, Lysle Patricia Montes, has gone on to earn a Master's Degree from the *University of Virginia*.

Bernie Del Hierro

Bernie Del Hierro was one of the boys brought to the Boys' Club by his friend and neighbor Joe Renteria. They lived in the 5 Points area of El Paso near *Austin High School*. The 5 Points area was decidedly a "nicer" neighborhood and even though their families had "escaped" from the south side of El Paso, these kids never completely disconnected themselves from the Boys' Club particularly after they discovered the *Linguistics Jr. Toastmasters Club*.

Bernie's parents never got past the 9th grade. Bernie was the second-oldest of seven siblings. He joined the Boys' Club in 1962 when Joe Renteria, a fellow freshman at Austin High School, invited him and two other buddies, Manny and Javier Alvarez, to check out what the boys were doing in this club known as the Jr. Toastmasters. Despite coming from a more affluent neighborhood and occasionally arriving at Jr. Toastmasters meetings in the head-turning, late-model Cadillac owned by the father of Manny and Javier, Bernie never felt insecure while at the Boys' Club. He attributes this to the Unit 1 Director, Sal "Huevo" Ramirez, who always made him and the others feel safe and welcome. Like so many of us, Bernie remembers that he was profoundly influenced to pursue higher education by our Jr. Toastmaster Club mentor and attorney, Mr. Eddie Marquez. Bernie remained an active member of the Boys' Club until he graduated from Austin High in 1966.

Bernie recently confirmed to me that the experiences that he had in the Jr. Toastmasters were life-changing. Even though he was a successful athlete in school, he always felt extremely shy and socially reticent. He acknowledged that after joining the Jr. Toastmasters and successfully competing in the *Optimist Oratorical Contest*, his self-confidence grew significantly and he became a much more mature teenager. He learned that he could "shine" as brightly in a large room while giving a speech as he could when he played well on the basketball court.

Bernie enrolled at the *University of Texas at El Paso* right after finishing high school and in 1971 was awarded a Bachelor's degree in Business Administration. From 1971 until 1974, he served in the US Army attaining the rank of E-4. From 1974 until 1987, he worked as a sales representative for *Pennwalt Pharmaceuticals*. It was then that Bernie decided to become an educator. Beginning in 1987, he started working for the *Socorro (Texas) Independent School District* finally receiving his certification as a bilingual education teacher in 1990. In 1995 he became the Athletic Director of the *Socorro Independent School District*. In 1998 he earned a Master's degree in Education from *Stephen F. Austin State University*. Bernie retired in 2013.

From 1971 until the present, Bernie has also been officiating high school football and basketball games in the El Paso area. In addition, he did a stint at officiating NCAA Division 1 football games in the *Western Athletic Conference* from 1988-1995.

Bernie still lives in El Paso. He has three children, the oldest of whom, Bernardo Mario Del Hierro, earned a Master's degree in Business Administration and presently works as Director of Operations for the *Borderplex Alliance* in El Paso. His younger children are still in grade school.

Ben Garcia

Ben Garcia was another one of those boys who did not grow up in the Projects but who saw the value of the Boys' Club from afar and got drawn into it. Ben and I were classmates at Jefferson High and, in many ways, we were friendly rivals. After I got involved in the Jr. Toastmasters Club and started getting some good publicity from winning speech contests, I invited

Ben to join. He was a pretty good public speaker and we quickly found ourselves competing with each other in the *Optimist Oratorical Contest*. In the summer of our sophomore year we were both invited to represent Jefferson High in the *Crossroads of the Americas* program in Parral, Mexico. The following year, we were both invited to again participate in that summer's *Crossroads* program but this time as Assistants to the Project Director. As seniors in high school, we again competed as rivals in student body elections. I ran for Student Body President in one ticket of candidates while he ran for Assembly Manager in the other ticket. His ticket beat us and so he became Assembly Manager that year.

Despite the competition, I always respected and admired Ben and I have always felt that he was another one of those kids who made me better. It was Ben who planted the seed in my mind to one day attend West Point. We were juniors in High School and were attending a function as representatives of the Boys' Club. Someone asked Ben what he planned to do after finishing high school. He replied that he was thinking about going to *West Point*. I remember hearing him say that and for the first time in my life, I wondered whether that might not be such a bad idea. From that day forward, I started looking at that possibility for myself. Eventually, Ben's life took him elsewhere but I did indeed graduate from *West Point*.

Ben finished in the top 2% of our high school class and went on to attend college receiving a Bachelor of Arts degree in Journalism from the *University of Texas at El Paso* in 1969. He passed away in 1999.

Julio Pellicano

Julio Pellicano and Ben Garcia were best friends and neighbors. They did everything together as kids and when I invited Ben to join the Jr. Toastmasters, it was a given that Julio would be welcome too. Julio was also in my high school class and one of the nicest kids that I have ever known. We did lots of things together while in the Boys' Club, in the Jr. Toastmasters, in the Jefferson High Band and in the *Crossroads of the Americas* programs. Julio was always the guy who could be counted on to do anything, particularly the unpleasant tasks. But perhaps more importantly, he always brought levity and cheer to any situation and, for that more than any other reason, he was extremely well-liked by everyone.

Julio earned a Bachelor of Science degree in Education from the *University of Texas at El Paso* in 1974. In a very strange coincidence, he--like his best friend Ben Garcia--also passed away in 1999.

The Anonymous One

One kid from the Boys' Club grew up to be extremely private and sensitive to any kind of publicity and he asked me not to disclose anything about him in my book. Yet, I think his story is interesting enough to be included and so I will by referring to him simply as "el Muchacho" (the Kid). El Muchacho was one of those kids who actually joined the Boys' Club in order to be able to get into the Jr. Toastmasters. He lived in that more affluent neighborhood called Clardy Fox where kids could choose to attend either the predominantly Anglo *Burges High School* or the predominantly Hispanic *Jefferson High School*. El Muchacho attended Burges. But he was a very good friend and neighbor of Ben Garcia, who attended Jefferson and had been a schoolmate and friend of mine in middle school. I invited Ben to join the Jr. Toastmasters and eventually, Ben invited el Muchacho to also join.

El Muchacho graduated from Burges High in 1967. He earned a Bachelor's degree in Accounting from the *University of Texas in El Paso* in 1972. From there, he went to *Notre Dame* and earned a law degree. Later, El Muchacho went to work as a litigator in the *Internal Revenue Service*. He retired from the IRS after 40 years of service.

Eddie Lerma

Eddie Lerma, my buddy who shot that guy on the Rio Grande levee with a pellet gun, graduated with me from Jefferson High in 1965. He went on to get a Bachelor of Science degree from *George Mason University* in 1974 and then a Juris Doctor degree from *Indiana State University* in 1977. He has been practicing law successfully in El Paso since then.

Luis Cesar Labrado

Luis Cesar Labrado was some 4 years younger than me when we shared the Boys' Club experience. He was therefore in the "Midget" age group while I was in the "Junior" group. He was known to all of us then and even now as "Chino" because he has a decidedly Asian look on his face. But I remember him as a very bright kid who was bound to amount to something.

The educational attainment of his parents was not unlike that of other parents who were bringing up their families in the Paisano Projects. Chino does not believe either of them went beyond the sixth grade as they were growing up in Mexico. He was determined to break that pattern and so upon graduation from Jefferson High in 1969, he enrolled at UTEP and received a Bachelor of Arts degree in 1973.

In 1977, he received a Juris Doctor degree from the *University of Houston* and soon thereafter launched his legal career. After working at the *El Paso Legal Aid* office for three years he embarked on a solo legal practice. Along the way, he became a municipal Judge. He continues to work in those capacities to this day.

His son, Daniel Cesar Labrado, received a degree in Economics from *St. John's University* in New York in 2012.

Chino is a member of the *Boys and Girls Clubs of El Paso Alumni Association* and participates in a variety of local activities that involve the kids who grew up at the Boys' Club with him in the 1960's.

Hector Armijo

Hector, known around the Paisano Projects as "Manito," was two years younger than me when we lived through the Boys' Club experience so we did not interact frequently either at the Club or at school. However, in the few times that we did, I could see that he was a bright kid who seemed to be on the right path. His parents were typical in that they both never went beyond high school in their educations. His mother, like mi Mamá, cared deeply about what happened to their kids while at the Club and, therefore, she became an active member of the Parent's Club.

Hector recently communicated to me that, like so many of us, he too was profoundly influenced by the Unit 2 Director, Mr. D. He specifically remembered "the pep talks Mr. D gave us about being a good son, a good student and about keeping God in our lives." He also credits Neto Madrid, another product of the Projects who later became a Club Staff member, as an influential leader and motivator in keeping him straight. When I asked him about how peers at the Club might have influenced him, he acknowledged that Checo and Chuy Reza and Lefty Chavez, 1963 National Boy of the Year, had been instrumental in motivating him to always keep trying to be better.

He graduated from Jefferson High in 1967 and went on to *UTEP* where he graduated with a Bachelor's degree in Business Administration in 1971. After spending 16 years with *JC Penny*, he joined the *Federal Bureau of Investigation* where he spent the next 24 years until he retired. His four kids all went on to also earn college degrees.

Hector still lives in El Paso, Texas, with his wife Linda.

The Tally

I wanted to write this book because I have always believed that an unusually high number of kids who grew up with me around the *El Paso Boys' Club* went on to finish high school, college and even graduate school. An informal tally reveals that of the 18 boys who were nominated by the El Paso Boys' Club to compete for Boy of the Year between 1961 and 1967, 12 obtained bachelor degrees, 6 went on to get masters degrees and 4 ultimately received doctorates (1 MD and 3 JD's.) Of the additional 12 "other inspired boys" that I found and interviewed, all 12 obtained bachelor degrees, 3 earned master's degrees and 3 earned JD degrees. And this was by no means an exhaustive survey of all of my peers but merely an informal review of those who were pretty close friends of mine at the Boys' Club and who I managed to track down as we all slide comfortably into our golden years. I submit that these numbers truly underscore the fact that something very unusual and amazingly salutary did indeed occur to us back in the 60's in South El Paso.

In getting ready to move up and away from South El Paso, my friends and I were very fortunate in being the beneficiaries of so many helpful people and organizations and of the "timing" that I mentioned earlier. However, I continue to be somewhat mystified as to why so many of us felt compelled to get those degrees. Somehow, during those amazing years, we all seemed to discover that an education was the best and—considering all the challenges that we faced in the barrio—the *easiest* way to ascend into a better life and into the mainstream of America. I do not think I will ever know exactly why or how we all came to that determination. The more important consideration is the fact that we *did* go out and get those degrees and, as a result, made ourselves, our community and our country so much better.

The Persistent Bond

"Curada Cincha" in South El Paso lingo roughly means "fun or laughs for certain." My good friend Sergio "Checo" Reza, coined that term in 1990 when a group of guys who grew up around the Boys' Club got together in El Paso for a day of golf. Most of us were well into careers, marriages and parenthood but absolute beginners at the game of golf. Nevertheless, we all felt that we had a really good time that day and made a sort of pledge to get together again and often to do the same. We agreed to call these events "Curada Cinchas."

Between 1990 and 1999, the Curada Cinchas were haphazardly planned, attendance was spotty and they were usually held in El Paso. But the enthusiasm that we felt and the comradery that we experienced each time we got together became compelling. Therefore, beginning in 2000, we integrated a little more formality into the annual event. We dubbed the event that year as Curada Cincha X, came up with a handicapping system, a rotating trophy for the winner, agreed to elect a new "Commish" each year to do all the planning and decided that we would, henceforth, only choose golf and hotel venues *outside* of El Paso. For the next 18 years, Curada Cincha has been held each year in places like Tucson, AZ, Scottsdale, AZ, San Antonio, TX, Houston, TX, Dallas, TX, Las Cruces, NM, Santa Fe, NM, Albuquerque, NM and Mescalero. NM. The usual number of attendees is between 16 and 24, and since 2000, thirteen different players have won the *Curada Cincha Grand Champion Cup*. In 2018, we played Curada Cincha XXVIII in Dallas-Fort Worth, TX.

Let me try to explain what exactly is so precious to me about Curada Cincha. First and foremost, I have known almost all of the participants since 1958 so there is a long history that binds us. With respect to Checo and Fernando Casas, the bond is more like that of a brother. Checo and 4 of his brothers (Chuy, Homer, Raul and Tony) are regular attendees at Curada Cinchas. My own brother, Lefty Chavez, is also a regular. Other regular attendees are Gilbert Montes, Antonio Anchondo, George Leon, Hector Lopez, Joe Arias, Carlos Rodriguez, Manny Ontiveros, Frank Hernandez, Louie and Robert Fierro, Oscar Garza, Omar Lopez, Nick Reza, Henry Tafoya, Hector Beltran, Henry Martinez, Willie Diaz, Wil Ordoñez, Juvi and Tony Celino, Lorenzo Cruz and Johnny Estrada, who passed away in 2014. Almost all of us went to Jefferson High or Bowie High and almost all of us were members of the *El Paso Boys' Club* during the late 50's and early 60's. Most of us also played together in athletic teams at school or at the Boys' Club for most of those years. We had the same after-school jobs, we were mentored by the same adults, we had the same girlfriends, we knew and deeply respected each other's parents, we shared the few cars that were available among us, we went to dances together, we participated in the same school clubs and many of us were in the high school band at the same time. After high school, we all went in different directions. We stayed in touch but we all became immersed in chasing careers or raising children and so we did not do much together until those matters became relatively settled. And that's when, in 1990, we had that fateful first Curada Cincha. We discovered that, as we reach middle age and beyond, it is a real thrill to get together and reminisce.

Being successful in a career or being good parents or spouses are all fine objectives in life. However, there comes a time when these objectives either are achieved or they become less important and the thrill we once felt as we pursued them becomes less palpable. In fact, the thrill may not have been as great as originally expected. I, for example, am extremely proud of what I have accomplished as a corporate lawyer, a father and a husband, but these accomplishments are what was expected. Contrast that with the experiences and expectations we had as boys and young men. In those times, every day brought a new and exciting challenge—each of them an opportunity to taste victory or success. To me--as well as to many of my Boys' Club peers--that feeling was intoxicating beyond belief. Therefore, one never forgets how good those years felt.

Now as aging baby boomers, we find ourselves giving priority to any opportunity to look back and to remember those good times. To be sure, we are probably recalling versions of past events that look much better than they actually were. But, so what? Every older person knows that it is so much more pleasant to recall the good times than the bad. Anyway, these Curada Cinchas indeed are opportunities for the group to look back and recall and actually reinforce just how good those times were.

In addition, by mixing in a little golf, we actually get to compete with each other to reassure ourselves that we have not lost the edge--even if we *have* lost it. We play strictly for the fun of it, although a modest amount of prize money is also awarded. Even though scores are kept and looked at over the years and even though a "trophy" is awarded each time, we have managed to come up with ways of assuring that luck more than skill determines the winner. The golf enables us to compete and, therefore, to use whatever testosterone and adrenaline each of us still has. This allows us at the end of each Curada Cincha to recognize a winner and to honor and praise him as we did many years ago back at the Boys' Club.

Yet, the real pleasure of the Curada Cinchas comes after we play each round of golf. At that point each day we are usually very tired and dehydrated. At times like those, nothing on earth tastes better than a cold beer. Along with the beer, the war stories start to flow. Soon, we invoke the glories of the past. Before we know it, we have whiled away long hours shooting the breeze. Then we sit down for dinner or whatever, where we continue doing more of the same for a few more hours. Remember, during this entire time spent at a Curada Cincha, none of us has been distracted by work or families. It has been pure fun with lots of old brothers of the heart (carnales de corazón) and even a few brothers of the blood (carnales de sangre).

In addition to the annual Curada Cincha golf outings, in 1990 the aging but still indomitable Boys' Clubbers from the 1960's re-organized that Boys' Club league softball team from the 1960's that used to be called the *Lancers*. The new team dubbed itself the *Soft Lancers* then joined one of the El Paso over-fifty softball leagues and, for the next 15 or so years, played two games every Saturday morning, year-round. On account of rising injury risk, the *Soft Lancers* were disbanded as a softball team in 2005 and they turned their attention to golf. Beginning in 2010, the *Soft Lancers*--plus a few newcomers--started playing regularly at different golf courses around El Paso. Eventually, they settled down at the *Fort Bliss Golf Club* where a group of 10-15 of them play regularly on Saturdays and Wednesdays.

My wife Licia and I live in Houston these days because that's where I finished my corporate law career. One of our sons, Chris, started his real estate career in Houston and lives there with his son, Vince. Our other son, Alex, also in real estate, lives in Tucson with his son Dashiell. In order to stay close to all of our sons and grandsons, Licia and I bought another house in Tucson and drive back and forth from Houston to Tucson every 60 days. The drive always includes a stop-over in El Paso. I always try to plan those trips so that we arrive in El Paso on a Friday evening. That enables me to join the *Soft Lancers* for their regular round of golf the following day. We have been doing that since 2012.

The *Alumni Association*

In 1998, some 35 to 40 years after many of the Boys' Club members who had lived through the experiences that I have described in this book, a few of us from the Unit 2 of the Boys' Club got together to honor and thank the one man whom we all acknowledged as perhaps the single individual at Unit 2 who way back then most ensured that we did not waste our lives. That man was Mr. Manuel De La Rosa. We all knew him as Mr. D.

Mr. D was 72 that year and had retired from his career as a Boys' Club Unit Director and Social Worker for El Paso County. The event that we planned was simply a luncheon where some 150 men and women who, as boys and girls at Unit 2, knew Mr. D took turns talking about what a fine man he was. When Mr. D's time came for him to accept the tributes and the commemorative plaque, he delivered a message that would resonate for many years to come. In essence, he politely admonished the gathered Boys' Club alumni for failing to ensure that the benefits that we all reaped while we were Club members remained available for kids that came after us.

He was absolutely correct. Of all of the alumni who had gathered to honor Mr. D, only two or three had remained in touch with the *El Paso Boys' Club* after high school. And that was because they had chosen careers within the Boys' Club. The rest of us had gone on to pursue the American Dream in other ways but had--for all practical purposes--completely forgotten about the Boys' Club.

Mr. D's message struck a chord in many of us but it was Boys' Club alumnus Eloiso De Avila who assumed the leadership in coming up with a means of correcting the miscue that Mr. D had brought to our attention. Once again, the same group of Boys' Clubbers that lived through the events that I have described in this book and who had started re-uniting to play golf at Curada Cinchas, rallied behind the guidance of Eloiso and the inspiration of Mr. D to somehow pay back for what we had received many years earlier. Shortly thereafter, the *Boys and Girls Clubs of El Paso Alumni Association* came into being. It was formed as a non-profit organization under IRS Code section 501(c)(3) and we decided that we would focus on helping kids from the Boys and Girls Clubs *after* they graduated from high school. However, the *El Paso Boys and Girls Clubs* could also look to the *Alumni Association* for operational financial assistance. The *Alumni Association* then created a scholarship program intended to provide modest financial assistance to worthy candidates with preference to applicants who also had some affiliation to the *Boys and Girls Clubs of El Paso.*

In order to fund these scholarships, the *Alumni Association* began organizing an annual charity golf tournament in 2000. In October, 2018, the 18th Annual Golf Tournament was held. Over the years, the *Alumni Association* has given out around $120,000 in scholarships and has also donated some $47,000 to the *El Paso Boys and Girls Clubs* for the purchase of equipment.

As I and my fellow Boys' Clubbers fade into our sunset years, we do so with wonderful memories of our lives in South El Paso. Those memories have certainly enriched our lives and we love to spend time talking about them to anyone who will listen. I thought it would be worthwhile to preserve my memories in writing so that my children and their children would forever have some idea of what these memories were all about. And so, now it is done.

Willie Chavez
June 1, 2019

www.ingramcontent.com/pod-product-compliance
Lightning Source LLC
Chambersburg PA
CBHW021847090426
42811CB00033B/2170/J